THE ETHICS
OF LIBERTY

THE ETHICS
OF LIBERTY

Murray N. Rothbard

with a new introduction
by Hans-Hermann Hoppe

NEW YORK UNIVERSITY PRESS

New York and London

The Center for Libertarian Studies and the Ludwig von Mises Institute thank all of their donors for making possible the republication of this classic of liberty, and in particular the following Patrons: Athena Tech, John H. Bolstad, William T. Brown, Willard Fischer, Douglas E. French, Frank W. Heemstra, Franklin Lee Johnson, Richard J. Kossmann, M.D., William W. Massey, Jr., Sam Medrano, Joseph Edward Paul Melville, Mason P. Pearsall, Conrad Schneiker, Eward Schoppe, Jr., Mr. and Mrs. Thomas W. Singleton, Mary Lou Stiebling, Loronzo H. Thomson, the L.H. Thomson Co., and Mr. and Mrs. Donald F. Warmbier.

For editorial assistance, thanks to Mark Brandly, Williamson Evers, Tony Flood, Jonnie Gilman, Scott Kjar, Judy Thommesen, and Jeffrey Tucker.

First published in paperback in 2002.

NEW YORK UNIVERSITY PRESS
New York and London

Library of Congress Cataloging-in-Publication Data
Rothbard, Murray Newton, 1926–1995
The ethics of liberty / Murray N. Rothbard.
p.   cm.
Originally published: Atlantic Highlands, N.J. : Humanities Press, 1982. With new introd.
Includes bibliographical references (p.   ) and index.
ISBN 0-8147-7506-3 (alk. paper) — ISBN 0-8147-7559-4 pbk.
1. Liberty. 2. Natural law. 3. Ethics.   I. Title.
JC585.R69 1998
323.44'01—dc21   98-10058
                         CIP

TO
THE MEMORY OF
FRANK CHODOROV
F.A. "BALDY" HARPER
and my father
DAVID ROTHBARD

CONTENTS

"As reason tells us, all are born thus naturally equal, i.e., with an equal right to their persons, so also with an equal right to their preservation . . . and every man having a property in his own person, the labour of his body and the work of his hands are properly his own, to which no one has right but himself; it will therefore follow that when he removes anything out of the state that nature has provided and left it in, he has mixed his labour with it, and joined something to it that is his own, and thereby makes it his property. . . . Thus every man having a natural right to (or being proprietor of) his own person and his own actions and labour, which we call property, it certainly follows, that no man can have a right to the person or property of another: And if every man has a right to his person and property; he has also a right to defend them . . . and so has a right of punishing all insults upon his person and property."

Rev. Elisha Williams
(1744)

INTRODUCTION

by

Hans-Hermann Hoppe

I n an age of intellectual hyperspecialization, Murray N. Rothbard was a grand system builder. An economist by profession, Rothbard was the creator of a system of social and political philosophy based on economics and ethics as its cornerstones. For centuries, economics and ethics (political philosophy) had diverged from their common origin into seemingly unrelated intellectual enterprises. Economics was a value-free "positive" science, and ethics (if it was a science at all) was a "normative" science. As a result of this separation, the concept of property had increasingly disappeared from both disciplines. For economists, property sounded too normative, and for political philosophers property smacked of mundane economics. Rothbard's unique contribution is the rediscovery of property and property rights as the common foundation of both economics and political philosophy, and the systematic reconstruction and conceptual integration of modern, marginalist economics and natural-law political philosophy into a unified moral science: libertarianism.

Following his revered teacher and mentor, Ludwig von Mises, Mises's teachers Eugen von Böhm-Bawerk and Carl Menger, and an intellectual tradition reaching back to the Spanish late-Scholastics and beyond, Rothbardian economics sets out from a simple and undeniable fact and experience (a single indisputable axiom): that man acts, i.e., that humans always and invariably pursue their most highly valued ends (goals) with scarce means (goods). Combined with a few empirical assumptions (such as that labor implies disutility), all of economic theory can be deduced from this incontestable starting point, thereby elevating its propositions to the status of apodictic, exact, or *a priori* true empirical laws and establishing economics as a logic of action (*praxeology*). Rothbard modeled his first *magnum opus, Man, Economy, and State*[1] on Mises's monumental *Human Action*.[2] In it, Rothbard developed the entire body of economic theory—from utility theory and the law of marginal utility to monetary theory and the theory of the business cycle—along praxeological lines, subjecting all variants of quantitative–empirical and mathematical economics to critique and logical

---

1. Murray N. Rothbard, *Man, Economy and State* (Princeton, N.J.: D. Van Nostrand, 1962).

2. Ludwig von Mises, *Human Action* (New Haven, Conn.: Yale University Press, 1949).

refutation, and repairing the few remaining inconsistencies in the Misesian system (such as his theory of monopoly prices and of government and governmental security production). Rothbard was the first to present the complete case for a pure-market economy or private-property anarchism as always and necessarily optimizing social utility. In the sequel, *Power and Market*,[3] Rothbard further developed a typology and analyzed the economic effects of every conceivable form of government interference in markets. In the meantime, *Man, Economy, and State* (including *Power and Market* as its third volume) has become a modern classic and ranks with Mises's *Human Action* as one of the towering achievements of the Austrian School of economics.

Ethics, or more specifically political philosophy, is the second pillar of the Rothbardian system, strictly separated from economics, but equally grounded in the acting nature of man and complementing it to form a unified system of rationalist social philosophy. *The Ethics of Liberty*, originally published in 1982, is Rothbard's second *magnum opus*. In it, he explains the integration of economics and ethics via the joint concept of property; and based on the concept of property, and in conjunction with a few general empirical (biological and physical) observations or assumptions, Rothbard deduces the corpus of libertarian law, from the law of appropriation to that of contracts and punishment.

Even in the finest works of economics, including Mises's *Human Action*, the concept of property had attracted little attention before Rothbard burst onto the intellectual scene with *Man, Economy, and State*. Yet, as Rothbard pointed out, such common economic terms as direct and indirect exchange, markets and market prices, as well as aggression, invasion, crime, and fraud, cannot be defined or understood without a prior theory of property. Nor is it possible to establish the familiar economic theorems relating to these phenomena without an implied notion of property and property rights. A definition and theory of property must precede the definition and establishment of all other economic terms and theorems.[4]

At the time when Rothbard had restored the concept of property to its central position within economics, other economists—most notably Ronald Coase, Harold Demsetz, and Armen Alchian—also began to redirect professional attention to the subject of property and property rights. However, the response and the lessons drawn from the simultaneous

---

3. Murray N. Rothbard, *Power and Market*, 2nd ed. (Kansas City: Sheed Andrews and McMeel, 1977).

4. See Rothbard, *Man, Economy, and State*, ch. 2, esp. pp. 78–80.

rediscovery of the centrality of the idea of property by Rothbard on the one hand, and Coase, Demsetz, and Alchian on the other, were categorically different.

The latter, as well as other members of the influential Chicago School of law and economics, were generally uninterested and unfamiliar with philosophy in general and political philosophy in particular. They unswervingly accepted the reigning positivistic dogma that no such thing as rational ethics is possible. Ethics was not and could not be a science, and economics was and could be a science only if and insofar as it was "positive" economics. Accordingly, the rediscovery of the indispensable role of the idea of property for economic analysis could mean only that the term property had to be stripped of all normative connotations attached to it in everyday "non-scientific" discourse. As long as scarcity and hence potential interpersonal conflict exists, every society requires a well-defined set of property rights assignments. But no absolute—universally and eternally—correct and proper or false and improper way of defining or designing a set of property rights exists; and there exists no such thing as absolute rights or absolute crimes, but only alternative systems of property rights assignments describing different activities as right and wrong. Lacking any absolute ethical standards, the choice between alternative systems of property rights assignments *will* be made—and in cases of interpersonal conflicts *should* be made by government judges—based on utilitarian considerations and calculations; that is, property rights *will* be so assigned or reassigned that the monetary value of the output produced is thereby maximized, and in all cases of conflicting claims government judges *should* so assign them.

Profoundly interested in and familiar with philosophy and the history of ideas, Rothbard recognized this response from the outset as just another variant of age-old self-contradictory ethical relativism. For in claiming ethical questions to be outside the realm of science and then predicting that property rights will be assigned in accordance with utilitarian cost–benefit considerations or should be so assigned by government judges, one is likewise proposing an ethic. It is the ethic of statism, in one or both of two forms: either it amounts to a defense of the status quo, whatever it is, on the grounds that lastingly existing rules, norms, laws, institutions, etc., must be efficient as otherwise they would already have been abandoned; or it amounts to the proposal that conflicts be resolved and property rights be assigned by state judges according to such utilitarian calculations.

Rothbard did not dispute the fact that property rights are and historically have been assigned in various ways, of course, or that the different ways in which they are assigned and reassigned have distinctly different economic consequences. In fact, his *Power and Market* is probably the most comprehensive economic analysis of alternative property rights arrangements to be found. Nor did he dispute the possibility or importance of monetary calculation and of evaluating alternative property rights arrangements in terms of money. Indeed, as an outspoken critic of socialism and as a monetary theorist, how could he? What Rothbard objected to was the argumentatively unsubstantiated acceptance, on the part of Coase and the Chicago law-and-economics tradition, of the positivistic dogma concerning the impossibility of a rational ethic (and by implication, their statism) and their unwillingness to even consider the possibility that the concept of property might in fact be an ineradicably normative concept which could provide the conceptual basis for a systematic reintegration of value-free economics and normative ethics.

There was little to be found in modern, contemporary political philosophy that Rothbard could lean on in support of such a contention. Owing to the dominance of the positivistic creed, ethics and political philosophy had long disappeared as a "science" or else degenerated into an analysis of the semantics of normative concepts and discourse. And when political philosophy finally made a comeback in the early 1970s, in the wake of John Rawls and his *Theory of Justice*,[5] the recognition of scarcity as a fundamental human condition and of private property and private property rights as a device for coordinating the actions of individuals constrained by scarcity was conspicuously absent. Neither "property" nor "scarcity" appeared in Rawls's elaborate index, for instance, while "equality" had several dozen entries.

In fact, Rawls, to whom the philosophy profession has in the meantime accorded the rank of the premier ethicist of our age, was the prime example of someone completely uninterested in what a human ethic must accomplish: that is, to answer the question of what I am permitted to do right now and here, given that I cannot *not* act as long as I am alive and awake and the means or goods which I must employ in order to do so are always scarce, such that there may be interpersonal conflicts regarding their use. Instead of answering this question, Rawls addressed an altogether different one: what rules would be agreed upon as "just" or "fair" by "parties situated behind a veil of ignorance"? Obviously, the answer to this question depends crucially on the description of the "original position" of "parties behind a veil of ignorance." How, then, was this situation defined? According to Rawls, behind the veil of ignorance "no

5. John Rawls, *A Theory of Justice* (Cambridge, Mass.: Harvard University Press, 1971).

one knows his place in society, his class position or social status; nor does he know his fortune in the distribution of natural assets and abilities, his intelligence and strength, and the like. . . . It is taken for granted, however, that they know the general facts about human society. They understand political affairs and the principles of economic theory; they know the basis of social organization and the laws of human psychology."[6]

While one would think that scarcity ranks among the general facts of society and economic theory, Rawls's parties, who supposedly knew *about* scarcity, were themselves strangely unaffected by this condition. In Rawls's construction of the "original position," there was no recognition of the fact that scarcity must be assumed to exist even here. Even in deliberating behind a veil of ignorance, one must still make use of scarce means— at least one's physical body and its standing room, i.e., labor and land. Even before beginning any ethical deliberation then, in order to make them possible, private or exclusive property in bodies and a principle regarding the private or exclusive appropriation of standing room must already be presupposed. In distinct contrast to this general fact of human nature, Rawls's moral "parties" were unconstrained by scarcities of any kind and hence did not qualify as actual humans but as free-floating wraiths or disembodied somnambulists. Such beings, Rawls concluded, cannot but "acknowledge as the first principle of justice one requiring an equal distribution (of all resources). Indeed, this principle is so obvious that we would expect it to occur to anyone immediately."[7] True; for if it is assumed that "moral parties" are not human actors but disembodied entities, the notion of private property must indeed appear strange. As Rawls admitted with captivating frankness, he had simply "define[d] the original position so that we get the desired result."[8] Rawls's imaginary parties had no resemblance whatsoever with human beings but were epistemological somnambulists; accordingly, his socialist–egalitarian theory of justice does not qualify as a human ethic, but something else entirely.

If anything useful could be found in Rawls in particular and contemporary political philosophy in general, it was only the continued recognition of the age-old universalization principle contained in the so-called Golden Rule as well as in the Kantian Categorical Imperative: that all rules aspiring to the rank of just rules must be general rules, applicable and valid for everyone without exception.

---

6. Ibid. p. 137.

7. Ibid, pp. 150–51.

8. Ibid, p. 141.

Rothbard sought and found support for his contention regarding the possibility of a rational ethic and the reintegration of ethics and economics based on the notion of private property in the works of the late Scholastics and, in their footsteps, such "modern" natural-rights theorists as Grotius, Pufendorf, and Locke. Building upon their work, in *The Ethics of Liberty* Rothbard gives the following answer to the question of what I am justified doing here and now: every person owns his own physical body as well as all nature-given goods which he puts to use with the help of his body before anyone else does; this ownership implies his right to employ these resources as one sees fit so long as one does not thereby uninvitedly change the physical integrity of another's property or delimit another's control over it without his consent. In particular, once a good has been first appropriated or homesteaded by "mixing one's labor" with it (Locke's phrase), then ownership of it can only be acquired by means of a voluntary (contractual) transfer of its property title from a previous to a later owner. These rights are absolute. Any infringement on them is subject to lawful prosecution by the victim of this infringement or his agent, and is actionable in accordance with the principles of strict liability and the proportionality of punishment.

Taking his cues from the very same sources, Rothbard then offered this ultimate proof for these rules as just rules: if a person A were not the owner of his physical body and all goods originally appropriated, produced or voluntarily acquired by him, there would only exist two alternatives. Either another person, B, must then be regarded as the owner of A and the goods appropriated, produced, or contractually acquired by A, or both parties, A and B, must be regarded as equal co-owners of both bodies and goods.

In the first case, A would be B's slave and subject to exploitation. B would own A and the goods originally appropriated, produced, or acquired by A, but A would not own B and the goods homesteaded, produced, or acquired by B. With this rule, two distinct classes of people would be created—exploiters (B) and exploited (A)—to whom different "law" would apply. Hence, this rule fails the "universalization test" and is from the outset disqualified as even a potential human ethic, for in order to be able to claim a rule to be a "law" (just), it is necessary that such a rule be universally—equally—valid for everyone.

In the second case of universal co-ownership, the requirement of equal rights for everyone is obviously fulfilled. Yet this alternative suffers from another fatal flaw, for each activity of a person requires the employment of scarce goods (at least his body and its standing room). Yet if all goods were the collective property of everyone, then no one, at any time and in any place, could ever do anything with anything unless he had every other co-owner's prior permission to do what he wanted to do. And how can one give such a permission if one is not even the sole owner of one's very own body (and vocal chords)? If one were to follow the rule of total collective ownership, mankind would die out instantly. Whatever this is, it is not a human ethic either.

Thus, one is left with the initial principles of self-ownership and first-use-first-own, i.e., original appropriation, homesteading. They pass the universalization test—they hold for everyone equally—and they can at the same time assure the survival of mankind. They and only they are therefore non-hypothetically or absolutely true ethical rules and human rights.

Rothbard did not claim that these fundamental principles of just conduct or proper action were new or his own discovery, of course. Equipped with near encyclopedic knowledge ranging over the entire field of the sciences of man, he knew that—at least as far as the social sciences are concerned—there is little new under the sun. In the fields of ethics and economics in particular, which form the cornerstones of the Rothbardian system and which are concerned with non-hypothetical truths, it must be expected that most of our knowledge consists of "old," long ago discovered insights. Newly discovered non-hypothetical truths, even if not impossible, should be expected to be rare intellectual events, and the newer they are, the more suspect they are. It must be expected that most non-hypothetical truths already have been discovered and learned long ago and merely need to be rediscovered and relearned by every successive generation. And it also should be expected that scientific progress in ethics and economics, as in other disciplines concerned with non-hypothetical propositions and relations such as philosophy, logic, and mathematics, will usually be extremely slow and painstaking. The danger is not that a new generation of intellectuals cannot add anything new or better to the stock of knowledge inherited from the past, but rather that it will not, or only incompletely, relearn whatever knowledge already exists, and will fall into old errors instead.

Accordingly, Rothbard saw himself in the role of a political philosopher as well as an economist essentially as a preserver and defender of old, inherited truths, and his claim to originality, like that of Mises, was one of utmost modesty. Like Mises, his achievement was to hold onto and restate long-ago established insights and repair a few errors within a fundamentally complete intellectual edifice. Yet this, as Rothbard knew well, was in fact the rarest and highest possible intellectual achievement. For, as Mises once remarked about economics which holds equally true for ethics, "there never lived at the same time more than a score of men whose work contributed anything essential to economics."[9] Rothbard was one of those rare individuals who did contribute to ethics as well as economics.

This is illustrated in *The Ethics of Liberty*. All elements and principles— every concept, analytical tool, and logical procedure—of Rothbard's private-property ethic are admittedly old and familiar. Even primitives and children intuitively understand the moral validity of the principle of self-ownership and original appropriation. And indeed, the list of Rothbard's acknowledged intellectual predecessors goes back to antiquity. Yet, it is difficult to find anyone who has stated a theory with greater ease and clarity than Rothbard. More importantly, due to the sharpened methodological awareness derived from his intimate familiarity with the praxeological, axiomatic–deductive method, Rothbard was able to provide more rigorous proof of the moral intuitions of self-ownership and original appropriation as ultimate ethical principles or "axioms," and develop a more systematic, comprehensive, and consistent ethical doctrine or law code than anyone before him. Hence, *The Ethics of Liberty* represents a close realization of the age-old *desideratum* of rationalist philosophy of providing mankind with an ethic which, as Hugo Grotius demanded more than 300 years ago, "even the will of an omnipotent being cannot change or abrogate" and which "would maintain its objective validity even if we should assume— *per impossibile*—that there is no God or that he does not care for human affairs."

When *The Ethics of Liberty* appeared in 1982, it initially attracted only a little attention in academia. Two factors were responsible for this neglect. First, there were the anarchistic implications of Rothbard's theory, and his argument that the institution of government—the state—is incompatible with the fundamental principles of justice. As defined by Rothbard, a state is an organization

> which possesses either or both (in actual fact, almost always both) of the following characteristics: (a) it acquires its revenue by physical coercion (taxation); and (b) it achieves a compulsory monopoly of force and of ultimate decision-making power over a given territorial area. Both of these essential activities of the State necessarily constitute criminal aggression and depredation of the just rights of private property of its subjects (including self-ownership). For the first constitutes and establishes theft

---

9. Mises, *Human Action*, p. 873.

on a grand scale; while the second prohibits the free competition of defense and decision-making agencies within a given territorial area—prohibiting the voluntary purchase and sale of defense and judicial services (p. 172–73).

"Without justice," Rothbard concluded as St. Augustine had before him, "the state was nothing but a band of robbers."

Rothbard's anarchism was not the sort of anarchism that his teacher and mentor Mises had rejected as hopelessly naive, of course. "The anarchists," Mises had written,

> contend that a social order in which nobody enjoys privileges at the expense of his fellow-citizens could exist without any compulsion and coercion for the prevention of action detrimental to society. . . . The anarchists overlook the undeniable fact that some people are either too narrow-minded or too weak to adjust themselves spontaneously to the conditions of social life. . . . An anarchistic society would be exposed to the mercy of every individual. Society cannot exist if the majority is not ready to hinder, by the application or threat of violent action, minorities from destroying the social order.[10]

Indeed, Rothbard wholeheartedly agreed with Mises that without resort to compulsion, the existence of society would be endangered and that behind the rules of conduct whose observance is necessary to assure peaceful human cooperation must stand the threat to force if the whole edifice of society is not to be continually at the mercy of any one of its members. One must be in a position to compel a person who will not respect the lives, health, personal freedom, or private property of others to acquiesce in the rules of life in society.[11]

Inspired in particular by the nineteenth-century American anarchist political theorists Lysander Spooner and Benjamin Tucker and the Belgian economist Gustave de Molinari, from the outset Rothbard's anarchism took it for granted that there will always be murderers, thieves, thugs, con artists, etc., and that life in society would be impossible if they were not punished by physical force. As a reflection of this fundamental realism—anti-utopianism—of his private-property anarchism, Rothbard, unlike most contemporary political philosophers, accorded central importance to the subject of punishment. For him, private property and the right to physical defense were inseparable. No one can be said to be

---

10. Ibid., p. 149.

11. Ludwig von Mises, *Liberalism* (Kansas City: Sheed Andrews and McMeel, 1978) p. 37.

the owner of something if he is not permitted to defend his property by physical violence against possible invaders and invasions. "Would," Rothbard asked, "somebody be allowed to 'take the law into his own hands'? Would the victim, or a friend of the victim, be allowed to exact justice personally on the criminal?" and he answered, "of course, Yes, since all rights of punishment derive from the victim's right of self-defense" (p. 90). Hence, the question is not whether or not evil and aggression exist, but how to deal with its existence justly and efficiently, and it is only in the answer to this question that Rothbard reaches conclusions which qualify him as an anarchist.

The classical-liberal answer, from the American *Declaration of Independence* to Mises, was to assign the indispensable task of protecting life, liberty, and property to government as its sole function. Rothbard rejected this conclusion as a *non sequitur* (*if* government was defined by its power to tax and ultimate decision-making [territorial monopoly of jurisdiction]). Private-property ownership, as the result of acts of original appropriation, production, or exchange from prior to later owner, implies the owner's right to exclusive jurisdiction regarding his property. In fact, it is the very purpose of private property to establish physically separate domains of exclusive jurisdiction (so as to avoid possible conflicts concerning the use of scarce resources). No private-property owner can possibly surrender his right to ultimate jurisdiction over and physical defense of his property to someone else—unless he sold or otherwise transferred his property (in which case someone else would have exclusive jurisdiction over it). That is, so long as something has not been abandoned, its owner must be presumed to retain these rights. As far as his relations to others are concerned, every property owner may further partake of the advantages of the division of labor and seek better and improved protection of his unalterable rights through cooperation with other owners and their property. Every property owner may buy from, sell to, or otherwise contract with anyone else concerning supplemental property protection and security products and services. Yet every property owner may also at any time unilaterally discontinue any such cooperation with others or change his respective affiliations. Hence, in order to satisfy the demand for protection and security among private property owners, it is permissible and possible that there will be specialized firms or agencies providing protection, insurance, and arbitration services for a fee to voluntarily buying or not buying clients. It is impermissible, however, for any such firm or agency to compel anyone to come exclusively to it for protection or to bar any other agency from likewise offering protection services; that is, no protection agency may be funded by taxes or exempted from competition ("free entry").

In distinct contrast, a territorial monopoly of protection and juris-diction—a state—rests from the outset on an impermissible act of expro-priation, and it provides the monopolist and his agents with a license to further expropriation (taxation). It implies that every property owner is prohibited from discontinuing his cooperation with his supposed pro-tector, and that no one except the monopolist may exercise ultimate juris-diction over his own property. Rather, everyone (except the monopolist) has lost his right to physical protection and defense against possible inva-sion by the state and is thus rendered defenseless *vis-à-vis* the actions of his own alleged protector. Consequently, the price of justice and protection will continually rise and the quality of justice and protection will contin-ually fall. A tax-funded protection agency is a contradiction in terms—an invasive protector—and will, if permitted, lead to increasingly more taxes and ever less protection. Likewise, the existence of a judicial mono-poly will lead to a steady deterioration of justice. For if no one can appeal for justice except to the state and its courts and judges, justice will be constantly perverted in favor of the state until the idea of immutable laws of human conduct ultimately disappears and is replaced with the idea of law as positive state-made legislation.

Based on this analysis, Rothbard considered the classical-liberal sol-ution to the fundamental human problem of protection—of a minimal or night-watchman state, or an otherwise "constitutionally limited" govern-ment—as a hopelessly confused and naive idea. Every minimal state has the inherent tendency to become a maximal state, for once an agency is permitted to collect *any* taxes, however small and for whatever purpose, it will naturally tend to employ its current tax revenue for the collection of ever more future taxes for the same and/or other purposes. Similarly, once an agency possesses *any* judiciary monopoly, it will naturally tend to employ this privileged position for the further expansion of its range of jurisdiction. Constitutions, after all, are state-constitutions, and what-ever limitations they may contain—what is or is not constit-utional—is determined by state courts and judges. Hence, there is no other possible way of limiting state power except by eliminating the state altogether and, in accordance with justice and economics, establishing a free market in protection and security services.

Naturally, Rothbard's anarchism appeared threatening to all statists, and his right-wing—that is, private-property—anarchism in particular could not but offend socialists of all stripes. However, his anarchistic con-clusions were not sufficient to explain the neglect of *The Ethics of Liberty* by academia. Rothbard's first handicap was compounded by an even weightier one. Not only had he come to unorthodox conclusions, worse, he had reached them by pre-modern intellectual means. Instead of suggesting, hypothesizing, pondering, or puzzling, Rothbard had offered axiomatic–deductive arguments and proofs. In the age of democratic egalitarianism and ethical relativism, this constituted the ultimate academic sin: intellectual absolutism, extremism, and intolerance.

The importance of this second methodological factor can be illustrated by contrasting the reception accorded to Rothbard's *The Ethics of Liberty* on the one hand and Robert Nozick's *Anarchy, State, and Utopia*[12] on the other. Nozick's book appeared in 1974, three years after the publication of Rawls's *A Theory of Justice*. Almost overnight Nozick was internationally famous, and to this day, in the field of political philosophy *Anarchy, State, and Utopia* ranks probably second only to Rawls's book in terms of academic recognition. Yet, while Rawls was a socialist, Nozick was a libertarian. In fact, Nozick was heavily influenced by Rothbard. He had read Rothbard's earlier *Man, Economy, and State, Power and Market*, and *For A New Liberty*,[13] and in the acknowledgments to his book he noted that "it was a long conversation about six years ago with Murray Rothbard that stimulated my interest in individualist anarchist theory." To be sure, the conclusions arrived at by Nozick were less radical than those proposed by Rothbard. Rather than reaching anarchistic conclusions, Nozick's

> main conclusions about the state are that the minimal state, limited to the narrow functions of protection against force, theft, fraud, enforcement of contracts, and so on, is justified; that any more extensive state will violate persons' rights not to be forced to do certain things, and is unjustified; and that the minimal state is inspiring as well as right.[14]

Nonetheless, in claiming "that the state may not use its coercive apparatus for the purpose of getting some citizens to aid others, or in order to prohibit activities to people for their *own* good or protection,"[15] even Nozick's conclusions placed him far outside the political–philosophical mainstream. Why, then, in distinct contrast to the long-lasting neglect of Rothbard's libertarian *The Ethics of Liberty*, the stupendous academic success of Nozick's libertarian *Anarchy, State, and Utopia*? The answer is method and style.

Rothbard was above all a systematic thinker. He set out from the most elementary human situation and problem—Crusoe-ethics—and then

---

12. Robert Nozick, *Anarchy, State, and Utopia* (New York: Basic Books, 1974).

13. Murray N. Rothbard, *For A New Liberty*, rev. ed. (New York: Macmillan, 1978).

14. Nozick, *Anarchy, State, and Utopia*, p. ix.

15. Ibid.

proceeded painstakingly, justifying and proving each step and argument along the way to increasingly more complex and complicated situations and problems. Moreover, his prose was characterized by unrivaled clarity. In distinct contrast, Nozick was a modern unsystematic, associationist, or even impressionistic thinker, and his prose was difficult and unclear. Nozick was explicit about his own method. His writing, he stated, was

> in the mode of much contemporary philosophical work in epistemology and metaphysics: there are elaborate arguments, claims rebutted by unlikely counterexamples, surprising theses, puzzles, abstract structural conditions, challenges to find another theory which fits a specified range of cases, startling conclusions, and so on. . . . One view about how to write a philosophy book holds that an author should think through all of the details of the view he presents, and its problems, polishing and refining his view to present to the world a finished, complete, and elegant whole. *This is not my view.* At any rate, I believe that there also is a place and a function in our ongoing intellectual life for a less complete work, containing unfinished presentations, conjectures, open questions and problems, leads, side connections, as well as a main line of argument. There is room for words on subjects other than last words.[16]

Methodologically, then, Nozick and Rothbard were poles apart. But *why* would Nozick's unsystematic ethical "explorations" find so much more resonance in academia than Rothbard's systematic ethical treatise, especially when their conclusions appeared to be largely congruent? Nozick touched upon the answer when he expressed the hope that his method "makes for intellectual interest and excitement."[17] But this was at best half of the answer, for Rothbard's *The Ethics of Liberty*, too, was an eminently interesting and exciting book, full of examples, cases, and scenarios from the full range of everyday experiences to extreme— life-boat—situations, spiced with many surprising conclusions, and above all solutions instead of merely suggestions to problems and puzzles.

Nozick's method rather made for interest and excitement of a particular kind. Rothbard's *The Ethics of Liberty* consisted essentially of one successively and systematically drawn out and elaborated argument, and thus required the long sustained attention of its reader. However, a reader of Rothbard's book could possibly get so excited that he would not want to put it down until he had finished it. The excitement caused by *Anarchy, State, and Utopia* was of a very different kind. The book was a

---

16. Ibid., pp. x–xii, emphasis added.

17. Ibid., p. x.

series of dozens of disparate or loosely jointed arguments, conjectures, puzzles, counterexamples, experiments, paradoxes, surprising turns, startling twists, intellectual flashes, and philosophical razzle-dazzle, and thus required only short and intermittent attention of its reader. At the same time, few if any readers of Nozick's book likely will have felt the urge to read it straight through. Instead, reading Nozick was characteristically done unsystematically and intermittently, in bits and pieces. The excitement stirred by Nozick was intense, short, and fleeting; and the success of *Anarchy, State, and Utopia* was due to the fact that at all times, and especially under democratic conditions, there are far more high time-preference intellectuals—intellectual thrill seekers—than patient and disciplined thinkers.[18]

Despite his politically incorrect conclusions, Nozick's libertarianism was deemed respectable by the academic masses and elicited countless comments and replies, because it was methodologically non-committal; that is, Nozick did not claim that his libertarian conclusions *proved* anything. Even though one would think that ethics is—and must be—an eminently practical intellectual subject, Nozick did not claim that his ethical "explorations" had any practical implications. They were meant to be

---

18. In his subsequent book, *Philosophical Explanations* (Oxford: Oxford University Press, 1981), Nozick further confirmed this judgment. There he wrote,

> I, too, seek an unreadable book: urgent thoughts to grapple with in agitation and excitement, revelations to be transformed by or to transform, a book incapable of being read straight through, a book, even, to bring reading to *stop*. I have not found that book, or attempted it. Still, I wrote and thought in awareness of it, in the hope that this book would bask in its light. . . . At no point is [the reader] forced to accept anything. He moves along gently, exploring his own and the author's thoughts. He explores together with the author, moving only where he is ready to; then he stops. Perhaps, at a later time mulling it over or in a second reading, he will move further. . . . I place no extreme obligation of attentiveness on my readers; I hope instead for those who read as I do, seeking what they can learn from, make use of, transform for their own purposes. . . . This book puts forward its explanations in a very tentative spirit; not only do I not ask you to believe they are correct, I do not think it important for me to believe them correct, either. Still, I do believe, and hope you will find it so, that these proposed explanations are illuminating and worth considering, that they are worth surpassing; also, that the process of seeking and elaborating explanations, being open to new possibilities, the new wonderings and wanderings, the free exploration, is itself a delight. Can any pleasure compare to that of a new idea, a new question? There is sexual experience, of course, not dissimilar, with its own playfulness and possibilities, its focused freedom, its depth, its sharp pleasures and its gentle ones, its ecstacies. What is the mind's excitement and sensuality? What is orgasm? Whatever, it unfortunately will frighten and offend the puritans of the mind (do the two puritanisms share a common root?) even as it expands others and brings them joy" (pp. 1, 7, 8, 24).

nothing more than fascinating, entertaining, or suggestive intellectual play. As such, libertarianism posed no threat to the predominantly social-democratic intellectual class. On account of his unsystematic method—his philosophical pluralism—Nozick was "tolerant" *vis-à-vis* the intellectual establishment (his anti-establishment conclusions notwithstanding). He did not insist that his libertarian conclusions were correct and, for instance, socialist conclusions were false and accordingly demand their instant practical implementation (that is, the immediate abolition of the social-democratic welfare state, including all of public tax-funded education and research). Rather, Nozick's libertarianism was, and claimed to be, no more than just an interesting thought. He did not mean to do any real harm to the ideas of his socialist opponents. He only wanted to throw an interesting idea into the democratic open-ended intellectual debate, while everything real, tangible, and physical could remain unchanged and everyone could go on with his life and thoughts as before.

Following the publication of *Anarchy, State, and Utopia*, Nozick took even further steps to establish his reputation as "tolerant." He never replied to the countless comments and criticisms of his book, including Rothbard's, which forms chapter 29 of this book. This confirmed that he took his non-committal method seriously, for why, indeed, should anyone reply to his critics, if he were not committed to the correctness of his own views in the first place? Moreover, in his subsequent book, *Philosophical Explanations*, Nozick removed all remaining doubts as to his supposed non-extremist tolerance. He went further than merely restating his commitment to the methodological non-committal:

> So don't look here for a knockdown argument that there is something wrong with knockdown arguments, for the knockdown argument to end all knockdown arguing. It will not do to argue you into the conclusion, even in order to reduce the total amount of presentation of argument. Nor may I hint that I possess the knockdown argument yet will not present it.[19]

Further, in a truly startling twist, Nozick went on to say that the use of knockdown arguments even constituted coercion and was hence morally offensive:

> The terminology of philosophical art is coercive: arguments are powerful and best when they are knockdown, arguments force you to a conclusion, if you believe the premises you have to or must believe the conclusion, some arguments do not carry

---

19. Ibid., p. 5.

much punch, and so forth. A philosophical argument is an attempt to get someone to believe something, whether he wants to believe it or not. A successful philosophical argument, a strong argument, forces someone to a belief. . . . Why are philosophers intent on forcing others to believe things? Is that a nice way to behave toward someone? I think we cannot improve people that way. . . . Philosophical argument, trying to get someone to believe something whether he wants to believe it or not, is not, I have held, a nice way to behave toward someone; also, it does not fit the original motivation for studying or entering philosophy. That motivation is puzzlement, curiosity, a desire to understand, not a desire to produce uniformity of belief. Most people do not want to become thought-police. The philosophical goal of explanation rather than proof not only is morally better, it is more in accord with one's philosophical motivation. Also it changes how one proceeds philosophically; at the macro-level . . . it leads away from constructing the philosophical tower; at the micro-level, it alters which philosophical "moves" are legitimate at various points.[20]

With this surprising redefinition of systematic axiomatic–deductive reasoning as "coercion," Nozick had pulled the last tooth from his libertarianism. If even the attempt of *proving* (or *demonstrating*) the ethical impermissibility and injustice of democratic socialism constituted "bad" behavior, libertarianism had been essentially disarmed and the existing order and its academic bodyguards rendered intellectually invincible. How could one not be nice to someone as nice as Nozick? It is no wonder that the anti-libertarian intellectual establishment took kindly to a libertarianism as gentle and kind as his, and elevated Nozick to the rank of the premier philosopher of libertarianism.[21]

---

20. Ibid., pp. 4, 5, 13.

21. In accordance with this non-methodical mindset, Nozick's philosophical interests continued to drift from one subject to another. Already in his *Philosophical Explanations*, he had confessed "I have found (and not only in sequence) many different philosophies alluring and appealing, cogent and impressive, tempting and wonderful." (p.20) Libertarianism—ethics—carried no particular or even unique weight within Nozick's philosophy. It was one exciting subject among innumerous others, to be taken up for "exploration" or dropped as one's curiosity demanded.

It was not entirely surprising then when, only a few years after the publication of the very book that had made him famous, it became increasingly obvious that Nozick had all but abandoned even his kind and gentle libertarianism. And when he at last acknowledged openly (in *The Examined Life*, a book of neo-Buddhist musings on the meaning of life) that he was no longer a libertarian and had converted to communitarian social democracy, he still felt under no obligation to give reasons for his change of mind

The interest stimulated and the influence exerted by Rothbard's libertarianism and *The Ethics of Liberty* was significantly different: slow, intensively growing, and lasting, and reaching and affecting academia from outside (rather than being picked up by it and from the ivory tower communicated "down" to the non-academic public).

Rothbard, as every reader of the following treatise will quickly recognize, was the prototype of a "coercive philosopher" (in the startling Nozickian definition of coercion). He demanded and presented proofs and exact and complete answers rather then tentative explanations, conjectures, and open questions. Regarding *Anarchy, State, and Utopia,* Nozick had written that "some may feel that the truth about ethics and political philosophy is too serious and important to be obtained by such 'flashy' tools."[22] This was certainly Rothbard's conviction. Because man cannot *not act* as long as he is alive, and he must use scarce means to do so, he must also permanently choose between right and wrong conduct. The fundamental question of ethics—what am I here and now rightfully allowed to do and what not— is thus the most permanent, important, and pressing intellectual concern confronting man. Whenever and wherever one acts, an actor must be able to determine and distinguish unambiguously and instantly right from wrong. Thus, any ethic worth its salt *must*—praxeologically—be a "coercive" one, because only proofs and knockdown arguments can provide such definite answers as are necessary. Man cannot temporarily suspend acting; hence, tentative conjectures and open questions simply are not up to the task of a human ethic.

Rothbard's "coercive" philosophizing—his insistence that ethics must be an axiomatic–deductive system, an ethic *more geometrico*—was nothing new or unusual, of course. As already noted, Rothbard shared this view concerning the nature of ethics with the entire tradition of rationalist philosophy. His had been the dominant view of Christian rationalism and of the Enlightenment. Nor did Rothbard claim infallibility regarding his ethics. In accordance with the tradition of rationalist philosophy he merely insisted that axiomatic–deductive arguments can be attacked, and possibly refuted, exclusively by other arguments of the same logical status (just as one would insist, without thereby claiming infallibility for logicians and mathematicians, that logical or mathematical proofs can be attacked only by other logical or mathematical arguments).

---

and explain why his previous ethical views had been false. Interestingly, this development seems to have had little effect on the status of *Anarchy, State, and Utopia* as prime libertarian philosophizing.

22. Ibid., p. x.

In the age of democratic socialism, however, such old-fashioned claims—certainly if made in conjunction with ethics and especially if this ethic turned out to be a libertarian one—were generally rejected and dismissed out of hand by academia. Unlike the modern Nozick, Rothbard was convinced that he had *proved* libertarianism—private-property anarchism—to be morally justified and correct, and that all statists and socialists were plain wrong. Accordingly, he advocated immediate and ongoing action. "Libertarianism," wrote Rothbard,

> is a philosophy seeking a policy. . . . The libertarian must be possessed of a passion for justice, an emotion derived from and channeled by his rational insight into what natural justice requires. Justice, not the weak reed of mere utility, must be the motivating force if liberty is to be attained; . . . (and) this means that the libertarian must be an "abolitionist," i.e., he must wish to achieve the goal of liberty as rapidly as possible . . . . [He] should be an abolitionist who would, if he could, abolish instantaneously all invasions of liberty (pp. 258–59).

To the tax-subsidized intellectual class and especially the academic establishment, Rothbard could not but appear to be an extremist, best to be ignored and excluded from mainstream academic discourse.[23]

Rothbard's "unkind" and "intolerant" libertarianism took first hold among the non-academic public: among professionals, businessmen, and educated laymen of all backgrounds. Whereas Nozick's "gentle" libertarianism never penetrated outside academia, Rothbard and his "extremist" libertarianism became the fountainhead and theoretical hardcore of an ideological movement. Rothbard became the creator of modern American libertarianism, the radical offspring of classical liberalism, which, in the course of some three decades, has grown from a handful of proponents into a genuine political and intellectual movement. Naturally, in the course

---

23. An interesting parallel exists between the treatment of Rothbard vs. Nozick by the philosophy establishment, and that of Mises vs. Hayek by the economics establishment. Even if Mises's conclusions were significantly more radical than Hayek's, both came to largely similar—politically "incorrect"—free-market conclusions. Based on the similarity of their conclusions, both Mises and Hayek were considered Austrian School economists. Yet the method by which they derived their conclusions fundamentally differed. Mises was a philosophical rationalist: systematic, rigorous, proving and demonstrating, and lucid as a writer. In comparison, Hayek was a philosophical skeptic: unsystematic, methodologically eclectic, tentative and probing, and a less than lucid writer. Consequently, Hayek's treatment by academia was significantly more friendly than that accorded to Mises. But also: it was the pre-modern "extremist Austrian" Mises, not the modern "moderate Austrian" Hayek, whose influence proved more intense and enduring, and whose work led to the formation of an ideological movement.

of this development and transformation, Rothbard and his libertarianism did not remain unchallenged or undisputed, and there were ups and downs in Rothbard's institutional career: of institutional alignments and realignments. Yet, until his death Rothbard, remained without doubt the single most important and respected moral authority within the entire libertarian movement, and his rationalist—axiomatic–deductive, praxeological, or "Austrian"—libertarianism provides to this day the intellectual benchmark in reference to which everyone and everything else in libertarianism is defined and positioned.

What proved to be unacceptable to academia—Rothbard's pre-modern method of axiomatic–deductive reasoning and system building—still found resonance among many people. Even if modern academics, freed of the obligation of having to provide a practical justification for their activities, can engage in unsystematic and open-ended "conversation," real men, and especially successful men, have to act and think systematically and methodically and such planning and future-oriented low-time-preference people also will not likely be satisfied with anything but systematic and methodical answers to their own practical moral concerns.

Nor did Rothbard's explicit political radicalism constitute a serious acceptance problem among such successful and independently minded men. Even if increasingly marginalized, significant remnants of the original American tradition of radical libertarianism still existed among the educated public. In fact, the American Revolution had been largely inspired by libertarian, radical Lockean ideas. And the *Declaration of Independence,* and in particular its author Thomas Jefferson, reflected and expressed the same rationalist spirit of the Enlightenment and the even older natural-law tradition that also characterized Rothbard and his political philosophy:

> We hold these truths to be self-evident, that all men are created equal, that they are endowed by their Creator with certain unalienable rights, that among these are life, liberty, and the pursuit of happiness. That to secure these rights, governments are instituted among men, deriving their just powers from the consent of the governed. That whenever any form of government becomes destructive of these ends, it is the right of the people to alter or to abolish it, and to institute new government, laying its foundation on such principles and organizing its powers in such form, as to them shall seem most likely to effect their safety and happiness. Prudence, indeed, will dictate that governments long established should not be changed for light and transient causes; and accordingly all experience has shown, that mankind are more disposed to suffer, while evils are sufferable, than

to right themselves by abolishing the forms to which they are accustomed. But when a long train of abuses and usurpations, pursuing invariably the same object evinces a design to reduce them under absolute despotism, it is their right, it is their duty, to throw off such government, and to provide new guards for their future security.

Rothbard, apart from his theoretical work as an economist and a political philosopher, was also an eminent historian. In his four-volume history of colonial America, *Conceived in Liberty*,[24] he gives a detailed narrative account of the predominance of libertarian thought in early America, and in many essays on critical episodes in U.S. history, he notes again and again the continuing importance of the original libertarian American spirit. To be sure, the original radical-libertarian impetus, which had led to the American Revolution and the *Declaration of Independence*, had subsequently suffered one setback after another: with the victory of the Federalists over the anti-Federalists and the transition from the original Confederacy to the Union, with the *de facto* abolition of the Union constitution by Abraham Lincoln in the course and as the result of the destruction of the secessionist Southern Confederacy, with the onset of Progressivism, with Franklin D. Roosevelt's New Deal, with Lyndon B. Johnson's Great Society, and so on with presidents Nixon, Carter, Reagan, Bush, and Clinton. Even if again and again defeated, however, the tradition of radical individualist libertarianism could not be eradicated from the American public consciousness. In harking back explicitly to Jefferson and the Jeffersonian tradition, Rothbard tapped into a still widespread if dormant pool of activists and lay intellectuals; and owing to the clarity, the logical rigor, the systematic and comprehensive character, and the passion of his writings, he succeeded almost single-handedly in reinvigorating, radicalizing, and channeling their sentiments into a unified political-philosophical movement.

It was only in light of "external" events—the emergence and advancement of a libertarian movement and the central role played by Rothbard in this movement—and with a considerable delay, that Rothbard and *The Ethics of Liberty* no longer could be overlooked by academia. Not surprisingly, even then the general reaction was cool. To be sure, there were also a fair and steadily growing number of highly respectful and appreciative academic treatments of Rothbard's political philosophy,[25] and around *The Journal of Libertarian Studies*, an interdisciplinary scholarly review Rothbard had founded in 1977 and for which he had served until

---

24. Murray N. Rothbard, *Conceived in Liberty* (New York: Arlington House, 1975).

his death as editor, he had assembled a formidable number of disciples. But in general, the academic reaction to Rothbard and his libertarianism was one of non- or mis-comprehension, indignant rejection, or even downright hostility.

In part, this was certainly due to Rothbard's unapologetic use of the language of natural rights. This had been the language of the *Declaration of Independence*; the same natural-rights language had been preserved to the present within the Christian and in particular the Catholic Church, and it had also been adopted by a handful of contemporary philosophers.[26] However, to most contemporary academics talk of "natural rights" was, in Jeremy Bentham's words, no more than "nonsense on stilts." In fact and more to the point, natural rights were incompatible with absolute state power, and they did not sit well with either democracy or socialism. Hence, in the course of the transformation of the Western world from an aristocratic or monarchical system to a modern mass democracy within the last 100 years, natural-rights teachings had been successively removed from the officially approved philosophical curriculum and replaced with modern positivistic doctrines. Confronted with a largely unfamiliar language, even many well-intentioned philosophers were simply befuddled or irritated by Rothbard's work. Moreover, Rothbard may even have overstated his own agreement with classical natural-rights theory, and not sufficiently emphasized his own distinct contribution of importing and applying the Misesian method of praxeology to ethics, and thus unintentionally have aggravated an already existing problem.

Typical and at the same time instructive were reactions like those of Peter D. McClelland, for instance, in a chapter in a book on economic justice entitled "The Market Defended: Confusions of the Right." "Murray Rothbard," McClelland noted:

> is one of the acknowledged intellectual leaders among contemporary libertarians, a group which, by American standards, is located on the far right. His views are interesting for purposes of this discussion for two reasons. First he provides a carefully reasoned defense of the income distribution generated by the market that makes no reference to the merits of recipients. Secondly, that defense proceeds from a handful of premises to a conclusion presumed to be universally applicable in any situation where

---

25. See, e.g., Norman P. Barry, *On Classical Liberalism and Libertarianism* (London: Macmillan, 1986).

26. See, e.g., Leo Strauss, *Natural Right and History* (Chicago: University of Chicago Press, 1970); also Henry Veatch, *Human Rights: Fact or Fancy?* (Baton Rouge: Louisiana State University Press, 1985).

the justice of the economic system is at stake. As such, it provides a classic example of how not to reason about economic justice. To put the second point a second way, Rothbard's approach flies in the face of key points made in earlier chapters: that to problems of economic justice we bring a multitude of values to be honored; these values can and do conflict; when conflicts arise, tradeoffs among competing values must be made; general rules for making such tradeoffs are difficult to formulate; and thus judgments about economic justice are difficult to make independent of the context of the situation in which such judgments must be made. Or, more simply put, in reaching decisions about economic justice in a concrete situation, we do not generally rely upon universal rules to determine the "right" or "just" choice.[27]

In all, McClelland finds that Rothbard's arguments are "somewhat strange"—"Aquinas viewpoint minus the theology"—and he then summarily dismisses them on the ground that:

> for most Americans, many of [Rothbard's] points are extreme or simplistic or both, and the argument in its entirety is more curious than compelling. The best evidence of that is the negligible importance of the Libertarian Party in American politics. . . . [Rothbard's "reduction" of moral dilemmas to one or few basic principles] is itself objectionable, precisely because it is achieved by ignoring much that is important—or at least much that is important to the vast majority of Americans.[28]

Several objections and questions arise immediately upon reading this, not least of which is the *truly* strange fact that our author apparently believes that empirical facts, such as that not many people believe *p*, have any bearing on the question whether or not *p* is true, valid, or justified. Would he also object to mathematical or logical proofs on the ground that most people are incapable of grasping them? Moreover, granting that "when conflicts arise, tradeoffs among competing values must be made," the decisive question is, *who* is to decide what these tradeoffs should be? Conflicting values invariably involve incompatible— mutually exclusive—views of at least two actors concerning the use of some scarce resources. Obviously then, not *both* of these parties can decide what these tradeoffs should be (after all, their respective values are incompatible), but only one *or* the other. But how can one party be

---

27. Peter D. McClelland, *The American Search for Economic Justice* (Oxford: Basil Blackwell, 1990), p. 74.

28. Ibid., pp. 75, 76, 80–81.

selected, and not the other, unless one possesses a theory of property? And if one cannot "rely upon universal rules to determine the 'right' or 'just' choice" and everything depends on the "context of the situation," how then does our critic think it possible for anyone to ever know *ex ante, before* taking it, whether or not some action qualifies as just? Or does he believe that justice is to be determined only *ex post*? How could such a theory of justice qualify as a human ethic?

All of these concerns may be left aside, however, because the ultimate error in McClelland's criticism—and by contrast the unique Rothbardian contribution to ethics—occurs at a logically prior stage, when McClelland claims that Rothbard's "reductionist"—that is, axiomatic–deductive—method "flies in the face" of the existence of a "multitude of values to be honored."

McClelland does not explain why this should be so. Nor could he have succeeded, even if he had tried. First off, surely Rothbard could not have been unaware of the fact of a multitude of conflicting values. Indeed, it is difficult to imagine anyone unaware of this fact. Yet this observation is no more than the starting point of ethics and moral reasoning. If no conflicting values existed, then, by definition, all actions would be in perfect harmony with each other. Everyone would always act in such a way as everyone else thought he should act. In this case of a pre-stabilized harmony of all interests, there is no need for an ethic and none would ever come into existence. The existence of conflicting values thus poses no problem whatsoever for Rothbard's ethic (or any other ethic, for that matter). Rather, it is from the outset taken for granted, and ethics is the very response to this universal and eternal human dilemma. Furthermore, if conflicts exist and if these can be resolved at all, then such a solution cannot possibly be found except by means of a "reductionist" method, i.e., the subsumption of specific cases or conflict-situations under general and abstract rules or principles. Rothbard's view in this regard is not essentially different from that of most other political and moral philosophers: ethics, if it is possible at all, must and can never be anything else but "reductionist."

Assuming for the sake of argument that no disagreement exists up to this point, McClelland's charge can only mean this: even if one were to follow such a reductionist strategy, it will not yield a single principle (or a single set of internally consistent principles) covering and resolving all cases of conflict. In other words, even if some disagreements may be resolved by reference to increasingly more general and abstract rules and principles, (many) other disagreements will remain unresolvable because, as a matter of empirical fact, even on the level of abstract rules and principles, disagreement persists and inescapably results in inconsistencies and incompatibilities (and leads to moral skepticism of some sort). This line of reasoning is indeed characteristic of a wide-ranging group of political philosophers (including Rawls) who, while they may disagree among themselves on how much conflict can or cannot be resolved in this way, all conceive of ethical principles as the *result* (outcome) of agreement or contract.

It is here that the fundamental error lies and Rothbard's unique contribution to ethics comes into play. Ethics—the validity of the principle of self-ownership and original appropriation—is demonstrably *not* dependent and contingent upon agreement or contract; and the universality claim connected with Rothbard's libertarianism is not affected in the slightest by the circumstance that moral discussants may or may not always come to an agreement or contract. Ethics is the logical–praxeological *presupposition*—in Kantian terminology: *die Bedingung der Moeglichkeit*—rather than the result of agreement or contract. The principles of self-ownership and original appropriation make agreement and contract—including that of not agreeing and contracting—possible. Set in motion and stimulated by the universal experience of conflict, moral discussion and argument can discover, reconstruct, explicate, and formulate the principles of self-ownership and original appropriation, but their validity in no way depends on whether or not this is the case, and if so whether or not these formulations then find universal assent.

Rothbard's distinct contribution to the natural-rights tradition is his reconstruction of the principles of self-ownership and original appropriation as the praxeological precondition—*Bedingung der Moeglichkeit*—of argumentation, and his recognition that whatever must be presupposed as valid in order to make argumentation possible in the first place cannot in turn be argumentatively disputed without thereby falling into a practical self-contradiction.[29]

As Rothbard explains in an unfortunately brief but centrally important passage of *The Ethics of Liberty*:

> a proposition rises to the status of an axiom when he who denies it may be shown to be using it in the very course of the supposed refutation. Now, *any* person participating in any sort of discussion, including one on values, is, by virtue of so participating, alive and affirming life. For if he were *really*

29. On this, and further-reaching philosophical investigations into the logic of axiomatic-deductive proofs and reasoning in ethics (and economics) as championed by Rothbard, see in particular Hans-Hermann Hoppe, *The Economics and Ethics of Private Property* (Boston: Kluwer Academic Publishers, 1993); also N. Stephan Kinsella, "New Rationalist Directions in Libertarian Rights Theory," *Journal of Libertarian Studies* 12, no. 2 (1996).

opposed to life, he would have no business in such a discussion, indeed he would have no business continuing to be alive. Hence, the supposed opponent of life is really affirming it in the very process of his discussion, and hence the preservation and furtherance of one's life takes on the stature of an incontestable axiom (pp. 32–33).

As an immediate implication of this insight into the status of the principles of self-ownership and original appropriation as ethical *axioms*, Rothbard rejected as nonsense all notions of "animal rights." Animals are incapable of engaging in propositional exchange with humans. Indeed, it is this inability which defines them as non-rational and distinguishes them categorically from men as rational animals. Unable to communicate, and without rationality, animals are by their very nature incapable of recognizing or possessing any rights. Rothbard noted,

> There is rough justice in the common quip that "we will recognize the rights of animals whenever they petition for them." The fact that animals can obviously not petition for their "rights" is part of their nature, and part of the reason why they are clearly not equivalent to, and do not possess the rights of, human beings (p. 156).

Rather than rightful moral agents, animals are objects of possible human control and appropriation. Thus Rothbard confirmed the biblical pronouncement that man had been given *dominion* over every living thing, in the sea, on earth, and in the sky.

As academia had little to do with Rothbard's success in creating and shaping a political–philosophical mass movement in the first place, its belated mostly negative reactions did little to change Rothbard's growing status as a public philosopher. To the contrary. The course of historical events—the spectacular collapse of the "great socialist experiment" in the Soviet Union and Eastern Europe from 1989–91, and the increasingly obvious crisis of the Western welfare states—provided ever-more support for fundamental libertarian insights. No one but his teacher Mises had given a more accurate account of the economic inefficiencies of socialism and social democracy than Rothbard, and no one had explained more clearly the moral hazards and perversions created by socialism and social democracy. Whereas the events in Eastern Europe and the economic and moral crisis of the Western states—of stagnating or falling real incomes, staggering public debt, imminently bankrupt social security systems, family and social disintegration, rising uncivility, moral degeneration, and crime—were an obvious embarrassment and intellectual debacle for the social-democratic academic

establishment,[30] they provided dramatic empirical confirmation for
Rothbard and his theoretical work. In this situation, libertarianism and
Rothbard's influence in particular could only grow and gain prominence.
By the mid-1990s, Rothbard's role as the *spiritus rector* of a steadily
growing and increasingly "threatening" revolutionary libertarian move-
ment was even acknowledged by the mainstream media.[31]

Nor did the academic rejection make any noticeable impression on
Rothbard or the further development of libertarian theory. *The Ethics of
Liberty* had been published at a low point in Rothbard's career. Though
one of the founders of the Cato Institute, Rothbard had been forced out
by the chief financial backer as too "extreme" and "intransigent." Despite
such unfavorable external circumstances and without any institutional
promotion, the book established itself quickly as the single most author-
itative and comprehensive work in libertarian theory. Long after the book
had gone out of print in the U.S., it was being translated into French,
Spanish, Italian, and German, further securing its status as an enduring
classic of political philosophy. Ironically, 1982 was also the year of the
founding of the Ludwig von Mises Institute, of which he served as academic head until his death. Together with a new academic position at
the University of Nevada, Las Vegas, these would prove to be the years of
Rothbard's greatest professional success.

After the original publication of *The Ethics of Liberty* and until his
death in 1995, Rothbard was working on a comprehensive and encom-
passing history of economic and political thought. Two massive volumes
of the unfinished three-volume project were published posthumously,
in 1995, under the titles *Economic Thought Before Adam Smith* and *Classical
Economics*.[32] Based on his prior theoretical work—with Austrian free-market
economics and libertarian political philosophy providing the conceptual
framework—Rothbard in these volumes gave a sweeping narrative account of the history of economic and political-philosophical ideas, from
the ancient Greeks to near the end of the nineteenth century, and the inter-
play of ideas and economic and political reality. Pure and abstract

---

30. E.g., Paul Samuelson, left-liberal Keynesian Nobel-prize economist, and author of
the world's all-time bestselling textbook, *Economics*, had characterized the Soviet Union
as a largely noble and successful experiment all the way up to the book's 1989 edition!

31. Thus, following the right-wing "Republican revolution" during the 1994 congressional
elections, the *Washington Post* identified Rothbard as the central intellectual figure behind
this event. In what is probably his last publication, Rothbard took this opportunity to
denounce the newly elected Republican House Speaker Newt Gingrich as an anti-
libertarian welfare-statist sell-out.

32. (Brookfield, Vt.: Edward Elgar, 1995).

Austrian and libertarian theory was illustrated with historical examples and illustrations, and at the same time intellectual and political history was presented as a systematically comprehensible subject, methodically and thematically unified and integrated. Rothbard here opened a panoramic view of the entire history of Western civilization, with new vistas and many surprising or even startling reinterpretations and reevaluations. History was unfolded as a permanent struggle between truth and falsehood and good (justice) and evil—of intellectual and political heroes great and small, and of economic and political break-throughs and progress, as well as of blunderers and villains, and of errors, perversions, and decline—and the civilizational ups and downs of human history were explained as the results of true and false ideas and the distribution and strength of ideologies in public consciousness. By complementing economic and political theory with history, Rothbard provided the Austrolibertarian movement with a grand historical perspective, sociological understanding, and strategic vision, and thus deepened and broadened libertarianism's popular anchoring and sociological base.

Besides his main work on the history of economic and political thought, however, Rothbard also returned repeatedly to political theory. In reaction to a growing environmentalist movement and its transformation into an anti-human and pro-animal movement, Rothbard wrote "Law, Property Rights, and Air Pollution,"[33] further elucidating the concepts of physical invasion, tort, causation, risk, burden of proof, and liability. In response to the rise of nationalism and separatism in the wake of the collapse of the Soviet Empire and U.S. multiculturalism and compulsory "non-discrimination," a decade later in an article on "Nations by Consent: Decomposing the Nation State,"[34] he further elaborated on the libertarian answers to the questions of nations, borders, immigration, separation, and secession. In the preface to the French edition of *The Ethics of Liberty*, he summarily reviewed several current contributions to libertarian theory— apart from Nozick's, utilitarian and contractarian libertarianisms, and natural-rights minarchisms—and rejected all of them as ultimately confused or inconsistent. In the monthly *Free Market* published by the Mises Institute, he provided political and economic analysis of current

---

33. *Cato Journal* (Spring 1982): 55–99.

34. *Journal of Libertarian Studies* 11, no. 1 (Fall 1994). Additional scholarly political articles published in his last year include "Bureaucracy and the Civil Service in the United States," *Journal of Libertarian Studies* 11, no. 2 (Summer 1995): 3–75; "Origin of the Welfare State in America," *Journal of Libertarian Studies* 12, no. 2 (Fall 1996): 193–230; "Egalitarianism and the Elites," *Review of Austrian Economics* 8, no. 2: 39–60; "The End of Socialism and the Calculation Debate Revisited," *Review of Austrian Economics* 2: 51–76.

events, beginning in 1982 and continuing until 1995. In addition, in 1989 he founded the monthly *Rothbard–Rockwell Report*, which served as the main outlet of Rothbard's political, sociological, cultural and religious commentary; he contributed dozens of articles in which he applied libertarian principles to the full range of human events and experiences—from war and criminal punishment to the appropriation of air space and waves, blackmail, affirmative action, and adoption, etc.—and thus constantly illustrated and reiterated the universal applicability and versatility of libertarian theory.

None of these later writings, however, brought any systematic changes as compared to *The Ethics of Liberty*, whether on principle or remote conclusions. Different and new problem aspects were analyzed and emphasized, but the essentials were already contained in his earlier treatise. In distinct contrast to Nozick, Rothbard did not change his mind on essential questions. Indeed, looking back over his entire career, it can be said that from the late 1950s, when he had first arrived at what would later become the Rothbardian system, until the end of his life, Rothbard did not waver on fundamental matters of economic or political theory. Yet owing to his long and intensive work in the history of economic and political thought, a different thematic emphasis became apparent in his later writings, most noticeably in the several hundred articles contributed during the last years of his life. Apart from economic and political concerns, Rothbard increasingly focused his attention on and stressed the importance of culture as a sociological prerequisite of libertarianism.

Libertarianism as developed in *The Ethics of Liberty* was no more and no less than a political philosophy. It provided an answer to the question of which actions are lawful and hence may not be legitimately threatened with physical violence, and which actions are unlawful and may be so punished. It did not say anything with respect to the further question whether or not all lawful actions should be equally tolerated or possibly punished by means other than—and below the threshold of—a threat of physical violence, such as public disapprobation, ostracism, exclusion, and expulsion.

Even given its explicitly limited scope, *The Ethics of Liberty* had a distinctly old-fashioned flavor and revealed libertarianism as a fundamentally conservative doctrine. The most obvious indicator of this was the already noted emphasis placed on punishment as the necessary complement to property. More specifically, Rothbard presented a rigorous modern defense of the traditional proportionality principle of punishment as contained in the *lex talionis*—of an eye for an eye, or rather, as he would correctively explain, two eyes for an eye. He rejected the deterrence and rehabilitation theories of punishment as incompatible with private property rights and championed instead the idea of victims' rights and of restitution (compensation) and/or retribution as essential to justice; he argued in favor of such old-fashioned institutions as compulsory labor and indentured servitude for convicted criminals, and for debtor's prisons; and his analyses of causation and liability, burden of proof, and proper assumption of risk invariably displayed a basic and staunch moral conservatism of strict individual responsibility and accountability.

This and Rothbard's own life-long cultural conservatism notwithstanding, however, from its beginnings in the late 1960s and the founding of a libertarian party in 1971, the libertarian movement had great appeal to many of the counter-cultural left that had then grown up in the U.S. in opposition to the war in Vietnam. Did not the illegitimacy of the state and the non-aggression axiom imply that everyone was at liberty to choose his very own non-aggressive lifestyle, no matter what it was?

Much of Rothbard's later writings, with their increased emphasis on cultural matters, were designed to correct this development and to explain the error in the idea of a leftist multi-counter-cultural libertarianism, of libertarianism as a variant of libertinism. It was false— empirically as well as normatively—that libertarianism could or should be combined with egalitarian multiculturalism. Both were in fact sociologically incompatible, and libertarianism could and should be combined exclusively with traditional Western bourgeois culture; that is, the old-fashioned ideal of a family-based and hierarchically structured society of voluntarily acknowledged rank orders of social authority.

Empirically, Rothbard did not tire to explain, the left-libertarians failed to recognize that the restoration of private-property rights and laissez-faire economics implied a sharp and drastic increase in social "discrimination." Private property means the right to exclude. The modern social-democratic welfare state has increasingly stripped private-property owners of their right to exclude.

In distinct contrast, a libertarian society where the right to exclude was fully restored to owners of private property would be profoundly unegalitarian. To be sure, private property also implies the owner's right to include and to open and facilitate access to one's property, and every private-property owner also faces an economic incentive of including (rather than excluding) so long as he expects this to increase the value of his property.

The Ethics of Liberty's chapter most difficult to accept for conservatives, on "Children and Rights," comes thus to appear in a different light. In this chapter Rothbard argued in favor of a mother's "absolute right to

her own body and therefore to perform an abortion." He rejected the
"right to life" argument not on the ground that a fetus was not life (in
fact, from the moment of conception, he agreed with the Catholic position,
it was human life), but rather on the fundamental ground that no such thing
as a universal "right to life," but exclusively a universal "right to live an
independent and separate life," can properly and possibly exist (and that
a fetus, while certainly human life, is just as certainly up to the moment
of birth not an independent but, biologically speaking, a "parasitic" life,
and thus has no rightful claim against the mother). Further, upon child
birth, a mother (and with her consent parents jointly),

> would have the trustee-ownership of her children, an
> ownership limited only by the illegality of aggressing against
> their persons and by their absolute right to run away or to
> leave home at any time. Parents would be able to sell their
> trustee-rights in children to anyone who wished to buy them
> at any mutually-agreed price (p. 104).

So long as children have not left home, a parent:

> does not have the right to aggress against his children, but also
> the parent should not have a legal obligation to feed, clothe,
> or educate his children, since such obligations would entail
> positive acts coerced upon the parent and depriving the parent
> of his rights. The parent therefore may not murder or mutilate
> his child . . . but the parent should have the legal right not to
> feed his child, i.e., to allow it to die" (p. 100).

So as to avoid any misunderstanding, in the next sentence Rothbard
reminded his reader of the strictly delineated scope of his treatise on political philosophy and noted that "whether or not a parent has a *moral*
rather than a legally enforceable obligation to keep his child alive is a completely separate question." However, this explicit qualification and the general thrust of *The Ethics of Liberty* notwithstanding, these pronouncements
were used in conservative circles in the attempt to prevent a libertarian
infiltration and radicalization of contemporary American conservatism.
Of course, conservative political theory was a contradiction in terms. Conservatism essentially meant not to have, and even reject, any abstract
theory and rigorous logical argument. Not surprisingly, Rothbard was
singularly unimpressed by conservative critics such as Russell Kirk,
whose "theoretical" work he considered devoid of analytical and argu-
mentative rigor. Consequently, Rothbard did not see any reason to abandon
his original conclusions. Until the end of his life, he would not budge on
the problem of abortion and child neglect and insisted on a mother's

absolute legal (lawful) right to an abortion and of letting her children die. In fact, if women did not have such rights and had committed instead a punishable crime, it would seem that their crime then must be equivalent to murder. Should abortion accordingly be threatened with capital punishment and convicted abortionist mothers be executed? But who, except its mother, can possibly claim a right to her fetus and child and thus be considered as the rightful victim of her actions? Who could bring a wrongful death suit against her? Surely not the state. For a conservative in particular, any state interference in the autonomy of families should be anathema. But who else, if indeed anyone?

Yet while Rothbard unchangingly held to his conclusions concerning the rights of children and parents, his later writings with an increased emphasis on moral–cultural matters and the exclusionary aspect of private property rights placed these conclusions in a wider—and characteristically conservative—social context. Thus, while in favor of a woman's right to have an abortion, Rothbard was nonetheless strictly opposed to the U.S. Supreme Court's decision in *Roe v. Wade,* which recognized such a right. This was not because he believed the court's finding concerning the legality of abortion wrong, but on the more fundamental ground that the U.S. Supreme Court had no jurisdiction in the matter and that, by assuming it, the court had engendered a systematic centralization of state power.

The right to have an abortion does not imply that one may have an abortion anywhere. In fact, there is nothing impermissible about private owners and associations discriminating against and punishing abortionists by every means other than physical punishment. Every household and property owner is free to prohibit an abortion on his own territory and may enter into a restrictive covenant with other owners for the same purpose. Moreover, every owner and every association of owners is free to fire or not to hire and to refuse to engage in any transaction whatsoever with an abortionist. It may indeed be the case that no civilized place can be found anywhere and that one must retire to the infamous "back alley" to have an abortion. Not only would there be nothing wrong with such a situation, it would be positively moral in raising the cost of irresponsible sexual conduct and helping to reduce the number of abortions. In distinct contrast, the Supreme Court's decision was not only unlawful by expanding its, i.e., the central state's, jurisdiction at the expense of state and local governments, but ultimately of every private-property owner's rightful jurisdiction regarding his own property, it was also positively immoral in facilitating the availability and accessibility of abortion.

Libertarians, Rothbard stressed in this connection, must be opposed, as are traditional conservatives (but unlike social democrats, neo-conservatives, and left-libertarians), on principled grounds to any and all centralization of state power, even and especially if such centralization involves a correct judgment (such as that abortion should be legal, or that taxes should be abolished). It would be anti-libertarian, for instance, to appeal to the United Nations to order the breakup of a taxi-monopoly in Houston, or to the U.S. government to order Utah to abolish its state-certification requirement for teachers, because in doing so one would have illegitimately granted these state agencies jurisdiction over property that they plainly do not own (but others do): not only Houston or Utah, but every city in the world and every state in the U.S. And while every state, small or large, violates the rights of private-property owners and must be feared and combated, large central states violate more people's rights and must be feared even more. They do not come into existence *ab ovo*, but are the outgrowth of a process of eliminative competition among originally numerous independent small local states. Central states, and ultimately a single world state, represent the successful expansion and concentration of state power, i.e., of evil, and must accordingly be regarded as especially dangerous.

Hence, a libertarian, as his second-best solution, must always discriminate in favor of local and against central government, and he must always try to correct injustices at the level and location where they occur rather than empowering some higher (more centralized) level of government to rectify a local injustice.

In fact, as a result of his increasing emphasis on cultural conservatism as a sociological presupposition of libertarianism, Rothbard succeeded in bringing about a fundamental reorientation of the libertarian movement during the last decade of his life. Symbolic of this change in direction was Rothbard's dissociation, in 1989, from the Libertarian Party. Rothbard's action did not, as some prominent left-libertarians vainly proclaimed at the time, mark the end of his association with libertarianism or his role as the libertarian movement's guiding star. Rather, it marked the beginning of a systematic ideological realignment to open libertarian access to the American "heartland" and foment there a rapidly growing and increasingly radicalized populist movement among "Middle Americans" disgusted with the welfare–warfare statism, and social disintegration produced and promoted by federal policies. The anti-central-state shift in American politics at the decisive end of the cold war was the first unmistakable sign of the burgeoning strength of the conservative–libertarian grassroots movement envisioned and shaped by Rothbard.[35]

---

35. The historical moment for Rothbardian scholarly tradition may at last have arrived, and his political movement is surely not too far in the distance. Rothbard had always

At the academic level, Rothbard's lifelong work for the scholarship of liberty has at long last come to serve as the foundational theoretical edifice for the modern successors of the old classical-liberal movement—the movement that originally influenced the development of the basic libertarian position. Today, this movement is truly international in scope, and includes thousands of lay intellectuals and professional scholars the world over, many of whom view Rothbard's voluminous writings over the entire course of his lifetime as the model and ideal of principled political and economic thinking.[36] After his death, his reputation as leader in libertarian political theory and Austrian School economics is increasingly obvious, even undeniable, to enthusiasts and critics alike. For his seminal *Ethics of Liberty* to be available once again should further solidify this status.

University of Nevada, Las Vegas
January 1998

---

been an optimist, grounded in the fact of human rationality and further strengthened by the Misesian–Rothbardian insight that one cannot violate moral and economic laws without having to pay a price and that one violation will, according to the "logic" of state action, lead to more violations until the price that must be paid becomes intolerable. Thus, the ethical and economic depredations of socialism finally ended in a spectacular collapse. Likewise, in the U.S. and the Western world, after nearly 100 years of social-democratic welfare statism, the moral and economic "reserve fund" inherited from the past has become visibly exhausted and has led to a manifest economic and moral crisis of stagnating or falling standards of living and societal breakdown, as well as a widespread loss of faith and trust in the central state as the organizing agent of society. In this situation of the obvious moral and economic bankruptcy of socialism and social democracy and an ever more strongly felt need for an explanation and a principle alternative, it can be safely predicted that Rothbard's *Ethics of Liberty* not only will endure as a classic but steadily gain in prominence.

36. *Journal des Economistes et des Etudes Humanines* 6, no. 2 (March 1995); *Murray N. Rothbard: In Memoriam* (Auburn, Ala.: Ludwig von Mises Institute, 1995).

ACKNOWLEDGMENTS

T his work has been literally a lifetime in the making, for my vital interest in libertarianism began in childhood, and has intensified ever since. Hence, it is simply impossible to mention and acknowledge all the people or influences from whom I have learned, and to whom I am deeply grateful. In particular, I have had the good fortune to benefit from countless discussions, interchanges, and correspondence with a large number of thoughtful and scholarly libertarians, all of whom have helped to form my ideas and hence to shape this work. This will have to be my apology for not mentioning each one of them. I will have to confine my acknowledgments to those who helped me specifically on this book. As the one exception to this rule, I would like to express my gratitude to my father, David Rothbard. Until my twenties, it seemed to me that he was the only other libertarian in the world, and so I am particularly grateful for his encouragement, endless patience, and enthusiasm. I first learned about the rudiments of liberty from him and then, after I became a full-fledged and consistent libertarian, in the winter of 1949–50, he was my first convert.

Turning then to the book itself, it too has been long in the making, and has undergone several wholesale transformations. It began, in discussion with Dr. Ivan R. Bierly of the William Volker Fund of Burlingame, California, in the early 1960s, with the idea of bringing natural rights to libertarians and liberty to conservatives. This concept of the book has long been abandoned, and transmuted into the far bolder task of setting forth a systematic theory of the ethics of liberty. On this long and rocky road, the patience and the encouragement of Floyd Arthur ("Baldy") Harper and of Kenneth S. Templeton, Jr., both initially of the William Volker Fund and then of the Institute of Humane Studies, Menlo Park, California, have never faltered.

I would like to thank the organizers and the commentators on parts of this book at the Libertarian Scholars Conference in New York City. I am grateful that Randy E. Barnett and John Hagel, III, saw fit to include my defense of proportionate punishment in their work, *Assessing the Criminal*. And *Ordo* is to be commended for publishing my critique of F.A. Hayek's concept of coercion.

Williamson M. Evers, of the department of political science, Stanford University, was immeasurably helpful during the year (1975) that I spent working on this book in Palo Alto, California. I am grateful to him for his stimulating discussions of libertarian theory, for his bibliographical erudition, and for numerous helpful suggestions. John N. Gray, fellow in politics, Jesus College, Oxford, and James A. Sadowsky, S.J. of the philosophy department of Fordham University, each read the entire manuscript and their kind comments greatly bolstered my morale in seeing it through to completion. Dr. David Gordon, of Los Angeles and of the Center for Libertarian Studies, read the entire manuscript and offered detailed and extremely helpful suggestions; his erudition and keen philosophical insights are an inspiration to all who know him. The devotion to and enthusiasm for this work by Leonard P. Liggio, now president of the Institute for Humane Studies, Menlo Park, were indispensable to its final publication. I would also like to thank Dr. Louis M. Spadaro, president emeritus of the Institute for Humane Studies, and George Pearson of the Koch Foundation and of the Institute.

I am grateful to the Volker Fund and to the Institute for Humane Studies for repeated research aid. I am particularly grateful to Charles G. Koch of Wichita, Kansas, for his devotion to this work and to the ideals of liberty, and for enabling me to take off the year 1974–75 from teaching to work on this book.

Despite my enormous gratitude to those friends and colleagues on the long and lonely struggle to develop libertarianism and to advance the cause of liberty, it cannot compare to the inexpressible debt that I owe my wife Joey, who for nearly thirty years has been an unflagging source of support, enthusiasm, insight, and happiness.

MURRAY N. ROTHBARD
New York City, May 1980

PREFACE

All of my work has revolved around the central question of human liberty. For it has been my conviction that, while each discipline has its own autonomy and integrity, in the final analysis all sciences and disciplines of human action are interrelated, and can be integrated into a "science" or discipline of individual liberty. In particular, my *Man, Economy, and State* (2 vols., 1962) set forth a comprehensive analysis of the free-market economy; while the analysis was praxeologic and value-free, and no political conclusions were directly upheld, the great virtues of the free market and the evils of coercive intervention into that market were evident to the discerning reader. The sequel to that work, *Power and Market* (1970), carried the analysis of *Man, Economy, and State* further in several ways: (a) a systematic analysis of the types of government intervention in the economy clearly shows the myriad of unfortunate consequences of such intervention; (b) for the first time in modern political economic literature, a model was outlined of the way in which a totally stateless and therefore purely free (or anarchistic) market economy could function successfully; and (c) a praxeological and therefore still value-free critique was conducted of the lack of meaningfulness and consistency of various types of ethical attacks on the free market. The latter section moved from pure economics to ethical criticism, but it remained within the bounds of value-freedom, and thus did not attempt a positive ethical theory of individual liberty. Yet, I was conscious that the latter task needed almost desperately to be done, for, as will be seen further in this work, I at no time believed that value-free analysis or economics or utilitarianism (the standard social philosophy of economists) can ever suffice to establish the case for liberty. Economics can help supply much of the *data* for a libertarian position, but it cannot establish that political philosophy itself. Political judgments are necessarily value judgments, political philosophy is therefore necessarily *ethical*, and hence a positive ethical system must be set forth to establish the case for individual liberty.

It was furthermore clear to me that no one was engaged in trying to fill this crying need. For one thing, until very recently in this century there have been virtually no libertarian political philosophers. And even in the far more libertarian nineteenth century, only Herbert Spencer's great *Social Statics* (1851) set forth a thorough and systematic theory of liberty. In *For A New Liberty* (1973), I was able for the first time to put forward at least the brief outlines of my theory of liberty, and also to expound and defend the "anarchocapitalist" political creed far more substantially than in *Power and Market*. But *For A New Liberty* was more popular than scholarly, and it concentrated mainly on the application of the libertarian creed to the important social and economic problem areas in American society. The great need for a systematic theory of liberty still remained.

The present work attempts to fill this gap, to set forth a systematic ethical theory of liberty. It is *not*, however, a work in ethics *per se*, but only in that subset of ethics devoted to political philosophy. Hence, it does not try to prove or establish the ethics or ontology of natural law, which provide the groundwork for the political theory set forth in this book. Natural law has been ably expounded and defended elsewhere by ethical philosophers. And so Part I simply explains the outlines of natural law which animates this work, without attempting a full-scale defense of that theory.

Part II is the substance of the work itself, setting forth my theory of liberty. It begins, as the best economic treatises have done, with a "Crusoe" world, except that the condition and actions of Crusoe are here analyzed not in order to establish economic concepts, but rather those of natural-rights morality—in particular, of the natural sphere of property and ownership, the foundation of liberty. The Crusoe model enables one to analyze the action of man *vis-à-vis* the external world around him, before the complications of interpersonal relations are considered.

The key to the theory of liberty is the establishment of the rights of private property, for each individual's justified sphere of free action can only be set forth if his rights of property are analyzed and established. "Crime" can then be defined and properly analyzed as a violent invasion or aggression against the just property of another individual (including his property in his own person). The positive theory of liberty then becomes an analysis of *what* can be considered property rights, and therefore *what* can be considered crimes. Various difficult but vitally important problems can then be dissected, including the rights of children, the proper theory of contracts as transfers of property titles, the thorny questions of enforcement and punishment, and many others. Since questions of property and crime are essentially *legal* questions, our theory of liberty necessarily sets forth an ethical theory of what law concretely *should* be. In short, as a natural-law theory should properly do, it sets forth a normative theory of law—in our case, a theory of "libertarian law." While the book establishes the general outlines of a system of libertarian law, however, it is only an outline, a prolegomenon to what I hope will be a fully developed libertarian law code of the future. Hopefully, libertarian jurists and legal theorists will arise to hammer out the system of libertarian law in detail, for such a law code will be necessary to the truly successful functioning of what we may hope will be the libertarian society of the future.

The focus of this work is on the positive ethical theory of liberty and of the outlines of libertarian law; for such a discussion, there is no need for a detailed analysis or critique of the State. Part III briefly sets forth my view of the State as the inherent enemy of liberty and, indeed, of genuine law. Part IV deals with the most important modern theories which attempt to establish a political philosophy of liberty: in particular, those of Mises, Hayek, Berlin, and Nozick. I do not attempt to review their works in detail, but rather to concentrate on why I think their theories fail at the task of establishing an ideology of liberty. Finally, Part V attempts the virtually pioneering task of beginning to set forth a theory of strategy of how to move from the present system to a world of liberty—and also my reasons for being highly optimistic about the long-run, and even short-run, prospects for the achievement of the noble ideal of a libertarian society, particularly in America.

PART I:

INTRODUCTION: NATURAL LAW

1. Natural Law and Reason

A mong intellectuals who consider themselves "scientific," the phrase "the nature of man" is apt to have the effect of a red flag on a bull. "Man has no nature!" is the modern rallying cry; and typical of the sentiment of political philosophers today was the assertion of a distinguished political theorist some years ago before a meeting of the American Political Science Association that "man's nature" is a purely theological concept that must be dismissed from any scientific discussion.[1]

In the controversy over man's nature, and over the broader and more controversial concept of "natural law," both sides have repeatedly proclaimed that natural law and theology are inextricably intertwined. As a result, many champions of natural law, in scientific or philosophic circles, have gravely weakened their case by implying that rational, philosophical methods alone cannot establish such law: that theological faith is necessary to maintain the concept. On the other hand, the opponents of natural law have gleefully agreed; since faith in the supernatural is deemed necessary to belief in natural law, the latter concept must be tossed out of scientific, secular discourse, and be consigned to the arcane sphere of the divine studies. In consequence, the idea of a natural law founded on reason and rational inquiry has been virtually lost.[2]

The believer in a rationally established natural law must, then, face the hostility of both camps: the one group sensing in this position an antagonism toward religion; and the other group suspecting that God

---

1. The political theorist was the late Hannah Arendt. For a typical criticism of natural law by a legal Positivist, see Hans Kelsen, *General Theory of Law and State* (New York: Russell and Russell, 1961), pp. 8ff.

2. And yet, Black's *Law Dictionary* defines the natural law in a purely rationalistic and non-theological manner:

> *Jus Naturale,* the natural law, or law of nature; law, or legal principles, supposed to be discoverable by the light of nature or abstract reasoning, or to be taught by nature to all nations and men alike, or law supposed to govern men and peoples in a state of nature, i.e., in advance of organized governments or enacted laws (3rd ed., p. 1044).

Professor Patterson, in *Jurisprudence: Men and Ideas of the Law* (Brooklyn: Foundation Press, 1953), p. 333, defines the natural law cogently and concisely as:

> Principles of human conduct that are discoverable by "reason" from the basic inclinations of human nature, and that are absolute, immutable and of universal validity for all times and places. This is the basic conception of scholastic natural law . . . and most natural law philosophers.

and mysticism are being slipped in by the back door. To the first group, it must be said that they are reflecting an extreme Augustinian position which held that faith rather than reason was the only legitimate tool for investigating man's nature and man's proper ends. In short, in this fideist tradition, theology had completely displaced philosophy.[3] The Thomist tradition, on the contrary, was precisely the opposite: vindicating the independence of philosophy from theology, and proclaiming the ability of man's reason to understand and arrive at the laws, physical and ethical, of the natural order. If belief in a systematic order of natural laws open to discovery by man's reason is *per se* anti-religious, then anti-religious also were St. Thomas and the later Scholastics, as well as the devout Protestant jurist Hugo Grotius. The statement that there is an order of natural law, in short, leaves open the problem of whether or not God has created that order; and the assertion of the viability of man's reason to discover the natural order leaves open the question of whether or not that reason was given to man by God. The assertion of an order of natural laws discoverable by reason is, by itself, neither pro- nor anti-religious.[4]

Because this position is startling to most people today, let us investigate this Thomistic position a little further. The statement of absolute independence of natural law from the question of the existence of God was implicit rather than flatly asserted in St. Thomas himself; but like so many implications of Thomism, it was brought forth by Suarez and the other brilliant Spanish Scholastics of the late sixteenth century. The Jesuit Suarez pointed out that many Scholastics had taken the position that the natural law of ethics, the law of what is good and bad for man, does not depend upon God's will. Indeed, some of the Scholastics had gone so far as to say that:

> even though God did not exist, or did not make use of His reason, or did not judge rightly of things, if there is in man such a dictate of right reason to guide him, it would have had the same nature of law as it now has.[5]

---

3. Supporters of theological ethics nowadays typically strongly oppose the concept of natural law. See the discussion of casuistry by the neo-orthodox Protestant theologian Karl Barth, *Church Dogmatics* 3, 4 (Edinburgh: T. and T. Clark, 1961), pp. 7ff.

4. For a discussion of the role of reason in the philosophy of Aquinas, see Etienne Gilson, *The Christian Philosophy of St. Thomas Aquinas* (New York: Random House, 1956). An important analysis of Thomistic natural law theory is Germain Grisez, "The First Principle of Practical Reason," in Anthony Kenny, ed., *Aquinas: A Collection of Critical Essays* (New York: Anchor Books, 1969), pp. 340–82. For a history of medieval natural law, see Odon Lottin, *Psychologie et morale aux xiie et xiiie siècles*, 6 vols. (Louvain, 1942–1960).

5. From Franciscus Suarez, *De Legibus ac Deo Legislatore* (1619), lib. II, Cap. vi. Suarez also noted that many Scholastics "seem therefore logically to admit that natural law does not

Or, as a modern Thomist philosopher declares:

> If the word "natural' means anything at all, it refers to the nature of a man, and when used with "law," "natural" must refer to an ordering that is manifested in the inclinations of a man's nature and to nothing else. Hence, taken in itself, there is nothing religious or theological in the "Natural Law" of Aquinas.[6]

Dutch Protestant jurist Hugo Grotius declared, in his *De Iure Belli ac Pacis* (1625):

> What we have been saying would have a degree of validity even if we should concede that which cannot be conceded without the utmost wickedness, that there is no God.

And again:

> Measureless as is the power of God, nevertheless it can be said that there are certain things over which that power does not extend. . . . Just as even God cannot cause that two times two should not make four, so He cannot cause that which is intrinsically evil be not evil.[7]

D'Entrèves concludes that:

> [Grotius's] definition of natural law has nothing revolutionary. When he maintains that natural law is that body of rules which Man is able to discover by the use of his reason, he does nothing but restate the Scholastic notion of a rational foundation of ethics. Indeed, his aim is rather to restore that notion which had been shaken by the extreme Augustinianism of certain Protestant currents of thought. When he declares that these rules are valid in themselves, independently of the fact that God willed them, he repeats an assertion which had already been made by some of the schoolmen.[8]

---

proceed from God as a lawgiver, for it is not dependent on God's will." Quoted in A. P. d'Entreves, *Natural Law* (London: Hutchinson University Library, 1951), p. 71.

6. Thomas E. Davitt, S.J., "St. Thomas Aquinas and the Natural Law," in Arthur L. Harding, ed., *Origins of the Natural Law Tradition* (Dallas, Tex.: Southern Methodist University Press, 1954), p. 39. Also see Brendan F. Brown, ed., *The Natural Law Reader* (New York: Oceana Pubs., 1960), pp. 101–4.

7. Quoted in d'Entrèves, *Natural Law.*, pp. 52–53. See also Otto Gierke, *Natural Law and the Theory of Society, 1500 to 1800* (Boston: Beacon Press, 1957), pp. 98–99.

8. D'Entrèves, *Natural Law*, pp. 51–52. Also see A.H. Chroust, "Hugo Grotius and the Scholastic Natural Law Tradition," *The New Scholasticism* (1943), and Frederick C. Copleston, S.J., *A History of Philosophy* (Westminster, Md.: Newman Press, 1959), 2, pp. 330f. On the neglected influence of the Spanish Scholastic Suarez on modern philosophers, see

Grotius's aim, d'Entrèves adds, "was to construct a system of laws which would carry conviction in an age in which theological controversy was gradually losing the power to do so." Grotius and his juristic successors—Pufendorf, Burlamaqui, and Vattel—proceeded to elaborate this independent body of natural laws in a purely secular context, in accordance with their own particular interests, which were not, in contrast to the Schoolmen, primarily theological.[9] Indeed, even the eighteenth-century rationalists, in many ways dedicated enemies of the Scholastics, were profoundly influenced in their very rationalism by the Scholastic tradition.[10]

Thus, let there be no mistake: in the Thomistic tradition, natural law is ethical as well as physical law; and the instrument by which man apprehends such law is his *reason*—not faith, or intuition, or grace, revelation, or anything else.[11] In the contemporary atmosphere of sharp dichotomy between natural law and reason—and especially amid the irrationalist sentiments of "conservative" thought—this cannot be underscored too often. Hence, St. Thomas Aquinas, in the words of the eminent historian of philosophy Father Copleston, "emphasized the place and function of reason in moral conduct. He [Aquinas] shared with Aristotle the view that it is the possession of reason which distinguished man from the animals" and which "enables him to act deliberately in view of the consciously apprehended end and raises him above the level of purely instinctive behavior."[12]

Aquinas, then, realized that men always act purposively, but also went beyond this to argue that ends can also be apprehended by reason

Jose Ferrater Mora, "Suarez and Modern Philosophy," *Journal of the History of Ideas* (October 1953): 528–47.

9. See Gierke, *Natural Law and the Theory of Society*, p. 289. Also see Herbert Spencer, *An Autobiography* (New York: D. Appleton, 1904), vol. 1, p. 415.

10. Thus, see Carl L. Becker, *The Heavenly City of the Eighteenth-Century Philosophers* (New Haven, Conn.: Yale University Press, 1957), p. 8.

11. The late realist philosopher John Wild, in his important article, "Natural Law and Modern Ethical Theory," *Ethics* (October 1952), states:

> Realistic [natural law] ethics is now often dismissed as theological and authoritarian in character. But this is a misunderstanding. Its ablest representatives, from Plato and Aristotle to Grotius, have defended it on the basis of empirical evidence alone without any appeal to supernatural authority (p. 2, and pp. 1–13).

Also see the denial of the existence of such a thing as "Christian philosophy" any more than "Christian hats and shoes" by the Catholic social philosopher Orestes Brownson. Thomas T. McAvoy, C.S.C., "Orestes A. Brownson and Archbishop John Hughes in 1860," *Review of Politics* (January 1962): 29.

12. Frederick C. Copleston, S.J., *Aquinas* (London: Penguin Books, 1955), p. 204.

as either objectively good or bad for man. For Aquinas, then, in the words of Copleston, "there is therefore room for the concept of 'right reason,' reason directing man's acts to the attainment of the objective good for man." *Moral* conduct is therefore conduct in accord with right reason: "If it is said that moral conduct is rational conduct, what is meant is that it is conduct in accordance with right reason, reason apprehending the objective good for man and dictating the means to its attainment."[13]

In natural-law philosophy, then, reason is not bound, as it is in modern post-Humean philosophy, to be a mere slave to the passions, confined to cranking out the discovery of the means to arbitrarily chosen ends. For the ends themselves are selected by the use of reason; and "right reason" dictates to man his proper ends as well as the means for their attainment. For the Thomist or natural-law theorist, the general law of morality for man is a special case of the system of natural law governing all entities of the world, each with its own nature and its own ends. "For him the moral law . . . is a special case of the general principles that all finite things move toward their ends by the development of their potentialities."[14] And here we come to a vital difference between inanimate or even non-human living creatures, and man himself; for the former are compelled to proceed in accordance with the ends dictated by their natures, whereas man, "the rational animal," possesses reason to discover such ends and the free will to choose.[15]

Which doctrine, natural law or those of its critics, is to be considered truly rational was answered incisively by the late Leo Strauss, in the course of a penetrating critique of the value-relativism in political theory of Professor Arnold Brecht. For, in contrast to natural law,

---

13. Ibid., pp. 204–05.

14. Ibid., p. 212.

15. Thus Copleston:

Inanimate bodies act in certain ways precisely because they are what they are, and they cannot act otherwise; they cannot perform actions which are contrary to their nature. And animals are governed by instinct. In fine, all creatures below man participate unconsciously in the eternal law, which is reflected in their natural tendencies, and they do not possess the freedom which is required in order to be able to act in a manner incompatible with this law. It is therefore essential that he [man] should know the eternal law in so far as it concerns himself. Yet, how can he know it? He cannot read, as it were, the mind of God . . . [but] he can discern the fundamental tendencies and needs of his nature, and by reflecting on them he can come to a knowledge of the natural moral law. . . . Every man possesses . . . the light of reason whereby he can reflect . . . and promulgate to himself the natural law, which is the totality of the universal precepts or dictates of right reason concerning the good which is to be pursued and the evil which is to be shunned (Ibid., pp. 213–14).

positivistic social science . . . is characterized by the abandonment of reason or the flight from reason. . . .

According to the positivistic interpretation of relativism
which prevails in present-day social science . . . reason can tell
us which means are conducive to which ends; it cannot tell us
which attainable ends are to be preferred to other attainable
ends. Reason cannot tell us that we ought to choose attainable
ends; if someone 'loves him who desires the impossible,' reason
may tell him that he acts irrationally, but it cannot tell him
that he ought to act rationally, or that acting irrationally is
acting badly or basely. If rational conduct consists in choosing
the right means for the right end, relativism teaches in effect
that rational conduct is impossible.[16]

Finally, the unique place of reason in natural-law philosophy has
been affirmed by the modern Thomistic philosopher, the late Father John
Toohey. Toohey defined sound philosophy as follows: "Philosophy, in
the sense in which the word is used when scholasticism is contrasted
with other philosophies, is an attempt on the part of man's unaided reason
to give a fundamental explanation of the nature of things."[17]

---

16. Leo Strauss, "Relativism," in H. Schoeck and J. W. Wiggins, eds., *Relativism and the Study of Man* (Princeton, N.J.: D. Van Nostrand, 1961), pp. 144–45. For a devastating critique of an attempt by a relativistic political scientist to present a "value-free" case for freedom and the self-development of the person, see Walter Berns, "The Behavioral Sciences and the Study of Political Things: The Case of Christian Bay's *The Structure of Freedom*," *American Political Science Review* (September 1961): 550–59.

17. Toohey adds that "scholastic philosophy is the philosophy which teaches the certitude of human knowledge acquired by means of sense experience, testimony, reflection, and reasoning." John J. Toohey, S.J., *Notes on Epistemology* (Washington, D.C.: Georgetown University, 1952), pp. 111–12.

2. Natural Law as "Science"

It is indeed puzzling that so many modern philosophers should sniff at the very term "nature" as an injection of mysticism and the supernatural. An apple, let fall, will drop to the ground; this we all observe and acknowledge to be *in the nature* of the apple (as well as the world in general). Two atoms of hydrogen combined with one of oxygen will yield one molecule of water—behavior that is uniquely in the *nature* of hydrogen, oxygen, and water. There is nothing arcane or mystical about such observations. Why then cavil at the concept of "nature"? The world, in fact, consists of a myriad number of observable *things*, or *entities*. This is surely an observable fact. Since the world does not consist of one homogenous thing or entity alone, it follows that each one of these different things possesses differing attributes, otherwise they would all be the same thing. But if A, B, C, etc., have different attributes, it follows immediately that they have different *natures*.[1,2] It also follows that when these various things meet and interact, a specifically delimitable and definable *result* will occur. In short, specific, delimitable *causes* will have specific, delimitable *effects*.[3]

---

1. Henry B. Veatch, in his *For an Ontology of Morals: A Critique of Contemporary Ethical Theory* (Evanston, Ill.: Northwestern University Press, 1971), p. 7, states:

> Recourse must be had to an older notion than that which has now come to be in fashion among contemporary scientists and philosophers of science.... Surely, in that everyday world of common-sense existence in which, as human beings, and for all of our scientific sophistication, we can hardly cease to live and move and have our being, we do indeed find ourselves constantly invoking an older and even a decidedly common sense notion of "nature" and "natural law." For don't we all recognize that a rose is different from an eggplant, and a man from a mouse, and hydrogen from manganese? To recognize such differences in things is surely to recognize that they behave differently: one doesn't expect of a man quite the same things that one does of a mouse, and *vice versa*. Moreover, the reason our expectations thus differ as to what various types of things or entities will do, or how they will act and react, is simply that they just are different kinds of things. They have different "natures," as one might say, using the old-fashioned terminology.

Leo Strauss (*Natural Right and History* [Chicago: University of Chicago Press, 1953]) adds:

> Socrates deviated from his predecessors by identifying the science of ... everything that is, with the understanding of what each of the beings is. For "to be" means "to be something" and hence to be different from things which are "something else": "to be" means therefore "to be a part" (p. 122).

2. For a defense of the concept of nature, see Alvin Plantinga, *The Nature of Necessity* (Oxford: Clarendon Press, 1974), pp. 71–81.

3. See H.W.B. Joseph, An *Introduction* to *Logic*, 2nd rev. ed (Oxford: Clarendon Press, 1916), pp. 407–9. For a hard-hitting defense of the view that causation states a necessary

The observable behavior of each of these entities is the law of their natures, and this law includes what happens as a result of the interactions. The complex that we may build up of these laws may be termed the structure of *natural law*. What is "mystical" about that?[4]

In the field of purely physical laws, this concept will usually differ from modern positivistic terminology only on high philosophical levels; applied *to man*, however, the concept is far more controversial. And yet, if apples and stones and roses each have their specific natures, is man the only entity, the only being, that cannot have one? And if man does have a nature, why cannot it too be open to rational observation and reflection? If all things have natures, then surely man's nature is open to inspection; the current brusque rejection of the concept of the nature of man is therefore arbitrary and *a priori*.

One common, flip criticism by opponents of natural law is: *who is* to establish the alleged truths about man? The answer is not *who* but *what*: man's reason. Man's reason is *objective*, i.e., it can be employed by all men to yield truths about the world. To ask *what* is man's nature is to invite the answer. Go thou and study and find out! It is as if one man were to assert that the nature of copper were open to rational investigation and a critic were to challenge him to "prove" this immediately by setting forth on the spot all the laws that have been discovered about copper.

Another common charge is that natural-law theorists differ among themselves, and that therefore all natural-law theories must be discarded. This charge comes with peculiar ill grace when it comes, as it often does, from utilitarian economists. For economics has been a notoriously contentious science—and yet few people advocate tossing all economics therefore into the discard. Furthermore, difference of opinion is no excuse for discarding all sides to a dispute; the responsible person is the one who uses his reason to examine the various contentions and make up his own mind.[5] He does not simply say *a priori*, "a plague on all your houses!" The fact of man's reason does not mean that error is impossible. Even

---

relation among entities, see R. Harre and E. H. Madden, *Causal Powers: A Theory of Natural Necessity* (Totowa, N.J.: Rowman and Littlefield, 1975).

4. See Murray N. Rothbard, *Individualism and the Philosophy of the Social Sciences* (San Francisco: Cato Institute, 1979), p. 5.

5. And there is a further point: the very existence of a difference of opinion seems to imply that there is something objective about which disagreement can take place; for otherwise, there would be no contradictions in the different "opinions" and no worry about these conflicts. For a similar argument in refutation of moral subjectivism see G.E. Moore, *Ethics* (Oxford, 1963 [1912]), pp. 63ff.

such "hard" sciences as physics and chemistry have had their errors and their fervent disputes.[6] No man is omniscient or infallible—a law, by the way, of man's nature.

The natural law ethic decrees that for all living things, "goodness" is the fulfillment of what is best for that type of creature; "goodness" is therefore relative to the nature of the creature concerned. Thus, Professor Cropsey writes:

> The classical [natural law] doctrine is that each thing is excellent in the degree to which it can do the things for which its species is naturally equipped. . . . Why is the natural good? . . . [Because] there is neither a way nor a reason to prevent ourselves from distinguishing between useless and serviceable beasts, for example; and . . . the most empirical and . . . rational standard of the serviceable, or the limit of the thing's activity, is set by its nature. We do not judge elephants to be good because they are natural; or because nature is morally good—whatever that would mean. We judge a particular elephant to be good by the light of what elephant nature makes it possible for elephants to do and to be.[7]

In the case of man, the natural-law ethic states that goodness or badness can be determined by what fulfills or thwarts what is best for man's nature.[8]

---

6. The psychologist Leonard Carmichael, in "Absolutes, Relativism and the Scientific Psychology of Human Nature," in H. Schoeck and J. Wiggins, eds., *Relativism and the Study of Man* (Princeton, N.J.: D. Van Nostrand, 1961), p. 16, writes:

> We do not turn aside from what we know about astronomy at any time because there is a great deal we do not know, or because so much that we once thought we knew is no longer recognized as true. May not the same argument be accepted in our thinking about ethical and esthetic judgments?

7. Joseph Cropsey, "A Reply to Rothman," *American Political Science Review* (June 1962): 355. As Henry Veatch writes, in *For an Ontology of Morals*, pp. 7–8:

> Moreover, it is in virtue of a thing's nature—i.e., of its being the kind of thing that it is— that it acts and behaves the way it does. Is it not also in virtue of a thing's nature that we often consider ourselves able to judge what that thing might or could be, but perhaps isn't? A plant, for example, may be seen to be underdeveloped or stunted in its growth. A bird with an injured wing is quite obviously not able to fly as well as others of the same species. . . . And so it is that a thing's nature may be thought of as being not merely that in virtue of which the thing acts or behaves in the way it does, but also as a sort of standard in terms of which we judge whether the thing's action or behavior is all that it might have been or could have been.

8. For a similar approach to the meaning of goodness, see Peter Geach, "Good and Evil," in Philippa R. Foot, ed., *Theories of Ethics* (London: Oxford University Press, 1967), pp. 74–82.

The natural law, then, elucidates what is best for man—what ends man should pursue that are most harmonious with, and best tend to fulfill, his nature. In a significant sense, then, natural law provides man with a "science of happiness," with the paths which will lead to his real happiness. In contrast, praxeology or economics, as well as the utilitarian philosophy with which this science has been closely allied, treat "happiness" in the purely formal sense as the fulfillment of those ends which people happen— for whatever reason—to place high on their scales of value. Satisfaction of those ends yields to man his "utility" or "satisfaction" or "happiness."[9] Value in the sense of valuation or utility is purely subjective, and decided by each individual. This procedure is perfectly proper for the formal science of praxeology, or economic theory, but not necessarily elsewhere. For in natural-law ethics, ends are demonstrated to be good or bad for man in varying degrees; value here is *objective*—determined by the natural law of man's being, and here "happiness" for man is considered in the commonsensical, *contentual* sense. As Father Kenealy put it:

> This philosophy maintains that there is in fact an *objective moral order* within the range of human intelligence, to which human societies are bound in conscience to conform and upon which the peace and happiness of personal, national and international life depend.[10]

And the eminent English jurist, Sir William Blackstone, summed up the natural law and its relation to human happiness as follows:

> This is the foundation of what we call ethics, or natural law . . . demonstrating that this or that action tends to man's real happiness, and therefore very justly concluding that the performance of it is a part of the law of nature; or, on the other hand, that this or that action is destruction of man's real happiness, and therefore that the law of nature forbids it.[11]

---

9. Contrast John Wild, in "Natural Law and Modern Ethical Theory," *Ethics* (October 1952): 2, who says:

Realistic ethics is founded on the basic distinction between human need and uncriticized individual desire or pleasure, a distinction not found in modern utilitarianism. The basic concepts of so-called "naturalistic" theories are psychological, whereas those of realism are existential and ontological.

10. William J. Kenealy, S.J., "The Majesty of the Law," *Loyola Law Review* (1949–50): 112–13; reprinted in Brendan F. Brown, ed., *The Natural Law Reader* (New York: Oceana, 1960), p. 123.

11. Blackstone, *Commentaries on the Laws of England*, Book 1: quoted in Brown, *Natural Law Reader*, p. 106.

Without using the terminology of natural law, psychologist Leonard Carmichael has indicated how an objective, absolute ethic can be established for man on scientific methods, based upon biological and psychological inquiry:

> because man has an unchanging and an age-old, genetically determined anatomical, physiological, and psychological make-up, there is reason to believe that at least some of the "values" that he recognized as good or bad have been discovered or have emerged as human individuals have lived together for thousands of years in many societies. Is there any reason to suggest that these values, once identified and tested, may not be thought of as essentially fixed and unchanging? For example, the wanton murder of one adult by another for the purely personal amusement of the person committing the murder, once it is recognized as a general wrong, is likely always to be so recognized. Such a murder has disadvantageous individual and social effects. Or to take a milder example from esthetics, man is always likely to recognize in a special way the balance of two complementary colors because he is born with specially constituted human eyes.[12]

One common philosophic objection to natural law ethics is that it confuses, or identifies, the realism of *fact* and *value*. For purposes of our brief discussion, John Wild's reply will suffice:

> In answer we may point out that their [natural law] view identifies value not with existence but rather with the fulfillment of tendencies determined by the structure of the existent entity. Furthermore, it identifies evil not with non-existence but rather with a mode of existence in which natural tendencies are thwarted and deprived of realization. . . . The young plant whose leaves are withering for lack of light is not nonexistent. It exists, but in an unhealthy or privative mode. The lame man is not nonexistent. He exists, but with a natural power partially unrealized. . . . This metaphysical objection is based upon the common assumption that existence is fully finished or complete. . . . [But] what is good is the fulfillment of being.[13]

---

12. Carmichael, "Absolutes," p. 9.

13. Wild, "Natural Law," pp. 4–5. Wild continues on p. 11:

Existence is . . . not a property but a structuralized activity. Such activities are a kind of fact. They can be observed and described by judgments that are true or false: human life needs material artifacts; technological endeavors need rational guidance; the child has cognitive faculties that need education. Value statements are founded on the directly verifiable fact of tendency or need. The value or realization is required not merely by us

After stating that ethics, for man as for any other entity, are determined by investigating verifiable existing tendencies of that entity, Wild asks a question crucial to all non-theological ethics: "why are such principles felt to be binding on me?" How do such universal tendencies of human nature become incorporated into a person's subjective value scale? Because

> the factual needs which underlie the whole procedure are common to man. The values founded on them are universal. Hence, if I made no mistake in my tendential analysis of human nature, and if I understand myself, I must exemplify the tendency and must feel it subjectively as an imperative urge to action.[14]

David Hume is the philosopher supposed by modern philosophers to have effectively demolished the theory of natural law. Hume's "demolition" was two-pronged: the raising of the alleged "fact-value" dichotomy, thus debarring the inference of value from fact,[15] and his view

---

but by the existent tendency for its completion. From a sound description and analysis of the given tendency we can infer the value founded upon it. This is why we do not say that moral principles are mere statements of fact, but rather that they are "founded" on facts.

On pp. 2–4, Wild says:

> The ethics of natural law . . . recognizes prescriptive moral laws but asserts that these are *founded* on tendential facts which may be described. . . . Goodness . . . must . . . be conceived dynamically as an existential mode, the realization of natural tendency. In this view, the world is not made up of determinate structures alone, but of determinate structures in an act of existing which they determine toward further appropriate acts of existing. . . . No determinate structure can be given existence without determining active tendencies. When such a tendency is fulfilled in accordance with natural law, the entity is said to be in a stable, healthy, or sound condition—adjectives of value. When it is obstructed or distorted, the entity is said to be in an unstable, diseased or unsound condition—adjectives of disvalue. Goodness and badness in their ontological sense are not phases of abstract structure, but rather modes of existence, ways in which the existential tendencies determined by such structures are either fulfilled or barely sustained in a deprived, distorted state.

14. Ibid., p. 12. For more on a defense of natural law ethics, see John Wild, *Plato's Modern Enemies and the Theory of Natural Law* (Chicago: University of Chicago Press, 1953); Henry Veatch, *Rational Man: A Modern Interpretation of Aristotelian Ethics* (Bloomington: University of Indiana Press, 1962); and Veatch, *For An Ontology of Morals.*

15. Hume in fact failed to prove that values cannot be derived from facts. It is frequently alleged that nothing can be in the conclusion of an argument which was not in one of the premises; and that therefore, an "ought" conclusion cannot follow from descriptive premises. But a conclusion follows from *both* premises taken together; the "ought" need not be present in either one of the premises so long as it has been validly deduced. To say that it cannot be so deduced simply begs the question. See Philippa R. Foot, *Virtues and Vices* (Berkeley: University of California Press, 1978), pp. 99–105.

that reason is and can only be a slave to the passions. In short, in contrast to the natural-law view that man's reason can discover the proper ends for man to follow, Hume held that only the emotions can ultimately set man's ends, and that reason's place is as the technician and handmaiden to the emotions. (Here Hume has been followed by modern social scientists since Max Weber.) According to this view, people's emotions are assumed to be primary and unanalyzable givens.

Professor Hesselberg has shown, however, that Hume, in the course of his own discussions, was compelled to reintroduce a natural-law conception into his social philosophy and particularly into his theory of justice, thus illustrating the gibe of Etienne Gilson: "The natural law always buries its undertakers." For Hume, in Hesselberg's words, "recognized and accepted that the social . . . order is an indispensable prerequisite to man's well-being and happiness: and that this is a statement of fact." The social order, therefore, *must* be maintained by man. Hesselberg continues:

> But a social order is not possible unless man is able to conceive what it is, and what its advantages are, and also conceive those norms of conduct which are necessary to its establishment and preservation, namely, respect for another's person and for his rightful possessions, which is the substance of justice. . . . But justice is the product of reason, not the passions. And justice is the necessary support of the social order; and the social order is necessary to man's well-being and happiness. If this is so, the norms of justice must control and regulate the passions, and not *vice versa.*[16]

Hesselberg concludes that "thus Hume's original 'primacy of the passions' thesis is seen to be utterly untenable for his social and political theory, and . . . he is compelled to reintroduce reason as a cognitive-normative factor in human social relations."[17]

Indeed, in discussing justice and the importance of the rights of private property, Hume was compelled to write that reason can establish such a social ethic: "nature provides a remedy in the judgment and understanding for what is irregular and uncommodious in the affections"—in short, reason can be superior to the passions.[18]

---

16. A. Kenneth Hesselberg, "Hume, Natural Law and Justice," *Duquesne Review* (Spring 1961): 46–47.

17. Ibid.

18. David Hume, *A Treatise of Human Nature,* quoted in Hesselberg, "Hume, Natural Law, and Justice," p. 61. Hesselberg adds perceptively that Hume's sharp ought-is dichotomy in the earlier chapters of Hume's *Treatise* stemmed from his restricting the

We have seen from our discussion that the doctrine of natural law—the view that an objective ethics can be established through reason—has had to face two powerful groups of enemies in the modern world: both anxious to denigrate the power of man's reason to decide upon his destiny. These are the fideists who believe that ethics can only be given to man by supernatural revelation, and the skeptics who believe that man must take his ethics from arbitrary whim or emotion. We may sum up with Professor Grant's harsh but penetrating view of

> the strange contemporary alliance between those who doubt the capacity of human reason in the name of scepticism (probably scientific in origin) and those who denigrate its capacity in the name of revealed religion. It is only necessary to study the thought of Ockham to see how ancient this strange alliance is. For in Ockham can be seen how philosophic nominalism, unable to face the question of practical certainty, solves it by the arbitrary hypothesis of revelation. The will detached from the intellect (as it must be in a nominalism) can seek certainty only through such arbitrary hypotheses. . . .
>
> The interesting fact historically is that these two anti-rationalist traditions—that of the liberal skeptic and the Protestant revelationist— should originally have come from two . . . opposite views of man. The Protestant dependence upon revelation arose from a great pessimism about human nature. . . . The immediately apprehended values of the liberal originate in a great optimism. Yet . . . after all, is not the dominating tradition in North America a Protestantism which has been transformed by pragmatic technology and liberal aspirations?[19]

---

meaning of "reason" to finding pleasure–pain objects, and determining the means to achieve them. But, in the later chapters on justice, the very nature of the concept compelled Hume "to assign a third role to reason, namely its power to judge actions in terms of their suitability, or conformity or disconformity, to man's social nature, and thus paved the way for the return to a natural law concept of justice." Ibid., pp. 61–62.

For some doubt whether or not Hume himself intended to assert the fact-value dichotomy, see A.C. MacIntyre, "Hume on 'Is' and 'Ought," in W.D. Hudson, ed., *The Is-Ought Question* (London: Macmillan, 1969), pp. 35–50.

19. George P. Grant, "Plato and Popper," *The Canadian Journal of Economics and Political Science* (May 1954): 191–92.

3. Natural Law versus Positive Law

If, then, the natural law is discovered by reason from "the basic inclinations of human nature . . . absolute, immutable, and of universal validity for all times and places," it follows that the natural law provides an objective set of ethical norms by which to gauge human actions at any time or place.[1] The natural law is, in essence, a profoundly "radical" ethic, for it holds the existing status quo, which might grossly violate natural law, up to the unsparing and unyielding light of reason. In the realm of politics or State action, the natural law presents man with a set of norms which may well be radically critical of existing *positive law* imposed by the State. At this point, we need only stress that the very existence of a natural law discoverable by reason is a potentially powerful threat to the status quo and a standing reproach to the reign of blindly traditional custom or the arbitrary will of the State apparatus.

In fact, the legal principles of any society can be established in three alternate ways: (a) by following the traditional custom of the tribe or community; (b) by obeying the arbitrary, *ad hoc* will of those who rule the State apparatus; or (c) by the use of man's reason in discovering the natural law—in short, by slavish conformity to custom, by arbitrary whim, or by use of man's reason. These are essentially the only possible ways for establishing positive law. Here we may simply affirm that the latter method is at once the most appropriate for man at his most nobly and fully human, and the most potentially "revolutionary" *vis-à-vis* any given status quo.

In our century, widespread ignorance of and scorn for the very existence of the natural law has limited people's advocacy of legal structures to (a) or (b), or some blend of the two. This even holds for those who try to hew to a policy of individual liberty. Thus, there are those libertarians who would simply and uncritically adopt the common law, despite its many anti-libertarian flaws. Others, like Henry Hazlitt, would scrap all constitutional limitations on government to rely solely on the majority will as expressed by the legislature. Neither group seems to understand the concept of a structure of rational natural law to be used as a guidepost for shaping and reshaping whatever positive law may be in existence.[2]

---

1. Edwin W. Patterson, *Jurisprudence: Men and Ideas of the Law* (Brooklyn, N.Y.: Foundation Press, 1953), p. 333.

2. Hazlitt's reaction to my own brief discussion of the legal norms essential to any free-market economy [in *Man, Economy, and State: A Treatise on Economic Principles* (Princeton,

17

While natural-law theory has often been used erroneously in defense of the political status quo, its radical and "revolutionary" implications were brilliantly understood by the great Catholic libertarian historian Lord Acton. Acton saw clearly that the deep flaw in the ancient Greek—and their later followers'—conception of natural law political philosophy was to identify politics and morals, and then to place the supreme social moral agent in the State. From Plato and Aristotle, the State's proclaimed supremacy was founded in their view that "morality was undistinguished from religion and politics from morals; and in religion, morality, and politics there was only one legislator and one authority."[3]

Acton added that the Stoics developed the correct, non-State principles of natural law political philosophy, which were then revived in the modern period by Grotius and his followers. "From that time it became possible to make politics a matter of principle and of conscience." The reaction of the State to this theoretical development was horror:

> When Cumberland and Pufendorf unfolded the true significance of [Grotius's] doctrine, every settled authority, every triumphant interest recoiled aghast. . . . It was manifest that all persons who had learned that political science is an affair of conscience rather than of might and expediency, must regard their adversaries as men without principle.[4]

Acton saw clearly that any set of objective moral principles rooted in the nature of man must inevitably come into conflict with custom and with positive law. To Acton, such an irrepressible conflict was an essential attribute of classical liberalism: "Liberalism wishes for what

---

N.J.: D. Van Nostrand, 1962] was a curious one. While critical of blind adherence to common law in other writers, Hazlitt could only react in puzzlement to my approach; calling it "abstract doctrinaire logic" and "extreme a priorism," he chided me for "trying to substitute his own instant jurisprudence for the common law principles built up through generations of human experience." It is curious that Hazlitt feels common law to be inferior to arbitrary majority will, and yet to be *superior* to human reason! Henry Hazlitt, "The Economics of Freedom," *National Review* (September 25, 1962): 232.

3. John Edward Emerich Dalberg-Acton, *Essays on Freedom and Power* (Glencoe, Ill.: Free Press, 1948), p. 45. Also see Gertrude Himmelfarb, *Lord Acton: A Study in Conscience and Politics* (Chicago: University of Chicago Press, 1962), p. 135.

4. Acton, *Essays*, p. 74. Himmelfarb correctly noted that "for Acton, politics was a science, the application of the principles of morality." Gertrude Himmelfarb, "Introduction," ibid., p. xxxvii.

ought to be, irrespective of what is."[5] As Himmelfarb writes of Acton's philosophy:

> the past was allowed no authority except as it happened to conform to morality. To take seriously this Liberal theory of history, to give precedence to "what ought to be" over "what is" was, he admitted, virtually to install a "revolution in permanence."[6]

And so, for Acton, the individual, armed with natural law moral principles, is then in a firm position from which to criticize existing regimes and institutions, to hold them up to the strong and harsh light of reason. Even the far less politically oriented John Wild has trenchantly described the inherently radical nature of natural-law theory:

> the philosophy of natural law defends the rational dignity of the human individual and his right and duty to criticize by word and deed any existent institution or social structure in terms of those universal moral principles which can be apprehended by the individual intellect alone.[7]

If the very idea of natural law is essentially "radical" and deeply critical of existing political institutions, then how has natural law become generally classified as "conservative"? Professor Parthemos considers natural law to be "conservative" because its principles are universal, fixed, and immutable, and hence are "absolute" principles of justice.[8] Very true—but how does fixity of principle imply "conservatism"? On

---

5. Himmelfarb, *Lord Acton*, p. 204. Contrast the exclamation of bewilderment and horror by the leading nineteenth-century German Conservative, Adam Muller: "A natural law which differs from the positive law!" See Robert W. Lougee, "German Romanticism and Political Thought," *Review of Politics* (October 1959): 637.

6. Himmelfarb, *Lord Acton*, p. 205.

7. John Wild, *Plato's Modern Enemies and the Theory of Natural Law* (Chicago: University of Chicago Press, 1953), p. 176. Note the similar assessment by the conservative Otto Gierke, in *Natural Law and the Theory of Society, 1500 to 1800* (Boston: Beacon Press, 1957), pp. 35–36, who was for that reason hostile to natural law:

> In opposition to positive jurisprudence, which still continued to show a Conservative trend, the natural-law theory of the State was Radical to the very core of its being. . . . It was also directed . . . not to the purpose of scientific explanation of the past, but to . . . the exposition and justification of a new future which was to be called into existence.

8. George S. Parthemos, "Contemporary Juristic Theory, Civil Rights, and American Politics," *Annals of the American Academy of Political and Social Science* (November 1962): 101–2.

the contrary, the fact that natural-law theorists derive from the very nature of man a fixed structure of law independent of time and place, or of habit or authority or group norms, makes that law a mighty force for radical change. The only exception would be the surely rare case where the positive law happens to coincide in every aspect with the natural law as discerned by human reason.[9]

---

9. The conservative political scientist Samuel Huntington recognizes the rarity of this event:

> No ideational theory can be used to defend existing institutions satisfactorily, even when those institutions in general reflect the values of that ideology. The perfect nature of the ideology's ideal and the imperfect nature and inevitable mutation of the institutions create a gap between the two. The ideal becomes a standard by which to criticize the institutions, much to the embarrassment of those who believe in the ideal and yet still wish to defend the institutions.

Huntington then adds the footnote: "Hence any theory of natural law as a set of transcendent and universal moral principles is inherently non-conservative.... Opposition to natural law [is] . . . a distinguishing characteristic of conservatism." Samuel P. Huntington "Conservatism as an Ideology," *American Political Science Review* (June 1957): 458–59. See also Murray N. Rothbard, "Huntington on Conservatism: A Comment," *American Political Science Review* (September 1957): 784–87.

4. Natural Law and Natural Rights

A s we have indicated, the great failing of natural-law theory—from Plato and Aristotle to the Thomists and down to Leo Strauss and his followers in the present day—is to have been profoundly statist rather than individualist. This "classical" natural-law theory placed the locus of the good and of virtuous action in the State, with individuals strictly subordinated to State action. Thus, from Aristotle's correct dictum that man is a " social animal," that his nature is best fitted for social cooperation, the classicists leaped illegitimately to a virtual identification of "society" and "the State," and thence to the State as the major locus of virtuous action.[1] It was, in contrast, the Levellers and particularly John Locke in seventeenth-century England who transformed classical natural law into a theory grounded on methodological and hence political individualism. From the Lockean emphasis on the individual as the unit of action, as the entity who thinks, feels, chooses, and acts, stemmed his conception of natural law in politics as establishing the natural rights of each individual. It was the Lockean individualist tradition that profoundly influenced the later American revolutionaries and the dominant tradition of libertarian political thought in the revolutionary new nation. It is this tradition of natural-rights libertarianism upon which the present volume attempts to build.

Locke' s celebrated "Second Treatise on Government" was certainly one of the first systematic elaborations of libertarian, individualistic, natural-rights theory. Indeed, the similarity between Locke' s view and the theory set forth below will become evident from the following passage:

> [E]very man has a *property* in his own *person*. This nobody has any
> right to but himself. The labour of his body and the *work* of his
> hands, we may say, are properly his. Whatsoever then he removes
> out of the state that nature hath provided, and left it in, he hath
> mixed his labour with, and joined to it something that is his own,
> and thereby makes it his *property*. It being by him removed from
> the common state nature placed it in, it hath by this *labour* some-
> thing annexed to it that excludes the common right of other men.

---

1. For a critique of such typical confusion by a modern Thomist, see Murray N. Rothbard, *Power and Market*, 2nd ed. (Kansas City: Sheed Andrews and McMeel, 1977), pp. 237–38. Leo Strauss's defense of classical natural law and his assault on individualistic natural-rights theory may be found in his *Natural Rights and History* (Chicago: University of Chicago Press, 1953).

For this *labour* being the unquestionable property of the labourer, no man but he can have a right to what that is once joined to. . . .

He that is nourished by the acorns he picked up under an oak, or the apples he gathered from the trees in the wood, has certainly appropriated them to himself. Nobody can deny but the nourishment is his. I ask then when did they begin to be his? . . . And 'tis plain, if the first gathering made them not his, nothing else could. That *labour* put a distinction between them and common. That added something to them more than nature, the common mother of all, had done: and so they become his private right. And will any one say he had no right to those acorns or apples he thus appropriated, because he had not the consent of all mankind to make them his? . . . If such a consent as that was necessary, man had starved, notwithstanding the plenty God had given him. We see in *commons*, which remain so by compact, that 'tis the taking part of what is common, and removing it out of the state Nature leaves it in, which *begins the property*; without which the common is of no use.[2]

It should not be surprising that Locke's natural-rights theory, as historians of political thought have shown, was riddled with contradictions and inconsistencies. After all, the pioneers of any discipline, any science, are bound to suffer from inconsistencies and lacunae that will be corrected by those that come after them. Divergences from Locke in the present work are only surprising to those steeped in the unfortunate modern fashion that has virtually abolished constructive political philosophy in favor of a mere antiquarian interest in older texts. In fact, libertarian natural-rights theory continued to be expanded and purified after Locke, reaching its culmination in the nineteenth century works of Herbert Spencer and Lysander Spooner.[3]

The myriad of post-Locke and post-Leveller natural-rights theorists made clear their view that these rights stem from the nature of man and

---

2. John Locke, *An Essay Concerning the True Origin, Extent, and End of Civil Government*, V. pp. 27–28, in *Two Treatises of Government*, P. Laslett, ed. (Cambridge: Cambridge University Press, 1960), pp. 305–7.

3. Current scholars, ranging from Marxists to Straussians, consider Thomas Hobbes rather than Locke as the founder of systematic individualist, natural rights theory. For a refutation of this view and a vindication of the older view of Hobbes as a statist and a totalitarian, see Williamson M. Evers, "Hobbes and Liberalism," *The Libertarian Forum* (May 1975): 4–6. Also see Evers, "Social Contract: A Critique," *The Journal of Libertarian Studies* 1 (Summer 1977): 187–88. For a stress upon Hobbes's absolutism by a pro-Hobbesian German political theorist, see Carl Schmitt, *Der Leviathan in der Staatslehre Thomas Hobbes* (Hamburg, 1938). Schmitt was for a time a pro-Nazi theorist.

of the world around him. A few strikingly worded examples: nineteenth-century German–American theorist Francis Lieber, in his earlier and more libertarian treatise, wrote: "The law of nature or natural law . . . is the law, the body of rights, which we deduce from the essential nature of man." And the prominent nineteenth-century American Unitarian minister, William Ellery Channing: "All men have the same rational nature and the same power of conscience, and all are equally made for indefinite improvement of these divine faculties and for the happiness to be found in their virtuous use." And Theodore Woolsey, one of the last of the systematic natural rights theorists in nineteenth-century America: natural rights are those "which, by fair deduction from the present physical, moral, social, religious characteristics of man, he must be invested with . . . in order to fulfill the ends to which his nature calls him."[4]

If, as we have seen, natural law is essentially a revolutionary theory, then so *a fortiori* is its individualist, natural-rights branch. As the nineteenth-century American natural-rights theorist Elisha P. Hurlbut put it:

> The laws shall be merely declaratory of natural rights and natural wrongs, and . . . whatever is indifferent to the laws of nature shall be left unnoticed by human legislation . . . and legal tyranny arises whenever there is a departure from this simple principle.[5]

A notable example of the revolutionary use of natural rights is, of course, the American Revolution, which was grounded in a radically revolutionary development of Lockean theory during the eighteenth century.[6] The famous words of the Declaration of Independence, as Jefferson himself made clear, were enunciating nothing new, but were simply a brilliantly written distillation of the views held by the Americans of the day:

> We hold these truths to be self-evident, that all men are created equal, that they are endowed by their Creator with certain unalienable Rights, that among these are Life, Liberty and the pursuit of Happiness [the more common triad at the time was "Life, Liberty and Property"]. That to secure these rights, Governments are instituted among Men, deriving their just powers

---

4. Francis Lieber, *Manual of Political Ethics* (1838); Theodore Woolsey, *Political Science* (1877); cited in Benjamin F. Wright, Jr., *American Interpretations of Natural Law* (Cambridge, Mass.: Harvard University Press, 1931), pp. 261ff., 255ff., 276ff. William Ellery Channing, *Works* (Boston: American Unitarian Association, 1895), p. 693.

5. Elisha P. Hurlbut, *Essays on Human Rights and Their Political Guarantees* (1845), cited in Wright, *American Interpretations*, pp. 257ff.

6. See Bernard Bailyn, *The Ideological Origins of the American Revolution* (Cambridge, Mass.: Belknap Press of Harvard University Press, 1967).

from the consent of the governed. That whenever any form of Government becomes destructive of these ends, it is the Right of the people to alter or to abolish it.

Particularly striking is the flaming prose of the great abolitionist William Lloyd Garrison, applying natural-rights theory in a revolutionary way to the question of slavery:

> The right to enjoy liberty is inalienable. . . . Every man has a right to his own body—to the products of his own labor—to the protection of law. . . . That all these laws which are now in force, admitting the right of slavery, are, therefore, before God, utterly null and void . . . and therefore they ought instantly to be abrogated.[7]

We shall be speaking throughout this work of "rights," in particular the rights of individuals to property in their persons and in material objects. But how do we define "rights"? "Right" has cogently and trenchantly been defined by Professor Sadowsky:

> When we say that one has the right to do certain things we mean this and only this, that it would be immoral for another, alone or in combination, to stop him from doing this by the use of physical force or the threat thereof. We do *not* mean that any use a man makes of his property within the limits set forth is necessarily a *moral* use.[8]

Sadowsky's definition highlights the crucial distinction we shall make throughout this work between a man's *right* and the morality or immorality of his exercise of that right. We will contend that it is a man's right to do whatever he wishes with his person; it is his right not to be molested or interfered with by violence from exercising that right. But what may be the moral or immoral ways of exercising that right is a question of personal ethics rather than of political philosophy—which is concerned solely with matters of right, and of the proper or improper exercise of physical violence in human relations. The importance of this crucial distinction cannot be overemphasized. Or, as Elisha Hurlbut concisely put it: "The exercise of a faculty [by an individual] is its only use. The *manner* of its exercise is one thing; *that* involves a question of morals. The *right* to its exercise is another thing.[9]

---

7. William Lloyd Garrison, "Declaration of Sentiments of the American Anti-Slavery Convention" (December 1833), cited in W. and J. Pease, eds., *The Antislavery Argument* (Indianapolis: Bobbs-Merrill, 1965).

8. James A. Sadowsky, S.J., "Private Property and Collective Ownership," in Tibor Machan, ed., *The Libertarian Alternative* (Chicago: Nelson-Hall, 1974), pp. 120–21.

9. Hurlbut, cited in Wright, *American Interpretations*, pp. 257ff.

5. The Task of Political Philosophy

I t is not the intention of this book to expound or defend at length the philosophy of natural law, or to elaborate a natural-law ethic for the personal morality of man. The intention is to set forth a social ethic of liberty, i.e., to elaborate that subset of the natural law that develops the concept of natural rights, and that deals with the proper sphere of "politics," i.e., with violence and non-violence as modes of interpersonal relations. In short, to set forth a political philosophy of liberty.

In our view the major task of "political science" or better, "political philosophy" is to construct the edifice of natural law pertinent to the political scene. That this task has been almost completely neglected in this century by political scientists is all too clear. Political science has either pursued a positivistic and scientistic "model building," in vain imitation of the methodology and content of the physical sciences, or it has engaged in purely empirical fact-grubbing. The contemporary political scientist believes that he can avoid the necessity of moral judgments, and that he can help frame public policy without committing himself to any ethical position. And yet as soon as anyone makes *any* policy suggestion, however narrow or limited, an ethical judgment— sound or unsound—has willy-nilly been made.[1] The difference between the political scientist and the political philosopher is that the "scientist's" moral judgments are covert and implicit, and therefore not subject to detailed scrutiny, and hence more likely to be unsound. Moreover, the avoidance of explicit ethical judgments leads political scientists to one overriding implicit value judgment—that in favor of the political status quo as it happens to prevail in any given society. At the very least, his lack of a systematic political ethics precludes the political scientist from persuading anyone of the value of any change from the status quo.

In the meanwhile, furthermore, present-day political philosophers generally confine themselves, also in a *Wertfrei* manner, to antiquarian descriptions and exegeses of the views of *other*, long gone political philosophers. In so doing, they are evading the major task of political philosophy, in the words of Thomas Thorson, "the philosophic justification of value positions relevant to politics."[2]

---

1. Cf. W. Zajdlic, "The Limitations of Social Sciences," *Kyklos* 9 (1956): 68–71.

2. Hence, as Thorson points out, political philosophy is a subdivision of the philosophy of ethics, in contrast to "political theory" as well as positivistic analytic philosophy. See Thomas Landon Thorson, "Political Values and Analytic Philosophy," *Journal of Politics* (November

In order to advocate public policy, therefore, a system of social or political ethics must be constructed. In former centuries this was the crucial task of political philosophy. But in the contemporary world, political theory, in the name of a spurious "science," has cast out ethical philosophy, and has itself become barren as a guide to the inquiring citizen. The same course has been taken in each of the disciplines of the social sciences and of philosophy by abandoning the procedures of natural law. Let us then cast out the hobgoblins of *Wertfreiheit*, of positivism, of scientism. Ignoring the imperious demands of an arbitrary *status quo*, let us hammer out— hackneyed cliché though it may be—a natural-law and natural-rights standard to which the wise and honest may repair. Specifically, let us seek to establish the political philosophy of liberty and of the proper sphere of law, property rights, and the State.

1961): 712n. Perhaps Professor Holton is right that "the decline in political philosophy is one part of a general decline," not only in philosophy itself, but also "in the status of rationality and ideas as such." Holton goes on to add that the two major challenges to genuine political philosophy in recent decades have come from historicism—the view that all ideas and truths are relative to particular historical conditions—and scientism, the imitation of the physical sciences. James Holton, "Is Political Philosophy Dead?" *Western Political Quarterly* (September 1961): 75ff.

PART II:
A THEORY OF LIBERTY

6. A Crusoe Social Philosophy

One of the most commonly derided constructions of classical economic theory is "Crusoe Economics," the analysis of an isolated man face-to-face with nature. And yet, this seemingly "unrealistic" model, as I have tried to demonstrate elsewhere, has highly important and even indispensable uses.[1] It serves to isolate man as against nature, thus gaining clarity by abstracting at the beginning from interpersonal relations. Later on, this man/nature analysis can be extended and applied to the "real world." The bringing in of "Friday,"or of one or more other persons, after analysis of strictly Robinsonian isolation, then serves to show how the addition of other persons affects the discussion. These conclusions can then also be applied to the contemporary world. Thus, the abstraction of analyzing a few persons interacting on an island enables a clear perception of the basic truths of interpersonal relations, truths which remain obscure if we insist on looking first at the contemporary world only whole and of a piece.

If Crusoe economics can and does supply the indispensable groundwork for the entire structure of economics and praxeology—the broad, formal analysis of human action—a similar procedure should be able to do the same thing for social philosophy, for the analysis of the fundamental truths of the nature of man *vis-à-vis* the nature of the world into which he is born, as well as the world of other men. Specifically, it can aid greatly in solving such problems of political philosophy as the nature and role of liberty, property, and violence.[2]

Let us consider Crusoe, who has landed on his island, and, to simplify matters, has contracted amnesia. What inescapable facts does Crusoe confront? He finds, for one thing, himself, with the primordial fact of his own consciousness and his own body. He finds, second, the natural world around him, the nature-given habitat and resources which economists sum up in the term "land."[3] He finds also that, in seeming contrast with animals,

---

1. See Murray N. Rothbard, *Man, Economy, and State* (Princeton, N.J.: D. Van Nostrand, 1962), vol. 1, chaps. 1 and 2.

2. Such seventeenth- and eighteenth-century constructs as "the state of nature" or "the social contract" were not wholly successful attempts to construct such a logical analysis. Such attempts were far more important than any actual *historical* assertions that may have been made in the course of developing these concepts.

3. This economic "land," including all nature-given resources, does not necessarily mean "land" in the popular sense, as it may include parts of the sea, e.g., fishing waters, and excludes man-made improvements on the earth.

he does not possess any innate instinctual knowledge impelling him into the proper paths for the satisfaction of his needs and desires. In fact, he begins his life in this world by knowing literally nothing; all knowledge must be *learned* by him. He comes to learn that he has numerous ends, purposes which he desires to achieve, many of which he *must* achieve to sustain his life: food, shelter, clothing, etc. After the basic needs are satisfied, he finds more "advanced" wants for which to aim. To satisfy any or all of these wants which he evaluates in accordance with their respective importance to him, Crusoe must also learn *how* to achieve them; he must, in short, acquire "technological knowledge,"or "recipes."

Crusoe, then, has manifold wants which he tries to satisfy, ends that he strives to attain. Some of these ends may be attained with minimal ef-fort on his part; if the island is so structured, he may be able to pick edible berries off nearby bushes. In such cases, his "consumption" of a good or service may be obtained quickly and almost instantaneously. But for almost all of his wants, Crusoe finds that the natural world about him does not satisfy them immediately and instantaneously; he is not, in short, in a Garden of Eden. To achieve his ends, he must, as quickly and productively as he can, take the nature-given resources and *transform* them into useful objects, shapes, and places most useful to him—so that he can satisfy his wants.

In short, he must (a) choose his goals; (b) learn how to achieve them by using nature-given resources; and then (c) exert his labor energy to transform these resources into more useful shapes and places: i.e., into "capital goods,"and finally into "consumer goods" that he can directly consume. Thus, Crusoe may build himself, out of the given natural raw materials, an axe (capital good) with which to chop down trees, in order to construct a cabin (consumer good). Or he may build a net (capital good) with which to catch fish (consumer good). In each case, he employs his learned technological knowledge to exert his labor effort in transforming land into capital goods and eventually into consumer goods. This process of transformation of land resources constitutes his "production." In short, Crusoe must *produce* before he can *consume*, and so that he may consume. And by this process of production, of transformation, man shapes and alters his nature-given environment to his own ends, instead of, animal-like, being simply determined by that environment.

And so man, not having innate, instinctive, automatically acquired knowledge of his proper ends, or of the means by which they can be achieved, must learn them, and to learn them he must exercise his powers of observation, abstraction, thought: in short, his reason. Reason is man's instrument of knowledge and of his very survival; the use and expansion of his mind, the acquisition of knowledge about what is best for him and how he can achieve it, is the uniquely *human* method of existence and of achievement. And this is uniquely man's nature; man, as Aristotle pointed out, is the rational animal, or to be more precise, the rational being. Through his reason, the individual man observes both the facts and ways of the external world, and the facts of his own consciousness, including his emotions: in short, he employs both extraspection and introspection.

Crusoe, we have said, learns about his ends and about how to attain them. But what specifically does his learning faculty, his reason, do in the process of obtaining such knowledge? It learns about the way things work in the world, i.e., the *natures* of the various specific entities and classes of entities that the man finds in existence; in short, he learns the *natural laws* of the way things behave in the world. He learns that an arrow shot from a bow can bring down a deer, and that a net can catch an abundance of fish. Further, he learns about his *own* nature, about the sort of events and actions that will make him happy or unhappy; in short, he learns about the ends he needs to achieve and those he should seek to avoid.

This process, this method necessary to man's survival and prosperity upon the earth, has often been derided as unduly or exclusively "material-istic." But it should be clear that what has happened in this activity proper to man's nature is a fusion of "spirit" and matter; man's mind, using the ideas it has learned, directs his energy in transforming and reshaping matter into ways to sustain and advance his wants and his life. Behind every "produced" good, behind every man-made transformation of natural resources, is an *idea* directing the effort, a manifestation of man's spirit.

The individual man, in introspecting the fact of his own consciousness, also discovers the primordial natural fact of his freedom: his freedom to choose, his freedom to use or not use his reason about any given subject. In short, the natural fact of his "free will." He also discovers the natural fact of his mind's command over his body and its actions: that is, of his natural *ownership* over his self.

Crusoe, then, owns his body; his mind is free to adopt whatever ends it wishes, and to exercise his reason in order to discover what ends he should choose, and to learn the recipes for employing the means at hand to attain them. Indeed, the very fact that the knowledge needed for man's survival and progress is not innately given to him or determined by external events, the very fact that he must use his mind to learn this knowledge, *demonstrates* that he is by nature free to employ or not to employ that reason—i.e., that he has free will.[4] Surely, there is nothing

---

4. See Murray N. Rothbard, *Individualism and the Philosophy of the Social Sciences* (San Francisco: Cato Institute, 1979), pp. 5–10. For one thing, a person cannot coherently believe

outré or mystical about the fact that men differ from stones, plants, or even animals, and that the above are crucial differences between them. The critical and unique facts about man and the ways in which he must live to survive—his consciousness, his free will and free choice, his faculty of reason, his necessity for learning the natural laws of the external world and of himself, his self-ownership, his need to "produce" by transforming nature-given matter into consumable forms—all these are wrapped up in what man's nature is, and how man may survive and flourish. Suppose now that Crusoe is confronted with a choice of either picking berries or picking some mushrooms for food, and he decides upon the pleasantly tasting mushrooms, when suddenly a previously shipwrecked inhabitant, coming upon Crusoe, shouts: "Don't do that! Those mushrooms are poisonous." There is no mystery in Crusoe's subsequent shift to berries. What has happened here? Both men have operated on an assumption so strong that it remained tacit, an assumption that poison is *bad*, bad for the health and even for the survival of the human organism—in short, bad for the continuation and the quality of a man's life. In this implicit agreement on the value of life and health for the person, and on the evils of pain and death, the two men have clearly arrived at the basis of an ethic, grounded on reality and on the natural laws of the human organism.

If Crusoe had eaten the mushrooms without learning of their poisonous effects, then his decision would have been *incorrect*—a possibly tragic error based on the fact that man is scarcely automatically determined to make correct decisions at all times. Hence, his lack of omniscience and his liability to error. If Crusoe, on the other hand, had known of the poison and eaten the mushrooms anyway—perhaps for "kicks" or from a very high time preference—then his decision would have been objectively *immoral*, an act deliberately set against his life and health. It may well be asked why life *should* be an objective ultimate value, why man should opt for life (in duration and quality).[5] In reply, we may note that a proposition rises to the status of an *axiom* when he who denies it may be shown to be using it in the very course of the supposed refutation.[6] Now, *any* person participating

---

that he is making judgments and at the same time that he is being determined by a foreign cause to do so. For if that were true, what would be the status of the judgment that he is determined? This argument was used by Immanuel Kant, *Groundwork of the Metaphysics of Morals*, trans. H. J. Paton (New York: Harper and Row, 1964), pp. 115f.

5. On the value of life not depending on whether it is perceived as one of happiness, see Philippa R. Foot, *Virtues and Vices* (Berkeley: University of California Press, 1978), p. 41.

6. Elsewhere, I have written: "if a man cannot affirm a proposition without employing its negation, he is not only caught in an inextricable self-contradiction; *he is conceding to the negation the status of an axiom.*" Rothbard, *Individualism*, p. 8. Also see R. P. Phillips, *Modern Thomistic Philosophy* (Westminster, Md.: Newman Bookshop, 1934–35), vol. 2, pp. 36–37.

in any sort of discussion, including one on values, is, by virtue of so participating, alive and affirming life. For if he were *really* opposed to life, he would have no business in such a discussion, indeed he would have no business continuing to be alive. Hence, the *supposed* opponent of life is really affirming it in the very process of his discussion, and hence the preservation and furtherance of one's life takes on the stature of an incontestable axiom.

We have seen that Crusoe, as in the case of any man, has freedom of will, freedom to choose the course of his life and his actions. Some critics have charged that this freedom is illusory because man is bound by natural laws. This, however, is a misrepresentation—one of the many examples of the persistent modern confusion between *freedom* and *power.* Man is free to adopt values and to choose his actions; but this does not at all mean that he may violate natural laws with impunity—that he may, for example, leap oceans at a single bound. In short, when we say that "man is not 'free' to leap the ocean,"we are really discussing not his lack of freedom but his lack of *power* to cross the ocean, given the laws of his nature and of the nature of the world. Crusoe's freedom to adopt ideas, to choose his ends, is inviolable and inalienable; on the other hand, man, not being *omnipotent* as well as not being omniscient, always finds his *power* limited for doing all the things that he would like to do. In short, his power is necessarily limited by natural laws, but not his freedom of will. To put the case another way, it is patently absurd to define the "freedom" of an entity as its power to perform an act impossible for its nature![7]

If a man's free will to adopt ideas and values is inalienable, his *freedom of action*—his freedom to put these ideas into effect in the world, is not in such a fortunate condition. Again, we are not talking about the limitations on man's power inherent in the laws of his own nature and of the natures of other entities. What we are talking about now is interference with his sphere of action by other people—but here we are getting a bit ahead of Robinson Crusoe and our discussion. Suffice it to say now that, in the sense of *social* freedom—of freedom as *absence of molestation by other persons*—Crusoe is *absolutely* free, but that a world of more than one person requires our further investigation.

Since, in this book, we are interested in social and political philosophy rather than in philosophy proper, we shall be interested in the term "freedom" in this social or interpersonal sense, rather than in the sense of freedom of will.[8]

---

7. See Rothbard, *Individualism*, p. 8, and F.A. Hayek, *The Road to Serfdom* (Chicago: University of Chicago Press, 1944), p. 26.

8. Perhaps the one great advantage of the term "liberty" over its synonym "freedom" is

Let us now return to our analysis of Crusoe's purposeful transformation of nature-given data through the understanding of natural laws. Crusoe finds virgin, unused land on the island; land, in short, unused and uncontrolled by anyone, and hence *unowned*. By finding land resources, by learning how to use them, and, in particular, by actually *transforming* them into a more useful shape, Crusoe has, in the memorable phrase of John Locke, "mixed his labor with the soil." In doing so, in stamping the imprint of his personality and his energy on the land, he has naturally converted the land and its fruits into his *property*. Hence, the isolated man *owns* what he *uses* and *transforms*; therefore, in his case there is no problem of what *should be* A's property as against B's. Any man's property is *ipso facto* what he *produces*, i.e., what he transforms into use by his own effort. His property in land and capital goods continues down the various stages of production, until Crusoe comes to *own* the consumer goods which he has produced, until they finally disappear through his consumption of them.

As long as an individual remains isolated, then, there is no problem whatever about how far his *property*—his ownership—extends; as a rational being with free will, it extends over his own body, and it extends further over the material goods which he transforms with his labor. Suppose that Crusoe had landed not on a small island, but on a new and virgin continent, and that, standing on the shore, he had claimed "ownership" of the entire new continent by virtue of his prior discovery. This assertion would be sheer empty vainglory, so long as no one else came upon the continent. For the *natural fact* is that his true property—his *actual control* over material goods—would extend only so far as his actual labor brought them into production. His true ownership could not extend beyond the power of his own reach.[9] Similarly, it would be empty and meaningless for Crusoe to trumpet that he does not "really" own some or all of what he has produced (perhaps this Crusoe happens to be a romantic opponent of the property concept), for in fact the use and *therefore* the ownership has already been his. Crusoe, in natural fact, owns his own self and the extension of his self into the material world, neither more nor less.

---

that liberty is generally used *only* in the social, and not in the purely philosophic free-will sense, and is also less confused with the concept of power. For an excellent discussion of free will, see J.R. Lucas, *The Freedom of the Will* (Oxford: Clarendon Press, 1970).

9. Later on, when other people arrived on the continent, they too, in *natural fact*, would own the lands which they transformed by their labor, the first man could only obtain ownership of them by the use of invasive force against their natural property, or by receiving them from the newcomers in voluntary gift or exchange.

7. Interpersonal Relations: Voluntary Exchange

I t is now time to bring other men into our Robinsonian idyll—to extend our analysis to interpersonal relations. The problem for our analysis is not simply more people: after all, we could simply postulate a world of a million Crusoes on a million isolated islands, and our analysis would not need to be expanded by one iota. The problem is to analyze the *interaction* of these people. Friday, for example, might land in another part of the island, and make contact with Crusoe, or he might land on a separate island, and then later construct a boat that could reach the other island.

Economics has revealed a great truth about the natural law of human interaction: that not only is *production* essential to man's prosperity and survival, but so also is exchange. In short, Crusoe, on his island or part thereof, might produce fish, while Friday, on his part, might grow wheat, instead of both trying to produce both commodities. By exchanging part of Crusoe's fish for some of Friday's wheat, the two men can greatly improve the amount of both fish and bread that both can enjoy.[1] This great gain for both men is made possible by two primordial facts of nature—natural laws—on which all of economic theory is based: (a) the great variety of skills and interests among individual persons; and (b) the variety of natural resources in geographic land areas. If all people were equally skilled and equally interested in all matters, *and* if all areas of land were homogeneous with all others, there would be no room for exchanges. But, in the world as it is, the opportunity for specialization in the best uses for land and people enables exchanges to multiply vastly and immensely to raise the productivity and the standard of living (the satisfaction of wants) of *all* those participating in exchange.

If anyone wishes to grasp how much we owe to the processes of exchange, let him consider what would happen in the modern world if every man were suddenly prohibited from exchanging anything with anyone else. Each person would be forced to produce all of his own goods and services himself. The utter chaos, the total starvation of the great bulk of the human race, and the reversion to primitive subsistence by the remaining handful of people, can readily be imagined.

Another remarkable fact of human action is that A and B can specialize and exchange for their mutual benefit *even if* one of them is superior to the other in *both lines* of production. Thus, suppose that Crusoe

---

1. On the economic analysis of all this, see Murray N. Rothbard, *Man, Economy, and State*, (Princeton, N.J.: D. Van Nostrand, 1962), chap. 2.

is superior to Friday in fish *and* wheat production. It still benefits Crusoe to concentrate on what he is *relatively* best at. If, for example, he is a far better fisherman than Friday but only a moderately better farmer, he can gain more of both products by concentrating on fishing, and then exchanging his produce for Friday's wheat. Or, to use an example from an advanced exchange economy, it will pay a physician to hire a secretary for typing, filing, etc. *even* if he is better at the latter jobs, in order to free his time for far more productive work. This insight into the advantages of exchange, discovered by David Ricardo in his Law of Comparative Advantage, means that, in the free market of voluntary exchanges, the "strong" do not devour or crush the "weak," contrary to common assumptions about the nature of the free-market economy. On the contrary, it is precisely on the free market where the "weak" reap the advantages of productivity because it benefits the "strong" to exchange with them.

The process of exchange enables man to ascend from primitive isolation to civilization: it enormously widens his opportunities and the market for his wares; it enables him to invest in machines and other "high-order capital goods"; it forms a pattern of exchanges—the free market—which enables him to calculate economically the benefits and the costs of highly complex methods and aggregates of production.

But economists too often forget, in contemplating the critical importance and the glories of the free market, *what* precisely is being exchanged. For apples are *not* simply being exchanged for butter, or gold for horses. What is really being exchanged is not the commodities themselves, but the *rights to ownership* of them. When Smith exchanges a bag of apples for Jones's pound of butter, he is actually transferring his *ownership rights* in the apples in exchange for the ownership rights to the butter, and vice versa. Now that Smith rather than Jones is the absolute controller of the butter, it is Smith who may eat it or not at his will; Jones now has nothing to say in its disposition, and is instead absolute owner of the apples.

Returning now to Crusoe and Friday, suppose that more people, C, D, E . . . join Crusoe and Friday on the island. Each specializes in different products; gradually one particular product emerges—because of such qualities as high value, steady demand, ready divisibility—as a *medium of exchange*. For it is discovered that the use of a medium enormously expands the scope of exchanges and the wants that can be satisfied on the market. Thus, a writer or an economics teacher would be hard put to exchange his teaching or writing services for loaves of bread, parts of a radio, a piece of a suit, etc. A generally acceptable medium is indispensable for any extensive network of exchange and hence for any civilized economy.

Such a generally acceptable medium of exchange is defined as a *money*. It has generally been found, on the free market, that the best commodities for use as a money have been the precious metals, gold and silver. The exchange sequence now appears as follows: A, owning his body and his labor, finds land, transforms it, produces fish which he then owns; B uses his labor similarly to produce wheat, which he then owns; C finds land containing gold, transforms it, produces the gold which he then owns. C then exchanges the gold for other services, say A's fish. A uses the gold to exchange for B's wheat, etc. In short, the gold "enters circulation," i.e., its ownership is transferred from person to person, as it is used as a general medium of exchange. In each case, the exchangers transfer ownership rights, and, in each case, ownership rights are acquired in two ways and two ways only: (a) by finding and transforming resources ("producing"), and (b) by exchanging one's produce for someone else's product—including the medium of exchange, or "money" commodity. And it is clear that method (b) *reduces* logically to (a), for the only way a person can obtain something in exchange is by giving up his own product. In short, there is only one route to ownership of goods: production-and-exchange. If Smith gives up a product in exchange for Jones's which Jones also acquired in a previous exchange, then *someone*, whether the person from whom Jones bought the product or someone else down the line, must have been the original finder-and-transformer of the resource.

A man then, can acquire "wealth"—a stock of useful capital or consumer goods—either by "producing" it himself, or by selling to its producer some other product in exchange. The exchange process reduces logically back to original production. Such production is a process by which a man "mixes his labor with the soil"—finding and transforming land resources *or*, in such cases as a teacher or writer, by producing and selling one's own labor services directly. Put another way: since all production of capital goods reduces ultimately back to the original factors of land and labor, all production reduces back either to labor services or to finding new and virgin land and putting it into production by means of labor energy.[2]

A man may also obtain wealth voluntarily in another way: through gifts. Thus Crusoe, upon stumbling on Friday at another end of the island, may give him some sustenance. In such a case, the giver receives, not another alienable good or service from the other party, but the psychic

---

2. That capital goods reduce back to land and labor as original factors is a fundamental insight of the Austrian School of economics. In particular, see Eugen von Böhm-Bawerk, *The Positive Theory of Capital*, vol. 2 of *Capital and Interest* (South Holland, Ill.: Libertarian Press, 1959).

satisfaction of having done something for the receiver. In the case of a
gift, also, the process of acquisition reduces back to production and exchange—and again ultimately to production itself, since a gift must be
preceded by production, if not directly as in this case, then somewhere
back down the line.

We have so far analyzed the exchange process for a multitude of exchanges of consumer goods. We must now complete our picture of the real
world by analyzing exchanges along the structure of production. For exchanges in an advanced economy are not only "horizontal" (of consumer
goods), but also "vertical": they proceed downward from the original transformation of land, down through the various types of capital goods, and
finally to the ultimate state of consumption.

Let us consider a simple vertical pattern as it occurs in the exchange
economy. Smith transforms land resources and constructs an axe; instead
of using the axe to make another product, Smith, as a specialist in a vast
exchange economy, sells his axe for gold (money). Smith, producer of
the axe, transfers his right of ownership to Jones, in exchange for a certain
amount of Jones's gold—the precise amount of gold being agreed upon
voluntarily by the two parties. Jones now takes the axe and fells lumber,
then sells the lumber to Johnson for gold; Johnson in turn sells the lumber
to Robbins, a contractor, for gold, and Robbins in his turn constructs a
house in exchange for the gold of his client, Benton. (It should be evident
that this vertical network of exchange could not take place without the
use of a monetary medium for the exchanges.)

To complete our picture of a market economy, let us suppose that
Jones has cut down his lumber, but has to ship it down-river to transfer
it to Johnson; Jones, then, sells the lumber to another intermediary, Polk,
who *hires* the labor services of X, Y, and Z to transport the logs to Johnson.
What has happened here, and why doesn't the use of X, Y, and Z's labor
in transforming and transporting the logs to a more useful place give
them rights to ownership of the logs?

What has happened is this: Polk transfers some gold to X and to Y,
and to Z, in return for their selling to him their labor services of
transporting the logs. Polk did *not* sell the logs to these men for money;
instead, he "sold" them money in exchange for employing their labor
services on his logs. In short, Polk may have bought the logs from Jones
for 40 gold ounces, and then paid X, Y, and Z 20 gold ounces each to
transport the logs, and *then* sold the logs to Johnson for 110 ounces of
gold. Hence, Polk netted a gain of 10 gold ounces on the entire transaction.
X, Y, and Z, if they had so desired, *could* have purchased the logs from
Jones themselves for the 40 ounces, and then shipped the logs themselves,

sold them to Johnson for 110 and pocketed the 10 extra ounces. Why didn't they? Because (a) they didn't have the *capital;* in short, they hadn't saved up the requisite money, by reducing their previous consumption sufficiently below their income to accumulate the 40 ounces; and/or (b) they wanted money payment *while they worked,* and were not willing to wait for the number of months it took for the logs to be shipped and sold; and/or (c) they were unwilling to be saddled with the *risk* that the logs might indeed not be saleable for 110 ounces. Thus, the indispensable and enormously important function of Polk, the *capitalist* in our example of the market economy, is to save the laborers from the necessity of restricting their consumption and thus saving up the capital themselves, and from waiting for their pay until the product would (hopefully) be sold at a profit further down the chain of production. Hence, the capitalist, far from somehow depriving the laborer of his rightful ownership of the product, makes possible a payment to the laborer considerably *in advance* of the sale of the product. Furthermore, the capitalist, in his capacity as forecaster or *entrepreneur,* saves the laborer from the risk that the product might not be sold at a profit, or that he might even suffer losses.

The capitalist, then, is a man who has labored, saved out of his labor (i.e. has restricted his consumption) and, in a series of voluntary contracts has (a) purchased ownership rights in capital goods, and (b) paid the laborers for their labor services in transforming those capital goods into goods nearer the final stage of being consumed. Note again that no one is preventing the laborers themselves from saving, purchasing capital goods from their owners and then working on their own capital goods, finally selling the product and reaping the profits. In fact, the capitalists are conferring a great benefit on these laborers, making possible the entire complex vertical network of exchanges in the modern economy. For they save the money needed to buy the capital goods and to pay the laborers in advance of sale for "producing" them further.[3]

At each step of the way, then, a man produces—by exerting his labor upon tangible goods. If this good was previously unused and unowned, then his labor automatically brings the good under his control, his "ownership." If the good was already owned by someone else, then the

---

3. In technical economic terms, the laborers, by choosing to take their money in advance of sale, earn the "discounted marginal value product" of their labor—the discount being the value which the laborers achieve by getting their money *now* instead of *later.* The capitalists, by advancing money *now* and relieving the laborers of the burden of waiting until later, earn the discount for "time-preference"; the farsighted ones also earn the reward for being better at forecasting the future under conditions of uncertainty, in the form of "pure profits." The less farsighted entrepreneurs suffer *losses* for poor handling of decisions under uncertainty. See Rothbard, *Man, Economy, and State,* passim.

owner may either sell this (capital) good to our laborer for money, after which his labor is exerted on the good; *or* the previous owner may purchase the labor service for money in order to produce the good further and then sell it to the next buyer. This process, too, reduces back to the original production of unused resources and to labor, since the capitalist—the previous owner in our example—ultimately derived his own ownership from: original production; voluntary exchange; and the saving of money. Thus, all ownership on the free market reduces ultimately back to: (a) ownership by each man of his own person and his own labor; (b) ownership by each man of land which he finds unused and transforms by his own labor; and (c) the exchange of the products of this mixture of (a) and (b) with the similarly-produced output of other persons on the market.

The same law holds true for all ownership, on the market, of the money commodity. As we have seen, money is either (1) produced by one's own labor transforming original resources (e.g., mining gold); or (2) obtained by selling one's own product—or selling goods previously purchased with the proceeds of one's own product—in exchange for gold owned by someone else. Again, just as (c) in the previous paragraph reduces logically back to (a) and (b) production coming before exchange— so here (2) ultimately reduces logically back to (1).

In the free society we have been describing, then, all ownership reduces ultimately back to each man's naturally given ownership over himself, *and* of the land resources that man transforms and brings into production. The *free market* is a society of voluntary and consequently mutually beneficial exchanges of ownership titles between specialized producers. It has often been charged that this market economy rests on the wicked doctrine that labor "is treated as a commodity." But the natural fact is that labor service is indeed a commodity, for, as in the case of tangible property, one's own labor service *can* be alienated and exchanged for other goods and services. A person's labor service is alienable, but his *will is* not. It is most fortunate, moreover, for mankind that this is so; for this alienability means (1) that a teacher or physician or whatever can sell his labor services for money; and (2) that workers can sell their labor services in transforming goods to capitalists for money. If this could not be done, the structure of capital required for civilization could not be developed, and no one's vital labor services could be purchased by his fellow men.

The distinction between a man's alienable labor service and his inalienable will may be further explained: a man can alienate his labor service, but he cannot *sell* the capitalized future value of that service. In short, he cannot, in nature, sell himself into slavery and have this sale enforced—for this would mean that his future will over his own person was being surrendered in advance. In short, a man can naturally expend his labor currently for someone else's benefit, but he cannot transfer himself, even if he wished, into another man's permanent capital good. For he cannot rid himself of his own will, which may change in future years and repudiate the current arrangement. The concept of "voluntary slavery" is indeed a contradictory one, for so long as a laborer remains totally subservient to his master's will voluntarily, he is not yet a slave since his submission is voluntary; whereas, if he later changed his mind and the master enforced his slavery by violence, the slavery would not then be voluntary. But more of coercion later on.

The society that we have been describing in this section—the society of free and voluntary exchanges—may be called the "free society" or the society of "pure liberty." The bulk of this work will be devoted to spelling out the implications of such a system. The term "free market," while properly signifying the critically important network of free and voluntary exchanges, is insufficient when going at all beyond the narrowly economic or praxeologic. For it is vital to realize that the free market is exchanges of titles to property, and that therefore the free market is necessarily embedded in a larger free society—with a certain pattern of property rights and ownership titles. We have been describing the free society as one where property titles are founded on the basic natural facts of man: each individual's ownership by his ego over his own person and his own labor, and his ownership over the land resources which he finds and transforms. The natural alienability of tangible property as well as man's labor service makes possible the network of free exchanges of ownership titles.

The regime of pure liberty—the libertarian society—may be described as a society where *no ownership titles are "distributed,"* where, in short, no man's property in his person or in tangibles is molested, violated, or interfered with by anyone else. But this means that *absolute freedom,* in the social sense, *can* be enjoyed, not only by an isolated Crusoe but by every man in any society, no matter how complex or advanced. For every man enjoys absolute freedom—pure liberty—if, like Crusoe, his "naturally" owned property (in his person and in tangibles) is free from invasion or molestation by other men. And, of course , being in a society of voluntary exchanges, each man can enjoy absolute liberty not in Crusoe-like isolation, but in a milieu of civilization, harmony, sociability, and enormously greater productivity through exchanges of property with his fellow men. Absolute freedom, then, need *not* be lost as the price we must pay for the advent of civilization; men *are* born free, and need *never* be in chains. Man may achieve liberty *and* abundance, freedom *and* civilization.

This truth will be obscured if we persist in confusing "freedom" or "liberty" with *power*. We have seen the absurdity of saying that man does not have free will because he has not the *power* to violate the laws of his nature—because he cannot leap oceans at a single bound. It is similarly absurd to say that a man is not "truly" free in the free society because, in that society, no man is "free" to aggress against another man or to invade his property. Here, again, the critic is not really dealing with freedom but with power; in a free society, no man would be permitted (or none would permit himself) to invade the property of another. This would mean that his *power* of action would be limited; as man's power is always limited by his nature; it would *not* mean any curtailment of his freedom. For if we define freedom, again, as the *absence of invasion* by another man of any man's person or property, the fatal confusion of freedom and power is at last laid to rest.[4] We then see clearly that a supposed "freedom to steal or assault"—in short, to aggress—would not be a state of freedom at all, because it would permit someone, the victim of an assault, to be deprived of his right to person and property—in short, to have his liberty violated.[5] Each man's power, then, is always necessarily limited by the facts of the human condition, by the nature of man and his world; but it is one of the glories of man's condition that each person *can* be absolutely free, even in a world of complex interaction and exchange. It is still true, moreover, that any man's power to act and do and consume is enormously greater in such a world of complex interaction than it could be in a primitive or Crusoe society.

A vital point: if we are trying to set up an ethic for man (in our case, the subset of ethics dealing with violence), then to be a valid ethic the theory must hold true for *all* men, whatever their location in time or place.[6] This is one of the notable attributes of natural law—its applicability to all men, regardless of time or place. Thus, ethical natural law takes its place alongside physical or "scientific" natural laws. But the society of liberty is the *only* society that can apply the same basic rule to every man,

---

4. We shall see later that this definition of freedom or liberty must be clarified to read "absence of molestation of a man's *just* property," with justice implying, once again, ownership title to one's own self, to one's own transformed property, and to the fruits of voluntary exchanges built upon them.

5. For a critique of the "freedom to steal or assault" argument against the libertarian position, see Murray N. Rothbard, *Power and Market*, 2nd ed. (Kansas City: Sheed Andrews and McMeel, 1977), p. 242.

6. On the requirement that ethical laws be universally binding, see R.M. Hare, *The Language of Morals* (Oxford: Clarendon Press, 1952), p. 162; Marcus Singer, *Generalization in Ethics* (New York: Knopf, 1961), pp. 13–33.

regardless of time or place. Here is one of the ways in which reason can select one theory of natural law over a rival theory—just as reason can choose between many economic or other competing theories. Thus, if someone claims that the Hohenzollern or Bourbon families have the "natural right" to rule everyone else, this kind of doctrine is easily refutable by simply pointing to the fact that there is here no uniform ethic for every person: one's rank in the ethical order being dependent on the accident of being, or not being, a Hohenzollern. Similarly, if someone says that every man has a "natural right" to three square meals a day, it is glaringly obvious that this is a fallacious natural law or natural rights theory; for there are innumerable times and places where it is physically impossible to provide three square meals for all, or even for the majority, of the population. Hence this cannot be set forth as some kind of "natural right." On the other hand, consider the universal status of the ethic of liberty, and of the natural right of person and property that obtains under such an ethic. For every person, at any time or place, can be covered by the basic rules: ownership of one's own self, ownership of the previously unused resources which one has occupied and transformed; and ownership of all titles derived from that basic ownership—either through voluntary exchanges or voluntary gifts. These rules—which we might call the "rules of natural ownership"—can clearly be applied, and such ownership defended, regardless of the time or place, and regardless of the economic attainments of the society. It is impossible for any other social system to qualify as universal natural law; for if there is any coercive *rule* by one person or group over another (and *all* rule partakes of such hegemony), then it is impossible to apply the same rule for all; only a rulerless, purely libertarian world can fulfill the qualifications of natural rights and natural law, or, more important, can fulfill the conditions of a universal ethic for all mankind.

8. Interpersonal Relations: Ownership and Aggression

We have so far been discussing the free society, the society of peaceful cooperation and voluntary interpersonal relations. There is, however, another and contrasting type of interpersonal relation: the use of aggressive violence by one man against another. What such aggressive violence means is that one man invades the property of another without the victim's consent. The invasion may be against a man's property in his person (as in the case of bodily assault), or against his property in tangible goods (as in robbery or trespass). In either case, the aggressor imposes his will over the natural property of another—he deprives the other man of his freedom of action and of the full exercise of his natural self-ownership.

Let us set aside for a moment the corollary but more complex case of tangible property, and concentrate on the question of a man's ownership rights to his own body. Here there are two alternatives: either we may lay down a rule that each man should be permitted (i.e. have the right to) the full ownership of his own body, or we may rule that he may *not* have such complete ownership. If he *does*, then we have the libertarian natural law for a free society as treated above. But if he does *not*, if each man is *not* entitled to full and 100 percent self-ownership, then what does this imply? It implies either one of two conditions: (1) the "communist" one of Universal and Equal Other-ownership, or (2) Partial Ownership of One Group by Another—a system of rule by one class over another. These are the only logical alternatives to a state of 100 percent self-ownership for all.[1]

Let us consider alternative (2); here, one person or group of persons, G, are entitled to own not only themselves but also the remainder of society, R. But, apart from many other problems and difficulties with this kind of system, we *cannot* here have a universal or natural-law ethic for the human race. We can only have a partial and arbitrary ethic, similar to the view that Hohenzollerns are by nature entitled to rule over non-Hohenzollerns. Indeed, the ethic which states that Class G is entitled to rule over Class R implies that the latter, R, are subhuman beings who

---

1. Professor George Mavrodes, of the department of philosophy of the University of Michigan, objects that there is another logical alternative: namely, "that no one owns anybody, either himself or anyone else, nor any share of anybody." However, since ownership signifies range of control, this would mean that no one would be able to *do* anything, and the human race would quickly vanish.

do not have a right to participate as full humans in the rights of self-ownership enjoyed by G—but this of course violates the initial assumption that we are carving out an ethic for human beings as such.

What then of alternative (1)? This is the view that, considering individuals A, B, C . . ., no man is entitled to 100 percent ownership of his own person. Instead, an equal part of the ownership of A's body should be vested in B, C . . ., and the same should hold true for each of the others. This view, at least, does have the merit of being a universal rule, applying to every person in the society, but it suffers from numerous other difficulties.

In the first place, in practice, if there are more than a very few people in the society, this alternative must break down and reduce to Alternative (2), partial rule by some over others. For it is physically impossible for everyone to keep continual tabs on everyone else, and thereby to exercise his equal share of partial ownership over every other man. In practice, then, this concept of universal and equal other-ownership is Utopian and impossible, and supervision and therefore ownership of others necessarily becomes a specialized activity of a ruling class. Hence, no society which does not have full self-ownership for everyone can enjoy a universal ethic. For this reason alone, 100 percent self-ownership for every man is the only viable political ethic for mankind.

But suppose for the sake of argument that this Utopia *could* be sustained. What then? In the first place, it is surely absurd to hold that no man is entitled to own himself, and *yet* to hold that each of these very men is entitled to own a part of all other men! But more than that, would our Utopia be desirable? Can we picture a world in which *no* man is free to take *any* action whatsoever without prior approval by *everyone else* in society? Clearly no man would be able to do anything, and the human race would quickly perish. But if a world of zero or near-zero self-ownership spells death for the human race, then any steps in that direction also contravene the law of what is best for man and his life on earth. And, as we saw above, any ethic where one group is given full ownership of another violates the most elemental rule for any ethic: that it apply to every man. No partial ethics are any better, though they may seem superficially more plausible, than the theory of all-power-to-the-Hohenzollerns.

In contrast, the society of absolute self-ownership for all rests on the primordial fact of natural self-ownership by every man, and on the fact that each man may only live and prosper as he exercises his natural freedom of choice, adopts values, learns how to achieve them, etc. By virtue of being a man, he must use his mind to adopt ends and means; if someone aggresses against him to change his freely-selected course, this violates his nature; it violates the way he must function. In short, an aggressor interposes violence to thwart the natural course of a man's freely adopted ideas and values, and to thwart his actions based upon such values.

We cannot fully explain the natural laws of property and of violence without expanding our discussion to cover tangible property. For men are not floating wraiths; they are beings who can only survive by grappling with and transforming material objects. Let us return to our island of Crusoe and Friday. Crusoe, isolated at first, has used his free will and self-ownership to learn about his wants and values, and how to satisfy them by transforming nature-given resources through "mixing" them with his labor. He has thereby produced and created property. Now suppose that Friday lands in another part of this island. He confronts two possible courses of action: he may, like Crusoe, become a producer, transform unused soil by his labor, and most likely exchange his product for that of the other man. In short, he may engage in production and exchange, in also creating property. Or, he may decide upon another course: he may spare himself the effort of production and exchange, and go over and seize by violence the fruits of Crusoe's labor. He may aggress against the producer.

If Friday chooses the course of labor and production, then he in natural fact, as in the case of Crusoe, will own the land area which he clears and uses, as well as the fruits of its product. But, as we have noted above, suppose that Crusoe decides to claim more than his natural degree of ownership, and asserts that, by virtue of merely landing first on the island, he "really" owns the entire island, even though he had made no previous use of it. If he does so, then he is, in our view, illegitimately pressing his property claim beyond its homesteading–natural law boundaries, and if he uses that claim to try to eject Friday by force, then he is illegitimately aggressing against the person and property of the second homesteader.

Some theorists have maintained—in what we might call the "Columbus complex"—that the first discoverer of a new, unowned island or continent can rightfully own the entire area by simply asserting his claim. (In that case, Columbus, if in fact he had actually landed on the American continent—and if there had been no Indians living there—could have rightfully asserted his private "ownership" of the entire continent.) In natural fact, however, since Columbus would only have been able actually to use, to "mix his labor with," a small part of the continent, the rest then properly continues to be unowned until the next homesteaders arrive and carve out their rightful property in parts of the continent.[2]

---

2. A modified variant of this "Columbus complex" holds that the first discoverer of a new island or continent could properly lay claim to the entire continent by himself walking

Let us turn from Crusoe and Friday and consider the question of a sculptor who has just created a work of sculpture by transforming clay and other materials (and let us for the moment waive the question of property rights in the clay and the tools). The question now becomes: who should properly own this work of art as it emerges from the fashioning of the sculptor? Once again, as in the case of the ownership of people's bodies, there are only three logical positions: (1) that the sculptor, the "creator" of the work of art, should have the property right in his creation; (2) that another man or group of men have the right in that creation, i.e. to expropriate it by force without the sculptor's consent; or (3) the "communist" solution—that every individual in the world has an equal, quotal right to share in the ownership of the sculpture.

Put this starkly, there are very few people who would deny the monstrous injustice in either a group or the world community seizing ownership of the sculpture. For the sculptor has in fact "created" this work of art—not of course in the sense that he has created matter, but that he has produced it by transforming nature-given matter (the clay) into another form in accordance with his own ideas and his own labor and energy. Surely, if every man has the right to own his own body, and if he must use and transform material natural objects in order to survive, then he has the right to own the product that he has made, by his energy and effort, into a veritable extension of his own personality. Such is the case of the sculptor, who has placed the stamp of his own person on the raw material, by "mixing his labor" with the clay. But if the sculptor has done so, then so has every producer who has "homesteaded" or mixed his labor with the objects of nature.

Any group of people who expropriated the work of the sculptor would be clearly aggressive and parasitical—benefitting at the expense of the expropriated. As most people would agree, they would be clearly violating the right of the sculptor to his product—to the extension of his personality. And this would be true whether a group or the "world commune" did the expropriation—except that, as in the case of communal ownership of persons. (In practice this expropriation would have to be performed by a group of men in the name of the "world community.") But, as we have indicated, if the sculptor has the right to his own product, or transformed materials of nature, then so have the other producers. So have the men who extracted the clay from the ground and sold it to the sculptor, or the

---

around it (or hiring others to do so), and thereby laying out a boundary for the area. In our view, however, their claim would still be no more than to the boundary *itself*, and not to any of the land within it, for only the boundary will have been transformed and used by man.

men who produced the tools with which he worked on the clay. For these men, too, were producers; they, too, mixed their ideas and their technological know-how with the nature-given soil to emerge with a valued product. They, too, have mixed their labor and energies with the soil. And so, they, too, are entitled to the ownership of the goods they produced.[3]

If every man has the right to own his own person and therefore his own labor, and if by extension he owns whatever property he has "created" or gathered out of the previously unused, unowned state of nature, then who has the right to own or control the earth itself? In short, if the gatherer has the right to own the acorns or berries he picks, or the farmer his crop of wheat, who has the right to own the land on which these activities have taken place? Again, the justification for the ownership of ground land is the same for that of any other property. For no man actually ever "creates" matter: what he does is to take nature-given matter and transform it by means of his ideas and labor energy. But this is precisely what the pioneer—the homesteader—does when he clears and uses previously unused virgin land and brings it into his private ownership. The homesteader—just as the sculptor, or miner—has transformed the nature-given soil by his labor and his personality. The homesteader is just as much a "producer" as the others, and therefore just as legitimately the owner of his property. As in the case of the sculptor, it is difficult to see the morality of some other group expropriating the product and labor of the homesteader. (And, as in the other cases, the "world communist" solution boils down in practice to a ruling group.) Furthermore, the land communalists, who claim that the entire world population really owns the land in common, run up against the natural fact that before the homesteader, no one really used and controlled, and hence owned the land. The pioneer, or homesteader, is the man who first brings the valueless unused natural objects into production and use.

And so, there are only two paths for man to acquire property and wealth: production or coercive expropriation. Or, as the great German sociologist Franz Oppenheimer perceptively put it, there are only two means to the acquisition of wealth. One is the method of production, generally followed by voluntary exchange of such products: this is what Oppenheimer called *the economic means*. The other method is the unilateral seizure of the products of another: the expropriation of another man's property by violence. This predatory method of getting wealth Oppenheimer aptly termed *the political means*.[4]

---

3. Cf. John Locke, *Two Treatises on Government*, pp. 307–8.

4. Franz Oppenheimer, in his book *The State* (New York: Free Life Editions, 1975), p. 12, said:

Now the man who seizes another's property is living in basic contradiction to his own nature as a man. For we have seen that man can *only* live and prosper by his own production and exchange of products. The aggressor, on the other hand, is not a producer at all but a predator; he lives *parasitically* off the labor and product of others. Hence, instead of living in accordance with the nature of man, the aggressor is a parasite who feeds unilaterally by exploiting the labor and energy of other men. Here is clearly a complete violation of any kind of universal ethic, for *man* clearly cannot live as a parasite; parasites must have non-parasites, producers, to feed upon. The parasite not only fails to add to the social total of goods and services, he depends completely on the production of the host body. And yet, any increase in coercive parasitism decreases *ipso facto* the quantity and the output of the producers, until finally, if the producers die out, the parasites will quickly follow suit.

Thus, parasitism cannot be a universal ethic, and, in fact, the growth of parasitism attacks and diminishes the production by which both host and parasite survive. Coercive exploitation or parasitism injure the processes of production for everyone in the society. Any way that it may be considered, parasitic predation and robbery violate *not only* the nature of the victim whose self and product are violated, but also the nature of the aggressor himself, who abandons the natural way of production—of using his mind to transform nature and exchange with other producers— for the way of parasitic expropriation of the work and product of others. In the deepest sense, the aggressor injures himself as well as his unfortunate victim. This is fully as true for the complex modern society as it is for Crusoe and Friday on their island.

There are two fundamentally opposed means whereby man, requiring sustenance, is impelled to obtain the necessary means for satisfying his desires. These are work and robbery, one's own labor and the forcible appropriation of the labor of others. . . . I propose . . . to call one's own labor and the equivalent exchange of one's own labor for the labor of others, the "economic means" for the satisfaction of needs, while the unrequited appropriation of the labor of others will be called the "political means."

9. Property and Criminality

We may define anyone who aggresses against the person or other produced property of another as a *criminal*. A criminal is anyone who initiates violence against another man and his property: anyone who uses the coercive "political means" for the acquisition of goods and services.[1]

Now, however, critical problems arise; we are now indeed at the very heart of the entire problem of liberty, property, and violence in society. A crucial question—and one which has unfortunately been almost totally neglected by libertarian theorists—may be illustrated by the following examples:

Suppose we are walking down the street and we see a man, A, seizing B by the wrist and grabbing B's wristwatch. There is no question that A is here violating both the person and the property of B. Can we then simply infer from this scene that A *is* a criminal aggressor, and B his innocent victim?

Certainly not—for we *don't know* simply from our observation whether A *is* indeed a thief, or whether A *is* merely repossessing his own watch from B who had previously stolen it from him. In short, while the watch had undoubtedly been B's property until the moment of A's attack, we don't know whether or not A had been the legitimate owner at some earlier time, and had been robbed by B. Therefore, we do not yet know which one of the two men is the *legitimate* or *just* property owner. We can only find the answer through investigating the concrete data of the particular case, i.e., through "historical" inquiry.

Thus, we *cannot* simply say that the great axiomatic moral rule of the libertarian society is the protection of property rights, *period*. For the criminal has no natural right whatever to the retention of property that he has stolen; the aggressor has no right to claim any property that he has acquired by aggression. Therefore, we must modify or

---

1. We are here using "crime" and "criminal" in the ordinary language, rather than technical, legal sense. In legal parlance, offenses or aggressions against individuals are not crimes but *torts*, with committers of torts being referred to as *tortfeasors*. The legal concept of "crime" is confined to offenses against the State or Community. It will be seen below that we deny the latter concept altogether, with all legally punishable offenses confined to invasions of the person or property of other individuals. In short, in the libertarian conception, its "crimes" correspond to legally designated "torts," although there is no particular reason for redress or punishment to be confined to monetary payment, as was the case in ancient tort law. See Sir Henry Maine, *Ancient Law* (New York: E.P. Dutton, 1917), pp. 217ff.

rather clarify the basic rule of the libertarian society to say that no one has the right to aggress against the *legitimate* or *just* property of another.

In short, we cannot simply talk of defense of "property rights" or of "private property" *per se*. For if we do so, we are in grave danger of defending the "property right" of a criminal aggressor—in fact, we logically must do so. We may therefore only speak of just property or legitimate property or perhaps "natural property."And this means that, in concrete cases, we must decide whether any single given act of violence is aggressive or defensive: e.g., whether it is a case of a criminal robbing a victim, or of a victim trying to repossess his property.

Another vital implication of this way of looking at the world is to invalidate totally the utilitarian way of looking at property rights and therefore of looking at the free market. For the utilitarian, who has *no conception*, let alone theory, of justice, must fall back on the pragmatic, *ad hoc* view that all titles to private property currently existing at any time or place *must* be treated as valid and accepted as worthy of defense against violation.[2] This, in fact, is the way utilitarian free-market economists invariably treat the question of property rights. Note, however, that the utilitarian *has* managed to smuggle into his discussion an unexamined ethic: that all goods "now" (the time and place at which the discussion occurs) considered private property must be accepted and defended as such. In practice, this means that all private property titles designated by any existing *government* (which has everywhere seized the monopoly of defining titles to property) must be accepted as such. This is an ethic that is blind to all considerations of justice, and, pushed to its logical conclusion, must also defend every criminal in the property that he has managed to expropriate. We conclude that the utilitarian's simply praising a free market based upon *all existing* property titles is invalid and ethically nihilistic.[3]

I am convinced, however, that the real motor for social and political change in our time has been a moral indignation arising from the fallacious theory of surplus value: that the capitalists have stolen the rightful property

---

2. For a criticism of utilitarianism on this point, see John Rawls, *A Theory of Justice* (Cambridge, Mass.: Harvard University Press, 1971), pp. 26–27, secs. 83–84. Utilitarianism is attacked more generally in Peter Geach, *The Virtues* (Cambridge: Cambridge University Press, 1977), pp. 91ff., 103ff. Geach points out the counter-intuitive nature of the formula, "the greatest happiness of the greatest number." For a utilitarian defense of existing property titles, see Ludwig von Mises, *Socialism* (New Haven, Conn.: Yale University Press, 1951), pp. 45–47.

3. For more on the role of government and existing property titles see below; for a more detailed critique of utilitarian free-market economics, see pp. 201–14 below.

of the workers, and therefore that existing titles to accumulated capital are unjust. Given this hypothesis, the remainder of the impetus for both Marxism and anarchosyndicalism follow quite logically. From an apprehension of what appears to be monstrous injustice flows the call for "expropriation of the expropriators," and, in both cases, for some form of "reversion" of the ownership and the control of the property to the workers.[4] Their arguments cannot be successfully countered by the maxims of utilitarian economics or philosophy, but only by dealing forthrightly with the moral problem, with the problem of the justice or injustice of various claims to property.

Neither can Marxist views be rebutted by utilitarian paeans to the virtues of "social peace." Social peace is all very well, but true peace is essentially the quiet, unmolested enjoyment of one's legitimate property, and if a social system is founded upon monstrously unjust property titles, not molesting them is not peace but rather the enshrinement and entrenchment of permanent aggression. Neither can the Marxists be rebutted by pointing the finger at their use of violent methods of overthrow. It is, to be sure, a consistent creed—though one that I do not share—that *no* violence should ever be used by anyone against anyone else: *even* by a victim against a criminal. But this Tolstoyan–Gandhian moral position is really irrelevant here. For the point at question is whether or not the victim has a moral *right* to employ violence in defending his person or property against criminal attack or in repossessing property from the criminal. The Tolstoyan may concede that the victim *has* such a right but may try to persuade him not to exercise that right in the name of a higher morality. But this takes us afield from our discussion into broader reaches of ethical philosophy. I would only add here that any such total objector to violence must then be consistent and advocate that *no* criminal ever be punished by the use of violent means. And this implies, let us note, not only abstaining from *capital* punishment but from all punishment whatsoever, and, indeed, from all methods of violent defense that might conceivably injure an aggressor. In short, to employ that horrid cliche to which we shall have occasion to return, the Tolstoyan may not use force to prevent someone from raping his sister.

The point here is that *only* Tolstoyans are entitled to object to the violent overthrow of an entrenched criminal group; for everyone who is *not* a Tolstoyan favors the use of force and violence to defend against

---

4. In this sense, the only proper carrying out of the Marxian ideal has partially occurred in Yugoslavia, where the Communist regime has turned the socialized sphere of production over to the control, and hence *de facto* ownership, of the workers in each particular plant.

and punish criminal aggression. He must therefore favor the morality, if not the wisdom, of using force to overthrow entrenched criminality. If so, then we are pushed immediately back to the really important question: *who* is the criminal, and therefore *who* is the aggressor? Or, in other words, against *whom* is it legitimate to use violence? And if we concede that capitalist property is morally illegitimate, then we cannot deny the right of the workers to employ whatever violence may be necessary to seize the property, just as A, in our above example, would have been within his rights in forcibly repossessing his watch if B had stolen it previously.

The only genuine refutation of the Marxian case for revolution, then, is that capitalists' property is just rather than unjust, and that therefore its seizure by workers or by anyone else would in itself be unjust and criminal. But this means that we *must* enter into the question of the justice of property claims, and it means further that we cannot get away with the easy luxury of trying to refute revolutionary claims by arbitrarily placing the mantle of "justice" upon any and all existing property titles. Such an act will scarcely convince people who believe that they or others are being grievously oppressed and permanently aggressed against. But this *also* means that we must be prepared to discover cases in the world where violent expropriation of existing property titles will be morally justified, because these titles are themselves unjust and criminal.

Let us again use an example to make our thesis clear. To use Ludwig von Mises's excellent device for abstracting from emotionalism, let us take a hypothetical country, "Ruritania." Let us say that Ruritania is ruled by a king who has grievously invaded the rights of persons and the legitimate property of individuals, and has regulated and finally seized their property. A libertarian movement develops in Ruritania, and comes to persuade the bulk of the populace that this criminal system should be replaced by a truly libertarian society, where the rights of each man to his person and his found and created property are fully respected. The king, seeing the revolt to be imminently successful, now employs a cunning stratagem. He proclaims his government to be dissolved, but just before doing so he arbitrarily parcels out the entire land area of his kingdom to the "ownership" of himself and his relatives. He then goes to the libertarian rebels and says: "all right, I have granted your wish, and have dissolved my rule; there is now no more violent intervention in private property. However, myself and my eleven relatives now each *own* one-twelfth of Ruritania, and if you disturb us in this ownership in any way, you shall be infringing upon the sanctity of the very fundamental principle that you profess: the inviolability of *private* property. Therefore, while we shall no longer be imposing 'taxes,' *you* must grant each of us the right to impose any 'rents' that we may wish upon our 'tenants,'or to regulate the lives of all the people who presume to live on 'our' property as we see fit. In this way, taxes shall be fully replaced by 'private rents'!"

Now what should be the reply of the libertarian rebels to this pert challenge? If they are consistent utilitarians, they must bow to this subterfuge, and resign themselves to living under a regime no less despotic than the one they had been battling for so long. Perhaps, indeed, *more* despotic, for now the king and his relatives can claim for themselves the libertarians' very principle of the absolute right of private property, an absoluteness which they might not have dared to claim before.

It should be clear that for the libertarians to refute this stratagem they must take their stand on a theory of *just* versus *unjust* property; they cannot remain utilitarians. They would then say to the king: "We are sorry, but we only recognize private property claims that are *just*— that emanate from an individual's fundamental natural right to own himself and the property which he has either transformed by his energy or which has been voluntarily given or bequeathed to him by such transformers. We do not, in short, recognize anyone's right to any given piece of property purely on his or anyone else's arbitrary say-so that it *is* his own. There can be no natural moral right derivable from a man's arbitrary claim that any property is his. Therefore, we claim the right to expropriate the 'private' property of you and your relations, and to return that property to the individual owners against whom you aggressed by imposing your illegitimate claim."

One corollary that flows from this discussion is of vital importance for a theory of liberty. This is that, in the deepest sense, *all* property is "private."[5] For all property belongs to, is controlled by, some individual persons or groups of persons. If B stole a watch from A, then the watch was B's private "property"—was under his control and *de facto* ownership—so long as he was allowed to possess and use it. Therefore, whether the watch was in the hands of A or B, it was in *private* hands—in some cases, legitimate-private, in others criminal-private, but private just the same.

As we shall see further below, the same holds for individuals forming themselves into any sort of group. Thus, when they formed the government, the king and his relatives controlled—and therefore at least partially "owned"—the property of the persons against whom they were aggressing. When they parcelled out the land into the "private" property of each, they again shared in owning the country, though in formally different

---

5. I owe this insight to Mr. Alan Milchman.

ways. The *form* of private property differed in the two cases, but not the essence. Thus, the crucial question in society is *not*, as so many believe, whether property should be private or governmental, but rather whether the *necessarily* "private" owners are legitimate owners or criminals. For, ultimately, there *is* no entity called "government"; there are only people forming themselves into groups called "governments" and acting in a "governmental" manner.[6] *All* property is therefore always "private"; the only and critical question is whether it should reside in the hands of criminals or of the proper and legitimate owners. There is really only one reason for libertarians to oppose the formation of governmental property or to call for its divestment: the realization that the rulers of government are unjust and criminal owners of such property.

In short, the *laissez-faire* utilitarian cannot simply oppose "government" ownership and defend private; for the trouble with governmental property is not so much that it is *governmental* (for what of "private" criminals like our watch-stealer?) but that it is illegitimate, unjust, and criminal—as in the case of our Ruritanian king. And since "private" criminals are also reprehensible, we see that the social question of property *cannot* ultimately be treated in utilitarian terms as *either* private *or* governmental. It must be treated in terms of justice or injustice: of legitimate property-owners vs. illegitimate, criminal invaders of such property, whether these invaders are called "private" or "public." The libertarian may now be getting rather worried. He may say: "granted that you are right in principle, that property titles must be validated by justice, and that neither the criminal may be allowed to keep the stolen watch, nor the king and his relatives 'their' country, how can your principle be applied in practice? Wouldn't this involve a chaotic inquiry into everyone's property title, and furthermore, what criterion can you establish for the justice of these titles?"

The answer is that the criterion holds as we have explained above: The right of every individual to own his person and the property that he has found and transformed, and therefore "created," and the property which he has acquired either as gifts from or in voluntary exchange with other such transformers or "producers." It is true that existing property titles must be scrutinized, but the resolution of the problem is much simpler than the question assumes. For remember always the basic principle: that all resources, all goods, in a state of no-ownership belong properly to the first person who finds and transforms them into a useful good (the "homestead" principle). We have seen this above in the case of

---

6. See pp. 159–98 below for a further discussion of the role of government.

unused land and natural resources: the first to find and mix his labor with them, to possess and use them, "produces" them and becomes their legitimate property owner. Now suppose that Mr. Jones has a watch; if we *cannot* clearly show that Jones or his ancestors to the property title in the watch were criminals, then we must say that since Mr. Jones has been possessing and using it, that *he* is truly the legitimate and just property owner.

Or, to put the case another way: if we do not *know* if Jones's title to any given property is criminally-derived, then we may assume that this property was, at least momentarily, in a state of no-ownership (since we are not sure about the original title), and therefore that the *proper* title of ownership reverted instantaneously to Jones as its "first" (i.e., current) possessor and user. In short, where we are not sure about a title but it cannot be clearly identified as criminally derived, then the title properly and legitimately reverts to its current possessor.

But now suppose that a title to property *is* clearly identifiable as criminal, does this necessarily mean that the current possessor must give it up? No, not necessarily. For that depends on two considerations: (a) whether the *victim* (the property owner originally aggressed against) or his heirs are clearly identifiable and can now be found; *or* (b) whether or not the current possessor is *himself* the criminal who stole the property. Suppose, for example, that Jones possesses a watch, and that we *can* clearly show that Jones's title is originally criminal, either because (1) his ancestor stole it, or (2) because he or his ancestor purchased it from a thief (whether wittingly or unwittingly is immaterial here). Now, *if* we can identify and find the victim or his heir, then it is clear that Jones's title to the watch is totally invalid, and that it must promptly revert to its true and legitimate owner. Thus, if Jones inherited or purchased the watch from a man who stole it from Smith, and if Smith or the heir to his estate can be found, then the title to the watch properly reverts immediately back to Smith or his descendants, *without* compensation to the existing possessor of the criminally derived "title."[7] Thus, if a current title to property is criminal in origin, *and* the victim or his heir can be found, then the title should immediately revert to the latter.

Suppose, however, that condition (a) is not fulfilled: in short, that we *know* that Jones's title is criminal, but that we cannot now find the victim or his current heir. Who now is the legitimate and moral property

---

7. Or it may revert to any other of Smith's assignees. Thus, Smith might have sold his claim or right to the watch to someone else, and then if this purchaser or his heirs can be found, the legitimate property title reverts to him.

owner? The answer to this question now depends on whether or not Jones himself is the criminal, whether Jones is the man who stole the watch. If Jones *was* the thief, then it is quite clear that he cannot be allowed to keep it, for the criminal cannot be allowed to keep the reward of his crime; and he loses the watch, and probably suffers other punishments besides.[8] In that case, who gets the watch? Applying our libertarian theory of property, the watch is *now*—after Jones has been apprehended—in a state of no-ownership, and it must therefore become the legitimate property of the first person to "homestead" it—to take it and use it, and therefore, to have converted it from an unused, no-ownership state to a useful, owned state. The first person who does so then becomes its legitimate, moral, and just owner.

But suppose that Jones is *not* the criminal, not the man who stole the watch, but that he had inherited or had innocently purchased it from the thief. And suppose, of course, that neither the victim nor his heirs can be found. In *that* case, the disappearance of the victim means that the stolen property comes properly into a state of no-ownership. But we have seen that any good in a state of no-ownership, with no legitimate owner of its title, reverts as legitimate property to the first person to come along and use it, to appropriate this now unowned resource for human use. But this "first" person is clearly Jones, who has been using it all along. Therefore, we conclude that even though the property was originally stolen, that *if* the victim or his heirs cannot be found, *and if* the current possessor was not the actual criminal who stole the property, then title to that property belongs properly, justly, and ethically to its current possessor.

To sum up, for any property currently claimed and used: (a) if we *know* clearly that there was no criminal origin to its current title, then obviously the current title is legitimate, just and valid; (b) if we *don't* know whether the current title had any criminal origins, but can't find out either way, then the hypothetically "unowned" property reverts instantaneously and justly to its current possessor; (c) if we *do* know that the title is originally criminal, but can't find the victim or his heirs, then (c1) if the current title-holder was not the criminal aggressor against the property, then it reverts to him justly as the first owner of a hypothetically unowned property. But (c2) if the current titleholder is himself the criminal or one of the criminals who stole the property, then clearly he is properly to be deprived of it, and it then reverts to the first man who takes it out of

8. We are assuming here that criminals suffer punishment beyond simple surrender of the property stolen: but how much the punishment should be or what theory it should be based upon—whether retributive, deterrent, or reform, for example—will be treated below.

its unowned state and appropriates it for his use. And finally, (d) if the current title is the result of crime, *and* the victim or his heirs can be found, then the title properly reverts immediately to the latter, without compensation to the criminal or to the other holders of the unjust title.

It might be objected that the holder or holders of the unjust title (in the cases where they are not themselves the criminal aggressors) should be entitled to the property which they *added* on to the property which was not justly theirs, or, at the very least, to be compensated for such additions. In reply, the criterion should be whether or not the addition is *separable* from the original property in question. Suppose, for example, that Brown steals a car from Black, and that Brown sells the car to Robinson. In our view, then, the car must be returned immediately to the true owner, Black, without compensation to Robinson. Being a victim of a theft should not impose obligations on Black to recompense someone else. Of course, Robinson has a legitimate complaint against the car-thief Brown, and should be able to sue Brown for repayment or damages on the basis of the fraudulent contract that Brown had foisted upon him (pretending that the car was really Brown's property to sell). But suppose that Robinson, in the course of his possession of the car, had added a new car radio; since the radio is separable from the car, he should be able to extract the radio as legitimately his own before returning the car to Black. On the other hand, if the addition is not separable, but an integral part of the property (e.g., a repaired engine), then Robinson should not be able to demand any payment or property from Black (although perhaps he may be able to do so by suing Brown). Similarly, if Brown had stolen a parcel of land from Black, and sold it to Robinson, the criterion should again be the separability of any additions Robinson had made to the property. If, for example, Robinson had built some buildings on the property, then he should be able to move the buildings or demolish them before turning the land over to the original landowner, Black.

Our example of the stolen car enables us to see immediately the injustice of the current legal concept of the "negotiable instrument." In current law, the stolen car would indeed revert to the original owner with no obligation on the owner's part to compensate the current holder of the unjust title. But the State has designated certain goods as "negotiable instruments" (e.g., dollar bills) which the non-criminal recipient or buyer is now deemed to own, and who cannot be forced to return them to the victim. Special legislation has also made pawnbrokers into a similarly privileged class; so that if Brown steals a typewriter from Black, and then pawns it with Robinson, the pawnbroker may not be forced to return the typewriter to its just property owner, Black.

To some readers, our doctrine may seem harsh on good-faith recipients of goods which later turn out to be stolen and unjustly possessed. But we should remember that, in the case of *land* purchase, title searches are a common practice, as well as title insurance against such problems. In the libertarian society, presumably the business of title search and title insurance will become more extensive to apply to the wider areas of the protection of the rights of just and private property.

We see, then, that, properly developed libertarian theory neither joins the utilitarians in placing an arbitrary and indiscriminate ethical blessing upon every current property title, *nor* does it open the morality of existing titles to total uncertainty and chaos. On the contrary, from the fundamental axiom of the natural right of every man to property in his self and in the unowned resources which he finds and transforms into use, libertarian theory deduces the absolute morality and justice of all current titles to property *except* where the origin of the current titles is criminal, *and* (1) the victim or his heirs can be identified and found, *or* (2) the victim cannot be found *but* the current title-holder is the criminal in question. In the former case, the property reverts in common justice to the victim or his heirs; in the latter, it becomes the property of the first appropriator to alter its unowned state.

We thus have a theory of the rights of property: that every man has an absolute right to the control and ownership of his own body, and to unused land resources that he finds and transforms. He also has the right to give away such tangible property (though he cannot alienate control over his own person and will) and to exchange it for the similarly derived properties of others. Hence, all legitimate property-right derives from every man's property in his own person, as well as the "homesteading" principle of unowned property rightly belonging to the first possessor.

We also have a theory of *criminality:* a criminal is someone who aggresses against such property. Any criminal titles to property should be invalidated and turned over to the victim or his heirs; if no such victims can be found, and if the current possessor is not himself the criminal, then the property justly reverts to the current possessor on our basic "homesteading" principle.

Let us now see how this theory of property may be applied to different categories of property. The simplest case, of course, is property *in persons*. The fundamental axiom of libertarian theory is that each person must be a self-owner, and that no one has the right to interfere with such self-ownership. From this there follows immediately the total impermissibility of property in another person.[9] One prominent example

9. The difficult case of *children* will be treated on pp. 97–112.

of this sort of property is the institution of *slavery*. Before 1865, for example, slavery was a "private property" title to many persons in the United States. The fact of such private title did not make it legitimate; on the contrary, it constituted a *continuing* aggression, a continuing criminality, of the masters (and of those who helped enforce their titles) against their slaves. For here the victims were immediately and clearly identifiable, and the master was every day committing aggression against his slaves. We should also point out that, as in our hypothetical case of the king of Ruritania, utilitarianism provides no firm basis for vacating the "property right" of a master in his slaves.

When slavery was a common practice, much discussion raged as to whether or how much the master should be monetarily compensated for the loss of his slaves if slavery were to be abolished. This discussion was palpably absurd. For what do we do when we have apprehended a thief and recovered a stolen watch: do we compensate the thief for the loss of the watch, or do we *punish* him? Surely, the enslavement of a man's very person and being is a far more heinous crime than the theft of his watch, and should be dealt with accordingly. As the English classical liberal Benjamin Pearson commented acidly: "the proposal had been made to compensate the slaveowners and he had thought it was the slaves who should have been compensated."[10] And clearly, such compensation could only justly have come from the slaveholders themselves, and not from the ordinary taxpayers.

It should be emphasized that on the question of slavery, whether or not it should have been abolished immediately is irrelevant to problems of social disruption, of the sudden impoverishing of slave masters, or of the flowering of Southern culture, let alone the question—interesting, of course, on other grounds—whether slavery was good for the soil, and for the economic growth of the South, or would have disappeared in one or two generations. For the libertarian, for the person who believes in justice, the sole consideration was the monstrous injustice and continuing aggression of slavery, and therefore the necessity of abolishing the institution as soon as it could be accomplished.[11]

---

10. Quoted in William D. Grampp, *The Manchester School of Economics* (Stanford, Calif.: Stanford University Press, 1969), p. 59. Also on compensation and slavery, see pp. 204, 237ff below.

11. For more on the general necessity for the libertarian to be an "abolitionist," see pp. 259ff below.

10. The Problem of Land Theft

A particularly important application of our theory of property titles is the case of *landed* property. For one thing, land is a fixed quotal portion of the earth, and therefore the ground land endures virtually permanently. Historical investigation of land titles therefore would have to go back much further than for other more perishable goods. However, this is by no means a critical problem, for, as we have seen, where the victims are lost in antiquity, the land properly belongs to any noncriminals who are in current possession. Suppose, for example, that Henry Jones I stole a piece of land from its legitimate owner, James Smith. What is the current status of the title of current possessor Henry Jones X? Or of the man who might be the current possessor by purchasing the land from Henry Jones X? If Smith and his descendants are lost to antiquity, then title to the land properly and legitimately belongs to the current Jones (or the man who has purchased it from him), in direct application of our theory of property titles.

A second problem, and one that sharply differentiates land from other property, is that the very *existence* of capital goods, consumers goods, or the monetary commodity, is at least a *prima facie* demonstration that these goods *had* been used and transformed, that human labor had been mixed with natural resources to produce them. For capital goods, consumer goods, and money do not exist by themselves in nature; they must be created by human labor's alteration of the given conditions of nature. But any area of land, which *is* given by nature, *might* never have been used and transformed; and therefore, *any* existing property title to never-used land would have to be considered invalid. For we have seen that title to an unowned resource (such as land) comes properly only from the expenditure of labor to transform that resource into use. Therefore, if any land has *never* been so transformed, no one can legitimately claim its ownership.

Suppose, for example, that Mr. Green legally owns a certain acreage of land, of which the northwest portion has never been transformed from its natural state by Green or by anyone else. Libertarian theory will morally validate his claim for the rest of the land—provided, as the theory requires, that there is no identifiable victim (or that Green had not himself stolen the land.) But libertarian theory must invalidate his claim to ownership of the northwest portion. Now, so long as no "settler" appears who will initially transform the northwest portion, there is no real difficulty; Brown's claim may be invalid but it is also mere meaningless verbiage. He is not yet a criminal aggressor against anyone else. But should *another* man appear who does transform the land, and should Green oust him by force from the property (or employ others to do so), then Green becomes at that point a criminal aggressor against land justly owned by another. The same would be true if Green should use violence to prevent another settler from entering upon this never-used land and transforming it into use.

Thus, to return to our Crusoe "model," Crusoe, landing upon a large island, may grandiosely trumpet to the winds his "ownership" of the entire island. But, in natural fact, he *owns* only the part that he settles and transforms into use. Or, as noted above, Crusoe might be a solitary Columbus landing upon a newly-discovered continent. But so long as no other person appears on the scene, Crusoe's claim is so much empty verbiage and fantasy, with no foundation in natural fact. But should a newcomer—a Friday—appear on the scene, and begin to transform unused land, then any *enforcement* of Crusoe's invalid claim would constitute criminal aggression against the newcomer and invasion of the latter's property rights.

Note that we are *not* saying that, in order for property in land to be valid, it must be *continually* in use.[1] The only requirement is that the land be *once* put into use, and thus become the property of the one who has mixed his labor with, who imprinted the stamp of his personal energy upon, the land.[2] After that use, there is no more reason to disallow the land's remaining idle than there is to disown someone for storing his watch in a desk drawer.[3]

---

1. This was the use-theory of landed property propounded by Joshua K. Ingalls in the nineteenth century. On Ingalls, see James J. Martin, *Men Against the State* (DeKalb, Ill.: Adrian Allen Associates, 1953), pp. 142–52.

2. As Leon Wolowski and Emile Levasseur have eloquently written in "Property," *Lalor's Cyclopedia of Political Science, etc.* (Chicago: M.B. Cary, 1884), vol. 3, p. 392:

Nature has been appropriated by . . . [man] for his use; she has become his *own;* she is his *property.* This property is legitimate; it constitutes a right as sacred for man as is the free exercise of his faculties. It is his because it has come entirely from himself, and is in no way anything but an emanation from his being. Before him, there was scarcely anything but matter, since him, and by him, there is interchangeable wealth. The producer has left a fragment of his own person in the thing which has thus become valuable, and may hence be regarded as a prolongation of the faculties of man acting upon external nature. As a free being he belongs to himself; now, the cause, that is to say, the productive force, is himself; the effect, that is to say, the wealth produced is still himself. Who shall dare contest his title of ownership so clearly marked by the seal of his personality?

3. There are, as I have demonstrated elsewhere, excellent economic reasons why land, in particular, may remain unused; for above-subsistence living standards depend on the supply of labor being scarcer than the supply of land, and, when that happy

One form of invalid land title, then, is any claim to land that has never been put into use. The enforcement of such a claim against a first-user then becomes an act of aggression against a legitimate property right. In practice, it must be noted, it is not at all difficult to distinguish land in its natural virgin state from land that has at some time been transformed by man for his use. The hand of man will in some way be evident.

One problem, however, that sometimes arises in the validity of land titles is the question of "adverse possession." Let us suppose that a man, Green, comes upon a section of land not obviously owned by someone—there is no fence perhaps, and no one on the premises. Green assumes that the land is unowned; he proceeds to work the land, uses it for a length of time, and then the original owner of the land appears on the scene and orders Green's eviction. Who is right? The common law of adverse possession arbitrarily sets a time span of twenty years, after which the intruder, despite his aggression against the property of another, retains absolute ownership of the land. But our libertarian theory holds that land needs only to be transformed *once* by man to pass into private ownership. Therefore, if Green comes upon land that in any way bears the mark of a former human use, it is his responsibility to *assume* that the land is owned by someone. Any intrusion upon his land, without further inquiry, must be done at the risk of the newcomer being an aggressor. It is of course possible that the previously owned land has been *abandoned;* but the newcomer must not assume blithely that land which has obviously been transformed by man is no longer owned by anyone. He must take steps to find out if his new title to the land is clear, as we have seen is in fact done in the title-search business.[4] On the other hand, if Green comes upon land that has obviously never been transformed by anyone, he can move onto it at once and with impunity, for in the libertarian society no one can have a valid title to land that has never been transformed.

In the present world, when most land areas have been pressed into service, the invalidating of land titles from never being used would not be very extensive. More important nowadays would be invalidating a

---

situation obtains, considerable land will be "sub-marginal" and therefore idle. See Murray N. Rothbard, *Man, Economy, and State* (Princeton, N.J.: D. Van Nostrand, 1962), pp. 504, 609. For a fascinating example of recurring property titles in land according to a migratory calendar worked out by numerous tribes in southern Persia, see Fredrik Barth, "The Land Use Pattern of Migratory Tribes of South Persia," *Norsk Geografisk Tidsskrift,* Bind 17 (1959–1960): 1–11.

4. Of course, everyone should have the *right* to abandon any property he wishes; in a libertarian society, no one can be forced to own property which he wishes to abandon.

land title because of a *continuing* seizure of landed property by aggressors. We have already discussed the case of Jones's ancestors having seized a parcel of land from the Smith family, while Jones uses and owns the land in the present day. But suppose that centuries ago, Smith was tilling the soil and therefore legitimately owning the land; and then that Jones came along and settled down near Smith, claiming by use of coercion the title to Smith's land, and extracting payment or "rent" from Smith for the privilege of continuing to till the soil. Suppose that now, centuries later, Smith's descendants (or, for that matter, other unrelated families) are now tilling the soil, while Jones's descendants, or those who purchased their claims, still continue to exact tribute from the modern tillers. Where is the true property right in such a case? It should be clear that here, just as in the case of slavery, we have a case of *continuing* aggression against the true owners—the true possessors—of the land, the tillers, or peasants, by the illegitimate owner, the man whose original *and continuing* claim to the land and its fruits has come from coercion and violence. Just as the original Jones was a continuing aggressor against the original Smith, so the modern peasants are being aggressed against by the modern holder of the Jones-derived land title. In this case of what we might call "feudalism" or "land monopoly," the feudal or monopolist landlords have no legitimate claim to the property. The current "tenants," or peasants, should be the absolute owners of their property, and, as in the case of slavery, the land titles should be transferred to the peasants, without compensation to the monopoly landlords.[5]

Note that "feudalism," as we have defined it, is not restricted to the case where the peasant is *also* coerced by violence to remain on the lord's land to keep cultivating it (roughly, the institution of *serfdom*).[6] Nor is it restricted to cases where additional measures of violence are used to bolster and maintain feudal landholdings (such as the State's prevention by violence of any landlord's sale or bequest of his land into smaller subdivisions).[7] All that "feudalism," in our sense, requires is the seizure

5. The term "feudalism," as used here, is not intended to apply to any specific landed or other relation during the Middle Ages; it is used here to cover a single kind of action: the seizure of land by conquest and the continuing assertion and enforcement of ownership over that land and the extraction of rent from the peasants continuing to till the soil. For a defense of such a broader use of the term "feudalism," see Robert A. Nisbet, *The Social Impact of the Revolution* (Washington, D.C.: American Enterprise Institute for Public Policy Research, 1974), pp. 4–7.

6. Serfdom, like slavery, constituted a continuing aggression by the lord against the *person* of the serf, as well as against his rightful property. For a discussion of various definitions of feudalism, see Marc Bloch, *Feudal Society* (Chicago: University of Chicago Press, 1961), chap. 1.

by violence of landed property from its true owners, the transformers of land, and the continuation of that kind of relationship over the years. Feudal land rent, then, is the precise equivalent of paying a continuing annual tribute by producers to their predatory conquerors. Feudal land rent is therefore a form of permanent tribute. Note also that the peasants in question need not be the descendants of the original victims. For since the aggression is continuing so long as this relation of feudal aggression remains in force, the current peasants are the contemporary victims and the currently legitimate property owners. In short, in the case of feudal land, or land monopoly, both of our conditions obtain for invalidating current property titles: For not only the original but also the current land title is criminal, *and* the current victims can very easily be identified.

Our above hypothetical case of the King of Ruritania and his relatives is one example of a means by which feudalism can get started in a land area. After the king's action, he and his relatives become feudal landlords of their quotal portions of Ruritania, each one extracting coercive tribute in the form of feudal "rent" from the inhabitants.

We do not of course mean to imply that all land rent is illegitimate and a form of continuing tribute. On the contrary, there is no reason, in a libertarian society, why a person transforming land may not then rent it out or sell it to someone else; indeed, that is precisely what will occur. How, then, can we distinguish between feudal rent and legitimate rent, between feudal tenancies and legitimate tenancies? Again, we apply our rules for deciding upon the validity of property titles: we look to see if the origin of the land title is criminal, and, in the current case, whether the aggression upon the producers of the land, the peasants, is still continuing. If we *know* that these conditions hold, then there is no problem, for the identification of both aggressor and victim is remarkably clear-cut. But if we *don't know* whether these conditions obtain, then (applying our rule), lacking a clear identifiability of the criminal, we conclude that the land title and the charge of rent is just and legitimate and not feudal. In practice, since in a feudal situation criminality is both old and continuing, *and* the peasant-victims are readily identifiable, feudalism is one of the easiest forms of invalid title to detect.

---

7. Such measures include *entail* (forcibly preventing the landowner from selling his land) and *primogeniture* (coercively preventing him from bequeathing his land except intact to his eldest son).

11. Land Monopoly, Past and Present

Thus, there are two types of ethically invalid land titles:[1] "feudalism," in which there is continuing aggression by titleholders of land against peasants engaged in transforming the soil; and land-engrossing, where arbitrary claims to virgin land are used to keep first-transformers out of that land. We may call both of these aggressions "land monopoly"—not in the sense that some one person or group owns all the land in society, but in the sense that arbitrary privileges to land ownership are asserted in both cases, clashing with the libertarian rule of non-ownership of land except by actual transformers, their heirs, and their assigns.[2]

Land monopoly is far more widespread in the modern world than most people—especially most Americans—believe. In the undeveloped world, especially in Asia, the Middle East, and Latin America, feudal landholding is a crucial social and economic problem—with or without quasi-serf impositions on the persons of the peasantry. Indeed, of the countries of the world, the United States is one of the very few virtually free from feudalism, due to a happy accident of its historical development.[3] Largely escaping feudalism itself, it is difficult for Americans to take the entire problem seriously. This is particularly true of American laissez-faire economists, who tend to confine their recommendations for the backward countries to preachments about the virtues of the free market. But these preachments naturally fall on deaf ears, because "free market" for American conservatives obviously does not encompass an end to feudalism and land monopoly and the transfer

---

1. In addition, of course, to *government* titles, for which see below.

2. As I have indicated in *Man, Economy, and State* (Princeton, N.J.: D. Van Nostrand, 1962), chap. 10, "monopoly" is properly defined as a receipt of exclusive privilege to a property *beyond* the libertarian rule of property rights.

3. This happy exception does not hold for those Mexican lands seized from their owners and redistributed by the conquering Yankees—as can be seen by the recent movement of Mexican–Americans, led by Reies Lopez Tijerina, to return to the heirs of the victims the land stolen from them by the U.S. conquerors. On the theft of land from the Mexican–Americans, see Clark S. Knowlton, "Land-Grant Problems Among the State's Spanish–Americans," *New Mexico Business* (June 1967): 1–13. Also see Clyde Eastman, Garrey Carruthers, and James A. Liefer, "Contrasting Attitudes Toward Land in New Mexico," *New Mexico Business* (March 1971): 3–20. On the Tijerina movement, see Richard Gardner, *Grito!: Reies Tuerina and the New Mexico Land Grant War of 1967* (New York: Harper and Row, 1971).

of title to these lands, *without compensation,* to the peasantry. And yet, since agriculture is always the overwhelmingly most important industry in the undeveloped countries, a *truly* free market, a truly libertarian society devoted to justice and property rights, can only be established there by ending unjust feudal claims to property. But utilitarian economists, grounded on no ethical theory of property rights, can only fall back on defending whatever status quo may happen to exist—in this case, unfortunately, the status quo of feudal suppression of justice and of any genuinely free market in land or agriculture. This ignoring of the land problem means that Americans and citizens of undeveloped countries talk in two different languages and that neither can begin to understand the other's position.

American conservatives, in particular, exhort the backward countries on the virtues and the importance of private foreign investment from the advanced countries, and of allowing a favorable climate for this investment, free from governmental harassment. This is all very true, but is again often unreal to the undeveloped peoples, because the conservatives persistently fail to distinguish between legitimate, free-market foreign investment, as against investment based upon monopoly concessions and vast land grants by the undeveloped states. To the extent that foreign investments are based on land monopoly and aggression against the peasantry, to that extent do foreign capitalists take on the aspects of feudal landlords, and must be dealt with in the same way.

A moving expression of these truths was delivered in the form of a message to the American people by the prominent left-wing Mexican intellectual, Carlos Fuentes:

> You have had four centuries of uninterrupted development within the capitalistic structure. We have had four centuries of underdevelopment within a feudal structure. . . . You had your own origin in the capitalistic revolution. . . . You started from zero, a virgin society, totally equal to modern times, without any feudal ballast. On the contrary, we were founded as an appendix of the falling feudal order of the Middle Ages; we inherited its obsolete structures, absorbed its vices, and converted them into institutions on the outer rim of the revolution in the modern world. . . . We come from . . . slavery to . . . *latifundio* [enormous expanses of land under a single landlord], denial of political, economic, or cultural rights for the masses, a customs house closed to modern ideas. . . . You must understand that the Latin American drama stems from the persistence of those feudal structures over four

centuries of misery and stagnation, while you were in the midst of the industrial revolution and were exercising a liberal democracy.[4]

We need not search far for examples of land aggression and monopoly in the modern world; they are indeed legion. We might cite one example not so very far removed from our hypothetical king of Ruritania: "The Shah owns more than half of all arable land in Iran, land originally taken over by his father. He owns close to 10,000 villages. So far, this great reformer has sold two of his villages."[5] A typical example of foreign investment combined with land aggression is a North American mining company in Peru, the Cerro de Pasco Corporation. Cerro de Pasco, having legitimately purchased its land from a religious convent a half century ago, began in 1959 to encroach upon and seize the lands of neighboring Indian peasants. Indians of Rancas refusing to leave their land were massacred by peasants in the pay of the company; Indians of Yerus Yacan tried to contest the company's action in the courts, while company men burned pastures and destroyed peasant huts. When the Indians retook their land through mass non-violent action, the Peruvian government, at the behest of the Cerro de Pasco and the regional *latifundia* owners, sent troops to eject, assault, and even murder the unarmed Indians.[6]

What, then, is to be our view toward investment in oil lands, one of the major forms of foreign investment in underdeveloped countries in today's world? The major error of most analyses is to issue either a blanket approval or a blanket condemnation, for the answer depends on the justice of the property title established in each specific case. Where, for example, an oil company, foreign or domestic, lays claim to the oil field which it discovers and drills, then this is its just "homesteaded" private property, and it is unjust for the undeveloped government to tax or regulate the company. Where the government insists on claiming ownership of the land itself, and only leases the oil to the company, then (as we will see further

---

4. Carlos Fuentes, "The Argument of Latin America: Words for the North Americans," in *Whither Latin America?* (New York: Monthly Review Press, 1963), pp. 10–12.

5. Michael Parrish, "Iran: The Portrait of a U.S. Ally," *The Minority of One* (December 1962): 12.

6. Sebastian Salazar Bondy, "Andes and Sierra Maestra," in *Whither Latin America?* p. 116, says:

> From time to time, the Lima newspapers publish stories about such and such a community's having "invaded" properties of latifundists or miners. The informed reader knows what is happening. Disgusted with being dispossessed, lacking official justice, the Indians have decided to take through their own effort what has always belonged to them.

below in discussing the role of government), the government's claim is illegitimate and invalid, and the company, in the role of homesteader, is properly the owner and not merely the renter of the oil land.

On the other hand, there are cases where the oil company uses the government of the undeveloped country to grant it, in advance of drilling, a monopoly concession to all the oil in a vast land area, thereby agreeing to the use of force to squeeze out all competing oil producers who might search for and drill oil in that area. In that case, as in the case above of Crusoe's arbitrarily using force to squeeze out Friday, the first oil company is illegitimately using the government to become a land-and-oil monopolist. Ethically, any new company that enters the scene to discover and drill oil is the proper owner of *its* "homesteaded" oil area. *A fortiori*, of course, our oil concessionaire who also uses the State to eject peasants from their land by force—as was done, for example, by the Creole Oil Co. in Venezuela—is a collaborator with the government in the latter' s aggression against the property rights of the peasantry.

We are now able to see the grave fallacy in the current programs for "land reform" in the undeveloped countries. (These programs generally involve minor transfers of the least fertile land from landlords to peasants, along with full compensation to the landlords, often financed by the peasants themselves via state aid.) If the landlord's title is just, then *any* land reform applied to such land is an unjust and criminal confiscation of his property; but, on the other hand, if his title is unjust, then the reform is picayune and fails to reach the heart of the question. For then the only proper solution is an immediate vacating of the title and its transfer to the peasants, with certainly no compensation to the aggressors who had wrongly seized control of the land. Thus, the land problem in the undeveloped countries can only be solved by applying the rules of justice that we have set forth; and such application requires detailed and wholesale empirical inquiry into present titles to land.

In recent years, the doctrine has gained ground among American conservatives that feudalism, instead of being oppressive and exploitative, was in fact a bulwark of liberty. It is true that feudalism, as these conservatives point out, was not as evil a system as "Oriental despotism," but that is roughly equivalent to saying that imprisonment is not as severe a penalty as execution. The difference between feudalism and Oriental despotism was really of degree rather than kind; arbitrary power over land and over persons on that land was, in the one case, broken up into geographical segments; in the latter case, land tended to concentrate into the hands of one imperial overlord over the land-area of the entire country, aided by his bureaucratic retinue. The systems of power and repression are similar in type; the Oriental despot is a single feudal overlord with the consequent power accruing into his hands. Each system is a variant of the other; neither is in any sense libertarian. And there is no reason to suppose that society must choose between one and the other—that these are the only alternatives.

Historical thinking on this entire matter was shunted onto a very wrong road by the statist German historians of the late nineteenth century: by men such as Schmoller, Bücher, Ehrenberg, and Sombart.[7] These historians postulated a sharp dichotomy and inherent conflict between feudalism on the one hand and absolute monarchy, or the strong State, on the other. They postulated that capitalist development *required* absolute monarchy and the strong State to smash local feudal and gild-type restrictions. In upholding this dichotomy of capitalism *plus* the strong central State vs. feudalism, they were joined, from their own special viewpoint, by the Marxists, who made no particular distinction between "bourgeoisie" who made use of the State, and bourgeoisie who acted on the free market. Now some modern conservatives have taken this old dichotomy and turned it on its head. Feudalism and the strong central state are still considered the critical polar opposites, except that feudalism is, on this view, considered the good alternative.

The error here is in the dichotomy itself. Actually, the strong state and feudalism were *not* antithetical; the former was a logical outgrowth of the latter, with the absolute monarch ruling as the super-feudal overlord. The strong state, when it developed in Western Europe, did not set about to smash feudal restrictions on trade; on the contrary, it *superimposed* its own central restrictions and heavy taxes on top of the feudal structure. The French Revolution, directed against the living embodiment of the strong state in Europe, was aimed at destroying *both* feudalism with its local restrictions, and the restrictions and high taxes imposed by the central government.[8] The true dichotomy was liberty on the one side *versus* the feudal lords *and* the absolute monarch on the other. Furthermore, the free market and capitalism flourished earliest and most strongly in those very countries where *both* feudalism and central government power were at their relative weakest: the Italian city-states, and seventeenth-century Holland and England.[9]

7. Ironically, Sombart's later years were marked by an attack on the notion of capitalist development. See e.g., Werner Sombart, *A New Social Philosophy* (Princeton, N.J.: Princeton University Press, 1937); also see Werner Sombart, *Vom Menschen* (Berlin, 1938).

8. On private property and feudalism in the French Revolution, see Gottfried Dietze, *In Defense of Property* (Chicago: Regnery, 1963), pp. 140–41.

9. On the neglected case of the Dutch, see Jelle C. Riemersma, "Economic Enterprise and Political Powers After the Reformation," *Economic Development and Cultural Change* (July 1955): 297–308.

North America's relative escape from the blight of feudal land and land monopoly was not for lack of trying. Many of the English colonies made strong attempts to establish feudal rule, especially where the colonies were chartered companies or proprietorships, as in New York, Maryland, and the Carolinas. The attempt failed because the New World was a vast and virgin land area, and therefore the numerous receivers of monopoly and feudal land grants—many of them enormous in size— could only gain profits from them by inducing settlers to come to the New World and settle on their property. Here were not, as in the Old World, previously existing settlers on relatively crowded land who could easily be exploited. Instead, the landlords, forced to encourage settlement, and anxious for a quick return, invariably subdivided and sold their lands to the settlers. It was unfortunate, of course, that by means of arbitrary claims and governmental grants, land titles were engrossed ahead of settlement. The settlers were consequently forced to pay a price for what should have been free land. But *once* the land was purchased by the settler, the injustice disappeared, and the land title accrued to its proper holder: the settler. In this way, the vast supply of virgin land, along with the desire of the land grantees for quick profits, led everywhere to the happy dissolution of feudalism and land monopoly, and the establishment in North America of a truly libertarian land system. Some of the colonial proprietors tried to keep collecting *quitrents* from the settlers—the last vestige of feudal exactions— but the settlers widely refused to pay or to treat the land as anything but their own. In every case, the colonial proprietors gave up trying to collect their *quitrents*, even before their charters were confiscated by the British Crown.[10] In only one minor case did feudal land tenure persist (apart from the vital case of slavery and the large Southern plantations) in the English colonies: in the Hudson Valley counties in New York, where the large grantees persisted in *not* selling the lands to settlers, but in renting them out. As a result, continuing resistance and even open warfare were waged by the farmers (who were even known as "peasants") against their feudal landlords. This resistance culminated in the "Anti-Rent" wars of the 1840s, when the quitrent exactions were finally ended by the state legislature, and the last vestige of feudalism outside the South finally disappeared.

The important exception to this agrarian idyll, of course, was the flourishing of the slave system in the Southern states. It was only the

---

10. On the American experience, see Murray N. Rothbard, *Conceived in Liberty* (New York: Arlington House, 1975), vol. 1.

coercion of slave labor that enabled the large plantation system in staple crops to flourish in the South. Without the ability to own and coerce the labor of others, the large plantations—and perhaps much of the tobacco and later the cotton culture—would not have pervaded the South.

We have indicated above that there was only one possible moral solution for the slave question: immediate and unconditional abolition, with no compensation to the slavemasters. Indeed, any compensation should have been the other way—to repay the oppressed slaves for their lifetime of slavery. A vital part of such necessary compensation would have been to grant the plantation lands not to the slavemaster, who scarcely had valid title to any property, but to the slaves themselves, whose labor, on our "homesteading" principle, was mixed with the soil to develop the plantations. In short, at the very least, elementary libertarian justice required not only the immediate freeing of the slaves, but also the immediate turning over to the slaves, again without compensation to the masters, of the plantation lands on which they had worked and sweated. As it was, the victorious North made the same mistake—though "mistake" is far too charitable a word for an act that preserved the essence of an unjust and oppressive social system—as had Czar Alexander when he freed the Russian serfs in 1861: the *bodies* of the oppressed were freed, but the property which they had worked and eminently deserved to own, remained in the hands of their former oppressors. With the economic power thus remaining in their hands, the former lords soon found themselves virtual masters once more of what were now free tenants or farm laborers. The serfs and the slaves had tasted freedom, but had been cruelly deprived of its fruits.[11]

---

11. In recent years, a new wave of pro-abolitionist historians—such as Staughton Lynd, James McPherson, and Willie Lee Rose—have recognized the critical importance of the abolitionist demand for "forty acres and a mule," for turning over the old plantations to the slaves. See James M. McPherson, *The Struggle for Equality: Abolitionists and the Negro in the Civil War and Reconstruction* (Princeton, N.J.: Princeton University Press, 1964); and Willie Lee Rose, *Rehearsal for Reconstruction: The Port Royal Experiment* (Indianapolis, Ind.: Bobbs-Merrill, 1964). Also see Claude F. Oubre, *Forty Acres and a Mule: The Freedmen's Bureau and Black Land Ownership* (Baton Rouge: Louisiana State University Press, 1978).

12. Self-Defense

If every man has the absolute right to his justly-held property, it then follows that he has the right to *keep* that property—to defend it by violence against violent invasion. Absolute pacifists who also assert their belief in property rights—such as Mr. Robert LeFevre—are caught in an inescapable inner contradiction: for if a man owns property and yet is denied the right to defend it against attack, then it is clear that a very important aspect of that ownership is being denied to him. To say that someone has the absolute right to a certain property but lacks the right to defend it against attack or invasion is also to say that he does *not* have total right to that property.

Furthermore, if every man has the right to defend his person and property against attack, then he must also have the right to hire or accept the aid of other people to do such defending: he may employ or accept defenders just as he may employ or accept the volunteer services of gardeners on his lawn.

How extensive is a man's right of self-defense of person and property? The basic answer must be: up to the point at which he begins to infringe on the property rights of someone else. For, in that case, his "defense" would in itself constitute a criminal invasion of the just property of some other man, which the latter could properly defend himself against.

It follows that defensive violence may only be used against an actual or directly threatened invasion of a person's property—and may not be used against any nonviolent "harm" that may befall a person's income or property value. Thus, suppose that A, B, C, D . . . etc. decide, for *whatever reason,* to boycott the sales of goods from Smith's factory or store. They picket, distribute leaflets, and make speeches—all in a non-invasive manner—calling on everyone to boycott Smith. Smith may lose considerable income, and they may well be doing this for trivial or even immoral reasons; but the fact remains that organizing such a boycott is perfectly within their rights, and if Smith tried to use violence to break up such boycott activities he would be a criminal invader of their property.

Defensive violence, therefore, must be confined to resisting invasive acts against person or property. But such invasion may include two corollaries to actual physical aggression: *intimidation,* or a direct threat of physical violence; and *fraud,* which involves the appropriation of someone else's property without his consent, and is therefore "implicit theft."

Thus, suppose someone approaches you on the street, whips out a gun, and demands your wallet. He might not have molested you physically during this encounter, but he has extracted money from you on the basis of a direct, overt threat that he *would* shoot you if you disobeyed his commands. He has used the threat of invasion to obtain your obedience to his commands, and this is equivalent to the invasion itself.

It is important to insist, however, that the threat of aggression be palpable, immediate, and direct; in short, that it be embodied in the initiation of an overt act. Any remote or indirect criterion—any "risk" or "threat"—is simply an excuse for invasive action by the supposed "defender" against the alleged "threat." One of the major arguments, for example, for the prohibition of alcohol in the 1920s was that the imbibing of alcohol increased the likelihood of (unspecified) people committing various crimes; therefore, prohibition was held to be a "defensive" act in defense of person and property. In fact, of course, it was brutally invasive of the rights of person and property, of the right to buy, sell, and use alcoholic beverages. In the same way, it could be held that (a) the failure to ingest vitamins makes people more irritable, that (b) the failure is therefore likely to increase crime, and that therefore (c) everyone should be forced to take the proper amount of vitamins daily. Once we bring in "threats" to person and property that are vague and future—i.e., are not overt and immediate—then all manner of tyranny becomes excusable. The only way to guard against such despotism is to keep the criterion of perceived invasion clear and immediate and overt. For, in the inevitable case of fuzzy or unclear actions, we must bend over backwards to require the threat of invasion to be direct and immediate, and therefore to allow people to do whatever they may be doing. In short, the burden of proof that the aggression has really begun must be on the person who employs the defensive violence.

Fraud as implicit theft stems from the right of free contract, derived in turn from the rights of private property. Thus, suppose that Smith and Jones agree on a contractual exchange of property titles: Smith will pay $1000 in return for Jones's car. If Smith appropriates the car and then refuses to turn over $1000 to Jones, then Smith has in effect stolen the $1000; Smith is an aggressor against $1000 now properly belonging to Jones. Thus, failure to keep a contract of this type is tantamount to theft, and therefore to a physical appropriation of another's property fully as "violent" as trespass or simple burglary without armed assault.

Fraudulent *adulteration* is equally implicit theft. If Smith pays $1000 and receives from Jones not a specified make of car but an older and poorer car, this too is implicit theft: once again, someone's property has been appropriated in a contract, without the other person's property being turned over to him as agreed.[1]

But we must not be led into the trap of holding that *all* contracts, whatever their nature, must be enforceable (i.e., that violence may properly be used in their enforcement). The only reason the above contracts are enforceable is that breaking such contracts involves an implicit theft of property. Those contracts which do *not* involve implicit theft should not be enforceable in a libertarian society.[2] Suppose, for example, that A and B make an agreement, a "contract," to get married in six months; or that A promises that, in six months' time, A will give B a certain sum of money. If A breaks these agreements, he may perhaps be morally reprehensible, but he has not implicitly stolen the other person's property, and therefore such a contract cannot be enforced. To use violence in order to force A to carry out such contracts would be *just as much* a criminal invasion of A's rights as it would be if Smith decided to use violence against the men who boycotted his store. Simple *promises*, therefore, are not properly enforceable contracts, because breaking them does not involve invasion of property or implicit theft.

Debt contracts are properly enforceable, not because a promise is involved, but because the creditor's property is appropriated without his consent—i.e., stolen—if the debt is not paid. Thus, if Brown lends Green $1000 this year in return for the delivery of $1100 next year, and Green fails to pay the $1100, the proper conclusion is that Green has appropriated $1100 of Smith's property, which Green refuses to turn over—in effect, has stolen. This legal way of treating a debt—of holding that the creditor has a *property* in the debt—should be applied to all debt contracts.

Thus, it is not the business of *law*—properly the rules and instrumentalities by which person and property are violently defended—to make people moral by use of legal violence. It is not the proper business of law to make people be truthful or to keep their promises. It is the business of legal violence to defend persons and their property from violent attack, from molestation or appropriation of their property

---

1. For a development of libertarian principles of the law of adulteration, see Wordsworth Donisthorpe, *Law In A Free State* (London: Macmillan, 1895), pp. 132–58.

2. For a further development of this thesis, see the section "Property Rights and the Theory of Contracts," pp. 133–48 below.

without their consent. To say more—to say, for example, that mere promises are properly enforceable—is to make an unwarranted fetish of "contracts" while forgetting *why* some of them are enforceable: in defense of the just rights of property.

Violent defense then must be confined to violent invasion—either actually, implicitly, or by direct and overt threat. But given this principle, *how far* does the right of violent defense go? For one thing, it would clearly be grotesque and criminally invasive to shoot a man across the street because his angry look seemed to you to portend an invasion. The danger must be immediate and overt, we might say, "clear and present"—a criterion that properly applies not to restrictions on freedom of speech (never permissible, if we regard such freedom as a subset of the rights of person and property) but to the right to take coercive action against a supposedly imminent invader.[3]

Secondly, we may ask: must we go along with those libertarians who claim that a storekeeper has the right to kill a lad as punishment for snatching a piece of his bubble gum? What we might call the "maximalist" position goes as follows: by stealing the bubble gum, the urchin puts himself outside the law. He demonstrates by his action that he does not hold or respect the correct theory of property rights. Therefore, he loses all of his rights, and the storekeeper is within his rights to kill the lad in retaliation.[4]

I propose that this position suffers from a grotesque lack of proportion. By concentrating on the storekeeper's right to his bubble gum, it totally ignores another highly precious property-right: every man's— including the urchin's— right of self-ownership. On what basis must we hold that a minuscule invasion of another's property lays one forfeit to the total loss of one's own? I propose another fundamental rule regarding crime: the criminal, or invader, loses his own right *to the extent* that he has deprived another man of his. If a man deprives another man of some of his self-ownership or its extension in physical property, to that extent does he lose his own rights.[5] From this principle immediately

---

3. This requirement recalls the scholastic doctrine of the double effect. See G.E.M. Anscombe, "The Two Kinds of Error in Action," *Journal of Philosophy* 60 (1963): 393–401; Philippa R. Foot, *Virtues and Vices* (Berkeley: University of California Press, 1978), pp. 19–25.

4. On the maximalist view, furthermore, socialists, interventionists and utilitarians would, by virtue of their views, be liable to execution. I am indebted to Dr. David Gordon for this point.

5. The great libertarian Auberon Herbert, in Auberon Herbert and J.H. Levy, *Taxation and Anarchism* (London: Personal Rights Association, 1912), p. 38, put it this way:

derives the proportionality theory of punishment—best summed up in the old adage: "let the punishment fit the crime."[6]

We conclude that the shopkeeper's shooting of the erring lad went beyond this proportionate loss of rights, to wounding or killing the criminal; this going beyond is *in itself* an invasion of the property right in his own person of the bubble gum thief. In fact, the storekeeper has become a far greater criminal than the thief, for he has killed or wounded his victim—a far graver invasion of another's rights than the original shoplifting.

Should it be illegal, we may next inquire, to "incite to riot"? Suppose that Green exhorts a crowd: "Go! Burn! Loot! Kill!" and the mob proceeds to do just that, with Green having nothing further to do with these criminal activities. Since every man is free to adopt or not adopt any course of action he wishes, we cannot say that in some way Green *determined* the members of the mob to their criminal activities; we cannot make him, because of his exhortation, at all responsible for *their* crimes. "Inciting to riot," therefore, is a pure exercise of a man's right to speak without being thereby implicated in crime. On the other hand, it is obvious that if Green happened to be involved in a plan or conspiracy with others to commit various crimes, and that then Green told them to proceed, he would then be just as implicated in the crimes as are the others—more so, if he were the mastermind who headed the criminal gang. This is a seemingly subtle distinction which in practice is clearcut—there is a world of difference between the head of a criminal gang and a soap-box orator during a riot; the former is not, properly, to be charged simply with "incitement."

It should further be clear from our discussion of defense that every man has the absolute right to bear arms—whether for self-defense or any other licit purpose. The crime comes not from *bearing* arms, but from *using* them for purposes of threatened or actual invasion. It is curious, by the way, that the laws have especially banned *concealed* weapons, when

---

Am I right in saying that a man has forfeited his own rights (to the extent of the aggression he has committed) in attacking the rights of others? . . . It may be very difficult to translate into concrete terms the amount of aggression, and of resulting restraint; but all just law seems to be the effort to do this. We punish a man in a certain way if he has inflicted an injury which lays me up for a day; in another way if he takes my life. . . . There is generally underlying it [the law] the view (which is, I think, true) that the punishment or redress—both in civil and criminal matters—should be measured by the amount of aggression; in other words that the aggressor—after a rough fashion—loses as much liberty as that of which he has deprived others.

6. For a development of this theory of punishment, see the section "Punishment and Proportionality," pp. 85–96 below.

it is precisely the *open* and unconcealed weapons which might be used
for intimidation.

In every crime, in every invasion of rights, from the most negligible
breach of contract up to murder, there are always two parties (or sets of
parties) involved: the victim (the plaintiff) and the alleged criminal (the
defendant). The purpose of every judicial proceeding is to find, as best
we can, *who* the criminal is or is not in any given case. Generally, these
judicial rules make for the most widely acceptable means of finding out
who the criminals may be. But the libertarian has one overriding *caveat*
on these procedures: no force may be used against non-criminals. For
any physical force used against a non-criminal is an invasion of that
innocent person's rights, and is therefore itself criminal and impermissible. Take, for example, the police practice of beating and torturing
suspects—or, at least, of tapping their wires. People who object to these
practices are invariably accused by conservatives of "coddling criminals." But the whole point is that we *don't know* if these are criminals
or not, and until convicted, they must be presumed not to be criminals
and to enjoy all the rights of the innocent: in the words of the famous
phrase, "they are innocent until proven guilty." (The only exception
would be a victim exerting self-defense on the spot against an aggressor, for he *knows* that the criminal is invading his home.) "Coddling
criminals" then becomes, in actuality, making sure that police do not
criminally invade the rights of self-ownership of presumptive
innocents whom they suspect of crime. In that case, the "coddler,"
and the restrainer of the police, proves to be far more of a genuine defender of property rights than is the conservative.

We may qualify this discussion in one important sense: police may
use such coercive methods *provided* that the suspect turns out to be
guilty, *and* provided that the police are treated as themselves criminal
if the suspect is not proven guilty. For, in that case, the rule of no force
against non-criminals would still apply. Suppose, for example, that
police beat and torture a suspected murderer to find information *(not*
to wring a confession, since obviously a coerced confession could never
be considered valid). If the suspect turns out to be guilty, then the police
should be exonerated, for then they have only ladled out to the murderer
a parcel of what he deserves in return; his rights had already been
forfeited by more than that extent. *But* if the suspect is not convicted,
then that means that the police have beaten and tortured an innocent
man, and that they in turn must be put into the dock for criminal assault.
In short, in all cases, police must be treated in precisely the same way
as anyone else; in a libertarian world, every man has equal liberty, equal

rights under the libertarian law. There can be no special immunities, special licenses to commit crime. That means that police, in a libertarian society, must take their chances like anyone else; if they commit an act of invasion against someone, that someone had better turn out to deserve it, otherwise *they* are the criminals.

As a corollary, police can *never* be allowed to commit an invasion that is worse than, or that is more than proportionate to, the crime under investigation. Thus, the police can never be allowed to beat and torture someone charged with petty theft, since the beating is far more proportionate a violation of a man's rights than the theft, *even* if the man is indeed the thief.

It should be clear that no man, in an attempt to exercise his right of self-defense, may coerce anyone else into defending him. For that would mean that the defender himself would be a criminal invader of the rights of others. Thus, if A is aggressing against B, B may not use force to compel C to join in defending him, for then B would be just as much a criminal aggressor against C. This immediately rules out *conscription* for defense, for conscription enslaves a man and forces him to fight on someone else's behalf. It also rules out such a deeply-embedded part of our legal system as *compulsory witnesses.* No man should have the right to force anyone else to speak on any subject. The familiar prohibition against coerced self-incrimination is all very well, but it should be extended to preserving the right not to incriminate *anyone else,* or indeed to say nothing at all. The freedom to speak is meaningless without the corollary freedom to keep silent.

If no force may be used against a noncriminal, then the current system of *compulsory jury duty* must also be abolished. Just as conscription is a form of slavery, so too is compulsory jury duty. Precisely because being a juror is so important a service, the service must not be filled by resentful serfs. And how can any society call itself "libertarian" that rests on a foundation of jury slavery? In the current system, the courts enslave jurors because they pay a daily wage so far below the market price that the inevitable shortage of jury labor has to be supplied by coercion. The problem is very much the same as the military draft, where the army pays far below the market wage for privates, cannot obtain the number of men they want at that wage, and then turns to conscription to supply the gap. Let the courts pay the market wage for jurors, and sufficient supply will be forthcoming.

If there can be no compulsion against jurors or witnesses, then a libertarian legal order will have to eliminate the entire concept of the *subpoena power.* Witnesses, of course, may be *requested to* appear. But this voluntarism must also apply to the defendants, since they have not yet been convicted of crime. In a libertarian society, the plaintiff would notify the defendant that the latter is being charged with a crime, and that a trial of the defendant will be underway. The defendant would be simply invited to appear. There would be no compulsion on him to appear. If he chose not to defend himself, then the trial would proceed *in absentia*, which of course would mean that the defendant's chances would be by that much diminished. Compulsion could only be used against the defendant *after* his final conviction. In the same way, a defendant could not be kept in jail before his conviction, unless, as in the case of police coercion, the jailer is prepared to face a kidnapping conviction if the defendant turns out to be innocent.[7]

---

7. This prohibition against coercing an unconvicted person would eliminate the blatant evils of the *bail* system, where the judge arbitrarily sets the amount of bail, and where, regardless of the amount, poorer defendants are clearly discriminated against.

13. Punishment and Proportionality[1]

F ew aspects of libertarian political theory are in a less satisfactory state than the theory of punishment.[2] Usually, libertarians have been content to assert or develop the axiom that no one may aggress against the person or property of another; what sanctions may be taken against such an invader has been scarcely treated at all. We have advanced the view that the criminal loses his rights *to the extent* that he deprives another of his rights: the theory of "proportionality." We must now elaborate further on what such a theory of proportional punishment may imply.

In the first place, it should be clear that the proportionate principle is a *maximum*, rather than a mandatory, punishment for the criminal. In the libertarian society, there are, as we have said, only two parties to a dispute or action at law: the victim, or plaintiff, and the alleged criminal, or defendant. It is the plaintiff that presses charges in the courts against the wrongdoer. In a libertarian world, there would be no crimes against an ill-defined "society," and therefore no such person as a "district attorney" who decides on a charge and then presses those charges against an alleged criminal. The proportionality rule tells us *how much* punishment a plaintiff *may* exact from a convicted wrongdoer, and no more; it imposes the maximum limit on punishment that may be inflicted before the punisher himself becomes a criminal aggressor.

Thus, it should be quite clear that, under libertarian law, capital punishment would have to be confined strictly to the crime of murder. For a criminal would only lose his right to life if he had first deprived some victim of that same right. It would not be permissible, then, for a merchant whose bubble gum had been stolen, to execute the convicted bubble gum thief. If he did so, then *he*, the merchant, would be an unjustifiable murderer, who could be brought to the bar of justice by the heirs or assigns of the bubble gum thief.

But, in libertarian law, there would be no *compulsion* on the plaintiff, or his heirs, to exact this maximum penalty. If the plaintiff or his heir, for

---

1. This section appeared in substantially the same form in Murray N. Rothbard, "Punishment and Proportionality," in *Assessing the Criminal: Restitution, Retribution, and the Legal Process*, R. Barnett and J. Hagel, eds. (Cambridge, Mass.: Ballinger Publishing, 1977), pp. 259–70.

2. It must be noted, however, that *all* legal systems, whether libertarian or not, must work out some theory of punishment, and that existing systems are in *at least* as unsatisfactory a state as punishment in libertarian theory.

example, did not believe in capital punishment, for whatever reason, he could voluntarily forgive the victim of part or all of his penalty. If he were a Tolstoyan, and was opposed to punishment altogether, he could simply forgive the criminal, and that would be that. Or—and this has a long and honorable tradition in older Western law—the victim or his heir could allow the criminal to *buy his way out* of part or all of his punishment. Thus, if proportionality allowed the victim to send the criminal to jail for ten years, the criminal could, if the victim wished, pay the victim to reduce or eliminate this sentence. The proportionality theory only supplies the upper bound to punishment—since it tells us how much punishment a victim may *rightfully* impose.

A problem might arise in the case of murder—since a victim's heirs might prove less than diligent in pursuing the murderer, or be unduly inclined to let the murderer buy his way out of punishment. This problem could be taken care of simply by people stating in their wills what punishment they should like to inflict on their possible murderers. The believer in strict retribution, as well as the Tolstoyan opponent of all punishment, could then have their wishes precisely carried out. The deceased, indeed, could provide in his will for, say, a crime insurance company to which he subscribes to be the prosecutor of his possible murderer.

If, then, proportionality sets the upper bound to punishment, how may we establish proportionality itself? The first point is that the emphasis in punishment must be *not* on paying one's debt to "society," whatever that may mean, but in paying one's "debt" to the victim. Certainly, the *initial* part of that debt is *restitution*. This works clearly in cases of theft. If A has stolen $15,000 from B, then the first, or initial, part of A's punishment must be to restore that $15,000 to the hands of B (plus damages, judicial and police costs, and interest foregone). Suppose that, as in most cases, the thief has already spent the money. In that case, the first step of proper libertarian punishment is to force the thief to work, and to allocate the ensuing income to the victim until the victim has been repaid. The ideal situation, then, puts the criminal frankly into a state of *enslavement* to his victim, the criminal continuing in that condition of just slavery until he has redressed the grievance of the man he has wronged.[3]

We must note that the emphasis of restitution-punishment is diametrically opposite to the current practice of punishment. What happens

---

3. Significantly, the only exception to the prohibition of involuntary servitude in the Thirteenth Amendment to the U.S. Constitution is the "enslavement" of criminals: "Neither slavery nor involuntary servitude except as a punishment for crime whereof the party shall have been duly convicted, shall exist within the United States, or any place subject to their jurisdiction."

nowadays is the following absurdity: A steals $15,000 from B. The government tracks down, tries, and convicts A, all at the expense of B, as one of the numerous taxpayers victimized in this process. Then, the government, instead of forcing A to repay B or to work at forced labor until that debt is paid, forces B, the victim, to pay taxes to support the criminal in prison for ten or twenty years' time. Where in the world is the justice here? The victim not only loses his money, but pays more money besides for the dubious thrill of catching, convicting, and then supporting the criminal; and the criminal is still enslaved, but *not* to the good purpose of recompensing his victim.

The idea of primacy for restitution to the victim has great precedent in law; indeed, it is an ancient principle of law which has been allowed to wither away as the State has aggrandized and monopolized the institutions of justice. In medieval Ireland, for example, a king was not the head of State but rather a crime-insurer; if someone committed a crime, the first thing that happened was that the king paid the "insurance" benefit to the victim, and then proceeded to force the criminal to pay the king in turn (restitution to the victim's insurance company being completely derived from the idea of restitution to the victim). In many parts of colonial America, which were too poor to afford the dubious luxury of prisons, the thief was indentured out by the courts to his victim, there to be forced to work for his victim until his "debt" was paid. This does not necessarily mean that prisons would disappear in the libertarian society, but they would undoubtedly change drastically, since their major goal would be to force the criminals to provide restitution to their victims.[4]

In fact, in the Middle Ages generally, restitution to the victim was the dominant concept of punishment; only as the State grew more powerful did the governmental authorities encroach ever more into the repayment process, increasingly confiscating a greater proportion of the criminal's property for themselves, and leaving less and less to the unfortunate victim. Indeed, as the emphasis shifted from restitution to the victim, from compensation by the criminal to his victim, to punishment for alleged crimes committed "against the State," the punishments exacted by the State became more and more severe. As the early twentieth-century criminologist William Tallack wrote,

> It was chiefly owing to the violent greed of feudal barons and medieval ecclesiastical powers that the rights of the injured

---

4. On the principles of restitution and "composition" (the criminal buying off the victim) in law, see Stephen Schafer, *Restitution to Victims of Crime* (Chicago: Quadrangle Books, 1960).

party were gradually infringed upon, and finally, to a large extent, appropriated by these authorities, who exacted a double vengeance, indeed, upon the offender, by forfeiting his property to themselves instead of to his victim, and then punishing him by the dungeon, the torture, the stake or the gibbet. But the original victim of wrong was practically ignored.

Or, as Professor Schafer has summed up: "As the state monopolized the institution of punishment, so the rights of the injured were slowly separated from penal law."[5]

But restitution, while the first consideration in punishment, can hardly serve as the complete and sufficient criterion. For one thing, if one man assaults another, and there is no theft of property, there is obviously no way for the criminal to make restitution. In ancient forms of law, there were often set schedules for monetary recompense that the criminal would have to pay the victim: so much money for an assault, so much more for mutilation, etc. But such schedules are clearly wholly arbitrary, and bear no relation to the nature of the crime itself. We must therefore fall back upon the view that the criterion must be: loss of rights by the criminal *to the same extent* as he has taken away.

But how are we to gauge the nature of the extent? Let us return to the theft of the $15,000. Even here, simple restitution of the $15,000 is scarcely sufficient to cover the crime (even if we add damages, costs, interest, etc.). For one thing, mere loss of the money stolen obviously fails to function in any sense as a deterrent to future such crime (although we will see below that deterrence itself is a faulty criterion for gauging punishment). If, then, we are to say that the criminal loses rights *to the extent that he deprives the victim*, then we must say that the criminal should not only have to return the $15,000, but that he must be forced to pay the victim *another* $15,000, so that he, in turn, loses those rights (to $15,000 worth of property) which he had taken from the victim. In the case of theft, then, we may say that the criminal must pay *double* the extent of theft: once, for restitution of the amount stolen, and once again for loss of what he had deprived another.[6]

But we are still not finished with elaborating the extent of deprivation of rights involved in a crime. For A had not simply stolen $15,000 from B, which can be restored and an equivalent penalty imposed.

---

5. William Tallack, *Reparation to the Injured and the Rights of the Victims of Crime to Compensation* (London, 1900), pp. 11–12; Schafer, *Restitution to Victims of Crime*, pp. 7–8.

6. This principle of libertarian double punishment has been pithily described by Professor Walter Block as the principle of "two teeth for a tooth."

He had also put B into a state of fear and uncertainty, of uncertainty as to the extent that B's deprivation would go. But the penalty levied on A is fixed and certain in advance, thus putting A in far better shape than was his original victim. So that for proportionate punishment to be levied we would also have to add *more* than double so as to compensate the victim in some way for the uncertain and fearful aspects of his particular ordeal.[7] What this extra compensation should be it is impossible to say exactly, but that does not absolve *any* rational system of punishment—including the one that would apply in the libertarian society—from the problem of working it out as best one can.

In the question of bodily assault, where restitution does not even apply, we can again employ our criterion of proportionate punishment; so that if A has beaten up B in a certain way, then B has the right to beat up A (or have him beaten up by judicial employees) to rather more than the same extent.

Here allowing the criminal to buy his way out of this punishment could indeed enter in, but *only* as a voluntary contract with the plaintiff. For example, suppose that A has severely beaten B; B now has the right to beat up A as severely, or a bit more, or to hire someone or some organization to do the beating for him (who in a libertarian society, could be marshals hired by privately competitive courts). But A, of course, is free to try to buy his way out, to pay B for waiving his right to have his aggressor beaten up.

The victim, then, has the right to exact punishment up to the proportional amount as determined by the extent of the crime, but he is also free either to allow the aggressor to buy his way out of punishment, *or* to forgive the aggressor partially or altogether. The proportionate level of punishment sets the *right* of the victim, the permissible upper bound of punishment; but how much or whether the victim decides to *exercise* that right is up to him. As Professor Armstrong puts it:

> [T]here should be a proportion between the severity of the crime and the severity of the punishment. It sets an upper limit to the punishment, suggests what is due. . . . Justice gives the appropriate authority [in our view, the victim] the right to punish offenders up to some limit, but one is not necessarily and invariably obliged to punish to the limit of justice. Similarly, if I lend a man money I have a right, in justice, to have it returned, but if I choose not to take it back I have

---

7. I am indebted to Professor Robert Nozick of Harvard University for pointing out this problem to me.

not done anything unjust. I cannot claim more than is owed
to me but I am free to claim less, or even to claim nothing.[8]

Or, as Professor McCloskey states: "We do not act unjustly if,
moved by benevolence, we impose less than is demanded by justice,
but there is a grave injustice if the deserved punishment is exceeded."[9]

Many people, when confronted with the libertarian legal system,
are concerned with this problem: would somebody be allowed to "take
the law into his own hands"? Would the victim, or a friend of the victim,
be allowed to exact justice personally on the criminal? The answer is, of
course, Yes, since *all* rights of punishment derive from the victim's right
of self-defense. In the libertarian, purely free-market society, however,
the victim will generally find it more convenient to entrust the task to
the police and court agencies.[10] Suppose, for example, that Hatfield$_1$
murders McCoy$_1$. McCoy$_2$ then decides to seek out and execute Hatfield$_1$
himself. This is fine, except that, just as in the case of the police coercion
discussed in the previous section, McCoy$_2$ may have to face the prospect
of being charged with murder in the private courts by Hatfield$_2$. The
point is that *if* the courts find that Hatfield$_1$ was indeed the murderer,
then nothing happens to McCoy$_2$ in our schema except public approbation
for executing justice. But if it turns out that there was not enough evidence
to convict Hatfield$_1$ for the original murder, or if indeed some other
Hatfield or some stranger committed the crime, then McCoy$_2$, as in the
case of the police invaders mentioned above, cannot plead any sort of
immunity; he then becomes a murderer liable to be executed by the courts
at the behest of the irate Hatfield heirs. Hence, just as in the libertarian
society, the police will be mighty careful to avoid invasion of the rights
of any suspect unless they are absolutely convinced of his guilt and willing
to put *their* bodies on the line for this belief, so also few people will "take

8. K.G. Armstrong, "The Retributivist Hits Back," *Mind* (1961), reprinted in Stanley E.
Grupp, ed., *Theories of Punishment* (Bloomington: Indiana University Press, 1971), pp.
35–36.

9. We would add that the "we" here should mean the victim of the particular crime.
H.J. McCloskey, "A Non-Utilitarian Approach to Punishment," *Inquiry* (1965), reprinted
in Gertrude Ezorsky, ed., *Philosophical Perspectives on Punishment* (Albany: State
University of New York Press, 1972), p. 132.

10. In our view, the libertarian system would not be compatible with monopoly State
defense agencies, such as police and courts, which would instead be privately
competitive. Since this is an ethical treatise, however, we cannot here go into the
pragmatic question of precisely *how* such an "anarcho-capitalist" police and court system
might work in practice. For a discussion of this question, see Murray N. Rothbard, *For
a New Liberty*, rev. ed. (New York: Macmillan, 1978), pp. 215–41.

the law into their own hands" unless they are similarly convinced. Furthermore, if Hatfield₁ merely beat up McCoy₁, and then McCoy kills him in return, this too would put McCoy up for punishment as a murderer. Thus, the almost universal inclination would be to leave the execution of justice to the courts, whose decisions based on rules of evidence, trial procedure, etc. similar to what may apply now, would be accepted by society as honest and as the best that could be achieved.[11]

It should be evident that our theory of proportional punishment— that people may be punished by losing their rights to the extent that they have invaded the rights of others—is frankly a *retributive* theory of punishment, a "tooth (or two teeth) for a tooth" theory.[12] Retribution is in bad repute among philosophers, who generally dismiss the concept quickly

---

11. All this is reminiscent of the brilliant and witty system of punishment for government bureaucrats devised by the great libertarian, H.L. Mencken. In *A Mencken Crestomathy* (New York: Alfred A. Knopf, 1949), pp. 386–87, he proposed that any citizen,

> having looked into the acts of a jobholder and found him delinquent may punish him instantly and on the spot, and in any manner that seems appropriate and convenient—and that in case this punishment involves physical damage to the jobholder, the ensuing inquiry by the grand jury or coroner shall confine itself strictly to the question whether the jobholder deserved what he got. In other words, I propose that it shall be no longer *malum in se* for a citizen to pummel, cowhide, kick, gouge, cut, wound, bruise, maim, burn, club, bastinado, flay or even lynch a jobholder, and that it shall be *malum prohibitum* only to the extent that the punishment exceeds the jobholder's deserts. The amount of this excess, if any, may be determined very conveniently by a petit jury, as other questions of guilt are now determined. The flogged judge, or Congressman, or other jobholder, on being discharged from the hospital— or his chief heir in case he has perished—goes before a grand jury and makes complaint, and, if a true bill is found, a petit jury is empaneled and all the evidence is put before it. If it decides that the jobholder deserves the punishment inflicted upon him, the citizen who inflicted it is acquitted with honor. If, on the contrary, it decides that this punishment was excessive, then the citizen is adjudged guilty of assault, mayhem, murder, or whatever it is, in a degree apportioned to the difference between what the jobholder deserved and what he got and punishment for that excess follows in the usual course.

12. Retribution has been interestingly termed "spiritual restitution." See Schafer, *Restitution to Victims of Crime*, pp. 120–21. Also see the defense of capital punishment for murder by Robert Gahringer, "Punishment as Language," *Ethics* (October 1960): 47–48:

> An absolute offense requires an absolute negation; and one might well hold that in our present situation capital punishment is the only effective symbol of absolute negation. What else could express the enormity of murder *in a manner accessible to men for whom murder is a possible act?* Surely a lesser penalty would indicate a less significant crime (Italics Gahringer's).

On punishment in general as negating an offense against right, cf. also F.H. Bradley, *Ethical Studies*, 2nd ed. (Oxford: Oxford University Press,1927), reprinted in Ezorsky, ed., *Philosophical Perspectives on Punishment*, pp. 109–10:

as "primitive" or "barbaric" and then race on to a discussion of the two other major theories of punishment: deterrence and rehabilitation. But simply to dismiss a concept as "barbaric" can hardly suffice; after all, it is possible that in this case, the "barbarians" hit on a concept that was superior to the more modern creeds.

Professor H.L.A. Hart describes the "crudest form" of proportionality, such as we have advocated here (the *lex talionis*), as

> the notion that what the criminal has done should be done to
> him, and wherever thinking about punishment is primitive,
> as it often is, this crude idea reasserts itself: the killer should
> be killed, the violent assailant should be flogged.[13]

But "primitive" is scarcely a valid criticism, and Hart himself admits that this "crude" form presents fewer difficulties than the more "refined" versions of the proportionality–retributivist thesis. His only reasoned criticism, which he seems to think dismisses the issue, is a quote from Blackstone:

> There are very many crimes, that will in no shape admit of
> these penalties, without manifest absurdity and wickedness.
> Theft cannot be punished by theft, defamation by defamation,
> forgery by forgery, adultery by adultery.

But these are scarcely cogent criticisms. Theft and forgery constitute robbery, and the robber can certainly be made to provide restitution and proportional damages to the victim; there is no conceptual problem there. Adultery, in the libertarian view, is not a crime at all, and neither, as will be seen below, is "defamation."[14]

Let us then turn to the two major modern theories and see if they provide a criterion for punishment which truly meets our conceptions of justice, as retribution surely does.[15] *Deterrence* was the principle put forth

---

Why . . . do I merit punishment? It is because I have been guilty. I have done "wrong" . . . the negation of "right," the assertion of not-right. . . . The destruction of guilt . . . is still a good in itself; and this, not because a mere negation is a good, but because the denial of wrong is the assertion of right. . . . Punishment is the denial of wrong by the assertion of right.

An influential argument for retributivism is found in Herbert Morris, *On Guilt and Innocence* (Berkeley: University of California Press, 1976), pp. 31–58.

13. For an attempt to construct a law code imposing proportionate punishments for crime—as well as restitution to the victim—see Thomas Jefferson, "A Bill for Proportioning Crimes and Punishments" in *The Writings of Thomas Jefferson*, A. Lipscomb and A. Bergh, eds. (Washington, D.C.: Thomas Jefferson Memorial Assn., 1904), vol. 1, pp. 218–39.

14. H.L.A. Hart, *Punishment and Responsibility* (New York: Oxford University Press, 1968), p. 161.

by utilitarianism, as part of its aggressive dismissal of principles of justice and natural law, and the replacement of these allegedly metaphysical principles by hard practicality. The practical goal of punishments was then supposed to be to deter further crime, either by the criminal himself or by other members of society. But this criterion of deterrence implies schemas of punishment which almost everyone would consider grossly unjust. For example, if there were no punishment for crime at all, a great number of people would commit petty theft, such as stealing fruit from a fruit-stand. On the other hand, most people have a far greater built-in inner objection to themselves committing murder than they have to petty shoplifting, and would be far less apt to commit the grosser crime. Therefore, if the object of punishment is to deter from crime, then a far greater punishment would be required for preventing shoplifting than for preventing murder, a system that goes against most people's ethical standards. As a result, with deterrence as the criterion there would have to be stringent capital punishment for petty thievery—for the theft of bubble gum—while murderers might only incur the penalty of a few months in jail.[16]

Similarly, a classic critique of the deterrence principle is that, if deterrence were our sole criterion, it would be perfectly proper for the police or courts to execute publicly for a crime someone whom *they* know to be innocent, but whom they had convinced the public was guilty. The knowing execution of an innocent man—provided, of course, that the knowledge can be kept secret—would exert a deterrence effect just as fully as the execution of the guilty. And yet, of course, such a policy, too, goes violently against almost everyone's standards of justice.

The fact that nearly everyone would consider such schemes of punishments grotesque, despite their fulfillment of the deterrence criterion,

---

15. Thus, *Webster's* defines "retribution" as "the dispensing or receiving of reward or punishment according to the desserts of the individual."

16. In his critique of the deterrence principle of punishment, Professor Armstrong, in "The Retributivist Hits Back," pp. 32–33, asks:

> [W]hy stop at the minimum, why not be on the safe side and penalize him [the criminal] in some pretty spectacular way—wouldn't that be more likely to deter others? Let him be whipped to death, publicly of course, for a parking offense; that would certainly deter me from parking on the spot reserved for the Vice-Chancellor!

Similarly, D.J.B. Hawkins, in "Punishment and Moral Responsibility," *The Modern Law Review* (November 1944), reprinted in Grupp, ed., *Theories of Punishment*, p. 14, writes:

> If the motive of deterrence were alone taken into account, we should have to punish most heavily those offenses which there is considerable temptation to commit and which, as not carrying with them any great moral guilt, people commit fairly easily. Motoring offenses provide a familiar example.

shows that people are interested in something more important than deterrence. What this may be is indicated by the overriding objection that
these deterrent scales of punishment, or the killing of an innocent man,
clearly invert our usual view of justice. Instead of the punishment "fitting the crime" it is now graded in inverse proportion to its severity
or is meted out to the innocent rather than the guilty. In short, the deterrence principle implies a gross violation of the intuitive sense that justice connotes some form of fitting and proportionate punishment to
the guilty party and to him alone.

The most recent, supposedly highly "humanitarian" criterion for
punishment is to "rehabilitate" the criminal. Old-fashioned justice,
the argument goes, concentrated on punishing the criminal, either in
retribution or to deter future crime; the new criterion humanely
attempts to reform and rehabilitate the criminal. But on further consideration, the "humanitarian" rehabilitation principle not only leads to
arbitrary and gross injustice, it also places enormous and arbitrary power
to decide men's fates in the hands of the dispensers of punishment.
Thus, suppose that Smith is a mass murderer, while Jones stole some
fruit from a stand. Instead of being sentenced in proportion to their crimes,
their sentences are now indeterminate, with confinement ending upon
their supposedly successful "rehabilitation." But this gives the power to
determine the prisoners' lives into the hands of an arbitrary group of
supposed rehabilitators. It would mean that instead of equality under
the law—an elementary criterion of justice—with equal crimes being
punished equally, one man may go to prison for a few weeks, if he is
quickly "rehabilitated," while another may remain in prison indefinitely. Thus, in our case of Smith and Jones, suppose that the mass murderer
Smith is, according to our board of "experts," rapidly rehabilitated. He
is released in three weeks, to the plaudits of the supposedly successful
reformers. In the meanwhile, Jones, the fruit-stealer, persists in being
incorrigible and clearly un-rehabilitated, at least in the eyes of the expert
board. According to the logic of the principle, he must stay incarcerated
indefinitely, perhaps for the rest of his life, for while the crime was negligible, he continued to remain outside the influence of his "humanitarian"
mentors.

Thus, Professor K.G. Armstrong writes of the reform principle:

> The logical pattern of penalties will be for each criminal to be
> given reformatory treatment until he is sufficiently changed
> for the experts to certify him as reformed. On this theory,
> every sentence ought to be indeterminate—"to be determined
> at the Psychologist's pleasure,"perhaps—for there is no longer

any basis for the principle of a definite limit to punishment. "You stole a loaf of bread? Well, we'll have to reform you, even if it takes the rest of your life." From the moment he is guilty the criminal loses his rights as a human being. . . . This is not a form of humanitarianism I care for.[17]

Never has the tyranny and gross injustice of the "humanitarian" theory of punishment-as-reform been revealed in more scintillating fashion than by C.S. Lewis. Noting that the "reformers" call their proposed actions "healing" or "therapy," rather than "punishment," Lewis adds:

> But do not let us be deceived by a name. To be taken without consent from my home and friends; to lose my liberty; to undergo all those assaults on my personality which modern psychotherapy knows how to deliver . . . to know that this process will never end until either my captors have succeeded or I grown wise enough to cheat them with apparent success—who cares whether this is called Punishment or not? That it includes most of the elements for which any punishment is feared—shame, exile, bondage, and years eaten by the locust—is obvious. Only enormous ill-desert could justify it; but ill-desert is the very conception which the Humanitarian theory has thrown overboard.

Lewis goes on to demonstrate the particularly harsh tyranny that is likely to be levied by "humanitarians" out to inflict their "reforms" and "cures" on the populace:

> Of all tyrannies a tyranny exercised for the good of its victims may be the most oppressive. It may be better to live under robber barons than under omnipotent moral busybodies. The robber baron's cruelty may sometimes sleep, his cupidity may at some point be satiated; but those who torment us for our own good will torment us without end for they do so with the approval of their own conscience. They may be more likely to go to Heaven yet at the same time likelier to make a Hell of earth. This very kindness stings with intolerable insult. To be "cured" against one's will and cured of states which we may not regard as disease is to be put on a level of those who have not yet reached the age of reason or those who never will; to be classed with infants, imbeciles, and domestic animals. But to be punished, however severely, because we have deserved it, because we "ought to have known better," is to be treated as a human person made in God's image.

---

17. Armstrong, "The Retributivist Hits Back," p. 33.

.

Furthermore, Lewis points out, the rulers can use the concept of "disease" as a means for terming any actions that they dislike as "crimes" and then to inflict a totalitarian rule in the name of Therapy.

> For if crime and disease are to be regarded as the same thing, it follows that any state of mind which our masters choose to call "disease" can be treated as crime; and compulsorily cured. It will be vain to plead that states of mind which displease government need not always involve moral turpitude and do not therefore always deserve forfeiture of liberty. For our masters will not be using concepts of Desert and Punishment but those of disease and cure. . . . It will not be persecution. Even if the treatment is painful, even if it is life-long, even if it is fatal, that will be only a regrettable accident; the intention was purely therapeutic. Even in ordinary medicine there were painful operations and fatal operations; so in this. But because they are "treatment," not punishment, they can be criticized only by fellow-experts and on technical grounds, never by men as men and on grounds of justice.[18]

Thus, we see that the fashionable reform approach to punishment can be at least as grotesque and far more uncertain and arbitrary than the deterrence principle. Retribution remains as our only just and viable theory of punishment and equal treatment for equal crime is fundamental to such retributive punishment. The barbaric turns out to be the just while the "modern" and the "humanitarian" turn out to be grotesque parodies of justice.

---

18. C.S. Lewis, "The Humanitarian Theory of Punishment," *Twentieth Century* (Autumn 1948–49), reprinted in Grupp, ed., *Theories of Punishment*, pp. 304–7. Also see Francis A. Allen, "Criminal Justice, Legal Values, and the Rehabilitative Ideal," in ibid., pp. 317–30.

14. Children and Rights

We have now established each man's property right in his own person and in the virgin land that he finds and transforms by his labor, and we have shown that from these two principles we can deduce the entire structure of property rights in all types of goods. These include the goods which he acquires in exchange or as a result of a voluntary gift or bequest.

There remains, however, the difficult case of *children.* The right of self-ownership by each man has been established for adults, for natural self-owners who must use their minds to select and pursue their ends. On the other hand, it is clear that a newborn babe is in no natural sense an existing self-owner, but rather a *potential* self-owner.[1] But this poses a difficult problem: for *when,* or in what way, does a growing child acquire his natural right to liberty and self-ownership? Gradually, or all at once? At what age? And what criteria do we set forth for this shift or transition?

First, let us begin with the prenatal child. What is the parent's, or rather the mother's, property right in the fetus? In the first place, we must note that the conservative Catholic position has generally been dismissed too brusquely. This position holds that the fetus is a living person, and hence that abortion is an act of murder and must therefore be outlawed as in the case of any murder. The usual reply is simply to demarcate *birth* as the beginning of a live human being possessing natural rights, including the right not to be murdered; before birth, the counter-argument runs, the child cannot be considered a living person. But the Catholic reply that the fetus is alive and is an imminently potential person then comes disquietingly close to the general view that a newborn baby cannot be aggressed against because *it* is a potential adult. While birth is indeed the proper line of demarcation, the usual formulation makes birth an arbitrary dividing line, and lacks sufficient rational groundwork in the theory of self-ownership.

---

1. John Locke, in his *Two Treatises on Government,* p. 322, put it this way:

    Children I confess are not born in this full state of equality (of right to their natural freedom), though they are born to it. Their parents have a sort of rule and jurisdiction over them when they come into the world, and for some time after, but 'tis but a temporary one. The bonds of this subjection are like the swaddling clothes they are wrapt up in, and supported by, in the weakness of their infancy. Age and reason as they grow up, loosen them till at length they drop quite off, and leave a man at his own free disposal.

The proper groundwork for analysis of abortion is in every man's absolute right of self-ownership. This implies immediately that every woman has the absolute right to her own body, that she has absolute dominion over her body and everything within it. This includes the fetus. Most fetuses are in the mother's womb because the mother consents to this situation, but the fetus is there by the mother's freely-granted consent. But should the mother decide that she does not *want* the fetus there any longer, then the fetus becomes a parasitic "invader" of her person, and the mother has the perfect right to expel this invader from her domain. Abortion should be looked upon, not as "murder" of a living person, but as the expulsion of an unwanted invader from the mother's body.[2] Any laws restricting or prohibiting abortion are therefore invasions of the rights of mothers.

It has been objected that since the mother originally consented to the conception, the mother has therefore "contracted" its status with the fetus, and may not "violate" that "contract" by having an abortion. There are many problems with this doctrine, however. In the first place, as we shall see further below, a mere promise is not an enforceable contract: contracts are only properly enforceable if their violation involves *implicit theft*, and clearly no such consideration can apply here. Secondly, there is obviously no "contract" here, since the fetus (fertilized ovum?) can hardly be considered a voluntarily and consciously contracting entity. And thirdly, as we have seen above, a crucial point in libertarian theory is the *inalienability of the will*, and therefore the impermissibility of enforcing voluntary slave contracts. Even if this *had been* a "contract," then, it could not be enforced because a mother's will is inalienable, and she cannot legitimately be enslaved into carrying and having a baby against her will.

Another argument of the anti-abortionists is that the fetus is a living human being, and is therefore entitled to all of the rights of human beings. Very good; let us concede, for purposes of the discussion, that fetuses are human beings—or, more broadly, potential human beings—and are therefore entitled to full human rights. But what *humans*, we may ask, have the right to be coercive parasites within the body of an unwilling human host? Clearly, no *born* humans have such a right, and therefore, *a fortiori*, the fetus can have no such right either.

---

2. What we are trying to establish here is not the *morality* of abortion (which may or may not be moral on other grounds), but its *legality*, i.e., the absolute right of the mother to have an abortion. What we are concerned with in this book is people's *rights* to do or not do various things, not whether they should or should not *exercise* such rights. Thus, we would argue that every person has the *right* to purchase and consume Coca-Cola from a willing seller, not that any person *should* or *should not* actually make such a purchase.

The anti-abortionists generally couch the preceding argument in terms of the fetus's, as well as the born human's, "right to life." We have not used this concept in this volume because of its ambiguity, and because any proper rights implied by its advocates are included in the concept of the "right to self-ownership"—the right to have one's person free from aggression. Even Professor Judith Thomson, who, in her discussion of the abortion question, attempts inconsistently to retain the concept of "right to life" along with the right to own one's own body, lucidly demonstrates the pitfalls and errors of the "right to life" doctrine:

> In some views, having a right to life includes having a right to be given at least the bare minimum one needs for continued life. But suppose that what in fact is the bare minimum a man needs for continued life is something he has no right at all to be given? If I am sick unto death, and the only thing that will save my life is the touch of Henry Fonda's cool hand on my fevered brow, then all the same, I have no right to be given the touch of Henry Fonda's cool hand on my fevered brow. It would be frightfully nice of him to fly in from the West Coast to provide it. . . . But I have no right at all against anybody that he should do this for me.

In short, it is impermissible to interpret the term "right to life," to give one an enforceable claim to the action of someone else to sustain that life. In our terminology, such a claim would be an impermissible violation of the other person's right of self-ownership. Or, as Professor Thomson cogently puts it, "having a right to life does not guarantee having either a right to be given the use of or a right to be allowed continued use of another person's body—even if one needs it for life itself."[3]

Suppose now that the baby has been born. Then what? First, we may say that the parents—or rather the mother, who is the only *certain* and visible parent—as the creators of the baby become its owners. A newborn baby cannot be an existent self-owner in any sense. Therefore, either the mother or some other party or parties may be the baby's owner, but to assert that a third party can claim his "ownership" over the baby would give that person the right to seize the baby by force from its natural or "homesteading" owner, its mother. The mother, then, is the natural and rightful owner of the baby, and any attempt to seize the baby by force is an invasion of her property right.

---

3. Judith Jarvis Thomson, "A Defense of Abortion," *Philosophy and Public Affairs* (Fall 1971): 55–56.

But surely the mother or parents may not receive the ownership of the child in absolute fee simple, because that would imply the bizarre state of affairs that a fifty-year old adult would be subject to the absolute and unquestioned jurisdiction of his seventy-year-old parent. So the parental property right must be limited *in time*. But it also must be limited *in kind*, for it surely would be grotesque for a libertarian who believes in the right of self-ownership to advocate the right of a parent to murder or torture his or her children.

We must therefore state that, even from birth, the parental ownership is not absolute but of a "trustee" or guardianship kind. In short, every baby, as soon as it is born and is therefore no longer contained within his mother's body, possesses the right of self-ownership by virtue of being a separate entity and a potential adult. It must therefore be illegal and a violation of the child's rights for a parent to aggress against his person by mutilating, torturing, murdering him, etc. On the other hand, the very concept of "rights" is a "negative" one, demarcating the areas of a person's action that no man may properly interfere with. No man can therefore have a "right" to compel someone to do a positive act, for in that case the compulsion violates the right of person or property of the individual being coerced. Thus, we may say that a man has a *right* to his property (i.e., a right not to have his property invaded), but we *cannot* say that anyone has a "right" to a "living wage," for that would mean that someone would be coerced into providing him with such a wage, and that would violate the property rights of the people being coerced. As a corollary, this means that, in the free society, no man may be saddled with the legal obligation to do anything for another, since that would invade the former's rights; the only legal obligation one man has to another is to respect the other man's rights.

Applying our theory to parents and children, this means that a parent does not have the right to aggress against his children, *but also* that the parent should not have a *legal obligation* to feed, clothe, or educate his children, since such obligations would entail positive acts coerced upon the parent and depriving the parent of his rights. The parent therefore may not murder or mutilate his child, and the law properly outlaws a parent from doing so. But the parent should have the legal right *not* to feed the child, i.e., to allow it to die.[4] The law, therefore, may not properly compel the parent to feed a child or to keep it alive.[5] (Again,

---

4. On the distinction between passive and active euthanasia, see Philippa R. Foot, *Virtues and Vices* (Berkeley: University of California Press, 1978), pp. 50ff.

5. Cf. the view of the individualist anarchist theorist Benjamin R. Tucker: "Under equal freedom, as it [the child] develops individuality and independence, it is entitled to

whether or not a parent has a *moral* rather than a legally enforceable obligation to keep his child alive is a completely separate question.) This rule allows us to solve such vexing questions as: should a parent have the right to allow a deformed baby to die (e.g. by not feeding it)?[6] The answer is of course yes, following *a fortiori* from the larger right to allow *any* baby, whether deformed or not, to die. (Though, as we shall see below, in a libertarian society the existence of a free baby market will bring such "neglect" down to a minimum.)

Our theory also enables us to examine the question of Dr. Kenneth Edelin, of Boston City Hospital, who was convicted in 1975 of manslaughter for allowing a fetus to die (at the wish, of course, of the mother) after performing an abortion. If parents have the legal right to allow a baby to die, then *a fortiori* they have the same right for extra-uterine fetuses. Similarly, in a future world where babies may be born in extra-uterine devices ("test tubes"), again the parents would have the legal right to "pull the plug" on the fetuses or, rather, to refuse to pay to continue the plug in place.

Let us examine the implications of the doctrine that parents *should have* a legally enforceable obligation to keep their children alive. The argument for this obligation contains two components: that the parents created the child by a freely-chosen, purposive act; and that the child is temporarily helpless and not a self-owner.[7] If we consider first the argument from helplessness, then first, we may make the general point that it is a philosophical fallacy to maintain that A's needs properly impose coercive obligations on B to satisfy these needs. For one thing, B's rights are then violated. Secondly, if a helpless child may be said to impose legal obligations on someone else, why specifically on its *parents*, and not on other people? What do the parents have to do with it? The answer, of course, is that they are the creators of the child, but this brings us to the second argument, the argument from creation.

---

immunity from assault or invasion, and that is all. If the parent neglects to support it, he does not thereby oblige anyone else to support it." Benjamin R. Tucker, *Instead of a Book* (New York: B.R. Tucker, 1893), p. 144.

6. The original program of the Euthanasia Society of America included the right of parents to allow monstrous babies to die. It has also been a common and growing practice for midwives and obstetricians to allow monstrous babies to die at birth by simply *not* taking positive acts to keep them alive. See John A. Robertson, "Involuntary Euthanasia of Defective Newborns: A Legal Analysis," *Stanford Law Review* (January 1975): 214–15.

7. The argument of this and succeeding paragraphs relies heavily on Williamson M. Evers, "Political Theory and the Legal Rights of Children," (unpublished manuscript), pp. 13–17. Also see Evers, "The Law of Omissions and Neglect of Children," *Journal of Libertarian Studies* 2 (Winter 1978): 1–10.

Considering, then, the creation argument, this immediately rules out any obligation of a mother to keep a child alive who was the result of an act of rape, since this was not a freely-undertaken act. It *also* rules out any such obligation by a step-parent, foster parent, or guardian, who didn't participate at all in creating the child.

Furthermore, if creation engenders an obligation to maintain the child, *why* should it stop when the child becomes an adult? As Evers states:

> The parents are still the creators of the child, why aren't they obliged to support the child forever? It is true that the child is no longer helpless; but helplessness (as pointed out above) is not in and of itself a cause of binding obligation. If the condition of being the creator of another is the source of the obligation, and this condition persists, why doesn't the obligation?[8]

And what of the case, in some future decade, when a scientist becomes able to create human life in the laboratory? The scientist is then the "creator." Must he also have a legal obligation to keep the child alive? And suppose the child is deformed and ill, scarcely human; does he still have a binding legal obligation to maintain the child? And if so, *how much* of his resources—his time, energy, money, capital equipment—should he be legally required to invest to keep the child alive? Where does his obligation stop, and by what criterion?

This question of resources is also directly relevant to the case of natural parents. As Evers points out:

> [L]et us consider the case of poor parents who have a child who gets sick. The sickness is grave enough that the parents in order to obtain the medical care to keep the baby alive, would have to starve themselves. Do the parents have an ... obligation to lessen the quality of their own lives even to the point of self-extinction to aid the child?[9]

And if not, we might add, *at what point* does the parents' legal obligation properly cease? And by what criterion? Evers goes on:

> One might want to argue that parents owe only the average minimal care (heat, shelter, nutrition) necessary to keep a child alive. But, if one is going to take the obligation position, it seems illogical—in view of the wide variety of human qualities and characteristics—to tie obligation to the Procrustean bed of the human average.[10]

---

8. Evers, "Political Theory," p. 17.

9. Ibid., p. 16.

10. Ibid., pp. 16–17.

A common argument holds that the voluntary act of the parents has created a "contract" by which the parents are obligated to maintain the child. But (a) this would also entail the alleged "contract" with the fetus that would prohibit abortion, and (b) this falls into all the difficulties with the contract theory as analyzed above.

Finally, as Evers points out, suppose that we consider the case of a person who voluntarily rescues a child from a flaming wreck that kills the child's parents. In a very real sense, the rescuer has brought life to the child; does the rescuer, then, have a binding legal obligation to keep the child alive from then on? Wouldn't this be a "monstrous involuntary servitude that is being foisted upon a rescuer?"[11] And if for the rescuer, why not also for the natural parent?

The mother, then, becomes at the birth of her child its "trustee-owner," legally obliged only not to aggress against the child's person, since the child possesses the potential for self-ownership. Apart from that, so long as the child lives at home, it must necessarily come under the jurisdiction of its parents, since it is living on property owned by those parents. Certainly the parents have the right to set down rules for the use of their home and property for all persons (whether children or not) living in that home.

But when are we to say that this parental trustee jurisdiction over children shall come to an end? Surely, any particular age (21, 18, or whatever) can only be completely arbitrary. The clue to the solution of this thorny question lies in the parental property rights in their home. For the child has his *full* rights of self-ownership *when he demonstrates that he has them in nature*—in short, when he leaves or "runs away" from home. Regardless of his age, we must grant to every child the absolute right to run away, and to find new foster parents who will voluntarily adopt him, or to try to exist on his own. Parents may try to persuade the runaway child to return, but it is totally impermissible enslavement and an aggression upon his right of self-ownership for them to use force to compel him to return. The absolute right to run away is the child's ultimate expression of his right of self-ownership, regardless of age.

Now if a parent may own his child (within the framework of non-aggression and runaway-freedom), then he may also transfer that ownership to someone else. He may give the child out for adoption, or he may *sell* the rights to the child in a voluntary contract. In short, we must face the fact that the purely free society will have a flourishing free market in children. Superficially, this sounds monstrous and inhuman. But closer thought will reveal the superior humanism of such a market. For we

---

11. Ibid., pp. 15–16.

must realize that there is a market for children now, but that since the government prohibits sale of children at a price, the parents may now only give their children away to a licensed adoption agency free of charge.[12] This means that we now indeed have a child-market, but that the government enforces a maximum price control of zero, and restricts the market to a few privileged and therefore monopolistic agencies. The result has been a typical market where the price of the commodity is held by government far below the free-market price: an enormous "shortage" of the good. The demand for babies and children is usually far greater than the supply, and hence we see daily tragedies of adults denied the joys of adopting children by prying and tyrannical adoption agencies. In fact, we find a large unsatisfied demand by adults and couples for children, along with a large number of surplus and unwanted babies neglected or maltreated by their parents. Allowing a free market in children would eliminate this imbalance, and would allow for an allocation of babies and children *away from* parents who dislike or do not care for their children, and *toward* foster parents who deeply desire such children. *Everyone* involved: the natural parents, the children, and the foster parents purchasing the children, would be better off in this sort of society.[13]

In the libertarian society, then, the mother would have the absolute right to her own body and therefore to perform an abortion; and would have the trustee-ownership of her children, an ownership limited only by the illegality of aggressing against their persons and by their absolute right to run away or to leave home at any time. Parents would be able to sell their trustee-rights in children to anyone who wished to buy them at any mutually agreed price.

---

12. It is now possible to make "independent placements" from one parent to another, but they can only be done with the approval of a judge, and such placements are officially discouraged. Thus, in *Petitions of Goldman,* the Supreme Court of Massachusetts refused to permit a Jewish couple to adopt twins born to Catholic parents, even though the natural parents were fully agreeable to the adoption. The ground of the refusal was that state regulations forbade cross-religious adoptions. See Lawrence List, "A Child and a Wall: A Study of 'Religious Protection' Laws," *Buffalo Law Review* (1963–64): 29; cited in Evers, "Political Theory," pp. 17–18.

13. Some years ago, the New York City authorities proudly announced that they had broken up an "illegal baby ring." Babies were being imported for a price from Greece by enterprising merchants, and then sold to eager parents in New York. No one seemed to realize that everyone involved in this supposedly barbaric transaction benefited: the poverty-stricken Greek parents gained money, as well as the satisfaction of knowing that their babies would be brought up in far more affluent homes; the new parents gained their heart's desire of having babies; and the babies were transferred to a far happier environment. And the merchants earned their profits as middlemen. Everyone gained; who lost?

The present state of juvenile law in the United States, it might be pointed out, is in many ways nearly the reverse of our desired libertarian model. In the current situation, both the rights of parents and children are systematically violated by the State.[14]

First, the rights of the parents. In present law, children may be seized from their parents by outside adults (almost always, the State) for a variety of reasons. Two reasons, physical abuse by the parent and voluntary abandonment, are plausible, since in the former case the parent aggressed against the child, and in the latter the parent voluntarily abandoned custody. Two points, however, should be mentioned: (a) that, until recent years, the parents were rendered immune by court decisions from ordinary tort liability in physically aggressing against their children—fortunately, this is now being remedied;[15] and (b) despite the publicity being given to the "battered child syndrome," it has been estimated that only 5 percent of "child abuse" cases involve physical aggression by the parents.[16]

On the other hand, the two other grounds for seizing children from their parents, both coming under the broad rubric of "child neglect," clearly violate parental rights. These are: failure to provide children with the "proper" food, shelter, medical care, or education; and failure to provide children with a "fit environment." It should be clear that both categories, and especially the latter, are vague enough to provide an excuse for the State to seize almost any children, since it is up to the State to define what is "proper" and "fit." Equally vague are other, corollary, standards allowing the State to seize children whose "optimal development" is not being promoted by the parents, or where the "best interests" of the child (again, all defined by the State) are promoted thereby. A few recent cases will serve as examples of how broadly the seizure power has been exercised. In the 1950 case of *In re Watson*, the state found a mother to have neglected three children by virtue of the fact that she was "incapable by reason of her emotional status, her mental condition, and her allegedly deeply religious feelings

---

14. On the current state of juvenile law in relation to the libertarian model, I am indebted to Evers, "Political Theory," *passim.*

15. Immunity was originally granted parents in the 1891 decision of a Mississippi court in *Hewlett v. Ragsdale.* Recently, however, courts have been allowing children their full rights to sue for injuries. See Lawrence S. Allen, "Parent and Child—Tort Liability of Parent to Unemancipated Child," *Case Western Reserve Law Review* (November 1967): 139; Dennis L. Bekemeyer, "A Child's Rights Against His Parent: Evolution of the Parental Immunity Doctrine," *University of Illinois Law Forum* (Winter 1967): 806–7; and Kenneth D. McCloskey, "Parental Liability to a Minor Child for Injuries Caused by Excessive Punishment," *Hastings Law Journal* (February 1960): 335–40.

16. Thus, see the report for Cook County in Patrick T. Murphy, *Our Kindly Parent—the State* (New York: Viking Press, 1974), pp. 153–54.

amounting to fanaticism." In its decision, fraught with totalitarian implications, the court stressed the alleged obligation of parents to bring up
children respecting and adjusting to "the conventions and the mores of the
community in which they are to live."[17] In 1954, in the case of *Hunter v. Powers*,
the court again violated religious freedom as well as parental rights by
seizing a child on the ground that the parent was too intensely devoted
to a nonconformist religion, and that the child should properly have been
studying or playing, rather than passing out religious literature. A year
later, in the case of *In re Black*, a Utah court seized eight children from
their parents because the parents had *failed to teach* the children that poly-
gamy was immoral.[18]

Not only religion, but also personal morality has been dictated by the
government. In 1962, five children were seized from their mother by a court
on the ground that the mother "frequently entertained male companions
in the apartment." In other cases, courts have held parents to have "neglected" the child, and thereupon seized the child, because parental quarrelling
or a child's sense of insecurity allegedly endangered the child's best interests.

In a recent decision, Justice Woodside of the Pennsylvania Superior
Court trenchantly warned of the massive coercive potential of the "best
interest" criterion:

> A court should not take the custody of a child from their par-
> ents solely on the ground that the state or its agencies can
> find a better home for them. If "the better home" test were
> the only test, public welfare officials could take children from
> half the parents in the state whose homes are considered to
> be the less desirable and place them in the homes of the other
> half of the population considered to have the more desirable
> homes. Extending this principle further, we would find that
> the family believed to have the best home would have the
> choice of any of our children.[19]

---

17. Compare the dictum of Sanford Katz, a prominent "child abuse" specialist: "child neglect connotes a parent's conduct, usually thought of in terms of passive behavior, that results in a failure to provide for the child's needs as defined by the preferred values of the community." Sanford Katz, *When Parents Fail* (Boston: Beacon Press, 1971), p. 22. On parental quarrelling, and on *In re Watson*, see Michael F. Sullivan, "Child Neglect: The Environmental Aspects," *Ohio State Law Journal* (1968): 89–90, 152–53.

18. See Sullivan, "Child Neglect," p. 90.

19. Quoted in Richard S. Levine, "Caveat Parens: A Demystification of the Child Protection System," *University of Pittsburgh Law Review* (Fall 1973): 32. Even more bizarre and total-itarian in its implications is the often proposed concept of a child's "right to be wanted." Apart from the impossibility of using violence to enforce an emotion on someone else, such a criterion would arm outside parties, in practice the State, with the power to

The rights of children, even more than those of parents, have been systematically invaded by the state. Compulsory school attendance laws, endemic in the United States since the turn of this century, force children either into public schools or into private schools officially approved by the state.[20] Supposedly "humanitarian" child labor laws have systematically forcibly prevented children from entering the labor force, thereby privileging their adult competitors. Forcibly prevented from working and earning a living, and forced into schools which they often dislike or are not suited for, children often become "truants," a charge used by the state to corral them into penal institutions in the name of "reform" schools, where children are in effect imprisoned for actions or non-actions that would never be considered "crimes" if committed by adults.

It has, indeed, been estimated that from one-quarter to one-half of "juvenile delinquents" currently incarcerated by the state did not commit acts that would be considered crimes if committed by adults (i.e. aggression against person and property).[21] The "crimes" of these children were in exercising their freedom in ways disliked by the minions of the state: truancy, "incorrigibility," running away. Between the sexes, it is particularly girl children who are jailed in this way for "immoral" rather than truly criminal actions. The percentage of girls jailed for immorality ("waywardness," sexual relations) rather than for genuine crimes ranges from 50 to over 80 percent.[22]

Since the U.S. Supreme Court's decision in the 1967 case of *In re Gault*, juvenile defendants, at least in theory, have been accorded the elementary procedural rights of adults (the right to notice of specific charges, the

---

determine when "wanting" exists and to seize children from parents who don't meet that scarcely definable criterion. Thus, Hillary Rodham, of the Children's Defense Fund, has challenged this criterion: "How should a 'right to be wanted' be defined and enforced? . . . The necessarily broad and vague enforcement guidelines could recreate the hazard of current laws, again requiring the State to make broad discretionary judgments about the quality of a child's life." Hillary Rodham, "Children Under the Law," *Harvard Educational Review* (1973): 496.

20. On compulsory education in the United States, see William F. Rickenbacker, ed., *The Twelve-Year Sentence* (LaSalle, Ill.: Open Court, 1974).

21. See William H. Sheridan, "Juveniles Who Commit Noncriminal Acts: Why Treat in a Correctional System?" *Federal Probation* (March 1967): 27. Also see Murphy, *Our Kindly Parent*, p. 104.

22. In addition to Sheridan, "Juveniles Who Commit Noncriminal Acts," p. 27, see Paul Lerman, "Child Convicts," *Transaction* (July–August 1971): 35; Meda Chesney-Lind, "Juvenile Delinquency: The Sexualization of Female Crime," *Psychology Today* (July 1974): 45; Colonel F. Betz, "Minor's Rights to Consent to an Abortion," *Santa Clara Lawyer* (Spring 1971): 469–78; Ellen M. McNamara, "The Minor's Right to Abortion and the Requirement of Parental Consent," *Virginia Law Review* (February 1974): 305–32; and Sol Rubin, "Children as Victims of Institutionalization," *Child Welfare* (January 1972): 9.

right to counsel, the right to cross-examine witnesses), but these have *only* been granted in cases where they have actually been accused of being *criminals*. As Beatrice Levidow writes, the *Gault* and similar decisions:

> do not apply to any adjudicatory hearings except those in which the offense charged to the juvenile would be violation of the criminal laws if committed by an adult. Therefore, the safeguards of *Kent, Gault,* and *Winship* do not protect the due process rights of juveniles who are dependent, neglected, in need of supervision, truant, run away, or accused of other offenses of which only juveniles can be guilty such as smoking, drinking, staying out late, etc.[23]

As a result, juveniles are habitually deprived of such elemental procedural rights accorded to adult defendants as the right to bail, the right to a transcript, the right to appeal, the right to a jury trial, the burden of proof to be on the prosecution, and the inadmissability of hearsay evidence. As Roscoe Pound has written, "the powers of the Star Chamber were a trifle in comparison with those of our juvenile courts." Once in a while, a dissenting judge has levelled a trenchant critique of this system. Thus, Judge Michael Musmanno stated in a 1954 Pennsylvania case:

> Certain constitutional and legal guarantees, such as immunity against self-incrimination, prohibition of hearsay, interdiction of ex parte and secret reports, all so jealously upheld in decisions from Alabama to Wyoming, are to be jettisoned in Pennsylvania when the person at the bar of justice is a tender-aged boy or girl.[24]

Furthermore, the state juvenile codes are studded with vague language that permits almost unlimited trial and incarceration for various forms of "immorality," "habitual truancy," "habitual disobedience," "incorrigibility," "ungovernability," "moral depravity," "in danger of becoming morally depraved," "immoral conduct," and even associating with persons of "immoral character."[25]

---

23. Beatrice Levidow, "Overdue Process for Juveniles: For the Retroactive Restoration of Constitutional Rights," *Howard Law Journal* (1972): 413.

24. Quoted in J. Douglas Irmen, "Children's Liberation—Reforming Juvenile Justice," *University of Kansas Law Review* (1972–73): 181–83. Also see Mark J. Green, "The Law of the Young," in B. Wasserstein and M. Green, eds., *With Justice for Some* (Boston: Beacon Press, 1970), p. 33; Sanford J. Fox, *Cases and Material on Modern Juvenile Justice* (St. Paul, Minn.: West, 1972), p. 68.

25. See the dissent of Justice Cadena in the 1969 Texas case of *E.S.G. v. State,* in Fox, *Cases and Material on Modern Juvenile Justice,* pp. 296–98. Also see Lawrence J. Wolk, "Juvenile

Moreover, the tyranny of indeterminate sentencing (see our chapter above on punishment) has been wielded against juveniles, with juveniles often receiving a longer sentence than an adult would have suffered for the same offense. Indeed the rule in contemporary juvenile justice has been to impose a sentence that may leave a juvenile in jail until he reaches the age of majority. Furthermore, in some states in recent years, this evil has been compounded by separating juvenile offenders into two categories—genuine criminals who are called "delinquents," and other, "immoral" children who are called "persons in need of supervision" or PINS. After which, the PINS "offenders" receive longer sentences than the actual juvenile criminals! Thus, in a recent study, Paul Lerman writes:

> The range of institutional stay was two to twenty-eight months for delinquents and four to forty-eight months for PINS boys; the median was nine months for delinquents and thirteen months for PINS; and the average length of stay was 10.7 months for delinquents and 16.3 months for PINS. . . .
>
> The results of length of stay do not include the detention period; the stage of correctional processing prior to placement in an institution. Analyses of recent detention figures for all five boroughs of New York City revealed the following patterns: (1) PINS boys and girls are more likely to be detained than delinquents (54 to 31 percent); and (2) once PINS youth are detained they are twice as likely to be detained for more than 30 days than are regular delinquents (50 to 25 percent).[26]

Again, it is mainly *female* juveniles that are punished for "immoral" offenses. A recent study of Hawaii, for example, found that girls charged merely with running away normally spend two weeks in pretrial detention, whereas boys charged with actual crimes are held for only a few days; and that nearly 70 percent of the imprisoned girls in a state training school were incarcerated for immorality offenses, whereas the same was true of only 13 percent for the imprisoned boys.[27]

Court Statutes—Are They Void for Vagueness?" *New York University Review of Law and Social Change* (Winter 1974): 53; Irmen, "Children's Liberation," pp. 181–83; and Lawrence R. Sidman, "The Massachusetts Stubborn Child Law: Law and Order in the Home," *Family Law Quarterly* (Spring 1972): 40–45.

26. Lerman, "Child Convicts," p. 38. Also see Nora Klapmuts, "Children's Rights: The Legal Rights of Minors in Conflict with Law or Social Custom," *Crime and Delinquency Literature* (September 1972): 471.

27. Meda Chesney-Lind, "Juvenile Delinquency," p. 46.

The current judicial view, which regards the child as having virtually no rights, was trenchantly analyzed by Supreme Court Justice Abe Fortas in his decision in the *Gault* case:

> The idea of crime and punishment was to be abandoned. The child was to be "treated" and "rehabilitated" and the procedures, from apprehension through institutionalization, were to be "clinical" rather than punitive.
>
> These results were to be achieved, without coming to conceptual and constitutional grief, by insisting that the proceedings were not adversary, but that the State was proceeding as *parens patriae* (the State as parent). The Latin phrase proved to be a great help to those who sought to rationalize the exclusion of juveniles from the constitutional scheme; but its meaning is murky and its historical credentials are of dubious relevance.
>
> . . . The right of the State, as *parens patriae*, to deny the child procedural rights available to his elders was elaborated by the assertion that a child, unlike an adult, has a right "not to liberty but to custody.". . . If his parents default in effectively performing their custodial functions—that is if the child is "delinquent"—the state may interfere. In doing so, it does not deprive the child of any rights, because he has none. It merely provides the "custody" to which the child is entitled. On this basis, proceedings involving juveniles were described as "civil" not "criminal" and therefore not subject to the requirements which restrict the State when it seeks to deprive a person of his liberty.[28]

It may be added that calling an action "civil" or "custody" does not make incarceration any more pleasant or any less incarceration for the victim of the "treatment" or the "rehabilitation." Criminologist Frederick Howlett has trenchantly criticized the juvenile court system, and placed it in a wider libertarian context. He writes of

> the denial of certain basic rights of individuals—the right to associate with those of their choice and to engage voluntarily in acts that harm no one but themselves. The drunk who clogs our courts should have the right to get drunk; the . . . prostitute and her client should not have to answer to the law for an act that is their personal decision. The misbehaving child likewise has a fundamental right to be a child, and if he has committed no act that would be considered criminal were he an adult, why seek recourse through the courts . . . ? Before rushing to treat or "help" a person outside the justice system,

---

28. Fox, *Cases and Material on Modern Juvenile Justice*, p. 14.

should not the community first consider the alternative of doing nothing? Should it not recognize the child's right, as a person, to nontreatment and noninterference by an outside authority?[29]

A particularly eloquent judicial defense of the rights of children occurred in an 1870 Illinois decision, years earlier than the modern assertion of state despotism in the juvenile court system, beginning with the turn of the century Progressive period. In his decision in *People ex rel. O'Connell v. Turner,* Justice Thornton declared:

The principle of the absorption of the child in, and its complete subjection to the despotism of, the State, is wholly inadmissible in the modern civilized world. . . .

These laws provide for the "safe keeping" of the child; they direct his "commitment," and only a "ticket of leave," of the uncontrolled discretion of a board of guardians, will permit the imprisoned boy to breathe the pure air of heaven outside his prison walls, and to feel the instincts of manhood by contact with the busy world. . . . The confinement may be from one to fifteen years, according to the age of the child. Executive clemency cannot open the prison doors, for no offense has been committed. The writ of *habeas corpus,* a writ for the security of liberty, can afford no relief, for the sovereign power of the State, as *parens patriae,* has determined the imprisonment beyond

29. Frederick W. Howlett, "Is the YSB All it's Cracked Up to Be?" *Crime and Delinquency* (October 1973): 489–91. In his excellent book, *The Child Savers,* Anthony Platt points out that the origin of the juvenile court–reform school system in the Progressive period at the turn of the twentieth century, was specifically designed to impose a despotic "reform" on the "immorality" of the nation's children on a massive scale. Thus, Platt in *The Child Savers* (Chicago: University of Chicago Press, 1970), pp. 99–100, writes that the "child savers"

were most active and successful in extending governmental control over a whole range of youthful activity that had been previously ignored or dealt with informally . . . The child savers were prohibitionists in a general sense who believed that social progress depended on efficient law enforcement, strict supervision of children's leisure and recreation, and the regulation of illicit pleasures. Their efforts were directed at rescuing children from institutions and situations (theaters, dance halls, saloons, etc.) which threatened their "dependency." The child saving movement also raised the issue of child protection in order to challenge a variety of "deviant" institutions: thus, children could only be protected from sex and alcohol by destroying the brothels and saloons.

Also see ibid., pp. 54, 67–68, 140. For earlier expressions of "child-saving," *parens patriae,* and the incarceration of juveniles for truancy, see J. Lawrence Schultz, "The Cycle of Juvenile Court History," *Crime and Delinquency* (October 1973): 468; and Katz, *When Parents Fail,* p. 188.

recall. Such a restraint upon natural liberty is tyranny and oppression. If, without crime, without the conviction of any offense, the children of the State are thus to be confined for the "good of society," then society had better be reduced to its original elements, and free government acknowledged a failure. . . .

The disability of minors does not make slaves or criminals of them. . . . Can we hold children responsible for crime; liable for their torts; impose onerous burdens upon them, and yet deprive them of their liberty, without charge or conviction of crime? [The Illinois Bill of Rights, following upon the Virginia Declaration of Rights and the Declaration of Independence, declares that] "all men are, by nature, free and independent, and have certain inherent and inalienable rights— among these life, liberty, and the pursuit of happiness." This language is not restrictive; it is broad and comprehensive, and declares a grand truth, that "all men," all people, everywhere, have the inherent and inalienable right to liberty. Shall we say to the children of the State, you shall not enjoy this right—a right independent of all human laws and regulations. . . . Even criminals cannot be convicted and imprisoned without due process of law.[30]

30. 55 Ill. 280 (1870), reprinted in Robert H. Bremner, ed., *Children and Youth in America* (Cambridge, Mass.: Harvard University Press, 1970–74), vol. 2, pp. 485–87. Naturally, the "child saving" reformers chafed at the results of the *O'Connell* decision, which the prominent Illinois social and child reformer Frederick Wines called "positively injurious. It proceeds from a morbid sensitivity on the subject of personal liberty." See Platt, *The Child Savers*, p. 106.

15. "Human Rights" As Property Rights

L iberals generally wish to preserve the concept of "rights" for such "human" rights as freedom of speech, while denying the concept to private property.[1] And yet, on the contrary, the concept of "rights" only makes sense as property rights. For not only are there no human rights which are not also property rights, but the former rights lose their absoluteness and clarity and become fuzzy and vulnerable when property rights are not used as the standard.

In the first place, there are two senses in which property rights are identical with human rights: one, that property can *only* accrue to humans, so that their rights to property are rights that belong to human beings; and two, that the person's right to his own body, his personal liberty, is a property right in his own person as well as a "human right." But more importantly for our discussion, human rights, when not put in terms of property rights, turn out to be vague and contradictory, causing liberals to weaken those rights on behalf of "public policy" or the "public good." As I wrote in another work:

> Take, for example, the "human right" of free speech. Freedom of speech is supposed to mean the right of everyone to say whatever he likes. But the neglected question is: Where? Where does a man have this right? He certainly does not have it on property on which he is trespassing. In short, he has this right only either on his own property or on the property of someone who has agreed, as a gift or in a rental contract, to allow him on the premises. In fact, then, there is no such thing as a separate "right to free speech"; there is only a man's property right: the right to do as he wills with his own or to make voluntary agreements with other property owners.[2]

In short, a person does not have a "right to freedom of speech"; what he *does* have is the right to hire a hall and address the people who enter the premises. He does not have a "right to freedom of the press"; what he *does* have is the right to write or publish a pamphlet, and to

---

1. A particularly stark and self-contradictory example is Professor Peter Singer, who explicitly calls for preserving the concept of rights for personal liberty, while shifting over to utilitarianism in economic affairs and in the realm of property. Peter Singer, "The Right to Be Rich or Poor," *New York Review of Books* (6 March 1975).

2. Murray N. Rothbard, *Power and Market*, 2nd ed. (Kansas City: Sheed Andrews and McMeel, 1977), pp. 238–39.

sell that pamphlet to those who are willing to buy it (or to give it away to those who are willing to accept it). Thus, what he has in each of these cases is property rights, including the right of free contract and transfer which form a part of such rights of ownership. There is no extra "right of free speech" or free press beyond the property rights that a person may have in any given case.

Furthermore, couching the analysis in terms of a "right to free speech" instead of property rights leads to confusion and the weakening of the very concept of rights. The most famous example is Justice Holmes's contention that no one has the right to shout "Fire" falsely in a crowded theater, and *therefore* that the right to freedom of speech cannot be absolute, but must be weakened and tempered by considerations of "public policy."[3] And yet, if we analyze the problem in terms of *property* rights we will see that no weakening of the absoluteness of rights is necessary.[4]

For, logically, the shouter is either a patron or the theater owner. If he is the theater owner, he is violating the property rights of the patrons in quiet enjoyment of the performance, for which he took their money in the first place. If he is another patron, then he is violating both the property right of the patrons to watching the performance *and* the property right of the owner, for he is violating the terms of his being there. For those terms surely include not violating the owner's property by disrupting the performance he is putting on. In either case, he may be prosecuted as a violator of property rights; therefore, when we concentrate on the *property* rights involved, we see that the Holmes case implies no need for the law to weaken the absolute nature of rights.

Indeed, Justice Hugo Black, a well-known "absolutist" on behalf of "freedom of speech," made it clear, in a trenchant critique of the Holmes "shouting 'fire' in a crowded theater" argument, that Black's advocacy of freedom of speech was grounded in the rights of private property. Thus Black stated:

---

3. On the Holmes dictum, see Murray N. Rothbard, *For A New Liberty*, rev. ed. (New York: MacMillan, 1978), pp. 43–44; and Rothbard, *Power and Market*, pp. 239–40. For a devastating critique of Holmes's unwarranted reputation as a civil libertarian, see H.L. Mencken, *A Mencken Chrestomathy* (New York: Alfred A. Knopf, 1947), pp. 258–64.

4. Furthermore, the view that the shout of "fire" causes a panic is deterministic and is another version of the "incitement to riot" fallacy discussed above. It is up to the people in the theater to assess information coming to them. If this were not so, why wouldn't *correctly* warning people of an actual fire in a theater be a crime, since it too might incite a panic? The disruption involved in falsely yelling "fire" is actionable only as a violation of property rights in the manner explained in the text below. I am indebted to Dr. David Gordon for this point.

I went to a theater last night with you. I have an idea if you and I had gotten up and marched around that theater, whether we said anything or not, we would have been arrested. Nobody has ever said that the First Amendment gives people a right to go anywhere in the world they want to go or say anything in the world they want to say. Buying the theater tickets did not buy the opportunity to make a speech there. We have a system of property in this country which is also protected by the Constitution. We have a system of property, which means that a man does not have a right to do anything he wants anywhere he wants to do it. For instance, I would feel a little badly if somebody were to try to come into my house and tell me that he had a constitutional right to come in there because he wanted to make a speech against the Supreme Court. I realize the freedom of people to make a speech against the Supreme Court, but I do not want him to make it in my house.

That is a wonderful aphorism about shouting "fire" in a crowded theater. But you do not have to shout "fire" to get arrested. If a person creates a disorder in a theater, they would get him there not because of what he hollered but because he hollered. They would get him not because of any views he had but because they thought he did not have any views that they wanted to hear there. That is the way I would answer not because of what he shouted but because he shouted.[5]

Some years ago, the French political theorist Bertrand de Jouvenel similarly called for the weakening of free speech and assembly rights in what he called the "chairman's problem"—the problem of allocating time or space in an assembly hall or newspaper, or in front of a microphone, where the writers or speakers believe that they have a "right" of free speech to the use of the resource.[6] What de Jouvenel overlooked was our solution to the "chairman's problem"—recasting the concept of rights in terms of private property rather than in terms of freedom of speech or assembly.

In the first place, we may notice that in each of de Jouvenel's examples—a man attending an assembly, a person writing to a letters-to-the-editor column, and a man applying for discussion time on the radio—the scarce time or space being offered is *free*, in the sense of costless. We

---

5. Irving Dillard, ed., *One Man's Stand for Freedom* (New York: Alfred A. Knopf, 1963), pp. 489–91.

6. Bertrand de Jouvenel, "The Chairman's Problem," *American Political Science Review* (June 1961): 305–32; The essence of this critique of de Jouvenel appeared in Italian in Murray N. Rothbard, "Bertrand de Jouvenel e i diritti di proprietá," *Biblioteca della Liberta*, no. 2 (1966): 41–45.

are in the midst of what economics calls "the rationing problem." A valuable, scarce resource has to be allocated: whether it be time at the podium, time in front of the microphone, or space in a newspaper. But since the use of the resource is free (costless), the demand for obtaining this time or space is bound greatly to exceed the supply, and hence a perceived "shortage" of the resource is bound to develop. As in all cases of shortages and of queueing up caused by low or nonexistent prices, the unsatisfied demanders are left with a feeling of frustration and resentment at not obtaining the use of the resource they believe they deserve.

A scarce resource, if not allocated by prices, must be allocated in some other way by its owner. It should be noted that the de Jouvenel cases *could* all be allocated by a price system, if the owner so desired. The chairman of an assembly *could* ask for price bids for scarce places at the podium and then award the places to the highest bidders. The radio producer *could* do the same with discussants on his program. (In effect, this is what producers do when they sell time to individual sponsors.) There would then be no shortages, and no feelings of resentment at a promise ("equal access" of the public to the column, podium, or microphone) reneged.

But beyond the question of prices, there is a deeper matter involved, for whether by prices or by some other criterion, the resource *must*, in all cases, be allocated *by its owner*. The owner of the radio station or the program (or his agent) rents, or donates, radio time in a way that he decides; the owner of the newspaper, or his editor–agent, allocates space for letters in any way that he chooses; the "owner" of the assembly, and his designated agent the chairman, allocates the space at the podium in any way he decides.

The fact that ownership is the ultimate allocator gives us the clue to the property solution of de Jouvenel's "chairman's problem." For the fellow who writes a letter to a newspaper is *not* the owner of the paper; he therefore has *no right to*, but only a request for, newspaper space, a request which it is the absolute right of the *owner* to grant or to deny. The man who asks to speak at an assembly has no *right* to speak, but only a request that the owner or his representative, the chairman, must decide upon. The solution is to recast the meaning of the "right to freedom of speech" or "assembly"; instead of using the vague, and, as de Jouvenel demonstrates, unworkable concept of some sort of equal right *to* space or time, we should focus on the right of private property. Only when the "right to free speech" is treated simply as a subdivision of property right does it become valid, workable, and absolute.

This can be seen in de Jouvenel's proposed "right to buttonhole." De Jouvenel says that there is a "sense in which the right of speech can be exercised by each and everyone; it is the right to buttonhole," to talk and to try to convince the people one meets, and then to collect these people in a hall, and thus to "constitute a congregation" of one's own. Here de Jouvenel approaches the proper solution without firmly attaining it. For what he is really saying is that "the right to free speech" is only valid and workable when used in the sense of the right to talk to people, to try to convince them, to hire a hall to address people who wish to attend, etc. But *this* sense of the right to free speech is, in fact, part of a person's general right to his property. (*Provided*, of course, we remember the right of another person *not* to be buttonholed if he doesn't want to, i.e., his right *not* to listen.) For property right *includes* the right to one's property and to make mutually agreed-upon contracts and exchanges with the owners of other properties. De Jouvenel's "buttonholer," who hires a hall and addresses his congregation, is exercising not a vague "right of free speech," but a part of his general right of property. De Jouvenel almost recognizes this when he considers the case of two men, "Primus" and "Secundus":

> Primus . . . has collected through toil and trouble a congregation of his own doing. An outsider, Secundus, comes in and claims the right to address this congregation on grounds of the right of free speech. Is Primus bound to give him the floor? I doubt it. He can reply to Secundus: "I have made up this congregation. Go thou and do likewise."

Precisely. In short, Primus *owns* the meeting; he has hired the hall, has called the meeting, and has laid down its conditions; and those who don't like these conditions are free not to attend or to leave. Primus has a property right in the meeting that permits him to speak at will; Secundus has no property right whatever, and therefore no right to speak at the meeting.

In general, those problems where rights seem to require weakening are ones where the *locus of ownership* is not precisely defined, in short where property rights are muddled. Many problems of "freedom of speech," for example, occur in the government-owned streets: e.g., *should* a government permit a political meeting which it claims will disrupt traffic, or litter streets with handbills? But all of such problems which seemingly require "freedom of speech" to be less than absolute, are actually problems due to the failure to define property rights. For the streets are generally *owned* by government; the government in these cases is "the chairman." And then government, like any other property owner, is faced with the problem of how to allocate its scarce resources. A political meeting on the streets *will*, let us say, block traffic; therefore, the decision of government involves not so much a right to freedom of speech as it involves the allocation of street space by its owner.

The whole problem would not arise, it should be noted, if the streets were owned by private individuals and firms—as they all would be in a libertarian society; for then the streets, like all other private property, could be rented by or donated to other private individuals or groups for the purpose of assembly. One would, in a fully libertarian society, have no more "right" to use someone else's street than he would have the "right" to preempt someone else's assembly hall; in both cases, the only *right* would be the property right to use one's money to rent the resource, *if* the landlord is willing. Of course, so long as the streets continue to be government-owned, the problem and the conflict remain insoluble; for government ownership of the streets means that all of one's other property rights, *including* speech, assembly, distribution of leaflets, etc., will be hampered and restricted by the ever-present necessity to traverse and use government-owned streets, which government may decide to block or restrict in any way. If the government allows the street meeting, it will restrict traffic; if it blocks the meeting in behalf of the flow of traffic, it will block the freedom of access to the government streets. In either case, and whichever way it chooses, the "rights" of some taxpayers will have to be curtailed.

The other place where the rights and locus of ownership are ill-defined and hence where conflicts are insoluble is the case of *government* assemblies (and their "chairmen"). For, as we have pointed out, where one man or group hires a hall, and appoints a chairman, the locus of ownership is clear and Primus has his way. But what of governmental assemblies? Who *owns* them? No one really knows, and therefore there is no satisfactory or non-arbitrary way to resolve who shall speak and who shall not, what shall be decided and what shall not. True, the government assembly forms itself under its own rules, but then what if these rules are not agreeable to a large body of the citizenry? There is no satisfactory way to resolve this question because there is no clear locus of property right involved. To put it another way: in the case of the newspaper or radio program, it is clear that the letter-writer or would-be discussant is the petitioner, and the publisher or producer the *owner* who makes the decision. But in the case of the governmental assembly, we do not know who the owner may be. The man who demands to be heard at a town meeting claims to be a part owner, and yet he has not established any sort of property right through purchase, inheritance, or discovery, as have property owners in all other areas.

To return to the streets, there are other vexed problems which would be quickly cleared up in a libertarian society where all property is private and clearly owned. In the current society for example, there is continuing conflict between the "right" of taxpayers to have access to government-owned streets, as against the desire of residents of a neighborhood to be free of people whom they consider "undesirable" gathering in the streets. In New York City, for example, there are now hysterical pressures by residents of various neighborhoods to prevent McDonald's food stores from opening in their area, and in many cases they have been able to use the power of local government to prevent the stores from moving in. These, of course, are clear violations of the right of McDonald's to the property which they have purchased. But the residents *do* have a point: the litter, and the attraction of "undesirable" elements who would be "attracted" to McDonald's and gather in front of it—on the *streets*. In short, what the residents are *really* complaining about is not so much the property right of McDonald's as what they consider the "bad" use of the government streets. They are, in brief, complaining about the "human right" of certain people to walk at will on the government streets. But as taxpayers and citizens, these "undesirables" surely have the "right" to walk on the streets, and of course they *could* gather on the spot, if they so desired, without the attraction of McDonald's. In the libertarian society, however, where the streets would all be privately owned, the entire con-flict could be resolved without violating anyone's property rights: for then the *owners of the streets* would have the right to decide who shall have access to those streets, and they could then keep out "undesirables" if they so wished.

Of course, those street-owners who decided to keep out "undesirables" would have to pay the price—both the actual costs of policing as well as the loss of business to the merchants on their street and the diminished flow of visitors to their homes. Undoubtedly, in the free society there would result a diverse pattern of access, with some streets (and therefore neigh-borhoods) open to all, and others with varying degrees of restricted access.

Similarly, the private ownership of all streets would resolve the prob-lem of the "human right" to freedom of immigration. There is no question about the fact that current immigration barriers restrict not so much a "human right" to immigrate, but the right of property owners to rent or sell property to immigrants. There can be no human right to immigrate, for on *whose* property does someone else have the right to trample? In short, if "Primus" wishes to migrate now from some other country to the United States, we cannot say that he has the absolute right to immigrate to this land area; for what of those property owners who don't *want* him on their property? On the other hand, there may be, and undoubtedly are, other property owners who would jump at the chance to rent or sell property to Primus, and the current laws now invade their property rights by preventing them from doing so.

The libertarian society would resolve the entire "immigration question" within the matrix of absolute property rights. For people only have the right to move to those properties and lands where the owners desire to rent or sell to them. In the free society, they would, in first instance, have the right to travel only on those streets whose owners agree to have them there, and then to rent or buy housing from willing owners. Again, just as in the case of daily movement on streets, a diverse and varying pattern of access of migration would undoubtedly arise.

16. Knowledge, True and False

Our theory of property rights can be used to unravel a tangled skein of complex problems revolving around questions of knowledge, true and false, and the dissemination of that knowledge. Does Smith, for example, have the right (again, we are concerned about his *right*, not the morality or esthetics of his *exercising* that right) to print and disseminate the statement that "Jones is a liar" or that "Jones is a convicted thief" or that "Jones is a homosexual"? There are three logical possibilities about the truth of such a statement: (a) that the statement about Jones is true; (b) that it is false and Smith knows it is false; or (c) most realistically, that the truth or falsity of the statement is a fuzzy zone, not certainly and precisely knowable (e.g., in the above cases, whether or not someone is a "liar" depends on how many and how intense the pattern of lies a person has told and is adjudged to add up to the category of "liar"—an area where individual judgments can and will properly differ).

Suppose that Smith's statement is definitely true. It seems clear, then, that Smith has a perfect right to print and disseminate the statement. For it is within his property right to do so. It is also, of course, within the property right of Jones to try to rebut the statement in his turn. The current libel laws make Smith's action illegal if done with "malicious" intent, even though the information be true. And yet, surely legality or illegality should depend not on the motivation of the actor, but on the objective nature of the act. If an action is objectively non-invasive, then it should be legal regardless of the benevolent or malicious intentions of the actor (though the latter may well be relevant to the *morality* of the action). And this is aside from the obvious difficulties in legally determining an individual's subjective motivations for any action.

It might, however, be charged that Smith does *not* have the right to print such a statement, because Jones has a "right to privacy" (his "human" right) which Smith does not have the right to violate. But is there really such a right to privacy? How can there be? How can there be a right to prevent Smith by force from disseminating knowledge which he possesses? Surely there can be no such right. Smith owns his own body, and therefore has the property right to own the knowledge he has inside his head, including his knowledge about Jones. And therefore he has the corollary right to print and disseminate that knowledge. In short, as in the case of the "human right" to free speech, *there is no such thing as a right to privacy except the right to protect one's property from invasion.* The *only* right "to privacy" is the right to protect one's property from being invaded by someone else. In brief, no one has the right to burgle someone else's home, or to wiretap someone's phone lines. Wiretapping is properly a crime *not* because of some vague and woolly "invasion of a 'right to privacy'," but because it is an invasion of the *property right* of the person being wiretapped.

At the present time, the courts distinguish between persons "in the public eye" who are adjudged not to have a right to privacy against being mentioned in the public press, and "private" persons who are considered to have such a right. And yet, such distinctions are surely fallacious. To the libertarian, everyone has the same right in his person and in the goods which he finds, inherits, or buys—and it is illegitimate to make distinctions in property right between one group of people and another. If there *were* some sort of "right to privacy," then simply being mentioned widely in the press (i.e. previous losses of the "right") could scarcely warrant being deprived of such right completely. No, the only proper course is to maintain that *no one* has any spurious "right to privacy," or right not to be mentioned publicly; while *everyone* has the right to protect his property against invasion. No one can have a property right in the knowledge in someone else's head.

In recent years, Watergate and the Pentagon Papers have brought to the fore such questions as privacy, the "privileges" of newspapermen, and the "public's right to know." Should, for example, a newspaperman have the right to "protect his sources of information" in court? Many people claim that newspapermen have such a right, basing that claim either (a) on special "privileges" of confidentiality allegedly accruing to newspapermen, lawyers, doctors, priests and psychoanalysts, and/or (b) on the "public's right to know" and hence on the widest possible knowledge as disseminated in the press. And yet, it should be clear by this point that both such claims are spurious. On the latter point, no one person or group of people (and therefore "the public") has the *right* to know anything. They have no right to knowledge which other people have and refuse to disseminate. For if a man has the absolute right to disseminate knowledge inside his head, he also has the corollary right *not* to disseminate that knowledge. There is no "right to know"; there is only the right of the knower to either disseminate his knowledge or to keep silent. Neither can any particular profession, be it newsmen or physicians, claim any particular right of confidentiality which is not possessed by anyone else. Rights to one's liberty and property must be universal.

The solution to the problem of the newsman's sources, indeed, rests in the right of the knower—*any* knower—to keep silent, to *not* disseminate knowledge if he so desires. Hence, not only newsmen and physicians, but *everyone* should have the right to protect their sources, or to be silent, in court or anywhere else. And this, indeed, is the other side of the coin of our previous strictures against the compulsory subpoena power. No one should be forced to testify at all, not only against himself (as in the Fifth Amendment) but against *or for* anyone else. Compulsory testimony itself is the central evil in this entire problem.

There is, however, an exception to the right to use and disseminate the knowledge within one's head: namely, if it was procured from someone else as a *conditional* rather than absolute ownership. Thus, suppose that Brown allows Green into his home and shows him an invention of Brown's hitherto kept secret, but *only* on the condition that Green keeps this information private. In that case, Brown has granted to Green not absolute ownership of the knowledge of his invention, but *conditional* ownership, with Brown retaining the ownership power to disseminate the knowledge of the invention. If Green discloses the invention anyway, he is violating the residual property right of Brown to disseminate knowledge of the invention, and is therefore to that extent a thief.

Violation of (common law) copyright is an equivalent violation of contract and theft of property. For suppose that Brown builds a better mousetrap and sells it widely, but stamps each mousetrap "copyright Mr. Brown." What he is then doing is selling *not* the entire property right in each mousetrap, but the right to do anything with the mousetrap *except* to sell it or an identical copy to someone else. The right to *sell* the Brown mousetrap is retained in perpetuity by Brown. Hence, for a mousetrap buyer, Green, to go ahead and sell identical mousetraps is a violation of his contract *and of* the property right of Brown, and therefore prosecutable as theft. Hence, our theory of property rights includes the inviolability of contractual copyright.

A common objection runs as follows: all right, it would be criminal for *Green* to produce and sell the Brown mousetrap; but suppose that someone else, Black, who had not made a contract with Brown, happens to see Green's mousetrap and then goes ahead and produces and sells the replica? Why should *he* be prosecuted? The answer is that, as in the case of our critique of negotiable instruments, no one can acquire a *greater* property title in something than has already been given away or sold. Green did not own the total property right in his mousetrap, in accordance with his contract with Brown—but only all rights *except* to sell it or a replica. But therefore Black's title in the mousetrap, the ownership of the ideas in Black's head, can be no greater than Green's, and therefore he too would be a violator of Brown's property even though he himself had not made the actual contract.

Of course, there may be some difficulties in the actual enforcement of Brown's property right. Namely, that, as in *all* cases of alleged theft or other crime, *every defendant is innocent until proven guilty.* It would be necessary for Brown *to prove* that Black (Green would not pose a problem) had access to Brown's mousetrap, and did not invent this kind of mousetrap by himself independently. By the nature of things, some products (e.g., books, paintings) are easier to prove to be unique products of individual minds than others (e.g., mousetraps).[1]

If, then, Smith has the absolute right to disseminate knowledge about Jones (we are still assuming that the knowledge is correct) and has the corollary right to keep silent about that knowledge, then, *a fortiori*, surely he *also* has the right to go to Jones and receive payment in exchange for not disseminating such information. In short, Smith has the right to "blackmail" Jones. As in all voluntary exchanges, both parties benefit from such an exchange: Smith receives money, and Jones obtains the service of Smith's not disseminating information about him which Jones does not wish to see others possess. The right to blackmail is deducible from the general property right in one's person and knowledge and the right to disseminate or not disseminate that knowledge. How can the right to blackmail be denied?[2]

Furthermore, as Professor Walter Block has trenchantly pointed out, on utilitarian grounds the consequence of outlawing blackmail—e.g., of preventing Smith from offering to sell his silence to Jones—will be to encourage Smith to disseminate his information, since he is coercively blocked from selling his silence. The result will be an increased dissemination of derogatory information, so that Jones will be worse off from the outlawry of blackmail than he would have been if blackmail had been permitted.

Thus Block writes:

> What, exactly, is blackmail? Blackmail is the offer of a trade; it is the offer to trade something, usually silence, for some other good, usually money. If the offer of the blackmail trade is accepted, then the blackmailer maintains his silence and the blackmailee pays the agreed amount of money. If the blackmail offer is

---

1. On the crucial legal and philosophical distinction between patents and copyrights, see Murray N. Rothbard, *Man, Economy, and State* (Princeton, N.J.: D. Van Nostrand, 1962), vol. 2, pp. 652–60. Also see Murray N. Rothbard, *Power and Market* (Kansas City: Sheed Andrews and McMeel, 1977), pp. 71–75. For instances of independent inventions of the same item, see S. Colum Gilfillan, *The Sociology of Invention* (Chicago: Follett Press, 1935), p. 75.

2. When I first briefly adumbrated the right to blackmail in *Man, Economy, and State,* vol. 1, p. 443, n. 49, I was met with a storm of abuse by critics who apparently believed that I was advocating the morality of blackmail. Again—a failure to make the crucial distinction between the legitimacy of a right and the morality or esthetics of exercising that right.

rejected, then the blackmailer may exercise his right of free speech, and perhaps announce and publicize the secret. . . .

The only difference between a gossip and blabbermouth and the blackmailer is that the blackmailer will refrain from speaking—for a price. In a sense, the gossip or the blabbermouth is much worse than the blackmailer, for the blackmailer at least gives you a chance to shut him up. The blabbermouth and gossip just up and spill the beans. A person with a secret he wants kept will be much better off if a blackmailer rather than a gossip or blabbermouth gets hold of it. With the blabbermouth or gossip, as we have said, all is lost. With the blackmailer, one can only gain, or at worst, be no worse off. If the price required by the blackmailer for his silence is worth less than the secret, the secret-holder will pay off, and accept the lesser of the two evils. He will gain the difference to him between the value of the secret and the price of the blackmailer. It is only in the case that the blackmailer demands more than the secret is worth that the information gets publicized. But in this case the secret-keeper is no worse off with the blackmailer than with the inveterate gossip. . . . It is indeed difficult, then, to account for the vilification suffered by the blackmailer, at least compared to the gossip who is usually dismissed with merely slight contempt.[3]

There are other, and less important problems, with the outlawry of a blackmail contract. Suppose that, in the above case, instead of Smith going to Jones with an offer of silence, Jones had heard of Smith's knowledge and his intent to print it, and went to Smith to offer to purchase the latter's silence? Should *that* contract be illegal? And if so, why? But if Jones's offer should be legal while Smith's is illegal, should it be illegal for Smith to turn down Jones's offer, and then ask for *more* money as the price of his silence? And, furthermore, should it be illegal for Smith to subtly let Jones know that Smith has the information and intends to publish, and then allow Jones to make the actual offer? But how could this simple letting Jones know in advance be considered as illegal? Could it not be rather construed as a simple act of courtesy to Jones? The shoals get muddier and muddier, and the support for outlawry of blackmail contracts—especially by libertarians who believe in property rights—becomes ever more flimsy.

Of course, if Smith and Jones make a blackmail contract, and then Smith violates it by printing the information anyway, then Smith has

---

3. Walter Block, "The Blackmailer as Hero," *Libertarian Forum* (December 1972): 3. Also see the version in Block, *Defending the Undefendable* (New York: Fleet Press, 1976), pp. 53–54.

stolen Jones's property (his money), and can be prosecuted as in the case of any other thief who has aggressed against property rights by violating a contract. But there is nothing unique about *blackmail* contracts in this regard.

In contemplating the law of a free society, therefore, the libertarian must look at people as acting within a general framework of absolute property rights and of the conditions of the world around them at any given time. In any exchange, any contract, that they make, they believe that they will be better off from making the exchange. Hence all of these contracts are "productive" in making them, at least prospectively, better off. And, of course, all of these voluntary contracts are legitimate and licit in the free society.[4]

We have therefore affirmed the legitimacy (the right) of Smith's either disseminating knowledge about Jones, keeping silent about the knowledge, or engaging in a contract with Jones to sell his silence. We have so far been assuming that Smith's knowledge is *correct*. Suppose, however, that the knowledge is false and Smith knows that it is false (the "worst" case). Does Smith have the right to disseminate false information about Jones? In short, should "libel" and "slander" be illegal in the free society?

And yet, once again, how can they be? Smith has a property right to the ideas or opinions in his own head; he also has a property right to print anything he wants and disseminate it. He has a property right to *say* that Jones is a "thief" even if he knows it to be false, and to print and sell that statement. The counter-view, and the current basis for holding libel and slander (especially of false statements) to be illegal is that every man has a "property right" in his own reputation, that Smith's falsehoods damage that reputation, and that therefore Smith's libels are invasions of Jones's property right in his reputation and should be illegal. Yet, again, on closer analysis this is a fallacious view. For everyone, as we have stated, owns his own body; he has a property right in his own head and person. But since every man owns his own mind, he cannot therefore own the minds of anyone else. And yet Jones's "reputation" is neither a physical entity nor is it something contained within or on his own person. Jones's "reputation" is purely a function of the subjective attitudes and beliefs about him contained in the minds *of other people*. But since these are beliefs in the minds of others, Jones can in no way legitimately own or control them. Jones can have no property right in the beliefs and minds of other people.

---

4. For a critique of Professor Robert Nozick's argument for the outlawry (or restriction) of blackmail contracts, see pp. 248–50 below.

Let us consider, in fact, the implications of believing in a property right in one's "reputation." Suppose that Brown has produced his mouse-trap, and then Robinson comes out with a better one. The "reputation" of Brown for excellence in mousetraps now declines sharply, as consumers shift their attitudes and their purchases, and buy Robinson's mousetrap instead. Can we not then say, on the principle of the "reputation" theory, that Robinson has injured the reputation of Brown, and can we not then outlaw Robinson from competing with Brown? If not, why not? Or should it be illegal for Robinson to advertise, and to tell the world that his mouse-trap is better?[5] In fact, of course, people's subjective attitudes and ideas about someone or his product will fluctuate continually, and hence it is impossible for Brown to stabilize his reputation by coercion; certainly it would be immoral and aggressive against other people's property right to *try*. Aggressive and criminal, then, either to outlaw one's competition *or* to outlaw false libels spread about one or one's product.

We can, of course, readily concede the gross immorality of spreading false libels about another person. But we must, nevertheless, maintain the legal right of anyone to do so. Pragmatically, again, this situation may well redound to the benefit of the people being libelled. For, in the current situation, when false libels are outlawed, the average person tends to believe that all derogatory reports spread about people are true, "otherwise they'd sue for libel." This situation discriminates against the poor, since poorer people are less likely to file suits against libelers. Hence, the reputations of poorer or less wealthy persons are liable to suffer more now, when libel is outlawed, then they would if libel were legitimate. For in that libertarian society, since everyone would know that false stories are legal, there would be far more skepticism on the part of the reading or listening public, who would insist on far more proof and believe fewer derogatory stories than they do now. Furthermore, the current system discriminates against poorer people in another way; for their own speech is restricted, since they are less likely to disseminate true but derogatory

5. Or, to take another example, suppose that Robinson publishes an investment advisory letter, in which he sets forth his opinion that a certain corporation's stock is unsound, and will probably decline. As a result of this advice, the stock falls in price. Robinson's opinion has "injured" the reputation of the corporation, and "damaged" its shareholders through the decline in price, caused by the lowering of confidence by investors in the market. Should Robinson's advice therefore be outlawed? Or, in yet another example, A writes a book; B reviews the book and states that the book is a bad one, the result is an "injury" to A's reputation and a decline in the sales of the book as well as A's income. Should all unfavorable book reviews therefore be illegal? Yet such are some of the logical implications of the "property in reputation" argument. I am indebted for the stock-market example to Williamson M. Evers.

knowledge about the wealthy for fear of having costly libel suits filed against them. Hence, the outlawing of libel harms people of limited means in two ways: by making them easier prey for libels and by hampering their own dissemination of accurate knowledge about the wealthy.

Finally, if anyone has the right knowingly to spread false libels about someone else, then, *a fortiori,* he of course has the right to disseminate those large numbers of statements about others which are in the fuzzy zone of not being clear or certain whether or not the statements are true or false.

17. Bribery

As in the case of blackmail, *bribery* has received a uniformly bad press, and it is generally assumed that bribery should be outlawed. But is this necessarily true? Let us examine a typical bribe contract. Suppose that Black wants to sell materials to the XYZ Company. In order to gain the sale, he pays a bribe to Green, the purchasing agent of the company. It is difficult to see what *Black* has done which libertarian law should consider as illegal. In fact, all he has done is to lower the price charged to the XYZ Company, by paying a rebate to Green. From Black's point of view, he would have been just as happy to charge a lower price directly, though presumably he did not do so because the XYZ executives would still not have purchased the materials from him. But the inner workings of the XYZ Company should scarcely be Black's responsibility. As far as he is concerned, he simply lowered his price to the Company, and thereby gained the contract.

The illicit action here is, instead, solely the behavior of Green, the taker of the bribe. For Green's employment contract with his employers implicitly requires him to purchase materials to the best of his ability in the interests of his company. Instead, he violated his contract with the XYZ company by not performing as their proper agent: for because of the bribe he *either* bought from a firm which he would not have dealt with otherwise, *or* he paid a higher price than he need have by the amount of his rebate. In either case, Green violated his contract and invaded the property rights of his employers.

In the case of bribes, therefore, there is nothing illegitimate about the briber, but there is much that is illegitimate about the bribee, the taker of the bribe. Legally, there should be a property right to pay a bribe, but not to take one. It is only the taker of a bribe who should be prosecuted. In contrast, liberals tend to hold the bribe-giver as somehow more reprehensible, as in some way "corrupting" the taker. In that way, they deny the free will and the responsibility of each individual for his own actions.

Let us now use our theory to analyze the problem of *payola*, which repeatedly arises on radio programs that play popular records. In a typical payola scandal, a record company bribes a disc jockey to play Record A. Presumably, the disc jockey would either not have played the record at all or would have played Record A fewer times; therefore, Record A is being played at the expense of Records B, C, and D which would have been played more frequently if the disc jockey had evaluated the records purely on the basis of his own and/or the public's taste. Surely, in a moral sense, the public is being betrayed in its trust in the disc jockey's sincerity. That trust turns out to have been a foolish one. But the public has no property rights in the radio program, and so they have no legal complaint in the matter. They received the program without cost. The other record companies, the producers of Records B, C, and D, were also injured since their products were not played as frequently, but they, too, have no property rights in the program, and they have no right to tell the disc jockey what to play.

Was anyone's property rights aggressed against by the disc jockey's taking of a bribe? Yes, for as in the case of the bribed purchasing agent, the disc jockey violated his contractual obligation to his employer— whether it be the station owner or the sponsor of the program—to play those records which in his view will most suit the public. Hence, the disc jockey violated the property of the station owner or sponsor. Once again, it is the disc jockey who accepts payola who has done something criminal and deserves to be prosecuted, but not the record company who paid the bribe.

Furthermore, if the record company had bribed the employer directly—whether the station owner or the sponsor—then there would have been no violation of anyone's property right and therefore properly no question of illegality. Of course, the public could easily feel cheated if the truth came out, and would then be likely to change their listening custom to another station or sponsor.

What about the case of *plugola*, where one sponsor pays for the program, and another company pays the producer of the program to plug its own product? Again, the property right being violated is that of the sponsor, who pays for the time and is entitled therefore to have sole advertising rights on the program. The violator of his property is not the maverick company that pays the bribe, but the producer who violates his contract with the sponsor by accepting it.

18. The Boycott

A *boycott* is an attempt to persuade other people to have nothing to do with some particular person or firm—either socially or in agreeing not to purchase the firm's product. Morally, a boycott may be used for absurd, reprehensible, laudatory, or neutral goals. It may be used, for example, to attempt to persuade people not to buy non-union grapes or not to buy union grapes. From our point of view, the important thing about the boycott is that it is purely voluntary, an act of attempted persuasion, and therefore that it is a perfectly legal and licit instrument of action. Again, as in the case of libel, a boycott may well diminish a firm's customers and therefore cut into its property values; but such an act is still a perfectly legitimate exercise of free speech and property rights. Whether we wish any particular boycott well or ill depends on our moral values and on our attitudes toward the concrete goal or activity. But a boycott is legitimate *per se*. If we feel a given boycott to be morally reprehensible, then it is within the rights of those who feel this way to organize a counter-boycott to persuade the consumers otherwise, or to boycott the boycotters. All this is part of the process of dissemination of information and opinion within the framework of the rights of private property.

Furthermore, "secondary" boycotts are also legitimate, despite their outlawry under our current labor laws. In a secondary boycott, labor unions try to persuade consumers not to buy from firms who deal with non-union (primary boycotted) firms. Again, in a free society, it should be their right to try such persuasion, just as it is the right of their opponents to counter with an opposing boycott. In the same way, it is the right of the League of Decency to try to organize a boycott of pornographic motion pictures, just as it would be the right of opposing forces to organize a boycott of those who give in to the League's boycott.

Of particular interest here is that the boycott is a device which can be used by people who wish to take action against those who engage in activities which we consider licit but which they consider immoral. Thus, while nonunion firms, pornography, libel, or whatever would be legal in a free society, so would it be the right of those who find such activities morally repugnant to organize boycotts against those who perform such activities. Any action would be legal in the libertarian society, provided that it does not invade property rights (whether of self-ownership or of material objects), and this would include boycotts against such activities, or counter-boycotts against the boycotters. The point is that coercion is not the only action that can be taken against what some consider to be immoral persons or activities; there are also such voluntary and persuasive actions as the boycott.

Whether *picketing* as a form of advertising a boycott would be legitimate in a free society is a far more complex question. Obviously, mass picketing that blocked entrance or egress from a building would be criminal and invasive of the rights of property—as would be sit-ins and sit-down strikes that forcibly occupied the property of others. Also invasive would be the type of picketing in which demonstrators threatened people who crossed the picket line—a clear case of intimidation by threat of violence. But even "peaceful picketing" is a complex question, for once again the use of government streets is involved. And, as in the case of assembly or street demonstrations generally, the government *cannot* make a nonarbitrary decision between the rights of taxpayers to use government streets to demonstrate their cause, and the right of the building owner and of traffic to use the streets as well. Again, it is impossible for government to decide in such a way as to eliminate conflict and to uphold rights in a clear-cut manner. If, on the other hand, the street in front of the picketed building were owned by private owners, then these owners would have the absolute right to decide on whether picketers could use their street in any way that the owners saw fit.[1]

Similarly, such employer devices as the *blacklist*—a form of boycott—would be legal in the free society. Before the Norris–LaGuardia Act of 1931, it was legal for employers to fire union organizers among their employees, and to circulate blacklists of such persons to other employers. Also legal would be the "yellow-dog contract," another device before the Norris–LaGuardia Act. In such a contract, the employee and the employer agree that, should the former join a union, the employer can fire him forthwith.

---

1. See Murray N. Rothbard, *For a New Liberty*, rev. ed. (New York: Macmillan, 1978), pp. 96–97.

19. Property Rights and the Theory of Contracts

The right of property implies the right to make contracts about that property: to give it away or to exchange titles of ownership for the property of another person. Unfortunately, many libertarians, devoted to the right to make contracts, hold the *contract itself* to be an absolute, and therefore maintain that *any* voluntary contract whatever must be legally enforceable in the free society. Their error is a failure to realize that the right to contract is strictly derivable from the right of private property, and therefore that the only *enforceable* contracts (i.e., those backed by the sanction of legal coercion) should be those where the failure of one party to abide by the contract implies the *theft* of property from the other party. In short, a contract should only be enforceable when the failure to fulfill it is an implicit theft of property. But this can only be true if we hold that validly enforceable contracts only exist where title to property has already been *transferred*, and therefore where the failure to abide by the contract means that the other party's property is retained by the delinquent party, without the consent of the former (implicit theft). Hence, this proper libertarian theory of enforceable contracts has been termed the "title-transfer" theory of contracts.[1]

Let us illustrate this point. Suppose that Smith and Jones make a contract, Smith giving $1000 to Jones at the present moment, in exchange for an IOU of Jones, agreeing to pay Smith $1100 one year from now. This is a typical debt contract. What has happened is that Smith has transferred his title to ownership of $1000 at present in exchange for Jones agreeing now to transfer title to Smith of $1100 one year from now. Suppose that, when the appointed date arrives one year later, Jones refuses to pay. Why should this payment now be enforceable at libertarian law? Existing law (which will be dealt with in greater detail below) largely contends that Jones must pay $1100 because he has "promised" to pay, and that this promise set up in Smith's mind the "expectation" that he would receive the money.

Our contention here is that mere *promises* are not a transfer of property title; that while it may well be the *moral* thing to keep one's promises, that it is not and cannot be the function of law (i.e., legal violence) in a libertarian system to enforce morality (in this case the keeping of promises).

---

1. In Williamson M. Evers, "Toward A Reformulation of the Law of Contracts," *Journal of Libertarian Studies* 1 (Winter 1977): 3–13. I am indebted in this section of the book to this excellent paper, particularly for its critique of existing and past laws and theories of enforceable contracts.

Our contention here is that Jones must pay Smith $1100 because he had already agreed to transfer title, and that nonpayment means that Jones is a thief, that he has stolen the property of Smith. In short, Smith's original transfer of the $1000 was not absolute, but *conditional,* conditional on Jones paying the $1100 in a year, and that, therefore, the failure to pay is an implicit theft of Smith's rightful property.

Let us examine, on the other hand, the implications of the now prevalent "promise" or "expectations" theory of contracts. Suppose that A promises to marry B; B proceeds to make wedding plans, incurring costs of preparing for the wedding. At the last minute, A changes his or her mind, thereby violating this alleged "contract." What should be the role of a legal enforcing agency in the libertarian society? Logically, the strict believer in the "promise" theory of contracts would have to reason as follows: A voluntarily promised B that he or she would marry the other, this set up the expectation of marriage in the other's mind; *therefore* this contract must be enforced. A must be *forced* to marry B.

As far as we know, no one has pushed the promise theory this far. Compulsory marriage is such a clear and evident form of involuntary slavery that no theorist, let alone any libertarian, has pushed the logic to this point. Clearly, liberty and compulsory slavery are totally incompatible, indeed are diametric opposites. But why *not*, if all promises must be enforceable contracts?

A milder form of enforcing such marriage promises *has,* however, been employed, let alone advocated, in our legal system. The old "breach of promise" suit forced the violator of his promise to pay damages to the promisee, to pay the expenses undergone because of the expectations incurred. But while this does not go as far as compulsory slavery, it is equally invalid. For there can be no property in someone's promises or expectations; these are only subjective states of mind, which do not involve transfer of title, and therefore do not involve implicit theft. They therefore should not be enforceable, and, in recent years, "breach of promise" suits, at least, have ceased to be upheld by the courts. The important point is that while enforcement of damages is scarcely as horrendous to the libertarian as compulsory enforcement of the promised service, it stems from the same invalid principle.

Let us pursue more deeply our argument that mere promises or expectations should not be enforceable. The basic reason is that the only valid transfer of title of ownership in the free society is the case where the property is, in fact and in the nature of man, *alienable* by man. All physical property owned by a person is alienable, i.e., in natural fact it can be given or transferred to the ownership and control of another party. I can give away or sell to another person my shoes, my house, my car, my money, etc. But there are certain vital things which, in natural fact and in the nature of man, are inalienable, i.e., they *cannot* in fact be alienated, even voluntarily. Specifically, a person cannot alienate his *will*, more particularly his control over his own mind and body. Each man has control over his own mind and body. Each man has control over his own will and person, and he is, if you wish, "stuck" with that inherent and inalienable ownership. Since his will and control over his own person are inalienable, then so also are his *rights to* control that person and will. That is the ground for the famous position of the Declaration of Independence that man's natural rights are inalienable; that is, they cannot be surrendered, *even if* the person wishes to do so.

Or, as Williamson Evers points out, the philosophical defenses of human rights

> are founded upon the natural fact that each human is the proprietor of his own will. To take rights like those of property and contractual freedom that are based on a foundation of the absolute self-ownership of the will and then to use those derived rights to destroy their own foundation is philosophically invalid.[2]

Hence, the unenforceability, in libertarian theory, of voluntary slave contracts. Suppose that Smith makes the following agreement with the Jones Corporation: Smith, for the rest of his life, will obey all orders, under whatever conditions, that the Jones Corporation wishes to lay down. Now, in libertarian theory there is nothing to prevent Smith from making this agreement, and from serving the Jones Corporation and from obeying

---

2. Evers, "Law of Contracts," p. 7. Rousseau argued trenchantly against the validity of a slave contract:

> When a man renounces his liberty he renounces his essential manhood, his rights, and even his duty as a human being. There is no compensation possible for such complete renunciation. It is incompatible with man's nature, and to deprive him of his free will is to deprive his actions of all moral sanction. The convention, in short, which sets up on one side an absolute authority, and on the other an obligation to obey without question, is vain and meaningless. Is it not obvious that where we can demand everything we owe nothing? Where there is no mutual obligation, no interchange of duties, it must, surely, be clear that the actions of the commanded cease to have any moral value? For how can it be maintained that my slave has any "right" against me when everything that he has is my property? His right being my right, it is absurd to speak of it as ever operating to my disadvantage.

Or, in short, if a man sells himself into slavery, then the master, being an absolute master, would then have the right to commandeer the funds with which he had "bought" the slave. Jean-Jacques Rousseau, *The Social Contract*, bk. 1, chap. 4, in E. Barker, ed., *Social Contract* (New York: Oxford University Press, 1948), p. 175.

the latter's orders indefinitely. The problem comes when, at some later date, Smith changes his mind and decides to leave. Shall he be held to his former voluntary promise? Our contention—and one that is fortunately upheld under present law—is that Smith's promise was not a valid (i.e., not an enforceable) contract. There is no transfer of title in Smith's agreement, because Smith's control over his own body and will are *inalienable*. Since that control *cannot* be alienated, the agreement was not a valid contract, and therefore should not be enforceable. Smith's agreement was a *mere* promise, which it might be held he is morally obligated to keep, but which should not be legally obligatory.

In fact, to enforce the promise would be just as much compulsory slavery as the compulsory marriage considered above. But should Smith at least be required to pay damages to the Jones Corporation, measured by the expectations of his lifelong service which the Jones Corporation had acquired? Again, the answer must be no. Smith is not an implicit thief; he has retained no just property of the Jones Corporation, for he *always* retains title to his own body and person.

What of the dashed expectations of the Jones Corporation? The answer must be the same as in the case of the disappointed suitor or bride. Life is always uncertain, always risky. Some people are better and some are poorer "entrepreneurs," i.e., forecasters of future human action and events of the world. The prospective bride or bridegroom, or the Jones Corporation, are the proper locus of risk in this matter; if their expectations are disappointed, well then, they were poor forecasters in this case, and they will remember the experience when dealing with Smith or the breacher-of-marriage-promise in the future.

If mere promises or expectations cannot be enforceable, but only contracts that transfer property titles, we can now see the application of the contrasting contract theories to an important real-life case: do enlistee-deserters from the army, as well as draftees, deserve total amnesty for their actions? Libertarians, being opposed to the draft as compulsory slavery, have no difficulty in calling for total exoneration for deserting draftees. But what of enlistees, who enlisted in the army voluntarily (and setting aside the case of those who may have enlisted only as an alternative to the compulsory draft)? The "promise" theorist must, strictly, advocate both punishment of the deserters and their compulsory return to the armed forces. The title-transfer theorist, on the contrary, maintains that every man has the inalienable right to control his own body and will, since he has that inalienable control in natural fact. And, therefore, that the enlistment was a mere promise, which cannot be enforceable, since every man has the right to change his mind at any time over the disposition of his body and will. Thus, seemingly minor and abstruse differences over the theory of contracts can and do imply vital differences over public policy.

In contemporary America, outside the glaring exception of the armed forces, everyone has the right to quit his job regardless of whatever promise or "contract" he had previously incurred.[3] Unfortunately, however, the courts, while refusing to compel specific personal performance of an employee agreement (in short, refusing to enslave the worker) *do prohibit* the worker from working at a similar task for another employer for the term of the agreement. If someone has signed an agreement to work as an engineer for ARAMCO for five years, and he then quits the job, he is prohibited by the courts from working for a similar employer for the remainder of the five years. It should now be clear that this prohibited employment is only one step removed from direct compulsory slavery, and that it should be completely impermissible in a libertarian society.

Have the employers, then, no recourse against the mind changer? Of course they do. They can, if they wish, voluntarily agree to blacklist the errant worker, and refuse to employ him. That is perfectly within their rights in a free society; what is *not* within their rights is to use violence to prevent him from working voluntarily for someone else. One more recourse would be permissible. Suppose that Smith, when making his agreement for lifelong voluntary obedience to the Jones Corporation, receives in exchange $1,000,000 in payment for these expected future services. Clearly, then, the Jones Corporation had transferred title to the $1,000,000 not absolutely, but *conditionally* on his performance of lifelong service. Smith has the absolute right to change his mind, but he no longer has the right to keep the $1,000,000. If he does so, he is a thief of the Jones Corporation's property; he must, therefore, be forced to return the $1,000,000 plus interest. For, of course, the title to the money was, and remains, *alienable*.

Let us take a seemingly more difficult case. Suppose that a celebrated movie actor agrees to appear at a certain theater at a certain date. For whatever reason, he fails to appear. Should he be forced to appear at that or at some future date? Certainly not, for that would be compulsory slavery. Should he be forced, at least, to recompense the theater owners for the publicity and other expenses incurred by the theater owners in anticipation of his appearance? No again, for his agreement was a mere promise concerning his inalienable will, which he has the right to change

---

3. On the importance of self-ownership and freedom of the will in forming the basis for the current judicial doctrine prohibiting the compulsion of specific performance to fulfill personal service contracts, see John Norton Pomeroy, Jr., and John C. Mann, *A Treatise on the Specific Performances of Contracts*, 3rd ed. (Albany, N.Y.: Banks, 1926), sec. 310, p. 683.

at any time. Put another way, since the movie actor has not yet received any of the theater owners' property, he has committed no theft against the owners (or against anyone else), and therefore he cannot be forced to pay damages. The fact that the theater owners may have made considerable plans and investments on the expectation that the actor would keep the agreement may be unfortunate for the owners, but that is their proper risk. The theater owners should not expect the actor to be forced to pay for their lack of foresight and poor entrepreneurship. The owners pay the penalty for placing too much confidence in the actor. It may be considered more *moral* to keep promises than to break them, but any coercive enforcement of such a moral code, since it goes beyond the prohibition of theft or assault, is *itself* an invasion of the property rights of the movie actor and therefore impermissible in the libertarian society.

Again, of course, if the actor received an *advance* payment from the theater owners, then his keeping the money while not fulfilling his part of the contract would be an implicit theft against the owners, and therefore the actor must be forced to return the money.

For utilitarians shocked at the consequences of this doctrine, it should be noted that many, if not all, of the problems could be easily surmounted in the libertarian society by the promisee's requiring a *performance bond* of the promissor in the original agreement. In short, if the theater owners wished to avoid the risk of nonappearance, they could refuse to sign the agreement unless the actor agreed to put up a performance bond in case of nonappearance. In that case, the actor, in the course of agreeing to his future appearance, agrees also to transfer a certain sum of money to the theater owners in case he fails to appear. Since money, of course, is alienable, and since such a contract would meet our title-transfer criterion, this would be a perfectly valid and enforceable contract. For what the actor would be saying is: "If I do not appear at Theater X at such and such a date, I hereby transfer as of the date the following sum _____, to the theater owners." Failure to meet the performance bond will then be an implicit theft of the property of the owners. If, then, the theater owners fail to require a performance bond as part of the agreement, then they must suffer the consequences.

Indeed, in an important article, A.W.B. Simpson has pointed out that performance bonds were the rule during the Middle Ages and in the early modern period, not only for personal services but for all contracts, including sales of land and money debts.[4] These performance bonds evolved on the market as voluntary penalty or *penal bonds*, in which

---

4. A.W.B. Simpson, "The Penal Bond With Conditional Defeasance," *Law Quarterly Review* (July 1966): 392–422.

the contractor obligated himself to pay what was usually twice the sum he owed in case of failure to pay his debt or fulfill his contract at the agreed-upon date. The voluntarily contracted penalty served as an incentive for him to fulfill his contract. Thus, if A agreed to sell a parcel of land in exchange for B's agreed upon payment of a money price, *each* would obligate himself to pay a certain sum, usually twice the value of his contractual obligation, in case of failure to pay. In the case of a money debt, called "a common money bond," someone who owed $1000 agreed to pay $2000 to the creditor if he failed to pay $1000 by a certain date. (Or, more strictly, the obligation to pay $2000 was *conditional* upon the debtor's paying $1000 by a certain date. Hence the term "conditional penal bond." In the above example of a contract to perform personal service, suppose that the failure of the actor to appear cost the theater owner $10,000 in damages; in that case, the actor would sign, or "execute," a penal performance bond, agreeing to pay $20,000 to the theater owner upon failure to appear. In this sort of contract, the theater owner is protected, and there is no improper enforcement of a mere promise. (Of course, the agreed-upon penalty does not *have* to be twice the estimated value; it can be any amount assented to by the contracting parties. The double amount became the custom in medieval and early modern Europe.)

In the course of his article, Simpson revises the orthodox historical account of the development of modern contract law: the view that the theory of *assumpsit*—of basing the enforcement of a contract upon a mere promise, albeit with consideration—was necessary to provide a workable system of contract enforcement in supplement to the crude property-rights concepts of the common law. For Simpson shows that the rise of *assumpsit* in the sixteenth and seventeenth centuries in England was *not* the result of new-found attention to the world of business contracts but rather a replacement for the rapid decline of the penal performance bond, which had served business needs well enough for centuries. Indeed, Simpson points out that the performance bond proved to be a remarkably flexible instrument for the handling of complex as well as simple contracts and agreements. And the performance bond was formal enough to guard against fraud, yet easy enough to execute for the convenience of commercial transactions. Furthermore, in its centuries of use, almost no creditors bothered to sue in the courts for "damages" (in a "writ of covenant"), since the "damages" had been fixed in advance in the contract itself. As Simpson writes:

> there are obvious attractions from a creditor's point of view in contracts which fix a penalty in advance, especially when the alternative is assessment of damages by juries.[5]

---

5. Ibid., p. 415.

But why the decline of the penal bond? Because the courts began to refuse to enforce these obligations. For whatever the reason, whether for misguided "humanitarian" or for more sinister reasons of special privilege, the courts began to balk at the toughness of the law, at the fact that they had been enforcing contracts to their full extent. For the bond meant that "for any default in performance the whole penalty was forfeit."[6] At first, during the Elizabethan era, the Courts of Chancery began intervening to relieve the debtor (the obligor) in cases of "extreme hardship." By the early seventeenth century, this relief was broadened to all cases in which misfortune befell the obligor and where he paid the contracted amount a short time later; in such cases, he only had to pay the principal (contracted amount) plus what the courts decided were "reasonable damages"—thus waiving the requirement to pay the agreed-on penalty. The intervention expanded further in later years until, finally, in the 1660s and early 1670s, the Chancery Courts simply outlawed penalty payments altogether, whatever the contract, and only required the defaulting obligor or debtor to pay the principal plus interest costs, as well as "reasonable damages" assessed by the court itself—usually by a jury. This rule was swiftly adopted by the common-law courts in the 1670s, and then formalized and regularized by statutes at the turn of the eighteenth century. Naturally, since bonded penalties were no longer enforced by the courts, the institution of the penal performance bond swiftly disappeared.

The unfortunate suppression of the performance bond was the result of a mistaken theory of contract enforcement that the courts had adopted in the first place: namely, that the purpose of enforcement was to *compensate* the creditor or obligee for the default of the debtor—i.e., to make him as well off as he would have been without the making of the contract.[7] In previous centuries, the courts had felt that "compensation" consisted of enforcing the penal bond; it then became fairly easy for the courts to change their minds, and to decide that court-assessed "damages" were compensation enough, relieving the "harshness" of the voluntarily stipulated penalty. The theory of contract enforcement should have had nothing to do with "compensation"; its purpose should always be to enforce property rights, and to guard against the implicit theft of breaking contracts which transfer titles to alienable property. Defense of property titles—and only such defense—is the business of enforcement agencies. Simpson writes perceptively of the

---

6. Ibid., p. 411.

7. For an expanded critique of the compensation concept see pp. 203–6, 238–51 below, especially the critique of Robert Nozick's *Anarchy, State, and Utopia*.

tension between two ideas. On the one hand we have the idea that the real function of contractual institutions is to make sure, so far as possible, that agreements are performed [e.g., the enforcement of the penal bond]. On the other hand we have the idea that it suffices for the law to provide compensation for loss suffered by failure to perform agreements.

The latter view places severe limits on the enthusiasm with which performance is required; moreover, in contracts for personal services (such as the actor example above), "a positive value is attached to the right to break the contract so long as the defaulting party is made to pay compensation.[8]

What of *gift*-contracts? Should they be legally enforceable? Again, the answer depends on whether a mere promise has been made, or whether an actual transfer of title has taken place in the agreement. Obviously, if A says to B, "I hereby give you $10,000," then title to the money has been transferred, and the gift is enforceable; A, furthermore, cannot later demand the money back as his right. On the other hand, if A says, "I promise to give you $10,000 in one year," then this is a mere promise, what used to be called a *nudum pactum* in Roman law, and therefore is not properly enforceable.[9] The receiver must take his chances that the donor will keep his promise. But if, on the contrary, A tells B: "I hereby agree to transfer $10,000 to you in one year's time," then this is a declared transfer of title at the future date, and should be enforceable.

It should be emphasized that this is not mere wordplay, much as it might seem so in particular cases. For the important question is always at stake: has title to alienable property been transferred, or has a mere promise been granted? In the former case, the agreement is enforceable because a failure to deliver the transferred property is

---

8. Simpson goes on to point out that while the enforcement of private, voluntarily agreed upon "penalties *in terrorem* of the party from whom performance is due" has now disappeared, the State and its courts themselves use this technique, and thus have arrogated a monopoly of such methods to themselves, e.g., in requiring bail, releasing someone on recognizance, or penalizing someone for contempt of court. Simpson, "Penal Bond," p. 420. The difference, of course, is that these state penalties are unilateral and compulsory rather than voluntarily agreed upon in advance by the obligor. All this is not to imply that the medieval courts were perfect; for one thing, they refused to enforce any contracts of money loans charging interest as committing the "sin of usury."

9. The Roman legal principle was that a "naked promise" (*nudum pactum*) could not be the subject of a legal action: *Ex nudo pacto non oritur actio.* On the *nudum pactum*, see John W. Salmond, *Jurisprudence*, 2nd ed. (London: Stevens and Haynes, 1907), p. 318; Pherozeshah N. Daruvala, *The Doctrine of Consideration* (Calcutta: Butterworth, 1914), p. 98; and Frederick Pollock, *Principles of Contract*, 12th ed., P. Winfield, ed. (London: Stevens and Sons, 1946), pp. 119–20.

theft; in the latter case, it is a mere promise which has not transferred title to property, a promise that may be morally binding, but cannot be legally binding on the promissor. Hobbes was not engaging in mere word-play when he correctly wrote:

> Words alone, if they be of the time to come, and contain a bare promise [*nudum pactum*], are an insufficient sign of a free gift and therefore not obligatory. For if they be of the time to come, as *tomorrow I will give*, they are a sign I have not yet given, and consequently that my right is not transferred, but remaineth till I transfer it by some other act. But if the words be of the time present, or past, as, *I have given*, or *do give to be delivered tomorrow*, then this is my tomorrow's right given away today. . . . There is a great difference in the signification of [the] words . . . between *I will that this be thine tomorrow*, and *I will give it thee tomorrow*: for the word *I will*, in the former manner of speech signifies a promise of an act of the will present; but in the latter, it signifies a promise of an act of the will to come: and therefore the former words, being of the present, transfer a future right; the latter, that be of the future, transfer nothing.[10]

Let us now apply the contrasting theories to a pure gift agreement, rather than an exchange. A grandfather promises to pay his grandson's way through college; after a year or two in college, the grandfather, whether from suffering business reverses or from any other reason, decides to revoke his promise. On the basis of the promise, the grandson has incurred various expenses in arranging his college career and foregoing other employment. Should the grandson be able to enforce the grandfather's promise through legal action?

In our title-transfer theory, the grandson has no right whatever to the grandfather's property, since the grandfather retained title to his money throughout. A mere naked promise can confer no title, and neither can any subjective expectations of the promisee. The costs incurred by the grandson are properly his own entrepreneurial risk. On the other hand, of course, if the grandfather transferred title, then it would be the grandson's property and he should be able to sue for his property. Such a transfer would have occurred if the grandfather had written: "I hereby transfer $8000 to you (the grandson)," *or* had written: "I hereby transfer $2000 to you at each of the following dates: 1 September 1975, 1 September 1976, etc."

On the other hand, on the expectations model of contracts, there are two possible variants: either that the grandson would have a binding legal claim on the grandfather because of the mere promise, *or* that the

---

10. Thomas Hobbes, *Leviathan*, pt. 1, chap. 14 [italics Hobbes's].

grandson would have a claim on the expenses that he had incurred on the expectation of the promise being fulfilled.[11]

Suppose, however, that the original statement of the grandfather was not a simple promise, but a conditional exchange: e.g., that the grandfather agreed to pay the grandson's full college tuition *provided that* the grandson made weekly progress reports to the grandfather. In that case, according to our title transfer theory, the grandfather has made a conditional transfer of title: agreeing to transfer title in the future provided that the grandson performed certain services. If the grandson in fact performed such services, and continues to perform them, then the tuition payment is his property and he should be legally entitled to collect from the grandfather.[12]

Under our proposed theory, would fraud be actionable at law? Yes, because fraud is failure to fulfill a voluntarily agreed upon transfer of property, and is therefore implicit theft. If, for example, A sells to B a package which A says contains a radio, and it contains only a pile of scrap metal, then A has taken B's money and not fulfilled the agreed upon conditions for such a transfer—the delivery of a radio. A has therefore stolen B's property. The same applies to a failure to fulfill any product warranty. If, for example, the seller asserts that the contents of a certain package include 5 ounces of product X, and they do not do so, then the seller has taken money without fulfilling the terms of the contract; he has in effect stolen the buyer's money. Once again, warranties of products would be legally enforceable, *not* because they are "promises," but because they describe one of the entities of the agreed-upon contract. If the entity is not as the seller describes, then fraud and hence implicit theft have taken place.[13]

Would bankruptcy laws be permissible in a libertarian legal system? Clearly not, for the bankruptcy laws compel the discharge of a debtor's

---

11. The present state of contract law is fuzzy on this kind of case. Whereas until recently a tuition promise was not actionable, it is now possible that recovery against the grandfather would be enforced for costs incurred on expectation of the promise being fulfilled. See Merton Ferson, *The Rational Basis of Contracts* (Brooklyn: Foundation Press, 1949), pp. 26–27; and Grant Gilmore, *The Death of Contract* (Columbus: Ohio State University Press, 1974), pp. 59ff.

12. See Evers, "Law of Contracts," pp. 5–6. On the other hand, as indicated above, the grandson could not be required to perform the service should he change his mind, for that would be compulsory slavery. He would be required, however, to repay the grandfather.

13. In older law, the action of deceit against the vendor of a chattel upon false warranty was, indeed, a pure action of tort (theft in our sense). James Barr Ames, "The History of Assumpsit," *Harvard Law Review* 2, no. 1 (15 April 1888): 8. For a contrasting promise view, see Roscoe Pound, *Jurisprudence* (St. Paul, Minn.: West, 1959), pp. 111, 200; and Oliver Wendell Holmes, Jr., *The Common Law*, Howe ed., (Cambridge, Mass.: Belknap Press of Harvard University Press, 1963), p. 216.

voluntarily contracted debts, and thereby invade the property rights of
the creditors. The debtor who refuses to pay his debt has stolen the property of the creditor. If the debtor is able to pay but conceals his assets, then
his clear act of theft is compounded by fraud. But even if the defaulting
debtor is not able to pay, he has *still* stolen the property of the creditor by
not making his agreed-upon delivery of the creditor's property. The function of the legal system should then be to enforce payment upon the debt-
or through, e.g., forced attachment of the debtor's future income for the
debt plus the damages and interest on the continuing debt. Bankruptcy
laws, which discharge the debt in defiance of the property rights of the
creditor, virtually confer a license to steal upon the debtor. In the pre-
modern era, the defaulting debtor was generally treated as a thief and
forced to pay as he acquired income. Doubtless the penalty of imprisonment went far beyond proportional punishment and hence was excessive,
but at least the old legal ways placed responsibility where it belonged:
on the debtor to fulfill his contractual obligations and to make the transfer
of the property owed to the creditor-owner. One historian of American
bankruptcy law, though a supporter of these laws, has conceded that
they trample on the property rights of the creditors:

> If the laws of bankruptcies were based on the legal rights of in-
> dividuals, there would be no warrant for the discharge of debt-
> ors from the payment of their debts as long as they lived, or
> their estates would continue to exist. . . . The creditor has rights
> which must not be violated even if adversity be the cause of
> the bankrupt's condition. His claims are part of his property.[14]

In defense of the bankruptcy laws, the utilitarian economist might
reply that, once these laws are on the books, the creditor knows what
may happen to him, that he compensates for that extra risk with a higher
interest rate, and that *therefore* actions under the bankruptcy law should
not be regarded as expropriation of the creditor's property. It is true that
the creditor knows the laws in advance, and that he will charge a higher
interest rate to compensate for the resulting risk. The "therefore," however, does not at all follow. Regardless of foreknowledge or forewarning,
bankruptcy laws are *still* violations and, hence, expropriations of the
property rights of the creditors. There are all sorts of situations on the

---

14. F. Regis Noel, "A History of the Bankruptcy Clause of the Constitution of the United
States of America" (Washington: doctoral dissertation, Catholic University of America,
1920), pp. 187, 191. Noel goes on to assert that the creditor's rights must be overridden
by "public policy," the "common good," and the "paramount rights of the community,"
whatever these may be. Quoted by Lawrence H. White, "Bankruptcy and Risk" (not
published), p. 13.

market where prospective victims may be able to maneuver so as to minimize the harm to themselves of institutionalized theft. The theft is no more moral or legitimate because of such praiseworthy maneuvering.

Moreover, the same utilitarian argument could be used about such crimes as mugging or burglary. Instead of deploring crime against store-keepers in certain sections of a city, we might then argue (as utilitarian economists) as follows: after all, the storekeepers knew what they were doing in advance. Before they opened the store, they knew of the higher crime rate at that location and were therefore able to adjust their insurance and their business practices accordingly. Should we say, therefore, that robbery of storekeepers is not to be deplored or even outlawed?[15]

In short, crime is crime, and invasions of property are invasions of property. Why should those farseeing property owners who took some advance measures to alleviate the effects of prospective crime be penalized by being deprived of a legal defense of their justly owned property? Why should the law penalize the virtue of forethought?

The problem of defaulting debtors may be met in another way: the creditor, taking account of the debtor's honest attempts to pay, may voluntarily decide to forgive part or all of the debt. Here it is important to stress that in a libertarian system which defends property rights, each creditor may forgive only *his own* debt, may only surrender his own property claims to the debtor. There can then be no legal situation in which a majority of creditors compel a minority to "forgive" their own claims.

Voluntary forgiveness of a debt may occur after the fact of default, *or* it may be incorporated *into the original* debt contract. In that case, A could lend B $1000 now, in exchange for $1000 a year from now, *provided that*, given certain conditions of unavoidable insolvency, A would forgive B part or all of that debt. Presumably, A would charge a higher interest rate to compensate for the additional risk of failure. But the important point is that in these legitimate situations of forgiveness, the discharge of debt has been *voluntarily* agreed upon, either in the original agreement or after default, by the individual creditor.

Voluntary forgiveness takes on the legal-philosophical status of a gift by the creditor to the debtor. Oddly enough, while title-transfer theorists see such a gift as a perfectly legitimate and valid agreement to transfer title to money from a creditor to a debtor, current legal doctrine has questioned the validity of such an agreement to forgive as a binding contract. For, in current theory, a binding contract must be a promise exchanged for a "consideration," and in the case of forgiveness, the creditor receives no consideration in exchange. But the title-transfer principle

15. I owe this example to Dr. Walter Block.

sees no problems with forgiveness: "The creditor's act by way of releasing a claim is of the same kind as an ordinary act of transfer. In either case the act is simply the manifested consent of the owner of the right."[16]

Another important point: in our title-transfer model, a person should be able to sell *not only* the full title of ownership to property, but also part of that property, retaining the rest for himself or others to whom he grants or sells that part of the title. Thus, as we have seen above, common-law copyright is justified as the author or publisher selling all rights to his property *except* the right to resell it. Similarly valid and enforceable would be restrictive covenants to property in which, for example, a developer sells all the rights to a house and land to a purchaser, *except* for the right to build a house over a certain height or of other than a certain design. The only proviso is that there must, at every time, be *some* existing owner or owners of *all* the rights to any given property. In the case of a restrictive covenant, for example, there must be *some* owners of the reserved right to build a tall building; if not the developer himself, then someone who has bought or received this right. If the reserved right has been abandoned, and no existing person possesses it, then the owner of the house may be considered to have "homesteaded" this right, and can then go ahead and build the tall build-ing. Covenants and other restrictions, in short, cannot simply "run with the property" forever, thereby overriding the wishes of *all* living owners of that property.

This proviso rules out *entail* as an enforceable right. Under entail, a property owner could bequeath this land to his sons and grandsons, with the proviso that *no future* owner could sell the land outside the family (a deed typical of feudalism). But this would mean that the living owners *could not* sell the property; they would be governed by the dead hand of the past. But *all* rights to any property must be in the hands of living, existing persons. It might be considered a moral requirement for the descendants to keep the land in the family, but it cannot properly be considered a legal obligation. Property rights must only be accorded to and can only be enjoyed by the living.

There is at least one case in which the "promised expectations" model is in grave internal contradiction, depending upon whether one stresses the "promise" or the "expectations" part of the theory. This is the legal problem of whether "purchase breaks hire." Thus, suppose that Smith owns a tract of land; he leases the land for five years to Jones. Smith, however, now sells the land to Robinson. Is Robinson bound to obey the terms of the

---

16. Ferson, *The Rational Basis of Contracts*, p. 159. On the absurd consequence of current contract theory in questioning the validity of voluntary forgiveness, see Gilmore, *The Death of Contract*, p. 33.

lease, or can he oust Jones immediately? On the promise theory, only Smith made the promise to lease the land; Robinson did not so promise, and therefore Robinson is not bound to respect the lease. On the expectations theory, the lease agreement generated expectations in Jones that the land would be his for five years. Therefore, on the former grounds, purchase breaks hire, whereas it cannot do so on the expectations model. The title-transfer theory, however, avoids this problem. On our model, Jones, the leaseholder, owns the use of the property for the contractual period of the lease; five years of property use has been transferred to Jones. Therefore Robinson cannot break the lease (unless, of course, the breaking of hire under such conditions was expressly included as a provision in the lease).

There is one vitally important political implication of our title-transfer theory, as against the promise theory of valid and enforceable contracts. It should be clear that the title-transfer theory immediately tosses out of court all variants of the "social contract" theory as a justification for the State. Setting aside the historical problem of whether such a social contract ever took place, it should be evident that the social contract, whether it be the Hobbesian surrender of all one's rights, the Lockean surrender of the right of self-defense, or any other, was a mere promise of future behavior (future will) and in no way surrendered title to alienable property. Certainly no past promise can bind later generations, let alone the actual maker of the promise.[17]

The current law of contracts is an inchoate mixture of the title-transfer and the promise-expectations approaches, with the expectations model predominating under the influence of nineteenth- and twentieth-century legal positivism and pragmatism. A libertarian, natural-rights, property-rights theory must therefore reconstitute contract law on the proper title-transfer basis.[18]

---

17. As Rousseau states, "Even if a man can alienate himself, he cannot alienate his children. They are born free, their liberty belongs to them, and no one but themselves has a right to dispose of it . . . for to alienate another's liberty is contrary to the natural order, and is an abuse of the father's rights." Rousseau in Barker, ed., *Social Contract*, pp. 174–75. And, four decades before Rousseau, in the early 1720s, the libertarian English writers John Trenchard and Thomas Gordon, in their *Cato's Letters*—widely influential in forming the attitudes of the American colonies—wrote as follows:

> All men are born free; liberty is a gift which they receive from God himself; nor can they alienate the same by consent, though possibly they may forfeit it by crimes. No man . . . can . . . give away the lives and liberties, religion or acquired property of his posterity, who will be born as free as he himself was born, and can never be bound by his wicked and ridiculous bargain.

Cato's Letters, no. 59, in D. L. Jacobson, ed., *The English Libertarian Heritage* (Indianapolis, Ind.: Bobbs-Merrill, 1965), p. 108.

18. The current requirement that there must be "consideration" for a promise to be enforceable is a philosophically confused injection of title-transfer principles into

the law of contracts. See Edward Jenks, *The History of the Doctrine of Consideration in English Law* (London: C.J. Clay and Sons, 1892), chap. 3. Contracts as enforceable promises entered English law by way of Church canon law, and the customary law merchant, as well as by the post-Norman Conquest doctrine of *assumpsit*. *Assumpsit* enforced such allegedly implied "promises" as innkeepers or common carriers in accepting customers. On *assumpsit*, see Jenks, *History of Doctrine of Consideration*, pp. 124–25; and James Barr Ames, "History of Assumpsit," in *Selected Readings on the Law of Contracts* (New York: Macmillan, 1931) pp. 37–40.

The pre-Norman Conquest law of England was on a property rights, title-transfer basis. Essentially, every debt was considered a bailment for a specific set of chattels. One problem with this variant is that people are not able to agree *now* to assign title to goods at some future date; as a result, creditors did not have a lien on debtors' future assets if the latter had no money to pay at the time of default. Moreover, the sole emphasis on *physical possession* of the property meant that the pre-Conquest English notion of "title" to property was highly defective. Thus, after a sale contract had been concluded, the seller, under that notion, did not have the right to sue for the money-price (since it had not been a previous physical possession of the seller and therefore could not be construed as a bailment, although the buyer could sue for delivery of the goods). It was partly because of such primitive defects in pre-Conquest contract theory that the promise model was able to take hold. Although see also the decline of the penal bond, pp. 139–40 above. See Robert L. Henry, *Contracts in the Local Courts of Medieval England* (London: Longmans, Green, 1926), pp. 238–41, 245. Also see Jenks, *History of the Doctrine of Consideration*, pp. 115–18; Frederick Pollock, "Contracts," *Encyclopedia Britannica*, 14th ed. (1929), vol. 6, pp. 339–40; Ames, "The History of Assumpsit," pp. 55–57; Ferson, *The Rational Basis of Contracts*, p. 121; and especially Evers, "Law of Contracts," pp. 1–2.

On views of debt in other cultures similar to those of pre-Conquest England, see Max Gluckman, *The Ideas in Barotse Jurisprudence* (New Haven, Conn.: Yale University Press, 1965), pp. 177, 182–83, 198; John D. Mayne, *Treatise on Hindu Law and Usage*, 11th ed., N.C. Aiyar, ed. (Madras: Higginbothams, 1953), pp. 395–447; Daruvala, *The Doctrine of Consideration*, p. 270; and E. Allan Farnsworth, "The Past of Promise: An Historical Introduction to Contract," *Columbia Law Review* 69, no. 4 (April 1969): 587.

Immanuel Kant, in contrast to numerous utilitarian and pragmatist philosophers, attempted to derive contract theory from a transfer rather than a promise basis. Immanuel Kant, *The Philosophy of Law: An Exposition of The Fundamental Principles of Jurisprudence as the Science of Right* (Edinburgh: T. and T. Clark, 1887), p. 101. Unfortunately, however, Kant's position had two major defects. First, he assumed that the voluntary transfers of property must take place within a framework of obedience to an imposed general will of civil society. But free choice and such civil obedience are inherently contradictory. And second, Kant emphasized that contracts are voluntary when the subjective mental states of the contracting parties are in agreement. But how can courts determine the subjective mental states of the parties to an agreement? Far better for libertarian contract theory is to hold that when two parties act to transfer titles, and neither is under threat of physical violence, then the contract is thereby revealed as voluntary, consensual, and valid. In short, consent by both parties is determined by observing actions under non-coercive conditions. See *Hallock v. Commercial Insurance Co.*, 26 N.J.L. 268 (1857); William Anson, *Principles of the English Law of Contract*, 2nd ed. (1882), p. 13; and Samuel Williston, "Mutual Assent in the Formation of Contracts," *Selected Readings on the Law of Contracts* (New York: Macmillan, 1931), pp. 119–27.

20. Lifeboat Situations

It is often contended that the existence of extreme, or "lifeboat," situations disproves any theory of absolute property rights, or indeed of any absolute rights of self-ownership whatsoever. It is claimed that since any theory of individual rights seems to break down or works unsatisfactorily in such fortunately rare situations, therefore there can be no concept of inviolable rights at all. In a typical lifeboat situation, there are, let us say, eight places in a lifeboat putting out from a sinking ship, and there are more than eight people wishing to be saved. Who then is to decide who should be saved and who should die? And what then happens to the right of self-ownership, or, as some people phrase it, the "right to life"? (The "right to life" is fallacious phraseology, since it could imply that A's "right to life" can justly involve an infringement on the life and property of someone else, i.e., on B's "right to life" and its logical extensions. A "right to self-ownership" of both A and B avoids such confusions.)

In the first place, a lifeboat situation is hardly a valid test of a theory of rights, or of any moral theory whatsoever. Problems of a moral theory in such an extreme situation do not invalidate a theory for normal situations. In any sphere of moral theory, we are trying to frame an ethic for man, based on his nature and the nature of the world—and this precisely means for normal nature, for the way life usually is, and not for rare and abnormal situations. It is a wise maxim of the law, for precisely this reason, that "hard cases make bad law." We are trying to frame an ethic for the way men generally live in the world; we are not, after all, interested in framing an ethic that focuses on situations that are rare, extreme, and *not* generally encountered.[1]

Let us take an example, to illustrate our point, outside the sphere of property rights or rights in general, and within the sphere of ordinary

---

1. A pragmatic point related to the rarity of the lifeboat case is that, as we know from economic science, a regime of property rights and the free-market economy would lead to a *minimum* of "lifeboat situations"—a minimum of cases where more than one person is battling over a scarce resource for survival. A free-market, property-rights economy raises the standard of living of all persons, and ever widens their sphere and range of choice—thereby harmonizing liberty and abundance, and rendering such extreme situations as negligible as humanly possible. But this sort of utilitarian argument, we must recognize, does not fully answer the questions of right and justice. For a sardonic protest against the use of grossly abnormal examples in moral philosophy, see G.E.M. Anscombe, "Does Oxford Moral Philosophy Corrupt the Youth?" *The Listener* (14 February 1957): 267.

ethical values. Most people would concede the principle that "it is ethical for a parent to save his child from drowning." But, then, our lifeboat skeptic could arise and hurl this challenge: "Aha, but suppose that two of your children are drowning and you can save only one. Which child would you choose? And doesn't the fact that you would *have* to let one child die negate the very moral principle that you *should* save your drowning child?" I doubt whether many ethicists would throw over the moral desirability or principle of saving one's child because it could not be fully applied in such a "lifeboat" situation. Yet why should the lifeboat case be different in the sphere of rights?

In a lifeboat situation, indeed, we apparently have a war of all against all, and there seems at first to be no way to apply our theory of self-ownership or of property rights. But, in the example cited, the reason is because the property right has so far been ill-defined. For the vital question here is: *who owns* the lifeboat? If the owner of the boat or his representative (e. g. the captain of the ship) has died in the wreck, *and* if he has not laid down known rules in advance of the wreck for allocation of seats in such a crisis,[2] then the lifeboat may be considered—at least temporarily for the emergency— abandoned and therefore *unowned*. At this point, our rules for unowned property come into play: namely, that unowned resources become the property of the first people possessing them. In short, the first eight people to reach the boat are, in our theory, the proper "owners" and users of the boat. Anyone who throws them out of the boat then commits an act of aggression in violating the property right of the "homesteader" he throws out of the boat. After he returns to shore, then, the aggressor becomes liable for prosecution for his act of violation of property right (as well, perhaps, for murder of the person he ejected from the boat).

Doesn't this homesteading principle sanction a mad scramble for the seats in the lifeboat? Scramble perhaps; but it should be pointed out that the scramble must not, of course, be violent, since any physical force used against another to keep him from homesteading is an act of criminal assault against him, and aggression may not be used to establish a homestead right (just as one would-be homesteader may not use force to prevent someone else from getting to a piece of land first).

To those who believe that such a homesteading principle is unduly harsh, we may reply (a) that we are *already* in an intolerably harsh and fortunately rare situation where *no* solution is going to be humane or comforting; and (b) that *any other* principle of allocation would be truly

---

2. If he *has* laid down such advance rules, then those rules for deciding on the use of his property—the lifeboat—must apply. I owe this point to Mr. Williamson M. Evers.

intolerable. The time-honored principle of "women and children first" is surely morally intolerable; by what principle of justice do men have inferior rights to life or self-ownership than women or children? The same is true of the view that the "superior" minds should be saved at the expense of the "inferior"; aside from the staggering objection of *who* is going to decide on who is superior or inferior, and by what criterion, this view implies that the "superior" have a right to live at the expense of the "inferior," and this violates any concept of equal rights and renders any ethic for mankind impossible.[3]

A far clearer outcome of the lifeboat case occurs where the owner or his representative still survives or has laid down rules for allocation in advance. For, in that case, our theory states that the *right* to allocate spaces in the lifeboat belongs to the owner of the boat. He may choose to carry out that allocation in various ways: whether by first come-first served, women and children first, or whatever. But though we may disagree with the morality of his criteria, we must concede his *right* to make the allocation in whatever way he wishes. Again, any forcible interference with such owner's allocation, e.g., by throwing people out of their allocated spaces, is at the very least an act of invasion of property right for which the aggressor may be repelled on the spot, and for which the aggressor would later be liable for prosecution. Our theory of absolute property right is therefore the most satisfactory—or , at the very minimum, the least unsatisfactory—way out of the tragic lifeboat example.

An even starker version of the "lifeboat" case—and one where there is no question of someone's prior ownership of the lifeboat—occurs when (to cite an example mentioned by Professor Eric Mack) two shipwrecked men are battling over a plank that can only support one. Does the concept

---

3. In 1884, a British court rejected the plea of "necessity" by which the defense sought to justify the murder and cannibalism of a shipwrecked boy by several of his adult companions. The judge, Lord Coleridge, asked:

Who is to be the judge of this sort of necessity? By what measure is the comparative value of lives to be measured? Is it to be strength or intellect or what? It is plain that the principle leaves to him who is to profit by it to determine the necessity which will justify him in deliberately taking another's life to save his own.

The Queen v. Dudley and Stephens, 14 Q.B.D. 273 (1884), quoted in John A. Robertson, "Involuntary Euthanasia of Defective Newborns: A Legal Analysis," *Stanford Law Review* (January 1975): 241. On the other hand, in a previous Pennsylvania case in 1842, *United States v. Holmes,* the court proposed to justify the murder of people in a lifeboat if the victims were chosen "by a fair procedure, such as lot." Why blind chance should be particularly "fair" was not adequately explained. 26 F. Cas. 360 (No. 15,383) (C.C.E.D. Pa. 1842). See ibid., pp. 240–41, 243n. For an interesting though inconclusive discussion clearly based on these two cases, see Lon L. Fuller, "The Case of the Speluncean Explorers," *Harvard Law Review* (February 1949): 616–45.

of aggression and property right apply even here? Yes, for again, our homestead principle of property right comes into play: i.e., the first person who reaches the plank "owns" it for the occasion, and the second person throwing him off is at the very least a violator of the former's property and perhaps also liable for prosecution for an act of murder. Again, neither of the persons may use force against the other in preventing the latter from reaching the plank, for this would be an act of physical aggression against his person.[4]

It may well be objected to our theory as follows: that a theory of property rights or even of self-ownership is derivable from the conditions by which man survives and flourishes in this world, and that therefore in this kind of extreme situation, where a man is faced with the choice of *either* saving himself *or* violating the property rights of the lifeboat owner (or, in the above example, of the "homesteader" in the boat), it is then ridiculous to expect him to surrender his life on behalf of the abstract principle of property rights. Because of this kind of consideration, many libertarians who otherwise believe in property rights gravely weaken them on behalf of the "contextualist" contention that, given a choice between his life and aggressing against someone else's property or even life, it is moral for him to commit the aggression *and* that therefore in such a situation, these property rights cease to exist. The error here on the part of the "contextualist" libertarians is to confuse the question of the *moral* course of action for the person in such a tragic situation with the totally separate question of whether or not his seizing of lifeboat or plank space by force constitutes an invasion of someone else's property right. For we are not, in constructing a theory of liberty and property, i.e., a "political" ethic, concerned with all *personal* moral principles. We are not herewith concerned whether it is moral or immoral for someone to lie, to be a good person, to develop his faculties, or be kind or mean to his neighbors. We are concerned, in this sort of discussion, solely with such "political ethical" questions as the proper role of violence, the sphere of rights, or the definitions of criminality and aggression. Whether or not it is moral or immoral for "Smith"—the fellow excluded by the owner from the plank or the lifeboat—to force someone else out of the lifeboat, or whether he *should* die heroically instead, is not our concern, and not the proper concern of a theory of political ethics.[5]

---

4. For a critique of the sort of "contextualism" employed by Mack in this example, see immediately below. Cf. Eric Mack, "Individualism, Rights, and the Open Society," in Tibor Machan, ed., *The Libertarian Alternative* (Chicago: Nelson-Hall, 1974), pp. 29–31.

5. Moreover, Eric Mack's example fails to show a necessary conflict between property rights and moral principles. The conflict in his example is between property rights and the dictates of prudence or self-interest. But the latter is only dominant in morality if one

The crucial point is that *even* if the contextualist libertarian may say that, given the tragic context, Smith *should* throw someone else out of the lifeboat to save his own life, he is *still* committing, at the very least, invasion of property rights, and probably also murder of the person thrown out. So that even if one says that he should try to save his life by forcibly grabbing a seat in the lifeboat, he is still, in our view, liable to prosecution as a criminal invader of property right, and perhaps as a murderer as well. After he is convicted, it would be the *right* of the lifeboat owner or the heir of the person tossed out to forgive Smith, to pardon him because of the unusual circumstances; but it would also be their right *not* to pardon and to proceed with the full force of their legal right to punish. Once again, we are concerned in this theory with the rights of the case, *not* with whether or not a person chooses voluntarily to exercise his rights. In our view, the property owner or the heir of the killed would have a right to prosecute and to exact proper punishment upon the aggressor. The fallacy of the contextualists is to confuse considerations of individual, personal morality (what should Smith do?) with the question of the rights of the case. The right of property continues, then, to be absolute, even in the tragic lifeboat situation.

Furthermore, if the lifeboat owner, Jones, is being aggressed against by Smith, and has the right to prosecute Smith later on, he therefore also has the right to use force to repel Smith's aggression on the spot. Should Smith try to use force to pre-empt a spot on the lifeboat, Jones, or his hired defense agent, certainly has the right to use physical force to repel Smith's act of invasion.[6]

To sum up the application of our theory to extreme situations: if a man aggresses against another's person or property to save his own life, he may or may not be acting morally in so doing. That is none of our particular concern in this work. Regardless of whether his action is moral or immoral, by any criterion, he is *still* a criminal aggressor against the property of another, and the victim is within his right to repel that aggression by force, and to prosecute the aggressor afterward for his crime.

---

adopts moral egoism, which indeed Professor Mack does, but which is only one possible moral theory.

6. Professor Herbert Morris takes a similar view of rights. Speaking of the concept of rights in general rather than merely in lifeboat situations, Morris defends the idea that rights must be absolute rather than merely a *prima facie* presumption; in those cases where it might perhaps be considered moral from a personal point of view to invade someone's rights, the point to stress is that those rights are nevertheless *invaded,* and that that infringement is therefore subject to punishment. See Herbert Morris, "Persons and Punishment," *The Monist* (October 1968): 475–501, esp. pp. 497ff.

21. The "Rights" of Animals

I t has lately become a growing fashion to extend the concept of rights from human beings to animals, and to assert that since animals have the full rights of humans, it is therefore impermissible—i.e., that no man has the right—to kill or eat them.

There are, of course, many difficulties with this position, including arriving at some criterion of *which* animals or living beings to include in the sphere of rights and which to leave out. (There are not many theorists, for example, who would go so far as Albert Schweitzer and deny the right of anyone to step on a cockroach. And, if the theory were extended further from conscious living beings to *all* living beings, such as bacteria or plants, the human race would rather quickly die out.)

But the fundamental flaw in the theory of animal rights is more basic and far-reaching.[1] For the assertion of human rights is not properly a simple emotive one; individuals possess rights *not* because we "feel" that they should, but because of a rational inquiry into the nature of man and the universe. In short, man has rights because they are *natural* rights. They are grounded in the nature of man: the individual man's capacity for conscious choice, the necessity for him to use his mind and energy to adopt goals and values, to find out about the world, to pursue his ends in order to survive and prosper, his capacity and need to communicate and interact with other human beings and to participate in the division of labor. In short, man is a rational and social animal. No other animals or beings possess this ability to reason, to make conscious choices, to transform their environment in order to prosper, or to collaborate consciously in society and the division of labor.

Thus, while natural rights, as we have been emphasizing, are absolute, there is *one* sense in which they are relative: they are relative *to the species man*. A rights-ethic for mankind is precisely that: for all men, regardless of race, creed, color or sex, but for the species man alone. The Biblical story was insightful to the effect that man was "given" or,—in natural

---

1. For an attack upon the supposed rights of animals, see Peter Geach, *Providence and Evil* (Cambridge: Cambridge University Press, 1977), pp. 79–80; and Peter Geach, *The Virtues* (Cambridge: Cambridge University Press, 1977), p. 19.

law, we may say "has"—dominion over all the species of the earth. Natural law is necessarily species-bound.

That the concept of a species ethic is part of the nature of the world may be seen, moreover, by contemplating the activities of other species in nature. It is more than a jest to point out that *animals*, after all, don't respect the "rights" of other animals; it is the condition of the world, and of all natural species, that they live by eating other species. Inter-species survival is a matter of tooth and claw. It would surely be absurd to say that the wolf is "evil" because he exists by devouring and "aggressing against" lambs, chickens, etc. The wolf is not an evil being who "aggresses against" other species; he is simply following the natural law of his own survival. Similarly for man. It is just as absurd to say that men "aggress against" cows and wolves as to say that wolves "aggress against" sheep. If, furthermore, a wolf attacks a man and the man kills him, it would be absurd to say either that the wolf was an "evil aggressor" or that the wolf was being "punished" for his "crime." And yet such would be the implications of extending a natural-rights ethic to animals. Any concept of rights, of criminality, of aggression, can *only* apply to actions of one man or group of men against other human beings.

What of the "Martian" problem? If we should ever discover and make contact with beings from other planets, could *they* be said to have the rights of human beings? It would depend on their nature. If our hypothetical "Martians" were like human beings—conscious, rational, able to communicate with us and participate in the division of labor, then presumably they too would possess the rights now confined to "earthbound" humans.[2] But suppose, on the other hand, that the Martians also had the characteristics, the nature, of the legendary vampire, and could only exist by feeding on human blood. In that case, regardless of their intelligence, the Martians would be our deadly enemy and we could not consider that they were entitled to the rights of humanity. Deadly enemy, again, not because they were wicked aggressors, but because of the needs and requirements of their nature, which would clash ineluctably with ours.

There is, in fact, rough justice in the common quip that "we will recognize the rights of animals whenever they petition for them." The fact that animals can obviously *not* petition for their "rights" is part of

---

2. Cf. the brief discussion of man and comparable creatures in John Locke,, *An Essay Concerning Human Understanding* (New York: Collier-Macmillan, 1965), p. 291.

their nature, and part of the reason why they are clearly not equivalent to, and do not possess the rights of, human beings.[3] And if it be protested that babies can't petition either, the reply of course is that babies are future human adults, whereas animals obviously are not.[4]

---

3. For the close connection between the use of language and the human species, see Ludwig Wittgenstein, *Philosophical Investigations* (New York: Macmillan, 1958), vol. 2, pp. xi, 223.

4. A fundamental error, then, of the advocates of "animal rights" is their failure to identify—or even to *attempt* to identify—the specific *nature* of the species man, and hence the differences between human beings and other species. Failing to think in such terms, they fall back on the shifting sands of subjective feelings. See Tibor R. Machan, *Human Rights and Human Liberties* (Chicago: Nelson-Hall, 1975), pp. 202–3, 241, 245ff., 256, 292. For a critique of the confusion between babies and animals by animal-rightists, see R.G. Frey, *Interests and Rights* (Oxford: Clarendon Press, 1980), pp. 22ff. Frey's book is a welcome recent critique of the animal-rights vogue in philosophy.

PART III:
THE STATE VERSUS LIBERTY

22. The Nature of the State

So far in this book, we have developed a theory of liberty and property rights, and have outlined the legal code that would be necessary to defend those rights. What of government, the State? What is its proper role, if any? Most people, including most political theorists, believe that once one concedes the importance, or even the vital necessity, of *some particular* activity of the State—such as the provision of a legal code—that one has *ipso facto* conceded the necessity of the State itself. The State indeed performs many important and necessary functions: from provision of law to the supply of police and fire fighters, to building and maintaining the streets, to delivery of the mail. But this in no way demonstrates that *only* the State can perform such functions, or, indeed, that it performs them even passably well.

Suppose, for example, that there are many competing cantaloupe stores in a particular neighborhood. One of the cantaloupe dealers, Smith, then uses violence to drive all of his competitors out of the neighborhood; he has thereby employed violence to establish a coerced monopoly over the sale of cantaloupes in a given territorial area. Does that mean that Smith's use of violence to establish and maintain his monopoly was *essential* to the provision of cantaloupes in the neighborhood? Certainly not, for there were existing competitors as well as potential rivals should Smith ever relax his use and threat of violence; moreover, economics demonstrates that Smith, as a coercive monopolist will tend to perform his service badly and inefficiently. Protected from competition by the use of force, Smith can afford to provide his service in a costly and inefficient manner, since the consumers are deprived of any possible range of alternative choice.[1] Furthermore, should a group arise to call for the abolition of Smith's coercive monopoly, there would be very few protesters with the temerity to accuse these "abolitionists" of wishing to deprive the consumers of their much desired cantaloupes.

And yet, the State is only our hypothetical Smith on a gigantic and all-encompassing scale. Throughout history, groups of men calling themselves "the government" or "the State" have attempted—usually successfully—to gain a compulsory monopoly of the commanding heights of

---

1. See Murray N. Rothbard, *Power and Market*, 2nd ed. (Kansas City: Sheed Andrews and McMeel, 1977), pp. 172–81; Murray N. Rothbard, *For a New Liberty*, rev. ed. (New York: Macmillan, 1978), pp. 194–201.

the economy and the society. In particular, the State has arrogated to itself a compulsory monopoly over police and military services, the provision of law, judicial decision-making, the mint and the power to create money, unused land ("the public domain"), streets and highways, rivers and coastal waters, and the means of delivering mail. Control of land and transportation has long been an excellent method of assuring overall control of a society; in many countries, highways began as a means of allowing the government to move its troops conveniently throughout its subject country. Control of the money supply is a way to assure the State an easy and rapid revenue, and the State makes sure that no private competitors are allowed to invade its self-arrogated monopoly of the power to counterfeit (i.e. create) new money. Monopoly of the postal service has long been a convenient method for the State to keep an eye on possibly unruly and subversive opposition to its rule. In most historical epochs, the State has also kept a tight control over religion, usually cementing a comfortable, mutually-supportive alliance with an Established Church: with the State granting the priests power and wealth, and the Church in turn teaching the subject population their divinely proclaimed duty to obey Caesar. But now that religion has lost much of its persuasive power in society, the State is often willing to let religion alone, and to concentrate on similar if looser alliances with more secular intellectuals. In either case, the State relies on control of the levers of propaganda to persuade its subjects to obey or even exalt their rulers.

But, above all, the crucial monopoly is the State's control of the use of violence: of the police and armed services, and of the courts—the locus of ultimate decision-making power in disputes over crimes and contracts. Control of the police and the army is particularly important in enforcing and assuring all of the State's other powers, including the all-important power to extract its revenue by coercion.

For there is one crucially important power inherent in the nature of the State apparatus. *All other* persons and groups in society (except for acknowledged and sporadic criminals such as thieves and bank robbers) obtain their income voluntarily: *either* by selling goods and services to the consuming public, *or* by voluntary gift (e.g., membership in a club or association, bequest, or inheritance). *Only* the State obtains its revenue by coercion, by threatening dire penalties should the income not be forthcoming. That coercion is known as "taxation," although in less regularized epochs it was often known as "tribute." Taxation is theft, purely and simply, even though it is theft on a grand and colossal scale which no acknowledged criminals could hope to match. It is a compulsory seizure of the property of the State's inhabitants, or subjects.

It would be an instructive exercise for the skeptical reader to try to frame a definition of taxation which does not *also* include theft. Like the robber, the State demands money at the equivalent of gunpoint; if the taxpayer refuses to pay, his assets are seized by force, and if he should resist such depredation, he will be arrested or shot if he should continue to resist. It is true that State apologists maintain that taxation is "really" voluntary; one simple but instructive refutation of this claim is to ponder what would happen if the government were to abolish taxation, and to confine itself to simple requests for voluntary contributions. Does anyone *really* believe that anything comparable to the current vast revenues of the State would continue to pour into its coffers? It is likely that even those theorists who claim that punishment never deters action would balk at such a claim. The great economist Joseph Schumpeter was correct when he acidly wrote that "the theory which construes taxes on the analogy of club dues or of the purchase of the services of, say, a doctor only proves how far removed this part of the social sciences is from scientific habits of mind."[2]

It has been recently maintained by economists that taxation is "really" voluntary because it is a method for everyone to make sure that everyone else pays for a unanimously desired project. Everyone in an area, for example, is assumed to desire the government to build a dam; but if A and B contribute voluntarily to the project, they cannot be sure that C and D will not "shirk" their similar responsibilities. Therefore, all of the individuals, A, B, C, D, etc., each of whom wish to contribute to building the dam, *agree* to coerce each other through taxation. Hence, the tax is not *really* coercion. There are, however, a great many flaws in this doctrine.

First is the inner contradiction between voluntarism and coercion; a coercion of all-against-all does not make any of this coercion "voluntary." Secondly, even if we assume for the moment that each individual would like to contribute to the dam, there is no way of assuring that the tax levied on each person is no more than he would be willing to pay voluntarily even if everyone else contributed. The government may levy $1000 on Jones even though he might have been willing to pay no more than $500. The point is that *precisely because* taxation is compulsory, there is no way to assure (as is done automatically on the free market) that the amount any person contributes is what he would "really" be willing to pay. In the free society, a consumer who voluntarily buys a TV set for $200

2. Joseph A. Schumpeter, *Capitalism, Socialism, and Democracy* (New York: Harper and Brothers, 1942), p. 198.

demonstrates by his freely chosen action that the TV set is worth more to him than the $200 he surrenders; in short, he demonstrates that the $200 is a voluntary payment. Or, a club member in the free society, by paying annual dues of $200, demonstrates that he considers the benefits of club membership worth at least $200. But, in the case of taxation, a man's surrender to the threat of coercion demonstrates no voluntary preference whatsoever for any alleged benefits he receives.

Thirdly, the argument proves far too much. For the supply of *any* service, not only dams, can be expanded by the use of the tax-financing arm. Suppose, for example, that the Catholic Church were established in a country through taxation; the Catholic Church would undoubtedly be larger than if it relied on voluntary contributions; but can it therefore be argued that such Establishment is "really" voluntary because everyone wants to coerce everyone else into paying into the Church, in order to make sure that no one shirks this "duty"?

And fourthly, the argument is simply a mystical one. How can anyone *know* that everyone is "really" paying his taxes voluntarily on the strength of this sophistical argument? What of those people— environmentalists, say—who are opposed to dams *per se*? Is their payment "really" voluntary? Would the coerced payment of taxes to a Catholic Church by Protestants or atheists *also* be "voluntary"? And what of the growing body of libertarians in our society, who oppose all action by the government on principle? In what way can this argument hold that *their* tax payments are "really voluntary"? In fact, the existence of at least *one* libertarian or anarchist in a country is enough *by itself to* demolish the "really voluntary" argument for taxation.

It is also contended that, in democratic governments, the act of *voting* makes the government and all its works and powers truly "voluntary." Again, there are many fallacies with this popular argument. In the first place, even if the majority of the public specifically endorsed each and every particular act of the government, this would simply be majority tyranny rather than a voluntary act undergone by every person in the country. Murder is murder, theft is theft, whether undertaken by one man against another, or by a group, or even by the majority of people within a given territorial area. The fact that a majority might support or condone an act of theft does not diminish the criminal essence of the act or its grave injustice. Otherwise, we would have to say, for example, that any Jews murdered by the democratically elected Nazi government were *not* murdered, but only "voluntarily committed suicide"—surely, the grotesque but logical implication of the "democracy as voluntary" doctrine. Secondly, in a republic as contrasted to a direct democracy, people vote not for specific measures but for "representatives" in a package deal; the representatives then wreak their will for a fixed length of time. In no legal sense, of course, are they truly "representatives" since, in a free society, the principal hires his agent or representative individually and can fire him at will. As the great anarchist political theorist and constitutional lawyer, Lysander Spooner, wrote:

> they [the elected government officials] are neither our servants, agents, attorneys, nor representatives . . . [for] we do not make ourselves responsible for their acts. If a man is my servant, agent, or attorney, I necessarily make myself responsible for all his acts done within the limits of the power I have intrusted to him. If I have intrusted him, as my agent, with either absolute power, or any power at all, over the persons or properties of other men than myself, I thereby necessarily make myself responsible to those other persons for any injuries he may do them, so long as he acts within the limits of the power I have granted him. But no individual who may be injured in his person or property, by acts of Congress, can come to the individual electors, and hold them responsible for these acts of their so-called agents or representatives. This fact proves that these pretended agents of the people, of everybody, are really the agents of nobody.[3]

Furthermore, even on its own terms, voting can hardly establish "majority" rule, much less of voluntary endorsement of government. In the United States, for example, less than 40 percent of eligible voters bother to vote at all; of these, 21 percent may vote for one candidate and 19 percent for another. 21 percent scarcely establishes even majority rule, much less the voluntary consent of all. (In *one* sense, and quite apart from democracy or voting, the "majority" always supports any existing government; this will be treated below.) And finally, how is it that taxes are levied on one and all, regardless of whether they voted or not, or, more particularly, whether they voted for the winning candidate? How can either nonvoting or voting for the loser indicate any sort of endorsement of the actions of the elected government?

Neither does voting establish any sort of voluntary consent even by the voters themselves to the government. As Spooner trenchantly pointed out:

> In truth, in the case of individuals their actual voting is not to be taken as proof of consent. . . . On the contrary, it is to be considered that, without his consent having even been asked

---

3. Lysander Spooner, *No Treason: The Constitution of No Authority,* James J. Martin ed., (Colorado Springs, Colo.: Ralph Myles, 1973), p. 29.

a man finds himself environed by a government that he cannot resist; a government that forces him to pay money, render service, and forego the exercise of many of his natural rights, under peril of weighty punishments. He sees, too, that other men practice this tyranny over him by the use of the ballot. He sees further, that, if he will but use the ballot himself, he has some chance of relieving himself from this tyranny of others, by subjecting them to his own. In short, he finds himself, without his consent, so situated that, if he uses the ballot, he may become a master, if he does not use it, he must become a slave. And he has no other alternative than these two. In self-defense, he attempts the former. His case is analogous to that of a man who has been forced into battle, where he must either kill others, or be killed himself. Because, to save his own life in battle, a man attempts to take the lives of his opponents, it is not to be inferred that the battle is one of his own choosing. Neither in contests with the ballot—which is a mere substitute for a bullet—because, as his only chance of self-preservation, a man uses a ballot, is it to be inferred that the contest is one into which he voluntarily entered; that he voluntarily set up all his own natural rights, as a stake against those of others, to be lost or won by the mere power of numbers. . . .

Doubtless the most miserable of men, under the most oppressive government in the world, if allowed the ballot would use it, if they could see any chance of meliorating their condition. But it would not, therefore, be a legitimate inference that the government itself, that crushes them, was one which they had voluntarily set up, or even consented to.[4]

If, then, taxation is compulsory, and is therefore indistinguishable from theft, it follows that the State, which subsists on taxation, is a vast criminal organization far more formidable and successful than any "private" Mafia in history. Furthermore, it should be considered criminal not only according to the theory of crime and property rights as set forth in this book, but *even* according to the common apprehension of mankind, which always considers theft to be a crime. As we have seen above, the nineteenth-century German sociologist Franz Oppenheimer put the matter succinctly when he pointed out that there are two and only two ways of attaining wealth in society: (a) by production and voluntary exchange with others—the method of the free market; and (b) by violent expropriation of the wealth produced by others. The latter is the method

4. Ibid., p. 15.

THE NATURE OF THE STATE

of violence and theft. The former benefits all parties involved; the latter parasitically benefits the looting group or class at the expense of the looted. Oppenheimer trenchantly termed the former method of obtaining wealth, "the economic means," and the latter "the political means." Oppenheimer then went on brilliantly to define the State as "the organization of the political means."[5]

Nowhere has the essence of the State as a criminal organization been put as forcefully or as brilliantly as in this passage from Lysander Spooner:

> It is true that the theory of our Constitution is, that all taxes are paid voluntarily; that our government is a mutual insurance company, voluntarily entered into by the people with each other. . . .
>
> But this theory of our government is wholly different from the practical fact. The fact is that the government, like a highwayman, says to a man: "Your money, or your life." And many, if not most, taxes are paid under the compulsion of that threat.
>
> The government does not, indeed, waylay a man in a lonely place, spring upon him from the roadside, and, holding a pistol to his head, proceed to rifle his pockets. But the robbery is none the less a robbery on that account; and it is far more dastardly and shameful.
>
> The highwayman takes solely upon himself the responsibility, danger, and crime of his own act. He does not pretend that he has any rightful claim to your money, or that he intends to use it for your own benefit. He does not pretend to be anything but a robber. He has not acquired impudence enough to profess to be merely a "protector," and that he takes men's money against their will, merely to enable him to "protect" those infatuated travellers, who feel perfectly able to protect themselves, or do not appreciate his peculiar system of protection. He is too sensible a man to make such professions as these. Furthermore, having taken your money, he leaves you, as you wish him to do. He does not persist in following you on the road, against your will; assuming to be your rightful "sovereign," on account of the "protection" he affords you. He does not keep "protecting" you, by commanding you to bow down and serve him; by requiring you to do this, and forbidding you to do that; by robbing you of more money as often as he finds it for his interest or pleasure to do so; and by branding you as a rebel, a traitor, and an enemy to your country, and shooting you down without

---

5. Franz Oppenheimer, *The State* (New York: Free Life Editions, 1975), p. 12.

mercy, if you dispute his authority, or resist his demands. He is too much of a gentleman to be guilty of such impostures, and insults, and villainies as these. In short, he does not, in addition to robbing you, attempt to make you either his dupe or his slave.[6]

It is instructive to inquire why it is that the State, in contrast to the highwayman, invariably surrounds itself with an ideology of legitimacy, why it must indulge in all the hypocrisies that Spooner outlines. The reason is that the highwayman is not a visible, permanent, legal, or legitimate member of society, let alone a member with exalted status. He is always on the run from his victims or from the State itself. But the State, in contrast to a band of highwaymen, is not considered a criminal organization; on the contrary, its minions have generally held the positions of highest status in society. It is a status that allows the State to feed off its victims while making at least most of them support, or at least be resigned to, this exploitative process. In fact, it is precisely the function of the State's ideological minions and allies to explain to the public that the Emperor does indeed have a fine set of clothes. In brief, the ideologists must explain that, while theft by one or more persons or groups is bad and criminal, that when the *State* engages in such acts, it is *not* theft but the legitimate and even sanctified act called "taxation." The ideologists must explain that murder by one or more persons or groups is bad and must be punished, but that when the *State* kills it is not murder but an exalted act known as "war" or "repression of internal subversion." They must explain that while kidnapping or slavery is bad and must be outlawed when done by private individuals or groups, that when the State commits such acts it is not kidnapping or slavery but "conscription"—an act necessary to the public weal and even to the requirements of morality itself. The function of the statist ideologists is to weave the false set of Emperor's clothes, to convince the public of a massive double standard: that when the State commits the gravest of high crimes it is really *not* doing so, but doing something else that is necessary, proper, vital, and even—in former ages—by divine command. The age-old success of the ideologists of the State is perhaps the most gigantic hoax in the history of mankind.

Ideology has always been vital to the continued existence of the State, as attested by the systematic use of ideology since the ancient Oriental empires. The specific *content* of the ideology has, of course, changed over time, in accordance with changing conditions and cultures. In the Oriental despotisms, the Emperor was often held by the Church to be himself divine; in our more secular age, the argument runs more to

---

6. Spooner, *No Treason*, p. 19.

"the public good" and the "general welfare." But the *purpose* is always the same: to convince the public that what the State does is not, as one might think, crime on a gigantic scale, but something necessary and vital that must be supported and obeyed. The reason that ideology is so vital to the State is that it always rests, in essence, on the support of the majority of the public. This support obtains whether the State is a "democracy," a dictatorship, or an absolute monarchy. For the support rests in the willingness of the majority (*not*, to repeat, of *every* individual) to go along with the system: to pay the taxes, to go without much complaint to fight the State's wars, to obey the State's rules and decrees. This support need not be active enthusiasm to be effective; it can just as well be passive resignation. But support there must be. For if the bulk of the public were *really* convinced of the illegitimacy of the State, if it were convinced that the State is nothing more nor less than a bandit gang writ large, then the State would soon collapse to take on no more status or breadth of existence than another Mafia gang. Hence the necessity of the State's employment of ideologists; and hence the necessity of the State's age-old alliance with the Court Intellectuals who weave the apologia for State rule.

The first modern political theorist who saw that all States rest on majority opinion was the sixteenth-century libertarian French writer, Etienne de la Boetie. In his *Discourse on Voluntary Servitude*, de la Boetie saw that the tyrannical State is always a minority of the population, and that therefore its continued despotic rule must rest on its legitimacy in the eyes of the exploited majority, on what would later come to be called "the engineering of consent." Two hundred years later, David Hume— though scarcely a libertarian—set forth a similar analysis.[7] The counter-argument that, with modern weapons, a minority force can permanently cow a hostile majority, ignores the fact that these weapons can be held by the majority, and that the armed force of the minority can mutiny or defect to the side of the populace. Hence, the permanent need for per-

---

7. Thus, as Hume stated:

> Nothing appears more surprising . . . than the easiness with which the many are governed by the few and the implicit submission with which men resign their own sentiments and passions to those of their rulers. When we inquire by what means this wonder is effected, we shall find, that, as Force is always on the side of the governed, the governors have nothing to support them but opinion. It is, therefore, on opinion that government is founded; and this maxim extends to the most despotic and most military governments.

David Hume, *Essays: Literary, Moral and Political* (London: Ward, Locke, and Taylor, n.d.), p. 23; also see, Etienne de la Boetie, *The Politics of Obedience: The Discourse of Voluntary Servitude* (New York: Free Life Editions, 1975); and Ludwig von Mises, *Human Action* (New Haven, Conn.: Yale University Press, 1949), pp. 188ff.

suasive ideology has always led the State to bring into its rubric the nation's opinion-moulding intellectuals. In former days, the intellectuals were invariably the priests, and hence, as we have pointed out, the age-old alliance between Church-and-State, Throne-and-Altar. Nowadays, "scientific" and "value-free" economists and "national security managers," among others, perform a similar ideological function in behalf of State power.

Particularly important in the modern world—now that an Established Church is often no longer feasible—is for the State to assume control over education, and thereby to mould the minds of its subjects. In addition to influencing the universities through all manner of financial subventions, and through state-owned universities directly, the State controls education on the lower levels through the universal institutions of the public school, through certification requirements for private schools, and through compulsory attendance laws. Add to this a virtually total control over radio and television—either through outright State ownership, as in most countries—or, as in the United States, by the nationalization of the airwaves, and by the power of a federal commission to license the right of stations to use those frequencies and channels.[8]

Thus, the State, by its very nature, *must* violate the generally accepted moral laws to which most people adhere. Most people are agreed on the injustice and criminality of murder and theft. The customs, rules, and laws of all societies condemn these actions. The State, then, is always in a vulnerable position, despite its seeming age-old might. What particularly needs to be done is to enlighten the public on the State's true nature, so that they can see that the State habitually violates the generally accepted injunctions against robbery and murder, that the State is the necessary violator of the commonly accepted moral and criminal law.

We have seen clearly why the State needs the intellectuals; but why do the intellectuals need the State? Put simply, it is because intellectuals, whose services are often not very intensively desired by the mass of consumers, can find a more secure "market" for their abilities in the arms of the State. The State can provide them with a power, status, and wealth which they often cannot obtain in voluntary exchange. For centuries, many (though, of course, not all) intellectuals have sought the goal of Power, the realization of the Platonic ideal of the "philosopher–king." Consider, for example, the cry from the heart by the distinguished Marxist scholar, Professor Needham, in protest against the acidulous critique by Karl Wittfogel of the alliance of State-and-intellectuals in Oriental despotisms:

---

8. See Rothbard, *For a New Liberty*, pp. 109–16.

"The civilization which Professor Wittfogel is so bitterly attacking was one which could make poets and scholars into officials." Needham adds that "the successive [Chinese] emperors were served in all ages by a great company of profoundly humane and disinterested scholars."[9] Presumably, for Professor Needham, this is enough to justify the grinding despotisms of the ancient Orient.

But we need not go back as far as the ancient Orient or even as far as the proclaimed goal of the professors at the University of Berlin, in the nineteenth century, to form themselves into "the intellectual bodyguard of the House of Hohenzollern." In contemporary America, we have the eminent political scientist, Professor Richard Neustadt, hailing the President as the "sole crownlike symbol of the Union." We have national security manager Townsend Hoopes writing that "under our system the people can look only to the President to define the nature of our foreign policy problem and the national programs and sacrifices required to meet it with effectiveness." And, in response, we have Richard Nixon, on the eve of his election as President, defining his role as follows: "He [the President] must articulate the nation's values, define its goals and marshall its will." Nixon's conception of his role is hauntingly similar to the scholar Ernst Huber's articulation, in the Germany of the 1930s, of the *Constitutional Law of the Greater German Reich*. Huber wrote that the head of State "sets up the great ends which are to be attained and draws up the plans for the utilization of all national powers in the achievement of the common goals . . . he gives the national life its true purpose and value."[10]

---

9. Joseph Needham, "Review of Karl A. Wittfogel, *Oriental Despotism*," *Science and Society* (1958): 61, 65. On the explicit search for power on the part of the "collectivist" intellectuals during the Progressive period of the twentieth century, see James Gilbert, *Designing the Industrial State* (Chicago: Quadrangle Books, 1972). For more on the alliance between intellectuals and the state, see Bertrand de Jouvenel, "The Treatment of Capitalism by Continental Intellectuals," and John Lukacs, "Intellectual Class or Intellectual Profession?" in George B. deHuszar, ed., *The Intellectuals* (Glencoe, Ill.: Free Press, 1960), pp. 385–99, and 521–22; Bertrand de Jouvenel, *On Power* (New York: Viking Press, 1949); Murray N. Rothbard, "The Anatomy of the State," in *Egalitarianism as a Revolt Against Nature and Other Essays* (Washington, D.C.: Libertarian Review Press, 1974), pp. 37–42; and Rothbard, *For a New Liberty*, pp. 59–70.

10. Richard Neustadt, "Presidency at Mid-Century," *Law and Contemporary Problems* (Autumn 1956): 609–45; Townsend Hoopes, "The Persistence of Illusion: The Soviet Economic Drive and American National Interest," *Yale Review* (March 1960): 336, cited in Robert J. Bresler, *The Ideology of the Executive State: Legacy of Liberal Internationalism* (Menlo Park, Calif.: Institute for Humane Studies, n.d.), pp. 4–5. Nixon and Huber cited in ibid., pp. 5, 16–17; and in Thomas Reeves and Karl Hess, *The End of the Draft* (New York: Vintage Books, 1970), pp. 64–65. On the national security managers, also see Marcus Raskin, "The Megadeath Intellectuals," *New York Review of Books* (14 November 1963): 6–7.

Thus, the State is a coercive criminal organization that subsists by a regularized large-scale system of taxation-theft, and which gets away with it by engineering the support of the majority (*not*, again, of everyone) through securing an alliance with a group of opinion-moulding intellectuals whom it rewards with a share in its power and pelf. But there is another vital aspect of the State that needs to be considered. There is one critical argument for the State that now comes into view: namely, the implicit argument that the State apparatus really and properly *owns* the territorial area over which it claims jurisdiction. The State, in short, arrogates to itself a monopoly of force, of ultimate decision-making power, over a given territorial area—larger or smaller depending on historical conditions, and on how much it has been able to wrest from other States. *If* the State may be said to properly *own* its territory, then it is proper for it to make rules for anyone who presumes to live in that area. It can legitimately seize or control private property because there is no private property in its area, because it really owns the entire land surface. *So long* as the State permits its subjects to leave its territory, then, it can be said to act as does any other owner who sets down rules for people living on his property. (This seems to be the only justification for the crude slogan, "America, love it or leave it!," as well as the enormous emphasis generally placed on an individual's right to emigrate from a country.) In short, this theory makes the State, as well as the King in the Middle Ages, a feudal overlord, who at least theoretically *owned* all the land in his domain. The fact that new and unowned resources—whether virgin land or lakes—are invariably claimed as owned by the State (its "public domain") is an expression of this implicit theory.

But our homesteading theory, outlined above, suffices to demolish any such pretensions by the State apparatus. For by what earthly right do the criminals of the State lay claim to the ownership of its land area? It is bad enough that they have seized control of ultimate decision-making for that area; what criterion can possibly give them the rightful ownership of the entire territory?

The State may therefore be defined as that organization which possesses either or both (in actual fact, almost always both) of the following characteristics: (a) it acquires its revenue by physical coercion (taxation); and (b) it achieves a compulsory monopoly of force and of ultimate decision-making power over a given territorial area. Both of these essential activities of the State necessarily constitute criminal aggression and depredation of the just rights of private property of its subjects (including self-ownership). For the first constitutes and establishes theft on a grand scale; while the second prohibits the free competition of defense and decision-making agencies within a given territorial area—prohibiting the voluntary purchase and sale of defense and judicial services.[11] Hence the justice of the vivid critique of the State by the libertarian theorist Albert Jay Nock: "The State claims and exercises the monopoly of crime" in a given territorial area. "It forbids private murder, but itself organizes murder on a colossal scale. It punishes private theft, but itself lays unscrupulous hands on anything it wants, whether the property of citizen or alien."[12]

It must be emphasized that the State does not merely use coercion to acquire its own revenue, to hire propagandists to advance its power, and to arrogate to itself and to enforce a compulsory monopoly of such vital services as police protection, firefighting, transportation, and postal service. For the State does many other things as well, none of which can in any sense be said to serve the consuming public. It uses its monopoly of force to achieve, as Nock puts it, a "monopoly of crime"—to control, regulate, and coerce its hapless subjects. Often it pushes its way into controlling the morality and the very daily lives of its subjects. The state uses its coerced revenue, not merely to monopolize and provide genuine services inefficiently to the public, but also to build up its own power at the expense of its exploited and harassed subjects: to redistribute income and wealth from the public to itself and to its allies, and to control, command, and coerce the inhabitants of its territory. In a truly free society, a society where individual rights of person and property are maintained, the State, then, would necessarily cease to exist. Its myriad of invasive and aggressive activities, its vast depredations on the rights of person and property, would then disappear. At the same time, those genuine services which it does manage badly to perform would be thrown open to free competition, and to voluntarily chosen payments by individual consumers.

The *grotesquerie* of the typical conservative call for the government to enforce conservative definitions of "morality" (e.g. by outlawing the alleged immorality of pornography) is therefore starkly revealed. Aside

---

11. "Given territorial area" in this context of course implicitly means "beyond the area of each property owner's just property." Obviously, in a free society, Smith has the ultimate decision-making power over his own just property, Jones over his, etc. The State, or government, claims and exercises a compulsory monopoly of defense and ultimate decision-making over an area larger than an individual's justly-acquired property. Smith, Jones, etc. are thereby prohibited by "the government" from having nothing to do with that "government" and from making their own defense contracts with a competing agency. I am indebted to Professor Sidney Morgenbesser for raising this point.

12. Albert Jay Nock, *On Doing the Right Thing, and Other Essays* (New York: Harper and Brothers, 1928), p. 143.

from other sound arguments against enforced morality (e.g., that no action not freely chosen can be considered "moral"), it is surely grotesque to entrust the function of guardian of the public morality to the most extensive criminal (and hence the most immoral) group in society—the State.

23. The Inner Contradictions of the State

A major problem with discussions of the necessity of government is the fact that all such discussions necessarily take place within a context of centuries of State existence and State rule—rule to which the public has become habituated. The wry coupling of the twin certainties in the popular motto "death and taxes" demonstrates that the public has resigned itself to the existence of the State as an evil but inescapable force of nature to which there is no alternative. The force of habit as the cement of State rule was seen as early as the sixteenth-century writings of de la Boetie. But, logically, and to cast off the scales of habit, we must not merely compare an existing State with an unknown quantity, but begin at the social zero point, in the logical fiction of the "state of nature," and compare the relative arguments for the establishment of the State with those on behalf of a free society.

Let us assume, for example, that a sizeable number of people suddenly arrive on Earth, and that they must now consider what sort of social arrangements to live under. One person or group of persons argues as follows (i.e., the typical argument for the State): "If each of us is allowed to remain free in all aspects, and particularly if each of us is allowed to retain weapons and the right of self-defense, then we will all war against each other, and society will be wrecked. Therefore, let us turn over all of our guns and all of our ultimate decision-making power and power to define and enforce our rights to the Jones family over there. The Jones family will guard us from our predatory instincts, keep social peace, and enforce justice." Is it conceivable that any one (except perhaps the Jones family itself) would spend one moment considering this clearly absurd scheme? The cry of "who would guard us from the Jones family, especially when we are deprived of our weapons?" would suffice to shout down such a scheme. And yet, given the acquisition of legitimacy from the fact of longevity, given the longtime rule of the "Jones family," this is precisely the type of argument to which we now blindly adhere. Employing the logical model of the state of nature aids us in casting off the fetters of habit to see the State plain—and to see that the Emperor, indeed, wears no clothes.

If, in fact, we cast a cold and logical eye on the theory of "limited government," we can see it for the chimera that it really is, for the unrealistic and inconsistent "Utopia" that it holds forth. In the first place, there is no reason to assume that a compulsory monopoly of violence, once acquired by the "Jones family" or by any State rulers, will remain "limited" to protection of person and property. Certainly, historically, no government has long remained "limited" in this way. And there are excellent reasons to suppose that it never will. First, once the cancerous principle of coercion— of coerced revenue and compulsory monopoly of violence—is established and legitimated at the very heart of society, there is every reason to suppose that this precedent will be expanded and embellished. In particular, it is in the economic *interest* of the State rulers to work actively for such expansion. The more the coercive powers of the State are expanded beyond the cherished limits of the laissez-faire theorists, the greater the power and pelf accruing to the ruling caste operating the State apparatus. Hence, the ruling caste, eager to maximize its power and wealth, will stretch State power—and will encounter only feeble opposition, given the legitimacy it and its allied intellectuals are gaining, and given the lack of any institutional free-market channels of resistance to the government's monopoly of coercion and the power of ultimate decision-making. On the free market, it is a happy fact that the maximization of the wealth of one person or group redounds to the benefit of all; but in the political realm, the realm of the State, a maximization of income and wealth can only accrue parasitically to the State and its rulers *at the expense of* the rest of society.

Advocates of a limited government often hold up the ideal of a government above the fray, refraining from taking sides or throwing its weight around, an "umpire" arbitrating impartially between contending factions in society. Yet, why *should* the government do so? Given the unchecked power of the State, the State and its rulers will act to maximize their power and wealth, and hence inexorably expand beyond the supposed "limits." The crucial point is that in the Utopia of limited government and laissez faire, there are no institutional mechanisms to *keep* the State limited. Surely the bloody record of States throughout history should have demonstrated that *any* power, once granted or acquired, *will* be used and therefore abused. Power corrupts, as the libertarian Lord Acton so wisely noted.

Furthermore, apart from the absence of institutional mechanisms to keep the ultimate decision-maker and force-wielder "limited" to protection of rights, there is a grave inner contradiction inherent in the very ideal of a neutral or impartial State. For there can be no such thing as a "neutral" tax, a taxing system that will be neutral to the market as it would have been without taxation. As John C. Calhoun trenchantly pointed out in the early nineteenth century, the very *existence* of taxation negates any possibility of such neutrality. For, given any level of taxation, the least that will happen will be the creation of two antagonistic social classes: the "ruling" classes who gain by and live off taxation, and the "ruled" classes who pay the taxes. In short, conflicting classes of net tax-*payers* and net tax-*consumers*. At the very least, the government bureaucrats will necessarily be net tax-consumers; other such will be those persons and groups subsidized by the inevitable expenditures of government. As Calhoun put it:

> [T]he agents and employees of the government constitute that portion of the community who are the exclusive recipients of the proceeds of the taxes. Whatever amount is taken from the community in the form of taxes, if not lost, goes to them in the shape of expenditures and disbursements. The two—disbursement and taxation—constitute the fiscal action of the government. They are correlatives. What the one takes from the community under the name of taxes is transferred to the portion of the community who are the recipients under that of disbursements. But as the recipients constitute only a portion of the community, it follows, taking the two parts of the fiscal process together, that its actions must be unequal between the payers of the taxes and the recipients of their proceeds. Nor can it be otherwise; unless what is collected from each individual in the shape of taxes shall be returned to him in that of disbursements, which would make the process nugatory and absurd. . . .
>
> The necessary result, then, of the unequal fiscal action of the government is to divide the community into two great classes: one consisting of those who, in reality, pay the taxes, and, of course, bear exclusively the burden of supporting the government; and the other, of those who are the recipients of their proceeds through disbursements, and who are, in fact, supported by the government; or, in fewer words, to divide it into tax-payers and tax-consumers.
>
> But the effect of this is to place them in antagonistic relations in reference to the fiscal action of the government—and the entire course of policy therewith connected. For the greater the taxes and disbursements, the greater the gain of the one and the loss of the other, and vice versa. . . . The effect, then, of every increase is to enrich and strengthen the one, and impoverish and weaken the other.[1]

Calhoun goes on to point out that a Constitution will not be able to keep the government limited; for given a monopoly Supreme Court

---

1. John C. Calhoun, *A Disquisition on Government* (New York: Liberal Arts Press, 1953), pp. 16–18.

selected by the self-same government and granted the power of ultimate decision- making, the political "ins" will always favor a "broad" or loose interpretation of the wording of the Constitution serving to expand the powers of government over the citizenry; and, over time, the "ins" will inexorably tend to win out over the minority of "outs" who will argue vainly for a "strict" interpretation limiting State power.[2]

But there are other fatal flaws and inconsistencies in the concept of limited, laissez-faire government. In the first place, it is generally accepted, by limited-government and by other political philosophers, that the State is necessary for the creation and development of *law*. But this is historically incorrect. For most law, but especially the most libertarian parts of the law, emerged not from the State, but out of non-State institutions: tribal custom, common-law judges and courts, the law merchant in mercantile courts, or admiralty law in tribunals set up by shippers themselves. In the case of competing common-law judges as well as elders of tribes, the judges were not engaged in making law, but in finding the law in existing and generally accepted principles, and then applying that law to specific cases or to new technological or institutional conditions.[3] The same was true in private Roman law. Moreover, in ancient Ireland, a society existing for a thousand years until the conquest by Cromwell, "there was no trace of State-administered justice"; competing schools of professional jurists interpreted and applied the common body of customary law, with enforcement undertaken by competing and voluntarily supported *tuatha*, or insurance agencies. Furthermore, these customary rules were not haphazard or arbitrary, but consciously rooted in *natural law*, discoverable by man's reason.[4]

But, in addition to the historical inaccuracy of the view that the State is needed for the development of law, Randy Barnett has brilliantly

---

2. Ibid., pp. 25–27.

3. See Bruno Leoni, *Freedom and the Law* (Los Angeles: Nash Publishing, 1972); F.A. Hayek, *Law, Legislation, and Liberty*, vol. 1, *Rules and Order* (Chicago: University of Chicago Press, 1973), pp. 72–93, and Murray N. Rothbard, *For A New Liberty*, rev. ed. (New York: Macmillan, 1978), pp. 234–43.

4. On ancient Ireland, see Joseph R. Peden, "Stateless Societies: Ancient Ireland," *The Libertarian Forum* (April 1971): 3. Cf., and more extensively, Peden, "Property Rights in Celtic Irish Law," *Journal of Libertarian Studies* 1 (Spring 1977): 81–95. Also see Daniel A. Binchy, *Anglo-Saxon and Irish Kingship* (London: Oxford University Press, 1970); Myles Dillon, *The Celtic Realms* (London: George Weidenfeld and Nicholson, 1967), and idem, *Early Irish Society* (Dublin, 1954). Irish law as based on natural law is discussed in Charles Donahue, "Early Celtic Laws" (unpublished paper, delivered at the Columbia University Seminar on the History of Legal and Political Thought, Autumn, 1964), pp. 13ff. Also see Rothbard, *For A New Liberty*, pp. 239–43.

pointed out that the State by its very nature *cannot* obey its own legal rules. But if the State cannot obey its own legal rules, then it is necessarily deficient and self-contradictory as a maker of law. In an exegesis and critique of Lon L. Fuller's seminal work *The Morality of Law*, Barnett notes that Professor Fuller sees in the current thinking of legal positivism a persistent error: "the assumption that law should be viewed as a . . . one-way projection of authority, originating with government and imposing itself upon the citizen."[5] Fuller points out that law is not simply "vertical"—a command from above from the State to its citizens, but also "horizontal," arising from among the people themselves and applied to each other. Fuller points to international law, tribal law, private rules, etc. as pervasive examples of such "reciprocal" and non-State law. Fuller sees the positivist error as stemming from failure to recognize a crucial principle of proper law, namely that the lawmaker should itself obey its own rules that it lays down for its citizens, or, in Fuller's words, "that enacted law itself presupposes a commitment by the government authority to abide by its own rules in dealing with its subjects."[6]

But Barnett correctly points out that Fuller errs significantly in failing to apply his own principle far enough: in limiting the principle to the procedural "rules by which laws are passed" rather than applying it to the *substance* of the laws themselves. Because of this failure to carry his principle to its logical conclusion, Fuller fails to see the inherent inner contradiction of the State as maker of law. As Barnett puts it,

> Fuller fails in his attempt because he has not followed his own principle far enough. If he did, he would see that the state legal system does not conform to the principle of official congruence with its own rules. It is because the positivists see that the State inherently violates its own rules that they conclude, in a sense correctly, that State-made law is *sui generis*.[7]

However, Barnett adds, if Fuller's principle were carried forward to assert that the "lawmaker must obey the *substance* of his own laws," then Fuller would see "that the State by its nature *must* violate this commitment."

For Barnett correctly points out that the two unique and essential features of the State are its power to tax—to acquire its revenue by

---

5. Lon L. Fuller, *The Morality of Law* (New Haven, Conn.: Yale University Press), p. 204; quoted in Randy E. Barnett, "Fuller, Law, and Anarchism," *The Libertarian Forum* (February 1976): 6.

6. Fuller, *Morality of Law*, p. 32.

7. Barnett, "Fuller, Law, and Anarchism," p. 66.

coercion and hence robbery—and to prevent its subjects from hiring any other defense agency (compulsory monopoly of defense).[8] But in doing so, the State violates its own laws that it sets down for its subjects. As Barnett explains,

> For example, the State says that citizens may not take from another by force and against his will that which belongs to another. And yet the State through its power to tax "legitimately" does just that. . . . More essentially, the State says that a person may use force upon another only in self-defense, i.e. only as a defense against another who initiated the use of force. To go beyond one's right of self-defense would be to aggress on the rights of others, a violation of one's legal duty. And yet the State by its claimed monopoly forcibly imposes its jurisdiction on persons who may have done nothing wrong. By doing so it aggresses against the rights of its citizens, something which its rules say citizens may not do.
>
> The State, in short, may steal where its subjects may not and it may aggress (initiate the use of force) against its subjects while prohibiting them from exercising the same right. It is to this that the positivists look when they say that the law (meaning State-made law) is a one-way, vertical process. It is this that belies any claim of true reciprocity.[9]

Barnett concludes that, interpreted consistently, Fuller's principle means that in a true and proper legal system, the lawmaker must "follow *all* of its rules, procedural and substantive alike." Therefore, "to the degree that it does not and cannot do this it is not and cannot be a legal system and its acts are outside the law. The State *qua* state, therefore, is an illegal system."[10]

Another inner contradiction of the theory of laissez-faire government deals again with taxation. For if government is to be limited to "protection" of person and property, and taxation is to be "limited" to providing that service only, then *how* is the government to decide *how much* protection to provide and how much taxes to levy? For, contrary to the limited government theory, "protection" is no more a collective, one-lump "thing" than any other good or service in society. Suppose, for example, that we might

---

8. Both features are essential to the historical category of the State; various Utopian schemes to dispense with the first trait and keep the second would still come under the present strictures as applied to the second trait.

9. Barnett, "Fuller, Law, and Anarchism," p. 7.

10. Ibid.

offer a competing theory, that government should be "limited" to supplying clothing free to all of its citizens. But this would scarcely be any sort
of viable limit, apart from other flaws in the theory. For how *much* clothing,
and at what cost? Must everyone be supplied with Balenciaga originals,
for example? And *who* is to decide how much and what quality of clothing
each person is to receive? Indeed, "protection" could conceivably imply
anything from one policeman for an entire country, to supplying an armed
bodyguard and a tank for every citizen—a proposition which would
bankrupt the society posthaste. But who is to decide on how much
protection, since it is undeniable that every person would be *better*
protected from theft and assault if provided with an armed bodyguard
than if he is not? On the free market, decisions on how much and what
quality of any good or service should be supplied to each person are
made by means of voluntary purchases by each individual; but what
criterion can be applied when the decision is made *by government*? The
answer is none at all, and such governmental decisions can only be purely
arbitrary.

Secondly, one searches in vain in the writings of laissez-faire theorists
for a cogent theory of taxation: not only how much taxation is to be levied,
but also *who* is to be forced to pay. The commonly adopted "ability to
pay" theory, for example, is, as the libertarian Frank Chodorov pointed
out, the philosophy of the highway robber to extract as much loot from
the victim as the robber can get away with—scarcely a cogent social
philosophy, and at total variance, of course, from the system of payment
on the free market. For if everyone were forced to pay for every good
and service in proportion to his income, then there would be no pricing
system at all, and no market system could work. (David Rockefeller, for
example, might be forced to pay $1 million for a loaf of bread.)[11]

Next, no laissez-faire writer has ever provided a theory of the size
of the State: if the State is to have a compulsory monopoly of force in a
given territorial area, *how large* is that area to be? These theorists have
not given full attention to the fact that the world has always lived in an
"international anarchy," with no one government, or compulsory monopoly of decision-making, *between* various countries. And yet, international
relations between *private citizens* of different countries have generally func-
tioned quite smoothly, despite the lack of a single government over them.
Thus, a contractual or a tort dispute between a citizen of North Dakota and

---

11. See Frank Chodorov, *Out of Step* (New York: Devin-Adair, 1962), p. 237. For a critique
of the ability to pay and other attempts to provide canons of "justice" for taxation, see
Murray N. Rothbard, *Power and Market*, 2nd ed. (Kansas City: Sheed Andrews and McMeel,
1977), pp. 135–67.

of Manitoba is usually handled quite smoothly, typically with the plaintiff suing or placing charges in his court, and the court of the other country recognizing the result. Wars and conflicts usually take place between the *governments*, rather than the private citizens, of the various countries.

But more profoundly, would a laissez-fairist recognize the right of a region of a country to *secede* from that country? Is it legitimate for West Ruritania to secede from Ruritania? If not, why not? And if so, then how can there be a logical stopping-point to the secession? May not a small district secede, and then a city, and then a borough of that city, and then a block, and then finally a particular individual?[12] Once admit *any* right of secession whatever, and there is no logical stopping-point short of the right of *individual* secession, which logically entails anarchism, since then individuals may secede and patronize their own defense agencies, and the State has crumbled.

Finally, there is a crucial inconsistency in the preferred criterion of laissez-faire itself: limiting the government to protection of person and property. For, if it is legitimate for a government to tax, why not tax its subjects to provide other goods and services that may be useful to consumers: why shouldn't the government, for example, build steel plants, provide shoes, dams, postal service, etc.? For each of these goods and services is useful to consumers. If the laissez-fairists object that the government should not build steel plants or shoe factories and provide them to consumers (either free or for sale) because tax-coercion had been employed in constructing these plants, well then the same objection can of course be made to governmental police or judicial service. The government should be acting no more immorally, from the laissez-faire point of view, when providing housing or steel than when providing police protection. Government limited to protection, then, cannot be sustained *even within* the laissez-faire ideal itself, much less from any other consideration. It is true that the laissez-faire ideal could still be employed to prevent such "second-degree" coercive activities of government (i.e., coercion *beyond* the initial coercion of taxation) as price control or outlawry of pornography; but the "limits" have now become flimsy indeed, and may be stretched to virtually complete collectivism, in which the government only supplies goods and services, yet supplies *all* of them.

---

12. Mises recognized this point, and supported the right of each individual to secede in theory, stopping short of the individual for merely "technical considerations." Ludwig von Mises, *Liberalism*, 2nd ed. (Kansas City: Sheed Andrews and McMeel, 1978), pp. 109–10.

24. The Moral Status of Relations to the State

I f the State, then, is a vast engine of institutionalized crime and aggression, the "organization of the political means" to wealth, then this means that the State is a criminal organization, and that therefore its moral status is radically different from any of the just property-owners that we have been discussing in this volume. And this means that the moral status of contracts with the State, promises to it and by it, differs radically as well. It means, for example, that no one is morally required to obey the State (except insofar as the State simply affirms the right of just private property against aggression). For, as a criminal organization with all of its income and assets derived from the crime of taxation, *the State cannot possess any just property.* This means that it cannot be unjust or immoral to fail to pay taxes to the State, to appropriate the property of the State (which is in the hands of aggressors), to refuse to obey State orders, or to break contracts with the State (since it cannot be unjust to break contracts with criminals). Morally, from the point of view of proper political philosophy, "stealing" from the State, for example, is removing property from criminal hands, is, in a sense, "homesteading" property, except that instead of homesteading unused land, the person is removing property from the criminal sector of society—a positive good.

Here a partial exception can be made where the State has clearly stolen the property of a specific person. Suppose, for example, that the State confiscates jewels belonging to Brown. If Green then steals the jewels from the State, he is not committing a criminal offense from the point of view of libertarian theory. However, the jewels are still not his, and Brown would be justified in using force to repossess the jewels from Green. In most cases, of course, the State's confiscations, taking place in the form of taxation, are mixed into a common pot, and it is impossible to point to specific owners of its specific property. *Who,* for example, properly owns a TVA dam or a post-office building? In these majority cases, then, Green's theft or "homesteading" from the State would be legitimate as well as noncriminal, and would confer a just homesteading property title upon Green.

Lying to the State, then, also becomes *a fortiori* morally legitimate. Just as no one is morally required to answer a robber truthfully when he asks if there are any valuables in one's house, so no one can be morally required to answer truthfully similar questions asked by the State, e.g., when filling out income tax returns.

All this does not mean, of course, that we must counsel or require civil disobedience, nonpayment of taxes, or lying to or theft from the State, for these may well be prudentially unwise, considering the *force majeure* possessed by the State apparatus. But what we are saying is that these actions are just and morally licit. Relations with the State, then, become purely prudential and pragmatic considerations for the particular individuals involved, who must treat the State as an enemy with currently prevailing power.

Many libertarians fall into confusion on specific relations with the State, even when they concede the general immorality or criminality of State actions or interventions. Thus, there is the question of default, or more widely, repudiation of government debt. Many libertarians assert that the government is morally bound to pay its debts, and that therefore default or repudiation must be avoided. The problem here is that these libertarians are analogizing from the perfectly proper thesis that *private* persons or institutions should keep their contracts and pay their debts. But government has no money of its own, and payment of its debt means that the taxpayers are further coerced into paying bondholders. Such coercion can never be licit from the libertarian point of view. For not only does increased taxation mean increased coercion and aggression against private property, but the seemingly innocent bondholder appears in a very different light when we consider that the purchase of a government bond is simply making an investment in the future loot from the robbery of taxation. As an eager investor in future robbery, then, the bondholder appears in a very different moral light from what is usually assumed.[1]

Another question to be placed in a new light is the problem of breaking contracts with the State. We have explained above our contention that since enforceable contracts are properly title-transfers and not promises, that therefore it would be legitimate in the free society to resign from an army, despite the signing of a voluntary contract for a longer term of enlistment. But regardless of which theory of contract we adopt, such considerations apply only to *private* armies in the free market. Since State armies are criminal aggressors—both in their actions as well as their means of revenue—it would be morally licit to leave the State's army at any time, regardless of the terms of enlistment. It is morally the individual's

---

1. On repudiation of government debt, see Frank Chodorov, "Don't Buy Government Bonds," in *Out of Step* (New York: Devin-Adair, 1962), pp. 170–77; and Murray N. Rothbard, *Man, Economy, and State* (Princeton, N.J.: D. Van Nostrand, 1962), vol. 2, pp. 881–83.

right to do so, although again whether such an action is prudential or not is another matter entirely.

Let us consider in this light the question of bribery of government officials. We saw above, that, in a free society or free market, the *briber* is acting legitimately, whereas it is the *bribee* who is defrauding someone (e.g. an employer) and therefore deserves prosecution. What of bribery of government officials? Here a distinction must be made between "aggressive" and "defensive" bribery; the first should be considered improper and aggressive, whereas the latter should be considered proper and legitimate. Consider a typical "aggressive bribe": a Mafia leader bribes police officials to exclude other, competing operators of gambling casinos from a certain territorial area. Here, the Mafioso acts in collaboration with the government to coerce competing gambling proprietors. The Mafioso is, in this case, an initiator, and accessory, to governmental aggression against his competitors. On the other hand, a "defensive bribe" has a radically different moral status. In such a case, for example, Robinson, seeing that gambling casinos are outlawed in a certain area, bribes policemen to allow his casino to operate—a perfectly legitimate response to an unfortunate situation.

Defensive bribery, in fact, performs an important social function throughout the world. For, in many countries, business could not be transacted at all without the lubricant of bribery; in this way, crippling and destructive regulations and exactions can be avoided. A "corrupt government," then, is not necessarily a bad thing; *compared* to an "incorruptible government" whose officials enforce the laws with great severity, "corruption" can at least allow a partial flowering of voluntary transactions and actions in a society. Of course, in neither case are either the regulations or prohibitions, or the enforcement officials themselves, justified, since neither they nor the exactions should be in existence at all.[2]

---

2. There is considerable evidence that the Soviet economy only works at all because of the pervasiveness of bribery, or "blat"; Margaret Miller calls it "the shadow system of private enterprise within planning." Margaret Miller, "Markets in Russia," in M. Miller, T. Piotrowicz, L. Sirc, and H. Smith, *Communist Economy Under Change* (London: Institute for Economic Affairs, 1963), pp. 23–30.

H. L. Mencken tells a charming and instructive story of the contrast between "corruption" and "reform":

> He [Mencken's father] believed that political corruption was inevitable under democracy, and even argued, out of his own experience, that it had its uses. One of his favorite anecdotes was about a huge swinging sign that used to hang outside his place of business in Paca Street. When the building was built in 1885, he simply hung out the sign, sent

In some areas, a radical distinction between private persons and government officials is acknowledged in existing law and opinion. Thus, a private individual's "right to privacy" or right to keep silent does not and should not apply to government officials, whose records and operations should be open to public knowledge and evaluation. There are two democratic arguments for denying the right to privacy to government officials, which, while not strictly libertarian, are valuable as far as they go: namely, (1) that in a democracy, the public can only decide on public issues and vote for public officials if they have complete knowledge of government operations; and (2) that since the taxpayers pay the bill for government, they should have the right to know what government is doing. The libertarian argument would add that, since government is an aggressor organization against the rights and persons of its citizens, then full disclosure of its operations is at least one right that its subjects might wrest from the State, and which they may be able to use to resist or whittle down State power.

Another area where the law now distinguishes between private citizens and public officials is the law of libel. We have maintained above that libel laws are illegitimate. But, even given laws against libel, it is important to distinguish between libeling a private citizen and a government official or agency. By the nineteenth century, we had fortunately gotten rid of the pernicious common law of "seditious libel," which had been used as a club to repress almost any criticisms of government. Currently, libel laws have now been fortunately weakened when applied, not merely to government *per se*, but also to politicians or government officials.

Many anarchist libertarians claim it immoral to vote or to engage in political action—the argument being that by participating in this way in State activity, the libertarian places his moral imprimatur upon the State apparatus itself. But a moral decision must be a free decision, and the State has placed individuals in society in an unfree environment,

---

for the city councilman of the district, and gave him $20. This was in full settlement forevermore of all permit and privilege fees, easement taxes, and other such costs and imposts. The city councilman pocketed the money, and in return was supposed to stave off any cops, building inspectors, or other functionaries who had any lawful interest in the matter, or tried to horn in for private profit. Being an honorable man according to his lights, he kept his bargain, and the sign flapped and squeaked in the breeze for ten years. But then, in 1895, Baltimore had a reform wave, the councilman was voted out of office, and the idealists in the City Hall sent word that a license to maintain the sign would cost $62.75 *a year*. It came down the next day. This was proof to my father that reform was mainly only a conspiracy of prehensile charlatans to mulct taxpayers.

H.L. Mencken, *Happy Days: 1880–1892* (New York: Alfred Knopf, 1947), pp. 251–52.

in a general matrix of coercion. The State—unfortunately—exists, and people must necessarily begin with this matrix to try to remedy their condition. As Lysander Spooner pointed out, in an environment of State coercion, voting does not imply voluntary consent.[3] Indeed, if the State allows us a periodic choice of rulers, limited though that choice may be, it surely cannot be considered immoral to make use of that limited choice to try to reduce or get rid of State power.[4]

The State, then, is not simply a part of society. The brunt of this part of the present volume, in fact, is to demonstrate that the State is *not*, as most utilitarian free-market economists like to think, a legitimate social institution that tends to be bumbling and inefficient in most of its activities. On the contrary, the State is an inherently illegitimate institution of organized aggression, of organized and regularized crime against the persons and properties of its subjects. Rather than necessary to society, it is a profoundly antisocial institution which lives parasitically off of the productive activities of private citizens. Morally, it must be considered as illegitimate and outside of the ordinary libertarian legal system (such as adumbrated in Part II above), which delimits and insures the rights and just properties of private citizens. Thus, from the point of view of justice and morality, the State can own no property, require no obedience, enforce no contracts made with it, and indeed, cannot exist at all.

A common defense of the State holds that man is a "social animal," that he must live in society, and that individualists and libertarians believe in the existence of "atomistic individuals" uninfluenced by and unrelated to their fellow men. But no libertarians have ever held individuals to be isolated atoms; on the contrary, all libertarians have recognized the necessity and the enormous advantages of living in society, and of participating in the social division of labor. The great *non sequitur* committed by defenders of the State, including classical Aristotelian and Thomist philosophers, is to leap from the necessity of *society* to the necessity of the *State*.[5] On the contrary, as we have indicated, the State is an antisocial instrument, crippling voluntary interchange, individual creativity, and the division of labor. "Society" is a convenient label for the voluntary interrelations of individuals, in peaceful exchange and on the market. Here we may point to Albert Jay Nock's penetrating distinction between "social power"—the fruits of voluntary interchange in the

---

3. For the relevant passage from Spooner, see pp. 165–66 above.

4. For more on the proper strategy for liberty, see pp. 257–74 below.

5. See Murray N. Rothbard, *Power and Market,* 2nd ed. (Kansas City: Sheed Andrews and McMeel, 1977), p. 237.

economy and in civilization—and "State power," the coercive interference and exploitation of those fruits. In that light, Nock showed that human history is basically a race between State power and social power, between the beneficent fruits of peaceful and voluntary production and creativity on the one hand, and the crippling and parasitic blight of State power upon the voluntary and productive social process.[6] All of the services commonly thought to require the State—from the coining of money to police protection to the development of law in defense of the rights of person and property—can be and have been supplied far more efficiently, and certainly more morally, by private persons. The State is in no sense required by the nature of man; quite the contrary.

---

6. See Albert Jay Nock, *Our Enemy, The State* (New York: Free Life Editions, 1973), pp. 3ff.

25. On Relations Between States

Each State has an assumed monopoly of force over a given territorial area, the areas varying in size in accordance with different historical conditions. *Foreign policy*, or *foreign relations*, may be defined as the relationship between any particular State, A, and other States, B, C, D, and the inhabitants living under those States. In the ideal moral world, no States would exist, and hence, of course, no foreign policy could exist. Given the existence of States, however, are there any moral principles that libertarianism can direct as criteria for foreign policy? The answer is broadly the same as in the libertarian moral criteria directed toward the "domestic policy" of States, namely, to reduce the degree of coercion exercised by States over individual persons as much as possible.

Before considering inter-State actions, let us return for a moment to the pure libertarian stateless world where individuals and their hired private protection agencies strictly confine their use of violence to the defense of person and property against violence. Suppose that, in this world, Jones finds that he or his property is being aggressed against by Smith. It is legitimate, as we have seen, for Jones to repel this invasion by the use of defensive violence. But, now we must ask: is it within the right of Jones to commit aggressive violence against innocent third parties in the course of his legitimate defense against Smith? Clearly the answer must be "No." For the rule prohibiting violence against the persons or property of innocent men is absolute; it holds regardless of the subjective *motives* for the aggression. It is wrong, and criminal, to violate the property or person of another, even if one is a Robin Hood, or is starving, or is defending oneself against a third man's attack. We may understand and sympathize with the motives in many of these cases and extreme situations. We (or, rather, the victim or his heirs) may later mitigate the guilt if the criminal comes to trial for punishment, but we cannot evade the judgment that this aggression is still a criminal act, and one which the victim has every right to repel, by violence if necessary. In short, A aggresses against B because C is threatening, or aggressing against, A. We may understand C's "higher" culpability in this whole procedure, but we still label this aggression by A as a criminal act which B has every right to repel by violence.

To be more concrete, if Jones finds that his property is being stolen by Smith, Jones has the right to repel him and try to catch him, but Jones has *no* right to repel him by bombing a building and murdering innocent people or to catch him by spraying machine gun fire into an innocent crowd. If he does this, he is as much (or more) a criminal aggressor as Smith is.

The same criteria hold if Smith and Jones each have men on his side, i.e. if "war" breaks out between Smith and his henchmen and Jones and his bodyguards. If Smith and a group of henchmen aggress against Jones, and Jones and his bodyguards pursue the Smith gang to their lair, we may cheer Jones on in his endeavor; and we, and others in society interested in repelling aggression, may contribute financially or personally to Jones's cause. But Jones and his men have *no* right, any more than does Smith, to aggress against anyone else in the course of their "just war": to steal others' property in order to finance their pursuit, to conscript others into their posse by use of violence, or to kill others in the course of their struggle to capture the Smith forces. If Jones and his men should do any of these things, they become criminals as *fully* as Smith, and they too become subject to whatever sanctions are meted out against criminality. In fact, if Smith's crime was theft, and Jones should use conscription to catch him, or should kill innocent people in the pursuit, then Jones becomes *more of* a criminal than Smith, for such crimes against another person as enslavement and murder are surely far worse than theft.

Suppose that Jones, in the course of his "just war" against the ravages of Smith, should kill some innocent people; and suppose that he should declaim, in defense of this murder, that he was simply acting on the slogan, "give me liberty or give me death." The absurdity of this "defense" should be evident at once, for the issue is not whether Jones was willing to risk death personally in his defensive struggle against Smith; the issue is whether he was willing to kill other innocent people in pursuit of his legitimate end. For Jones was in truth acting on the completely indefensible slogan: "Give me liberty or give *them* death"—surely a far less noble battle cry.

War, then, even a just defensive war, is only proper when the exercise of violence is rigorously limited to the individual criminals themselves. We may judge for ourselves how many wars or conflicts in history have met this criterion.

It has often been maintained, and especially by conservatives, that the development of the horrendous modern weapons of mass murder (nuclear weapons, rockets, germ warfare, etc.) is only a difference of *degree* rather than *kind* from the simpler weapons of an earlier era. Of course, one answer to this is that when the degree is the number of human lives, the difference is a very big one. But a particularly libertarian reply is that while the bow and arrow, and even the rifle, can be pinpointed, if the will be there, against actual criminals, modern nuclear weapons cannot. Here is a crucial difference in kind. Of course, the bow and arrow could be used for aggressive purposes, but it could also be pinpointed to use only against aggressors. Nuclear weapons, even "conventional" aerial bombs, cannot be. These weapons are *ipso facto* engines of indiscriminate mass destruction. (The only exception would be the extremely rare case where a mass of people who were *all* criminals inhabited a vast geographical area.) We must, therefore, conclude that the use of nuclear or similar weapons, or the threat thereof, is a crime against humanity for which there can be no justification.[1]

This is why the old cliche no longer holds that it is not the arms but the will to use them that is significant in judging matters of war and peace. For it is precisely the characteristic of modern weapons that they *cannot* be used selectively, cannot be used in a libertarian manner. Therefore, their very existence must be condemned, and nuclear disarmament becomes a good to be pursued for its own sake. Indeed, of all the aspects of liberty, such disarmament becomes the highest political good that can be pursued in the modern world. For just as murder is a more heinous crime against another man than larceny, so mass murder—indeed murder so widespread as to threaten human civilization and human survival itself—is the worst crime that any man could possibly commit. And that crime is now all too possible. Or are libertarians going to wax properly indignant about price controls or the income tax, and yet shrug their shoulders at or even positively advocate the ultimate crime of mass murder?

If nuclear warfare is totally illegitimate even for individuals defending themselves against criminal assault, how much more so is nuclear or even "conventional" warfare between States!

Let us now bring the State into our discussion. Since each State arrogates to itself a monopoly of violence over a territorial area, so long as its depredations and extortions go unresisted, there is said to be "peace" within the area, since the only violence is continuing and one-way, directed by the State downward against its people. Open conflict within the area only breaks out in the case of "revolutions," in which people resist the use of State power against them. Both the quiet case of the State unresisted and the case of open revolution may be termed "vertical violence": violence of the State against its public or vice versa.

In the existing world, each land area is ruled over by a State organization, with a number of States scattered over the earth, each with a monopoly

---

1. For a clear statement of the moral validity of the distinction between combatants and noncombatants, see G.E.M. Anscombe, *Mr. Truman's Degree* (Oxford: privately printed, 1956). The pamphlet was issued as a protest against the granting of an honorary doctorate to President Truman by Oxford University.

of violence over its own territory. No super-State exists with a monopoly of violence over the entire world; and so a state of "anarchy" exists between the several States.[2] And so, except for revolutions, which occur only sporadically, the open violence and two-sided conflict in the world takes place *between* two or more States, i.e., what is called "international war" or "horizontal violence."

Now there are crucial and vital differences between inter-State warfare on the one hand and revolutions against the State or conflicts between private individuals on the other. In a revolution the conflict takes place *within* the same geographical area: both the minions of the State and the revolutionaries inhabit the same territory. Inter-State warfare, on the other hand, takes place between two groups, each having a monopoly over its own geographical area, i.e. it takes place between inhabitants of different territories. From this difference flow several important consequences:

(1) In inter-State war, the scope for the use of modern weapons of mass destruction is far greater. For if the escalation of weaponry in an intra-territorial conflict becomes too great, each side will blow itself up with the weapons directed against the other. Neither a revolutionary group nor a State combatting revolution, for example, can use nuclear weapons against the other. But, on the other hand, when the warring parties inhabit different territorial areas, the scope for modern weaponry becomes enormous, and the entire arsenal of mass devastation can come into play.

A second corollary consequence (2) is that while it is *possible* for revolutionaries to pinpoint their targets and confine them to their State enemies, and thus avoid aggressing against innocent people, pinpointing is far less possible in an inter-State war. This is true even with older weapons; and, of course, with modern weapons there can be no pinpointing whatever.

Furthermore, (3) since each State can mobilize all the people and resources in its territory, the other State comes to regard all the citizens of the opposing country as at least temporarily its enemies and to treat them accordingly by extending the war to them. Thus, all of the consequences of inter-territorial war make it almost inevitable that inter-State war will involve aggression by each side against the innocent civilians—the private individuals—of the other. This inevitability becomes absolute with modern weapons of mass destruction.

If one distinct attribute of inter-State war is inter-territoriality, another unique attribute stems from the fact that each State lives by taxation over

---

2. It is curious and inconsistent that conservative advocates of "limited government" denounce as absurd any proposal for eliminating a monopoly of violence over a given territory, thus leaving private individuals without an overlord, and *yet* are equally insistent on leaving nation-*States* without an overlord to settle disputes between them.

its subjects. Any war against another State, therefore, involves the increase and extension of taxation-aggression against its own people. Conflicts between private individuals can be, and usually are, voluntarily waged and financed by the parties concerned. Revolutions can be, and often are, financed and fought by voluntary contributions of the public. But State wars can only be waged through aggression against the taxpayer.

All State wars, therefore, involve increased aggression against the State's own taxpayers, and almost all State wars (*all*, in modern warfare) involve the maximum aggression (murder) against the innocent civilians ruled by the enemy State. On the other hand, revolutions are often financed voluntarily and *may* pinpoint their violence to the State rulers; and private conflicts may confine their violence to the actual criminals. We must therefore conclude that, while some revolutions and some private conflicts *may* be legitimate, State wars are *always* to be condemned.

Some libertarians might object as follows: "While we too deplore the use of taxation for warfare, and the State's monopoly of defense service, we have to recognize that these conditions exist, and while they do, we must support the State in just wars of defense." In the light of our discussion above, the reply would go as follows: "Yes, States exist, and as long as they do, the libertarian attitude toward the State should be to say to it, in effect: 'All right, you exist, but so long as you do, *at least* confine your activities to the area which you monopolize.'" In short, the libertarian is interested in reducing as much as possible the area of State aggression against all private individuals, "foreign" and "domestic." The only way to do this, in international affairs, is for the people of each country to pressure their own State to confine its activities to the area which it monopolizes, and not to aggress against other State-monopolists—particularly the *people* ruled by other States. In short, the objective of the libertarian is to confine any existing State to as small a degree of invasion of person and property as possible. And this means the total avoidance of war. The people under each State should pressure "their" respective States not to attack one another, and, if a conflict should break out, to negotiate a peace or declare a cease-fire as quickly as physically possible.

Suppose further that we have that rarity—an unusually clear-cut case in which the State is actually trying to defend the property of one of its citizens. A citizen of country A travels or invests in country B, and then State B aggresses against his person or confiscates his property. Surely, our libertarian critic might argue, here is a clear-cut case where State A should threaten or commit war against State B in order to defend the property of "its" citizen. Since, the argument runs, the State has taken upon itself the monopoly of defense of its citizens, it then has the obligation to go to war on behalf of any citizen, and libertarians must support such a war as a just one.

But the point again is that each State has a monopoly of violence, and therefore of defense, *only* over its territorial area. It has no such monopoly—in fact it has no power at all—over any other geographical area. Therefore, if an inhabitant of country A should move to or invest in country B, the libertarian must argue that he thereby takes his chances with the State monopolist of country B, and that it would be immoral and criminal for State A to tax people in country A *and* to kill numerous innocents in country B in order to defend the property of the traveller or investor.[3]

It should also be pointed out that there is *no* defense against nuclear weapons (the only current "defense" being the threat of "mutually assured destruction") and, therefore, that the State *cannot* fulfill any sort of international defense function so long as these weapons exist.

The libertarian objective, then, should be, regardless of the specific causes of any conflict, to pressure States not to launch wars against other States and, should a war break out, to pressure them to sue for peace and negotiate a cease-fire and a peace treaty as quickly as physically possible. This objective, incidentally, was enshrined in the old-fashioned international law of the eighteenth and nineteenth centuries, i.e., the ideal that no State aggress against the territory of another—which is now called the "peaceful coexistence" of States.

Suppose, however, that despite libertarian opposition, war has begun and the warring States are not negotiating a peace. What, then, should be the libertarian position? Clearly, to reduce the scope of assault against innocent civilians as much as possible. Old-fashioned international law had two excellent devices for this purpose: the "laws of war," and the "laws of neutrality" or "neutrals' rights." The laws of neutrality were designed to keep any war that breaks out strictly confined to the warring States themselves, without aggression against the States, or particularly the peoples, of the other nations. Hence, the importance of such ancient and now forgotten American principles as "freedom of the seas" or severe limitations upon the rights of warring States to repress neutral trade with the enemy country. In short, the libertarian position is to induce the warring States to observe fully the rights of neutral citizens.

---

3. There is another consideration which applies rather to "domestic" defense within a State's territory: the *less* the State can successfully defend the inhabitants of its area against attack by (non-State) criminals, the *more* these inhabitants may come to learn the inefficiency of State operations, and the more they will turn to non-State methods of defense. Failure by the State to defend, therefore, may have educative value for the public.

For their part, the "laws of war" were designed to limit as much as possible the invasion by warring States of the rights of the civilians of the respective warring countries. As the British jurist F.J.P. Veale put it:

> The fundamental principle of this code was that hostilities between civilized peoples must be limited to the armed forces actually engaged. . . . It drew a distinction between combatants and noncombatants by laying down that the sole business of the combatants is to fight each other and, consequently, that noncombatants must be excluded from the scope of military operations.[4]

In condemning all wars, regardless of motive, the libertarian knows that there may well be varying degrees of guilt among States for any specific war. But his overriding consideration is the condemnation of any State participation in war. Hence, his policy is that of exerting pressure on all States not to start or engage in a war, to stop one that has begun, and to reduce the scope of any persisting war in injuring civilians of either side or no side.

One corollary of the libertarian policy of peaceful coexistence and nonintervention between States is the rigorous abstention from any foreign aid, aid from one State to another. For any aid given by State A to State B (1) increases the tax aggression against the people of country A, and (2) aggravates the suppression by State B of its own people.

Let us see how libertarian theory applies to the problem of *imperialism*, which may be defined as the aggression of State A over the people of country B, and the subsequent maintenance of this foreign rule. This rule could either be directly over country B, or indirectly through a subsidiary client State B. Revolution by the people of B against the imperial rule of A (either directly or against client State B) is certainly legitimate, provided again that the revolutionary fire be directed only against the rulers. It has often been maintained by conservatives—and even by some libertarians— that Western imperialism over undeveloped countries should be supported as more watchful of property rights than any successor native government might be. But first, judging what might follow the status quo is purely speculative, whereas the oppression of existing imperial rule over the people of country B is all too real and culpable. And secondly, this analysis neglects the injuries of imperialism suffered by the Western taxpayer, who is mulcted and burdened to pay

---

4. F.J.P. Veale, *Advance to Barbarism* (Appleton, Wisc.: C.C. Nelson, 1953), p. 58.

for the wars of conquest and then for the maintenance of the imperial bureaucracy. On this latter ground alone, the libertarian must condemn imperialism.[5]

Does opposition to all inter-State war mean that the Libertarian can never countenance change of geographical boundaries—that he is consigning the world to a freezing of unjust territorial regimes? Certainly not. Suppose, for example, that the hypothetical State of "Walldavia" has attacked "Ruritania" and annexed the western part of the country. The Western Ruritanians now long to be reunited with their Ruritanian brethren (perhaps because they wish to use their Ruritanian language undisturbed). How is this to be achieved? There is, of course, the route of peaceful negotiations between the two powers; but suppose that the Walldavian imperialists prove adamant. Or, libertarian Walldavians can put pressure on their State to abandon its conquest in the name of justice. But suppose that this, too, does not work. What then? We must still maintain the illegitimacy of the Ruritanian State's mounting a war against Walldavia. The legitimate routes to geographical change are (1) revolutionary uprisings by the oppressed Western Ruritanian people, and (2) aid by private Ruritanian groups (or, for that matter, by friends of the Ruritanian cause in other countries) to the Western rebels— either in the form of equipment or volunteer personnel.

Finally, we must allude to the domestic tyranny that is the inevitable accompaniment of inter-State war, a tyranny that usually lingers long after the war is over. Randolph Bourne realized that "war is the health of the State."[6] It is in war that the State really comes into its own: swelling in power, in number, in pride, in absolute dominion over the economy and the society. The root myth that enables the State to wax fat off war is the canard that war is a defense *by* the State *of* its subjects. The facts are

---

5. Two further empirical points may be made about Western imperialism. First, the property rights respected were largely those of the Europeans; the *native* population often found their best lands stolen from them by the imperialists, and their labor coerced by violence into working mines or landed estates acquired by this theft.

Second, another myth holds that the "gunboat diplomacy" of the turn of the twentieth century was, after all, a defense of the property rights of Western investors in backward countries. But, apart from our above strictures against going beyond any given State's monopolized land area, it is generally overlooked that the bulk of gunboat actions were in defense *not* of private investments, but of Western holders of native government bonds. The Western powers coerced the native governments into increasing tax aggression upon their own people in order to pay off foreign bondholders. This was no action on behalf of private property—quite the contrary.

6. Randolph Bourne, *War and the Intellectuals,* C. Resek, ed. (New York: Harper and Row, 1964), p. 69.

precisely the reverse. For if war is the health of the State, it is also its greatest danger. A State can only "die" by defeat in war or by revolution. In war, therefore, the State frantically mobilizes the people to fight for it against another State, under the pretext that it is fighting for them. Society becomes militarized and statized, it becomes a herd, seeking to kill its alleged enemies, rooting out and suppressing all dissent from the official war effort, happily betraying truth for the supposed public interest. Society becomes an armed camp, with the values and the morale—as Albert Jay Nock once phrased it—of an "army on the march."[7]

7. An earlier version of this view can be found in Murray N. Rothbard, "War, Peace, and the State," in *Egalitarianism as a Revolt Against Nature, and Other Essays* (Washington, D.C.: Libertarian Review Press, 1974), pp. 70–80.

PART IV:

MODERN ALTERNATIVE THEORIES OF LIBERTY

Having presented our theory of liberty and property rights, and discussed the inherent role of the State *vis-à-vis* liberty, we turn in this part of the work to a discussion and critique of several leading alternative theories of liberty brought forth in the modern world, by those who are very roughly in the free-market, or classical liberal, tradition. Whatever the other merits of these theories, they will be seen to provide a flawed and inadequate foundation for a systematic theory of liberty and the rights of the individual.

26. Utilitarian Free-Market Economics

A. Introduction: Utilitarian Social Philosophy

E conomics emerged as a distinct, self-conscious science or discipline in the nineteenth century, and hence this development unfortunately coincided with the dominance of utilitarianism in philosophy. The social philosophy of economists, therefore, whether the laissez-faire creed of the nineteenth century or the statism of the twentieth, has almost invariably been grounded in utilitarian social philosophy. Even today, political economy abounds with discussion of the weighing of "social costs" and "social benefits" in deciding upon public policy.

We cannot engage here in a critique of utilitarianism as an ethical theory.[1] Here we are interested in analyzing certain attempts to use a utilitarian ethic to provide a defensible groundwork for a libertarian or laissez-faire ideology. Our brief criticisms will concentrate, then, on utilitarianism insofar as it has been used as a groundwork for a libertarian, or quasi-libertarian, political philosophy.[2]

In brief, utilitarian social philosophy holds the "good" policy to be the one that yields the "greatest good for the greatest number": in which each person counts for one in making up that number, and in which "the good" is held to be the fullest satisfaction of the purely subjective desires of the individuals in society. Utilitarians, like economists (see further below) like to think of themselves as "scientific" and "value-free," and their doctrine supposedly permits them to adopt a virtually value-free stance; for they are presumably not imposing their own values, but simply recommending the greatest possible satisfaction of the desires and wants of the mass of the population.

But this doctrine is hardly scientific and by no means value-free. For one thing, why the "greatest number"? Why is it ethically better to follow the wishes of the greater as against the lesser number? What's so good about the "greatest number"?[3] Suppose that the vast majority of

---

1. For the beginning of a critique of utilitarianism in the context of the alternative of a natural-law ethics, see John Wild, *Plato's Modern Enemies and the Theory of Natural Law* (Chicago: University of Chicago Press, 1953); Henry B. Veatch, *For An Ontology of Morals: A Critique of Contemporary Ethical Theory* (Evanston, Ill.: Northwestern University Press, 1971). On utilitarianism's inadequacy as a libertarian political philosophy, see Herbert Spencer, *Social Statics* (New York: Robert Schalkenbach Foundation, 1970) pp. 3–16.

2. For preceding criticisms of utilitarian approaches in this work, see pp. 11–13 above.

3. And what if, even in utilitarian terms, more happiness can be obtained by following the wishes of the *smaller* number? For a discussion of this problem, see Peter Geach, *The Virtues* (Cambridge: Cambridge Univeristy Press, 1977), pp. 91ff.

people in a society hate and revile redheads, and greatly desire to murder them; and suppose further that there are only a few redheads extant at any time. Must we then say that it is "good" for the vast majority to slaughter redheads? And if not, why not? At the very least, then, utilitarianism scarcely suffices to make a case for liberty and laissez-faire. As Felix Adler wryly put it, utilitarians

> pronounce the greatest happiness of the greatest number to be the social end, although they fail to make it intelligible why the happiness of the greater number should be cogent as an end upon those who happen to belong to the lesser number.[4]

Secondly, what is the justification for each person counting for one? Why not some system of weighting? This, too, seems to be an unexamined and therefore unscientific article of faith in utilitarianism.

Thirdly, why is "the good" only fulfilling the subjective emotional desires of each person? Why can there be no supra-subjective critique of these desires? Indeed, utilitarianism implicitly assumes these subjective desires to be absolute givens which the social technician is somehow duty-bound to try to satisfy. But it is common human experience that individual desires are *not* absolute and unchanging. They are not hermetically sealed off from persuasion, rational or otherwise; experience and other individuals can and do persuade and convince people to change their values. But how could that be so if all individual desires and values are pure givens and therefore not subject to alteration by the inter-subjective persuasion of others? But if these desires are not givens, and they *are* changeable by the persuasion of moral argument, it would then appear that inter-subjective moral principles *do* exist that can be argued and can have an impact on others.

Oddly enough, while utilitarianism assumes that morality, the good, is purely subjective to each individual, it assumes on the other hand that these subjective desires can be added, subtracted, and weighed across the various individuals in society. It assumes that individual subjective utilities and costs can be added, subtracted, and measured so as to arrive at a "net social utility" or social "cost," thus permitting the utilitarian to advise for or against a given social policy.[5] Modern welfare economics

---

4. Felix Adler, "The Relation of Ethics to Social Science," in H.J. Rogers, ed., *Congress of Arts and Science* (Boston: Houghton Mifflin, 1906), vol. 7, p. 673.

5. Furthermore, some preferences, such as someone's desire to see an innocent person suffer, seem immoral on objective grounds. Yet a utilitarian must hold that they, fully as much as the most innocuous or altruistic preferences, must be included in the quantitative reckoning. I am indebted to Dr. David Gordon for this point.

is particularly adept at arriving at estimates (even allegedly precise quantitative ones) of "social cost" and "social utility." But economics does correctly inform us, not that *moral principles* are subjective, but that utilities and costs *are* indeed subjective: individual utilities are purely subjective and ordinal, and therefore it is totally illegitimate to add or weight them to arrive at any estimate for "social" utility or cost.

B. The Unanimity and Compensation Principles

Utilitarian economists, even more than their philosophic confreres, are eager to make "scientific" and "value free" pronouncements on public policy. Believing, however, that ethics are purely arbitrary and subjective, how may economists then take policy positions? This chapter will explore ways in which utilitarian free-market economists presume to favor a free market while attempting to refrain from taking ethical positions.[6]

One important utilitarian variant is the Unanimity Principle, based on the criterion of "Pareto optimality" that a political policy is "good" if one or more people are "better off" (in terms of satisfying utilities) from that policy while no one is "worse off." A strict version of Pareto optimality implies unanimity: that every person agrees to, hence believes that he will be better off or at least no worse off, from a particular government action. In recent years, the Unanimity Principle as groundwork for a free market of voluntary and contractual agreements has been stressed by Professor James Buchanan. The Unanimity Principle has great attractions for "value-free" economists eager to make policy judgments, for far more than in the case of mere majority rule; surely the economist can safely advocate a policy if *everyone* in the society favors it. While the Unanimity Principle may at first appear superficially attractive to libertarians, however, there is at its heart a vital and irredeemable flaw: that the goodness of free contracts or unanimously approved changes from the existing situation depends completely on the goodness or justice of that existing situation *itself*. Yet neither Pareto Optimality, nor its Unanimity Principle variant, can say anything about the goodness or justice of the existing status quo, concentrating as they do solely on *changes from* that situation, or zero point.[7] Not only that, but the requirement of unanimous approval of changes

---

6. For an extended analysis of the relationship between economics, value judgments, and government policy, see Murray N. Rothbard, "Praxeology, Value Judgments, and Public Policy," in E. Dolan, ed., *The Foundations of Modern Austrian Economics* (Kansas City: Sheed and Ward, 1976), pp. 89–111.

7. Neither does the Unanimity Principle, as will be shown further below, keep the economist from making his own value judgments and thus breaching his "value freedom";

necessarily *freezes* the existing status quo. If the status quo is unjust or
repressive of liberty, then the Unanimity Principle is a grave barrier to
justice and liberty rather than a bulwark on its behalf. The economist
who advocates the Unanimity Principle as a seemingly value-free pronouncement for liberty is instead making a massive and totally unsupported value judgment on behalf of freezing the status quo.

The commonly accepted "Compensation Principle" variant of
Pareto optimality contains all the flaws of the strict Unanimity Principle, while adding many of its own. The Compensation Principle asserts
that a public policy is "good" if the gainers (in utility) from that policy
can compensate the losers and still enjoy net gains. So that while there *are*
losers in utility from this policy at the beginning, there are no such losers after the compensations take place. But the Compensation Principle
assumes that it is conceptually possible to add and subtract utilities in-
terpersonally, and thereby to measure gains and losses; it also assumes
that each individual's gains and losses can be precisely estimated. But
economics informs us that "utility," and hence gains and losses in utility, are purely subjective and psychic concepts, and that they cannot
possibly be measured or even estimated by outside observers. Gains and
losses in utility therefore cannot be added, measured, or weighted against
each other, and much less can precise compensations be discovered.
The usual assumption by economists is to measure psychic losses in utility by the monetary price of an asset; thus, if a railroad damages the
land of a farmer by smoke, it is assumed by the compensationists that
the farmer's loss can be measured by the market price of the land. But
this assumption ignores the fact that the farmer may well have a psychic
attachment to that land which is far greater than the market price, and
that, furthermore, it is impossible to find out what the farmer's psychic
attachment to the land may be. *Asking* the farmer is useless, since he
may *say*, for example, that his attachment to the land is much higher
than the market price, but he may well be lying. The government, or
other outside observer, has no way of finding out one way or the other.[8]
Furthermore, the existence in the society of just *one* militant anarchist,

for even if the economist merely shares in *everyone else's* value judgment, he is making a
value judgment nevertheless.

8. Individuals *demonstrate* part of their utility rankings when they make free-market
exchanges, but government actions, of course, are non-market phenomena. For a further
analysis of this question, see Walter Block, "Coase and Demsetz on Private Property
Rights," *Journal of Libertarian Studies* 1 (Spring 1977): 111–15. For more on demonstrated
preference as opposed to the concept of social utility, see Rothbard, "Praxeology, Value
Judgments, and Public Policy"; and Murray N. Rothbard, *Toward A Reconstruction of Utility
and Welfare Economics* (New York: Center for Libertarian Studies, 1977).

whose psychic grievance against government is such that he *cannot* be compensated for his psychic disutility from the existence or activity of government, is enough by itself to destroy the Compensation Principle case for any government action whatsoever. And surely at least one such anarchist exists.

A stark but not atypical example of the fallacies and the unjust devotion to the status quo of the Compensation Principle was the debate in the British Parliament during the early nineteenth century on the abolition of slavery. Early adherents of the Compensation Principle were there maintaining that the masters must be compensated for the loss of their investment in slaves. At which point, Benjamin Pearson, a member of the libertarian Manchester School, declared that he "had thought it was the slaves who should have been compensated."[9] Precisely! Here is a striking example of the need, in advocating public policy, to have some ethical system, some concept of justice. Those of us ethicists who hold that slavery is criminal and unjust would always oppose the idea of compensating the masters, and would rather think in terms of requiring the masters to compensate the slaves for their years of oppression. But the "value-free economist," resting on the Unanimity and Compensation Principles, is, on the contrary, implicitly placing his unsupported and arbitrary value imprimatur on the unjust status quo.

In a fascinating exchange with a critic of the Unanimity Principle, Professor Buchanan concedes that

> I am defending the status quo . . . not because I like it, I do not . . . . But my defense of the status quo stems from my unwillingness, indeed inability, to discuss changes other than those that are contractual in nature. I can, of course, lay down my own notions. . . . But, to me, this is simply wasted effort.

Thus, tragically, Buchanan, admitting that his idea of ethics is one of purely subjective and arbitrary "notions," is yet willing to promulgate what can only be an equally subjective and arbitrary notion *on his own grounds*— a defense of the status quo. Buchanan concedes that his procedure:

> does allow me to take a limited step toward normative judgments or hypotheses, namely to suggest that the changes seem to be potentially agreeable to everyone. Pareto efficient changes, which must, of course, include compensations. The criterion in my scheme is agreement.

---

9. William D. Grampp, *The Manchester School of Economics* (Stanford, Calif.: Stanford University Press, 1969), p. 59. See above, p. 60. Also see Murray N. Rothbard, "Value Implications of Economic Theory," *The American Economist* (Spring 1973): 38–39.

But what is the justification for this "limited step"? What's so great about agreement on changes from a possibly unjust status quo? Isn't such a limited step also an arbitrary "notion" for Buchanan? And if willing to proceed to such an unsatisfactory limit, why not go still further to question the status quo?

Buchanan proceeds to assert that:

> [O]ur task is really . . . that of trying to find, locate, invent, schemes that can command unanimous or quasi-unanimous consent and propose them. [What in the world is "quasi-unanimity?"] Since persons disagree on so much, these schemes may be a very limited set, and this may suggest to you that few changes are possible. Hence, the status quo defended indirectly. The status quo has no propriety at all save for its existence and it is all that exists. The point I always emphasize is that we start from here not from somewhere else.[10]

Here one longs for Lord Acton's noble dictum: "Liberalism wishes for what ought to be, irrespective of what is."[11] Buchanan's critic, though far from a libertarian or a free-market liberal, here properly has the last word: "I certainly do not totally object to seeking contractual solutions; but I do think that they can't be projected in a vacuum which allows the status quo power structure to go unspecified and unexamined."[12]

C. Ludwig von Mises and "Value-Free" Laissez Faire[13]

Let us now turn to the position of Ludwig von Mises on the entire matter of praxeology, value-judgments, and the advocacy of public policy. The case of Mises is particularly interesting, for he was, of all the economists in the twentieth century, at one and the same time the most uncompromising and passionate adherent of laissez faire and the most rigorous and uncompromising advocate of value-free economics and opponent of any sort of objective ethics. How then did he attempt to reconcile these two positions?[14]

---

10. James M. Buchanan, in Buchanan and Warren J. Samuels, "On Some Fundamental Issues in Political Economy: An Exchange of Correspondence," *Journal of Economic Issues* (March 1975): 27f.

11. Gertrude Himmelfarb, *Lord Acton* (Chicago: University of Chicago Press, 1962), p. 204.

12. Samuels, in Buchanan and Samuels, "Some Fundamental Issues," p. 37.

13. This section is adapted from my "Praxeology, Value Judgments, and Public Policy."

14. For a posing of this question, see William E. Rappard "On Reading Von Mises," in M. Sennholz, ed., *On Freedom and Free Enterprise* (Princeton, N.J.: D. Van Nostrand, 1956), pp. 17–33.

Mises offered two separate and very different solutions to this problem. The first is a variant of the Unanimity Principle. Essentially this variant affirms that an economist *per se* cannot say that a given governmental policy is "good" or "bad." However, if a given policy will lead to consequences, as explained by praxeology, which every one of the supporters of the policy will agree is bad, *then* the value-free economist is justified in calling the policy a "bad" one. Thus, Mises writes:

> An economist investigates whether a measure *a* can bring about the result *p* for the attainment of which it is recommended, and finds that *a* does not result in *p* but in *g*, an effect which even the supporters of the measure *a* consider undesirable. If the economist states the outcome of his investigation by saying that *a* is a bad measure, he does not pronounce a judgment of value. He merely says that from the point of view of those aiming at the goal *p*, the measure *a* is inappropriate.[15]

And again:

> Economics does not say that . . . government interference with the prices of only one commodity . . . is unfair, bad, or unfeasible. It says, that it makes conditions worse, not better, from the point of view of the government and those backing its interference.[16]

Now this is surely an ingenious attempt to allow pronouncements of "good" or "bad" by the economist without making a value judgment; for the economist is supposed to be only a praxeologist, a technician, pointing out to his readers or listeners that *they* will all consider a policy "bad" once he reveals its full consequences. But ingenious as it is, the attempt completely fails. For how does Mises know *what* the advocates of the particular policy consider desirable? How does he know what their value-scales are now or what they will be when the consequences of the measure appear? One of the great contributions of praxeologic economics is that the economist realizes that he doesn't *know* what anyone's value scales are except as those value preferences are *demonstrated by* a person's concrete action. Mises himself emphasized that:

> one must not forget that the scale of values or wants manifests itself only in the reality of action. These scales have no independent existence apart from the actual behavior of individuals. The only source from which our knowledge concerning these

---

15. Ludwig von Mises, *Human Action* (New Haven, Conn.: Yale University Press 1949), p. 879.

16. Ibid., p. 758. Italics in original.

scales is derived is the observation of a man's actions. Every
action is always in perfect agreement with the scale of values
or wants because these scales are nothing but an instrument
for the interpretation of a man's acting.[17]

Given Mises's own analysis, then, how can the economist *know* what the
motives for advocating various policies really are, or how people will
regard the consequences of these policies?

Thus, Mises, *qua* economist, may show that price control (to use his
example) will lead to unforeseen shortages of a good to the consumers.
But how does Mises know that some advocates of price control do not
want shortages? They may, for example, be socialists, anxious to use the
controls as a step toward full collectivism. Some may be egalitarians who
prefer shortages because the rich will not be able to use their money to
buy more of the product than poorer people. Some may be nihilists, eager
to see shortages of goods. Others may be one of the numerous legion of
contemporary intellectuals who are eternally complaining about the "excessive affluence" of our society, or about the great "waste" of energy; they
may all delight in the shortages of goods. Still others may favor price
control, even after learning of the shortages, because they, or their political
allies, will enjoy well-paying jobs or power in the price-control bureaucracy. All sorts of such possibilities exist, and *none* of them is compatible
with Mises asserting, *as a value-free economist,* that all the supporters of
the price control—or of any other government intervention—must
concede, after learning economics, that the measure is bad. In fact, once
Mises concedes that even a *single* advocate of price control or any other
interventionist measure may acknowledge the economic consequences
and *still* favor it, *for whatever reason,* then Mises, as a praxeologist and
economist, can no longer call any of these measures "bad" or "good," or
even "appropriate" or "inappropriate," without inserting into his economic policy pronouncements the very value judgments that Mises himself holds to be inadmissible in a scientist of human action.[18] For then he
is no longer being a technical reporter to all advocates of a certain policy, but himself an advocate participating on one side of a value conflict.

Moreover, there is another fundamental reason for advocates of
"inappropriate" policies to refuse to change their minds even after
hearing and acknowledging the praxeological chain of consequences.
For praxeology may indeed show that all types of government policies

---

17. Ibid., p. 95.

18. Mises himself concedes at one point that a government or a political party may advocate policies for "demagogic," i.e., for hidden and unannounced reasons. Ibid., p. 104n.

will have consequences that *most* people, at least, will tend to abhor; however, (and this is a vital qualification) most of these consequences take *time*, some a great deal of time. No economist has done more than Ludwig von Mises to elucidate the universality of *time-preference* in human affairs—the praxeologic law that everyone prefers to attain a given satisfaction *sooner* than *later*. And certainly, Mises, as a value-free scientist, could never presume to criticize anyone's *rate* of time preference, to say that A's was "too high" or B's "too low." But, in that case, what about the high-time-preference people in society who may retort to the praxeologist: "perhaps this high tax and subsidy policy will lead to a decline of capital; perhaps even the price control will lead to shortages, but I don't care. Having a high time-preference, I value more highly the short-run subsidies, or the short-run enjoyment of buying the current good at cheaper prices, than the prospect of suffering the future consequences." And Mises, as a value-free scientist and opponent of any concept of objective ethics, *cannot* call them wrong. There is no way that he can assert the superiority of the long-run over the short-run without overriding the values of the high time-preference people; and this cannot be cogently done without abandoning his own subjectivist ethics.

In this connection, one of Mises's basic arguments for the free market is that, on the market, there is a "harmony of the rightly understood interests of all members of the market society." It is clear from his discussion that he doesn't merely mean "interests" after learning the praxeological consequences of market activity or of government intervention. He also, and in particular, means people's "long-run" interests, for, as Mises states, "For 'rightly understood' interests we may as well say interests 'in the long run.'"[19] But what about the high-time-preference folk, who prefer to consult their short-run interests? How can the long-run be called "better" than the short-run; why must "right understanding" necessarily be the long-run?[20] We see, therefore, that Mises's attempt to advocate laissez-faire while remaining value-free, by assuming that *all* of the advocates of government intervention will abandon their position once they learn of its consequences, falls completely to the ground.

There is another and very different way, however, that Mises attempts to reconcile his passionate advocacy of laissezfaire with the absolute value

---

19. Ibid., pp. 670 and 670n.

20. For a challenge to the notion that pursuit of one's desires against one's long-term interests is irrational, see Derek Parfit, "Personal Identity," *Philosophical Review* 80 (January 1971): 26.

freedom of the scientist. This is to take a position much more compatible with praxeology: by recognizing that the economist *qua* econ-omist can only trace chains of cause and effect and may not engage in value judgments or advocate public policy. This route of Mises concedes that the economic scientist cannot advocate laissez faire, but then adds that he as a *citizen* can do so. Mises, as a citizen, then proposes a value-system but it is a curiously scanty one. For he is here caught in a dilemma. As a praxeologist he knows that he cannot (as an economic scientist) pronounce value judgments or advocate policy; yet he cannot bring himself simply to assert and inject arbitrary value judgments. And so, as a utilitarian (for Mises, along with most economists, is indeed a utilitarian in ethics, although a Kantian in epistemology), what he does is to make *only one* narrow value judgment: that he desires to fulfill the goals of the major-ity of the public (happily, in this formulation, Mises does not presume to know the goals of *everyone*).

As Mises explains, in his second variant:

> Liberalism [i.e. laissez-faire liberalism] is a political doctrine. . . .
> As a political doctrine liberalism (in contrast to economic science) is not neutral with regard to values and ultimate ends sought by action. It assumes that all men or at least the majority of people are intent upon attaining certain goals. It gives them information about the means suitable to the realization of their plans. The champions of liberal doctrines are fully aware of the fact that their teachings are valid only for people who are committed to their valuational principles. While praxeology, and therefore economics too, uses the terms happiness and removal of uneasiness in a purely formal sense, liberalism attaches to them a concrete meaning. It presuppos-es that people prefer life to death, health to sickness . . . abun-dance to poverty. It teaches men how to act in accordance with these valuations.[21]

In this second variant, Mises has successfully escaped the self-contradiction of being a value-free praxeologist advocating laissez faire. Granting in this variant that the economist may not make such advocacy, he takes his stand as a "citizen" willing to make value judgments. But he is not willing to simply assert an *ad hoc* value judgment; presumably he feels that a valuing intellectual must present *some* sort of ethical system to justify such value judgments. But, as a utilitarian, Mises's system is a curiously bloodless one; even as a valuing laissez-faire liberal, he is only

---

21. Mises, *Human Action*, pp. 153–54.

willing to make *the one* value judgment that he joins the majority of the
people in favoring their common peace, prosperity, and abundance. In
this way, as an opponent of objective ethics, and uncomfortable as he
must be with making any value judgments even as a citizen, he makes
the minimal possible degree of such judgments. True to his utilitarian
position, his value judgment is the desirability of fulfilling the subjectively
desired goals of the bulk of the populace.

A few points in critique of this position may here be made. In the
first place, while praxeology can indeed demonstrate that laissez faire
will lead to harmony, prosperity, and abundance, whereas government
intervention leads to conflict and impoverishment,[22] and while it is
probably true that most people value the former highly, it is *not* true that
these are their *only* goals or values. The great analyst of ranked value
scales and diminishing marginal utility should have been more aware of
such competing values and goals. For example, many people, whether
through envy or a misplaced theory of justice, may prefer far more
equality of income than will be attained on the free market. Many people,
pace the aforementioned intellectuals, may want less abundance in order
to whittle down our allegedly " excessive" affluence. Others, as we have
mentioned above, may prefer to loot the capital of the rich or the
businessman in the short-run, while acknowledging but dismissing the
long-run ill effects, because they have a high time-preference. Probably
very few of these people will want to push statist measures to the point
of total impoverishment and destruction—although this may well happen. But a majority coalition of the above might well opt for *some* reduction in wealth and prosperity on behalf of these other values. They may
well decide that it is worth sacrificing a modicum of wealth and efficient
production because of the high opportunity cost of *not* being able to enjoy
an alleviation of envy, or a lust for power or submission to power, or, for
example, the thrill of "national unity" which they might enjoy from a
(short-lived) economic crisis.

What can Mises reply to a majority of the public who have indeed
considered all the praxeological consequences, and still prefer a modicum—or, for that matter, even a drastic amount—of statism in order
to achieve some of their competing goals? As a utilitarian, he *cannot*
quarrel with the ethical nature of their chosen goals, for, as a utilitarian,
he must confine himself to the *one* value judgment that he favors the
majority achieving their chosen goals. The only reply that Mises can

---

22. See Murray N. Rothbard, *Power and Market*, 2nd ed. (Kansas City: Sheed Andrews
and McMeel, 1977), pp. 262–66.

make within his own framework is to point out that government intervention has a cumulative effect, that eventually the economy must move either toward the free market or toward full socialism, which praxeology shows will bring chaos and drastic impoverishment, at least to an industrial society. But this, too, is not a fully satisfactory answer. While many or most programs of statist intervention— especially price controls—are indeed cumulative, others are not. Furthermore, the cumulative impact takes such a long time that the time-preferences of the majority might well lead them, in full acknowledgment of the consequences, to ignore the effect. And then what?

Mises attempted to use the cumulative argument to answer the contention that the majority of the public prefer egalitarian measures even knowingly at the expense of a portion of their own wealth. Mises's comment was that the "reserve fund" was on the point of being exhausted in Europe, and therefore that any further egalitarian measures would have to come directly out of the pockets of the masses through increased taxation. Mises assumed that once this became clear, the masses would no longer support interventionist measures.[23] But, in the first place, this is not a strong argument against the *previous* egalitarian measures, nor in favor of their repeal. But secondly, while the masses *might well* be convinced, there is certainly no apodictic certainty involved; and the masses have certainly in the past, and presumably will in the future continue knowingly to support egalitarian and other statist measures on behalf of others of their goals, despite the knowledge that their income and wealth would be reduced.

Thus, Dean Rappard pointed out in his thoughtful critique of Mises's position:

> Does the British voter, for instance, favor confiscatory taxation of large incomes primarily in the hope that it will redound to his material advantage, or in the certainty that it tends to reduce unwelcome and irritating social inequalities? In general, is the urge towards equality in our modern democracies not often stronger than the desire to improve one's material lot?

And, on his own country, Switzerland, Dean Rappard pointed out that the urban industrial and commercial majority of the country have repeatedly, and often at popular referenda, endorsed measures to subsidize the minority of farmers in a deliberate effort to retard industrialization and the growth of their own incomes.

---

23. Thus, see Mises, *Human Action*, pp. 851ff.

Rappard noted that the urban majority did not do so in the "absurd belief that they were thereby increasing their real income." Instead,

> quite deliberately and expressly, political parties have sacrificed the immediate material welfare of their members in order to prevent, or at least somewhat to retard, the complete industrialization of the country. A more agricultural Switzerland, though poorer, such is the dominant wish of the Swiss people today.[24]

The point here is that Mises, not only as a praxeologist but even as a utilitarian liberal, can have no word of criticism against these statist measures *once* the majority of the public have taken their praxeological consequences into account and chosen them anyway on behalf of goals other than wealth and prosperity.

Furthermore, there are other types of statist intervention which clearly have little or no cumulative effect,.and which may even have very little effect in diminishing production or prosperity. Let us for example assume again—and this assumption is not very farfetched in view of the record of human history—that the great majority of a society hate and revile redheads. Let us further assume that there are very few redheads in the society. This large majority then decides that it would like very much to murder all redheads. Here they are; the murder of redheads is high on the value-scales of the great majority of the public; there are few redheads so that there will be little loss in production on the market. How can Mises rebut this proposed policy either as a praxeologist or as a utilitarian liberal? I submit that he cannot do so.

Mises makes one further attempt to establish his position, but it is even less successful. Criticizing the arguments for state intervention on behalf of equality or other moral concerns, he dismisses them as "emotional talk." After reaffirming that "praxeology and economics . . . are neutral with regard to any moral precepts," and asserting that "the fact that the immense majority of men prefer a richer supply of material goods to a less ample supply is a datum of history; it does not have any place in economic theory," he concludes by insisting that "he who disagrees with the teachings of economics ought to refute them by discursive reasoning, not by . . . the appeal to arbitrary, allegedly ethical standards."[25]

But I submit that this will not do. For Mises must concede that no one can decide upon *any* policy whatever unless he makes an ultimate

---

24. Rappard, "On Reading von Mises," pp. 32–33.

25. Ludwig von Mises, "Epistemological Relativism in the Sciences of Human Action," in H. Schoeck and J.W. Wiggins, eds., *Relativism and the Study of Man* (Princeton, N.J.: D. van Nostrand, 1961), p. 133.

ethical or value judgment. But since this is so, and since according to Mises *all* ultimate value judgments or ethical standards are arbitrary, how then can he denounce *these particular* ethical judgments as "arbitrary"? Furthermore, it is hardly correct for Mises to dismiss these judgments as "emotional," since for him as a utilitarian, reason cannot establish ultimate ethical principles; which can therefore only be established by subjective emotions. It is pointless for Mises to call for his critics to use "discursive reasoning," since he himself denies that discursive reasoning can ever be used to establish ultimate ethical values. Furthermore, the man whose ultimate ethical principles would lead him to support the free market should *also* be dismissed by Mises as equally "arbitrary" and "emotional," even if he has taken the laws of praxeology into account before making his ultimately ethical decision. And we have seen above that the majority of the public very often has other goals which they hold, at least to a certain extent, higher than their own material well-being.

Thus, while praxeological economic theory is extremely useful for providing data and knowledge for framing economic policy, it cannot be sufficient by itself to enable the economist to make any value pronouncements or to advocate any public policy whatsoever. More specifically, Ludwig von Mises to the contrary notwithstanding, neither praxeological economics *nor* Mises's utilitarian liberalism is sufficient to make the case for laissez faire and the free-market economy. To make such a case, one must go beyond economics and utilitarianism to establish an objective ethics which affirms the overriding value of liberty, and morally condemns all forms of statism, from egalitarianism to "the murder of redheads," as well as such goals as the lust for power and the satisfaction of envy. To make the full case for liberty, one cannot be a methodological slave to every goal that the majority of the public might happen to cherish.

27. Isaiah Berlin on Negative Freedom

One of the best-known and most influential present-day treatments of liberty is that of Sir Isaiah Berlin. In his *Two Concepts of Liberty*, Berlin upheld the concept of "negative liberty"—absence of interference with a person's sphere of action—as against "positive liberty," which refers not to liberty at all but to an individual's effective power or mastery over himself or his environment. Superficially, Berlin's concept of negative liberty seems similar to the thesis of the present volume: that liberty is the absence of physically coercive interference or invasion of an individual's person and property. Unfortunately, however, the vagueness of Berlin's concepts led to confusion and to the absence of a systematic and valid libertarian creed.

One of Berlin's fallacies and confusions he himself recognized in a later essay and edition of his original volume. In his *Two Concepts of Liberty*, he had written that "I am normally said to be free to the degree to which no human being interferes with my activity. Political liberty in this sense is simply the area within which a man can do what he wants."[1] Or, as Berlin later phrased it, "In the original version of *Two Concepts of Liberty* I speak of liberty as the absence of obstacles to the fulfillment of a man's desires."[2] But, as he later realized, one grave problem with this formulation is that a man can be held to be "free" in proportion as his wants and desires are extinguished, for example by external conditioning. As Berlin states in his corrective essay,

> If degrees of freedom were a function of the satisfaction of desires, I could increase freedom as effectively by eliminating desires as by satisfying them; I could render men (including myself) free by conditioning them into losing the original desires which I have decided not to satisfy.[3]

---

1. Isaiah Berlin, *Two Concepts of Liberty* (Oxford: Oxford University Press, 1958), p. 7.

2. Isaiah Berlin, "Introduction," *Four Essays on Liberty* (Oxford: Oxford University Press, 1969), p. xxxviii.

3. Ibid., p. xxxviii. Also see William A. Parent, "Some Recent Work on the Concept of Liberty," *American Philosophical Quarterly* (July 1974): 149–53. Professor Parent adds the criticism that Berlin neglects the cases in which men act in ways which they do not "truly" want or desire, so that Berlin would have to concede that a man's freedom is not abridged if he is forcibly prevented from doing something he "dislikes." Berlin may be salvaged on this point however, if we interpret "want" or "desire" in the formal sense of a person's

In his later (1969) version, Berlin has expunged the offending passage, altering the first statement above to read: "Political liberty in this sense is simply the area within which a man can act unobstructed by others."[4] But grave problems still remain with Berlin's later approach. For Berlin now explains that what he means by freedom is "the absence of obstacles to possible choices and activities," obstacles, that is, put there by "alterable human practices."[5] But this comes close, as Professor Parent observes, to confusing "freedom" with "opportunity," in short to scuttling Berlin's own concept of negative freedom and replacing it with the illegitimate concept of "positive freedom." Thus, as Parent indicates, suppose that X refuses to hire Y because Y is a redhead and X dislikes redheads; X is surely reducing Y's range of opportunity, but he can scarcely be said to be invading Y's "freedom."[6] Indeed, Parent goes on to point out a repeated confusion in the later Berlin of freedom with opportunity; thus Berlin writes that "the freedom of which I speak is opportunity for action" (xlii), and identifies increases in liberty with the "maximization of opportunities" (xlviii). As Parent points out, "The terms 'liberty' and 'opportunity' have distinct meanings"; someone, for example, may lack the *opportunity* to buy a ticket to a concert for numerous reasons (e.g., he is too busy) and yet he was still in any meaningful sense "free" to buy such a ticket.[7]

Thus, Berlin's fundamental flaw was his failure to define negative liberty as the absence of physical interference with an individual's person and property, with his *just property rights* broadly defined. Failing to hit on this definition, Berlin fell into confusion, and ended by virtually abandoning the very negative liberty he had tried to establish and to fall, willy-nilly, into the "positive liberty" camp. More than that, Berlin, stung by his critics with the charge of upholding laissez-faire, was moved into frenetic and self-contradictory assaults on laissez-faire as somehow injurious to negative liberty. For example, Berlin writes that the "evils of unrestricted laissez faire . . . led to brutal violations of 'negative' liberty . . . including that of free expression or association." Since laissez faire precisely

---

freely chosen goal, rather than in the sense of something he emotionally or hedonistically "likes" or enjoys doing or achieving. Ibid., pp. 150–52.

4. Berlin, *Four Essays on Liberty*, p. 122.

5. Ibid., pp. xxxix–xl.

6. Furthermore, if one were to prohibit X from refusing to hire Y because the latter is a redhead, then X has had an obstacle imposed upon his action by an alterable human practice. On Berlin's revised definition of liberty, therefore, the *removing of* obstacles cannot increase liberty, for it can only benefit some people's liberty at the expense of others. I am indebted to Dr. David Gordon for this point.

7. Parent, "Some Recent Work," pp. 152–53.

means full freedom of person and property, including of course free expression and association as a subset of private property rights, Berlin has here fallen into absurdity. And in a similar canard, Berlin writes of

> the fate of personal liberty during the reign of unfettered eco-
> nomic individualism—about the condition of the injured maj-
> ority, principally in the towns, whose children were destroyed
> in mines or mills, while their parents lived in poverty, disease,
> and ignorance, a situation in which the enjoyment by the poor
> and the weak of legal rights . . . became an odious mockery.[8]

Unsurprisingly, Berlin goes on to attack such pure and consistent laissez-faire libertarians as Cobden and Spencer on behalf of such confused and inconsistent classical liberals as Mill and de Tocqueville.

There are several grave and basic problems with Berlin's fulminations. One is a complete ignorance of the modern historians of the Industrial Revolution, such as Ashton, Hayek, Hutt, and Hartwell, who have demonstrated that the new industry alleviated the previous poverty and starvation of the workers, including the child laborers, rather than the contrary.[9] But on a conceptual level, there are grave problems as well. First, that it is absurd and self-contradictory to assert that laissez-faire or economic individualism could have injured personal *liberty*; and, second, that Berlin is really explicitly scuttling the very concept of "negative" liberty on behalf of concepts of positive power or wealth.

Berlin reaches the height (or depth) of this approach when he attacks negative liberty directly for having been

> used to . . . arm the strong, the brutal, and the unscrupulous
> against the humane and the weak. . . . Freedom for the wolves
> has often meant death to the sheep. The bloodstained story of
> economic individualism and unrestrained capitalist compe-
> tition does not . . . today need stressing.[10]

The crucial fallacy of Berlin here is insistently to identify freedom and the free market economy with its opposite—with coercive aggression. Note his repeated use of such terms as "arm," "brutal," "wolves and sheep," and "bloodstained," all of which are applicable *only* to coercive

---

8. Berlin, *Four Essays on Liberty*, pp. xlv–xlvi.

9. See F.A. Hayek, ed., *Capitalism and the Historians* (Chicago: University of Chicago Press, 1954); and R.M. Hartwell, *The Industrial Revolution and Economic Growth* (London: Methuen, 1971).

10. Berlin, *Four Essays on Liberty*, p. xlv.

aggression such as has been universally employed by the *State.* Also, he then identifies such aggression with its opposite—the peaceful and voluntary processes of free exchange in the market economy. Unrestrained economic individualism led, on the contrary, to peaceful and harmonious exchange, which benefitted most precisely the "weak" and the "sheep"; it is the latter who could *not* survive in the statist rule of the jungle, who reap the largest share of the benefits from the freely competitive economy. Even a slight acquaintance with economic science, and particularly with the Ricardian Law of Comparative Advantage, would have set Sir Isaiah straight on this vital point.[11]

---

11. See also Murray N. Rothbard, "Back to the Jungle?" in *Power and Market,* 2nd ed. (Kansas City: Sheed Andrews and McMeel, 1977), pp. 226–28.

28. F.A. Hayek and The Concept of Coercion[1]

In his monumental work *The Constitution of Liberty*, F.A. Hayek attempts to establish a systematic political philosophy on behalf of individual liberty.[2] He begins very well, by defining freedom as the absence of coercion, thus upholding "negative liberty" more cogently than does Isaiah Berlin. Unfortunately, the fundamental and grievous flaw in Hayek's system appears when he proceeds to define "coercion." For instead of defining coercion as is done in the present volume, as the invasive use of physical violence or the threat thereof against someone else's person or (just) property, Hayek defines coercion far more fuzzily and inchoately: e.g., as "control of the environment or circumstances of a person by another (so) that, in order to avoid greater evil, he is forced to act not according to a coherent plan of his own but to serve the ends of another"; and again: "Coercion occurs when one man's actions are made to serve another man's will, not for his own but for the other's purpose."[3]

For Hayek, "coercion" of course includes the aggressive use of physical violence, but the term unfortunately *also* includes peaceful and non-aggressive actions as well. Thus, Hayek states that "the threat of force or violence is the most important form of coercion. But they are not synonymous with coercion, for the threat of physical force is not the only way in which coercion can be exercised."[4]

What, then, are the other, nonviolent "ways" in which Hayek believes coercion can be exercised? One is such purely voluntary ways of interacting as "a morose husband" or "a nagging wife," who can make someone else's "life intolerable unless their every mood is obeyed." Here Hayek concedes that it would be absurd to advocate legal outlawry of sulkiness or nagging; but he does so on the faulty grounds that such outlawry would involve "even greater coercion." But "coercion" is not really an additive quantity; how can we quantitatively compare different "degrees"of coercion, especially when they involve comparisons among different people? Is there no fundamental qualitative difference, a difference in *kind*, between a nagging wife and using the apparatus of physical violence to outlaw or restrict such nagging? It seems clear that the fundamental problem

---

1. A version of this section appeared in the 1980 issue of *Ordo* (Stuttgart).

2. F.A. Hayek, *The Constitution of Liberty* (Chicago: University of Chicago Press, 1960).

3. Ibid., pp. 20–21, 133.

4. Ibid., p. 135.

is Hayek's use of " coercion" as a portmanteau term to include, not only physical violence but *also* voluntary, nonviolent, and non-invasive actions such as nagging. The point, of course, is that the wife or husband is free to leave the offending partner, and that staying together is a voluntary choice on his or her part. Nagging might be morally or aesthetically unfortunate, but it is scarcely "coercive" in any sense similar to the use of physical violence.

Only confusion can be caused by lumping the two types of action together.

But not only confusion but also self-contradiction, for Hayek includes in the concept of "coercion" not only invasive physical violence, i.e. a compulsory action or exchange, but also certain forms of peaceful, voluntary *refusal* to make exchanges. Surely, the freedom to make an exchange *necessarily implies* the equivalent freedom *not* to make an exchange. Yet, Hayek dubs certain forms of peaceful refusal to make an exchange as "coercive," thus lumping them together with compulsory exchanges. Specifically, Hayek states that

> there are, undeniably, occasions when the condition of employment creates opportunity for true coercion. In periods of acute unemployment the threat of dismissal may be used to enforce actions other than those originally contracted for. And in conditions such as those in a mining town the manager may well exercise an entirely arbitrary and capricious tyranny over a man to whom he has taken a dislike.[5]

Yet, "dismissal" is simply a refusal by the capital-owning employer to make any further exchanges with one or more people. An employer may refuse to make such exchanges for many reasons, and there are none but subjective criteria to enable Hayek to use the term "arbitrary." Why is one reason any more "arbitrary" than another? If Hayek means to imply that any reasons other than maximizing monetary profit are "arbitrary," then he ignores the Austrian School insight that people, even in business, act to maximize their "psychic" rather than monetary profit, and that such psychic profit may include all sorts of values, none of which is more or less arbitrary than another. Furthermore, Hayek here seems to be implying that employees have some sort of "right" to continuing employment, a "right" which is in overt contradiction to the property rights of employers to their own money. Hayek concedes that dismissal is ordinarily not "coercive"; why then, in conditions of "acute unemployment"

---

5. Ibid., pp. 136–37.

(surely, in any case, not of the employer's making), or of the mining town? Again, miners have moved voluntarily to the mining town and are free to leave whenever they like.

Hayek commits a similar error when he deals with the refusal to exchange made by a "monopolist" (the single owner of a resource). He admits that "if . . . I would very much like to be painted by a famous artist and if he refused to paint me for less than a very high fee [or at all?], it would clearly be absurd to say that I am coerced." Yet he *does* apply the concept of coercion to a case where a monopolist owns water in an oasis. Suppose, he says, that people had "settled there on the assumption that water would always be available at a reasonable price," that then other water sources had dried up, and that people then "had no choice but to do whatever the owner of the spring demanded of them if they were to survive: here would be a clear case of coercion,"[6] since the good or service in question is "crucial to [their] existence." Yet, since the owner of the spring did not aggressively poison the competing springs, the owner is scarcely being "coercive"; in fact, he is supplying a vital service, and should have the right either to refuse a sale or to charge whatever the customers will pay. The situation may well be unfortunate for the customers, as are many situations in life, but the supplier of a particularly scarce and vital service is hardly being "coercive" by either refusing to sell or by setting a price that the buyers are willing to pay. Both actions are within his rights as a free man and as a just property owner. The owner of the oasis is responsible only for the existence of his own actions and his own property; he is not accountable for the existence of the desert or for the fact that the other springs have dried up.[7]

---

6. Hayek, *The Constitution of Liberty*, p. 136.

7. Furthermore, as Professor Ronald Hamowy points out in a brilliant critique of Hayek's concept of coercion, and of the "rule of law,"

> we are faced with what appears to be an insurmountable problem—what constitutes a "reasonable" price? By "reasonable" Hayek might mean "competitive." But how is it possible to determine what the competitive price is in the absence of competition? Economics cannot predict the cardinal magnitude of any market price in the absence of a market. What, then, can we assume to be a "reasonable" price, or, more to the point, at what price does the contract alter its nature and become an instance of "coercion"? Is it at one cent a gallon, at one dollar a gallon, at ten dollars a gallon? What if the owner of the spring demands nothing more than the friendship of the settlers? Is such a "price" coercive? By what principle can we decide when the agreement is a simple contractual one and when it is not?

Moreover, as Hamowy states,

> we must face yet a further difficulty. Is the owner acting coercively if he refuses to sell his water at *any* price? Suppose that he looks upon his spring as sacred and its water as

Let us postulate another situation. Suppose that there is only one physician in a community, and an epidemic breaks out; only *he* can save the lives of numerous fellow-citizens—an action surely crucial to their existence. Is he "coercing" them if (a) he refuses to do anything, or leaves town; or (b) if he charges a very high price for his curative services? Certainly not. There is, for one thing, nothing wrong with a man charging the value of his services to his customers, i.e., what they are willing to pay. He further has every right to refuse to do anything. While he may perhaps be criticized morally or aesthetically, as a self-owner of his own body he has every right to refuse to cure or to do so at a high price; to say that he is being "coercive" is furthermore to imply that it is proper and *not* coercive for his customers or their agents to *force* the physician to treat them: in short, to justify his enslavement. But surely enslavement, compulsory labor, must be considered "coercive" in any sensible meaning of the term.

All this highlights the gravely self-contradictory nature of including a forced activity or exchange in the same rubric of "coercion" with someone's peaceful *refusal to* make an exchange.

As I have written elsewhere:

> A well-known type of "private coercion" is the vague but ominous sounding "economic power." A favorite illustration of the wielding of such "power" is the case of a worker fired from his job. . . .
>
> Let us look at this situation closely. What exactly has the employer done? He has refused to continue to make a certain exchange which the worker preferred to continue making. Specifically, A, the employer, refuses to sell a certain sum of money in exchange for the purchase of B's labor services. B would like to make a certain exchange; A would not. The same principle may apply to all the exchanges throughout the length and breadth of the economy. . . .

---

holy. To offer the water to the settlers would contravene his deepest religious sentiments. Here is a situation which would not fall under Hayek's definition of coercion, since the owner of the spring forces *no* action on the settlers. Yet it would appear that, within Hayek's own framework, this is a far worse situation, since the only "choice" left open to the settlers now is dying of thirst.

Ronald Hamowy, "Freedom and the Rule of Law in F.A. Hayek," *Il Politico* (1971–72): 355–56. Also see Hamowy, "Hayek's Concept of Freedom: A Critique," *New Individualist Review* (April 1961): 28–31.

For the latest work on this subject, see Hamowy, "Law and the Liberal Society: F.A. Hayek's Constitution of Liberty," *Journal of Libertarian Studies* 2 (Winter 1978): 287–97; and John N. Gray, "F.A. Hayek on Liberty and Tradition," *Journal of Libertarian Studies* 4 (Fall 1980).

"Economic power," then, is simply the right under freedom to refuse to make an exchange. Every man has this power. Every man has the same right to make a preferred exchange.

Now, it should become evident that the "middle-of-the-road" statist, who concedes the evil of violence but adds that the violence of government is sometimes necessary to counteract the "private coercion of economic power," is caught in an impossible contradiction. A refuses to make an exchange with B. What are we to say, or what is the government to do, if B brandishes a gun and orders A to make the exchange? This is the crucial question. There are only two positions we may take on the matter: either that B is committing violence and should be stopped at once, or that B is perfectly justified in taking this step because he is simply "counteracting the subtle coercion" of economic power wielded by A. Either the defense agency must rush to the defense of A, or it deliberately refuses to do so, perhaps aiding B (or doing B's work for him). There is no middle ground!

B is committing violence; there is no question about that. In the terms of both doctrines (the libertarian and the "economic power" arguments), this violence is either invasive and therefore unjust, or defensive and therefore just. If we adopt the "economic power" argument, we must choose the latter position; if we reject it, we must adopt the former. If we choose the "economic-power" concept, we must employ violence to combat any refusal of exchange; if we reject it, we employ violence to prevent any violent imposition of exchange. There is no way to escape this either-or choice. The "middle-of-the-road" statist cannot logically say that there are "many forms" of unjustified coercion. He must choose one or the other and take his stand accordingly. Either he must say that there is only one form of illegal coercion—overt physical violence—or he must say that there is only one form of illegal coercion—refusal to exchange.[8]

And outlawing the refusal to work is, of course, a society of general slavery. Let us consider another example that Hayek quickly dismisses as *non*coercive: "If a hostess will invite me to her parties only if I conform to certain standards of conduct and dress . . . this is certainly not coercion."[9] Yet, as Professor Hamowy has shown, this case may well be considered "coercion" on Hayek's own criteria. For,

---

8. Murray N. Rothbard, *Power and Market*, 2nd ed. (Kansas City: Sheed Andrews and McMeel, 1977), pp. 228–30.

9. Hayek, *The Constitution of Liberty*, pp. 136–37.

it might be that I am a very socially conscious person and that my not attending this party would greatly endanger my social standing. Further, my dinner jacket is at the cleaners and will not be ready for a week . . . yet the party is tomorrow. Under these conditions could it be said that my host's action in demanding my wearing formal attire as the price of access to his home *is*, in fact, a coercive one, inasmuch as it clearly threatens the preservation of one of the things I most value, my social prestige?

Furthermore, Hamowy points out that if the host should demand, as a price of invitation to the party, "that I wash all the silver and china used at the party," Hayek would even more clearly have to call such a voluntary contract "coercive" on his own criteria.[10]

In attempting to rebut Hamowy's trenchant critique, Hayek later added that "to constitute coercion it is also necessary that the action of the coercer should put the coerced in a position which he regards as worse than that in which he would have been without that action."[11] But, as Hamowy points out in reply, this does not salvage Hayek's inconsistent refusal to adopt the patent absurdity of calling a conditional invitation to a party "coercive." For,

the case just described seems to meet this condition as well; for while it is true that, in a sense, my would-be host has widened my range of alternatives by the invitation, the *whole* situation (which must include my inability to acquire formal attire and my consequent frustration) is worse from my point of view than the situation which had obtained before the invitation, certainly worse than had existed before my would-be host had decided to have a party at that particular time.[12]

Thus, Hayek, and the rest of us, are duty-bound to do one of two things: either to confine the concept of "coercion" strictly to the invasion of another's person or property by the use or threat of physical violence; or to scrap the term "coercion" altogether, and simply define "freedom" not as the "absence of coercion" but as the "absence of aggressive physical violence or the threat thereof." Hayek indeed concedes that "coercion can be so defined as to make it an all-pervasive and unavoidable phenomenon."[13]

---

10. Hamowy, "Freedom and the Rule of Law," pp. 353–54.

11. F.A. Hayek, "Freedom and Coercion: Some Comments on a Critique by Mr. Ronald Hamowy," *Studies in Philosophy, Politics, and Economics* (Chicago: University of Chicago Press, 1967), p. 349.

12. Hamowy, "Freedom and the Rule of Law," p. 354n.

13. Hayek, *The Constitution of Liberty*, p. 139.

Unfortunately, his middle-of-the-road failure to confine coercion strictly to violence pervasively flaws his entire system of political philosophy. He cannot salvage that system by attempting to distinguish, merely quantitatively, between "mild" and "more severe" forms of coercion.

Another fundamental fallacy of Hayek's system is not only his defining coercion beyond the sphere of physical violence, but also in failing to distinguish between "aggressive" and "defensive" coercion or violence. There is all the world of distinction in kind between aggressive violence—assault or theft—against another, and the use of violence to defend oneself and one's property against such aggression. Aggressive violence is criminal and unjust; defensive violence is perfectly just and proper; the former invades the rights of person and property, the latter defends against such invasion. Yet Hayek again fails to make this crucial qualitative distinction. For him, there are only relative degrees, or quantities, of "coercion." Thus, Hayek states that "coercion, however, cannot be altogether avoided because the only way to prevent it is by the threat of coercion."[14] From this, he goes on to compound the error by adding that "free society has met this problem by conferring the monopoly of coercion on the state and by attempting to limit this power of the state to instances where it is required to prevent coercion by private persons."[15] Yet, we are not here comparing varying degrees of an undifferentiated lump we can call "coercion" (even if we define this as "physical violence"). For we *can* avoid *aggressive* violence completely by preventing it through purchasing the services of defense agencies, agencies which are empowered to use only *defensive* violence. We are not helpless in the throes of "coercion" if we define such coercion only as *aggressive* violence (or, alternatively, if we abandon the term "coercion" altogether, and keep the distinction between aggressive and defensive violence).

Hayek's crucial second sentence in the above paragraph compounds his error many times further. In the first place, in any and all historical cases, "free society" did not "confer" any monopoly of coercion on the State; there has never been any form of voluntary "social contract." In all historical cases, the State has seized, by the use of aggressive violence and conquest, such a monopoly of violence in society. And further, what

---

14. Ibid., p. 21. One fallacy of Hayek here is in holding that if unjust coercion is wrong, then it should be minimized. Instead, being immoral and criminal, unjust coercion should be prohibited altogether. That is, the point is not to minimize a certain quantity (unjust coercion) by any means possible, including new acts of unjust coercion; the point is to impose a rigorous side-constraint on all action. For this distinction, see Robert Nozick, "Moral Complications and Moral Structures," *Natural Law Forum* (1968): 1ff.

15. Hayek, *The Constitution of Liberty*, p. 21.

the State has is not so much a monopoly of "coercion" as of *aggressive* (as well as defensive) violence, and that monopoly is established and maintained by systematically employing two particular forms of aggressive violence: taxation for the acquisition of State income, and the compulsory outlawry of competing agencies of defensive violence within the State's acquired territorial area. Therefore, since liberty requires the elimination of aggressive violence in society (while maintaining defensive violence against possible invaders), the State is not, and can never be, justified as a defender of liberty. For the State lives by its very existence on the twofold and pervasive employment of aggressive violence against the very liberty and property of individuals that it is *supposed* to be defending. The State is qualitatively unjustified and unjustifiable.

Thus, Hayek's justification of the existence of the State, as well as its employment of taxation and other measures of aggressive violence, rests upon his untenable obliteration of the distinction between aggressive and defensive violence, and his lumping of all violent actions into the single rubric of varying degrees of "coercion." But this is not all. For, in the course of working out his defense of the State and State action, Hayek not only widens the concept of coercion beyond physical violence; he *also* unduly narrows the concept of coercion to *exclude* certain forms of aggressive physical violence. In order to "limit" State coercion (i.e., to justify State action *within* such limits), Hayek asserts that coercion is either minimized or even does *not* exist if the violence-supported edicts are not personal and arbitrary, but are in the form of general, universal rules, knowable to all in advance (the "rule of law"). Thus, Hayek states that

> The coercion which a government must still use . . . is reduced to a minimum and made as innocuous as possible by restraining it through known general rules, so that in most instances the individual need never be coerced unless he has placed himself in a position where he knows he will be coerced. Even where coercion is not avoidable, it is deprived of its most harmful effects by being confined to limited and foreseeable duties, or at least made independent of the arbitrary will of another person. Being made impersonal and dependent upon general, abstract rules, whose effect on particular individuals cannot be foreseen at the time they are laid down, even the coercive acts of government become data on which the individual can base his own plans.[16]

Hayek's avoidability criterion for allegedly "noncoercive" though violent actions is put baldly as follows:

---

16. Ibid., p. 21.

Provided that I know beforehand that if I place myself in a particular position, I shall be coerced and provided that I can avoid putting myself in such a position, I need never be coerced. At least insofar as the rules providing for coercion are not aimed at me personally but are so framed as to apply equally to all people in similar circumstances, they are no different from any of the natural obstacles that affect my plans.[17]

But, as Professor Hamowy trenchantly points out:

It follows from this that if Mr. X warns me that he is going to kill me if I buy anything from Mr. Y, and if the products available from Mr. Y are also available elsewhere (probably from Mr. X), such action on the part of Mr. X is noncoercive!

For purchasing from Mr. Y is "avoidable." Hamowy continues:

Avoidability of the action is sufficient, according to this criterion, to set up a situation theoretically identical to one in which a threat does not occur at all. The threatened party is no *less* free than he was before the threat was made, if he can avoid the threatener's action. According to the logical structure of this argument, "threatening coercion" is not a coercive act. Thus, if I know in advance that I will be attacked by hoodlums if I enter a certain neighborhood, and if I can avoid that neighborhood, then I need never be coerced by the hoodlums. . . . Hence, one could regard the hoodlum-infested neighborhood . . . in the same way as a plague-infested swamp, both avoidable obstacles, neither personally aimed at me . . .

—and hence, for Hayek, not "coercive."[18]

Thus, Hayek's avoidability criterion for non-coercion leads to a patently absurd weakening of the concept of "coercion," and the inclusion of aggressive and patently coercive actions under a benign, noncoercive rubric. And yet, Hayek is even willing to scuttle his own weak avoidability limitation on government; for he concedes that taxation and conscription, for example, are not, and are not supposed to be, "avoidable." But these too become "noncoercive" because:

---

17. Ibid., p. 142.

18. Hamowy, "Freedom and the Rule of Law," pp. 356–57, 356n. Indeed, in *The Constitution of Liberty*, p. 142, Hayek explicitly states that

this threat of coercion has a very different effect from that of actual and unavoidable coercion, if it refers only to known circumstances which can be avoided by the potential object of coercion. The great majority of the threats of coercion that a free society must employ are of this avoidable kind.

they are at least predictable and enforced irrespective of how the individual would otherwise employ his energies; this deprives them largely of the evil nature of coercion. If the known necessity of paying a certain amount in taxes becomes the basis of all my plans, if a period of military service is a foreseeable part of my career, then I can follow a general plan of life of my own making and am as independent of the will of another person as men have learned to be in society.[19]

The absurdity of relying on general, universal ("equally applicable"), predictable rules as a criterion, or as a defense, for individual liberty has rarely been more starkly revealed.[20] For this means that, e.g., if there is a general governmental rule that *every* person shall be enslaved one year out of every three, then such universal slavery is not at all "coercive." In what sense, then, are Hayekian general rules superior or more libertarian than *any conceivable* case of rule by arbitrary whim? Let us postulate, for example, two possible societies. One is ruled by a vast network of Hayekian general rules, equally applicable to all, e.g., such rules as: everyone is to be enslaved every third year; no one may criticize the government under penalty of death; no one may drink alcoholic beverages; everyone must bow down to Mecca three times a day at specified hours; everyone must wear a specified green uniform, etc. It is clear that such a society, though meeting all the Hayekian criteria for a noncoercive rule of law, is thoroughly despotic and totalitarian. Let us postulate, in contrast, a second society which is totally free, where every person is free to employ his person and property, make exchanges, etc. as he sees fit, *except* that, once a year, the monarch (who does literally nothing the rest of the year), commits one arbitrary invasive act against one individual that he selects.

As Professor Watkins points out, on Hayek's avoidability criterion for "noncoercion," a person may be confronted by a

> "general abstract rule, equally applicable to all" which forbids foreign travel; and suppose he has an ailing father abroad whom he wants to visit before he dies. On Hayek's argument, there is no coercion or loss of freedom here. This agent is not subject to anyone's will. He is just confronted by the fact that if he tries to go abroad he will be apprehended and punished.

J.W.N. Watkins, "Philosophy," in A. Seldon, ed., *Agenda for a Free Society: Essays on Hayek's The Constitution of Liberty* (London: Institute for Economic Affairs, 1961), pp. 39–40.

19. Hayek, *The Constitution of Liberty*, p. 143.

20. On the problem of the universal rule changing as more and more types of specific circumstances are added to the rule, see G.E.M. Anscombe, "Modern Moral Philosophy," *Philosophy* 33 (1958): 2.

Which society is to be considered more free, more libertarian?[21]

Thus, we see that Hayek's *Constitution of Liberty* can in no sense provide the criteria or the groundwork for a system of individual liberty. In addition to the deeply flawed definitions of "coercion," a fundamental flaw in Hayek's theory of individual rights, as Hamowy points out, is that they do not stem from a moral theory or from "some independent nongovernmental social arrangement," but instead flow from government itself. For Hayek, government—and its rule—of law *creates* rights, rather than ratifies or defends them.[22] It is no wonder that, in the course of his book, Hayek comes to endorse a long list of government actions clearly invasive of the rights and liberties of the individual citizens.[23]

---

21. For a thorough critique of the generality, equal applicability, and predictability criteria of Hayek's rule of law, as well as of Hayek's admitted departures from his own criteria, see Hamowy, "Freedom and the Rule of Law," pp. 359–76. This includes Bruno Leoni's fundamental criticism that given the existence (which Hayek accepts) of a legislature changing laws daily, no given law can be more than predictable or "certain" at any given moment; there is no certainty *over time*. See Bruno Leoni, *Freedom and the Law* (Princeton, N.J.: D. Van Nostrand, 1961), p. 76.

22. See Hamowy, "Freedom and the Rule of Law," p. 358.

23. In his more recent treatise, Hayek does not deal with the problem of coercion or freedom. He does, however, try in passing to meet the criticism of Hamowy and others by amending his concept of general and certain rules to exempt solitary actions and acts that are not "toward others." While the problem of religious rules might then be avoided, most of the problems in the above discussion *do* involve interpersonal actions and therefore continue to prevent Hayek's rule of law from being a satisfactory bulwark of individual liberty. F.A. Hayek, *Law, Legislation, and Liberty,* vol. 1 (Chicago: University of Chicago Press, 1973), pp. 101–2, 170n. In general, the new Hayek volume is a welcome retreat from Hayek's previous reliance on legislation and a turn toward the processes of judge-found common law; however, the analysis is greatly marred by a predominant emphasis on the purpose of law as "fulfilling expectations," which still concentrates on social ends rather than on the justice of property rights. Relevant here is the discussion above of the "title-transfer" theory vs. the expectations theory of contracts; see pp. 133–48 above.

29. Robert Nozick and the
Immaculate Conception of the State[1]

Robert Nozick's *Anarchy, State, and Utopia*[2] is an "invisible hand"variant of a Lockean contractarian attempt to justify the State, or at least a minimal State confined to the functions of protection. Beginning with a free-market anarchist state of nature, Nozick portrays the State as emerging, by an invisible hand process that violates no one's rights, first as a dominant protective agency, then to an "ultraminimal state," and then finally to a minimal state.

Before embarking on a detailed critique of the various Nozickian stages, let us consider several grave fallacies in Nozick's conception itself, *each of which* would in itself be sufficient to refute his attempt to justify the State.[3] First, despite Nozick's attempt[4] to cover his tracks, it is highly relevant to see whether Nozick's ingenious logical construction has ever indeed occurred in historical reality: namely, whether any State, or most or all States, have *in fact* evolved in the Nozickian manner. It is a grave defect in itself, when discussing an institution all too well grounded in historical reality, that Nozick has failed to make a single mention or reference to the history of actual States. In fact, there is no evidence whatsoever that any State was founded or developed in the Nozickian manner. On the contrary, the historical evidence cuts precisely the other way: for every State where the facts are available originated by a process of violence, conquest, and exploitation: in short, in a manner which Nozick himself would have to admit violated individual rights. As Thomas Paine wrote in *Common Sense*, on the origin of kings and of the State:

---

1. A version of this section appeared in Murray N. Rothbard, "Robert Nozick and the Immaculate Conception of the State," *Journal of Libertarian Studies* 1 (Winter 1977): 45–57.

2. Robert Nozick, *Anarchy, State, and Utopia* (New York: Basic Books, 1974).

3. For other criticisms of Nozick, see Randy E. Barnett, "Whither Anarchy? Has Robert Nozick Justified the State?" *Journal of Libertarian Studies* 1 (Winter 1977): 15–21; Roy A. Childs, Jr., "The Invisible Hand Strikes Back," *Journal of Libertarian Studies* 1 (Winter 1977): 23–33; John T. Sanders, "The Free Market Model Versus Government: A Reply to Nozick," *Journal of Libertarian Studies* 1 (Winter 1977): 35–44; Jeffrey Paul, "Nozick, Anarchism and Procedural Rights," *Journal of Libertarian Studies* 1, no. 4 (Fall 1977): 337–40; and James Dale Davidson, "Note on *Anarchy, State, and Utopia*," *Journal of Libertarian Studies* 1, no. 4 (Fall 1977): 341–48.

4. Nozick, *Anarchy, State, and Utopia*, pp. 6–9.

could we take off the dark covering of antiquity and trace them to their first rise, we should find the first of them nothing better than the principal ruffian of some restless gang; whose savage manners or preeminence in subtilty obtained him the title of chief among plunderers; and who by increasing in power and extending his depredations, overawed the quiet and defenceless to purchase their safety by frequent contributions.[5]

Note that the "contract" involved in Paine's account was of the nature of a coerced "protection racket" rather than anything recognizable to the libertarian as a voluntary agreement.

Since Nozick's justification of existing States—provided they are or become minimal—rests on their alleged immaculate conception, and since no such State exists, then none of them can be justified, *even* if they should later become minimal. To go further, we can say that, *at best,* Nozick's model can *only* justify a State which indeed did develop by his invisible hand method. Therefore, it is incumbent upon Nozick to join anarchists in calling for the abolition of all existing States, and *then* to sit back and wait for his alleged invisible hand to operate. The only minimal State, then, which Nozick *at best* can justify is one that will develop out of a future anarcho-capitalist society.

Secondly, *even if* an existing State had been immaculately conceived, this would *still* not justify its present existence. A basic fallacy is endemic to all social-contract theories of the State, namely, that any contract based on a promise is binding and enforceable. If, then, *everyone*—in itself of course a heroic assumption—in a state of nature surrendered all or some of his rights to a State, the social-contract theorists consider this promise to be binding forevermore.

A correct theory of contracts, however, termed by Williamson Evers the "title-transfer" theory, states that the only valid (and therefore binding) contract is one that surrenders what is, in fact, philosophically *alienable,* and that *only* specific titles to property are so alienable, so that their ownership can be ceded to someone else. While, on the contrary, *other* attributes of man—specifically, his self-ownership over his own will and body, and the *rights* to person and property which stem from that self-ownership—are "inalienable" and therefore cannot be surrendered in a binding contract. If no one, then, can surrender his own will, his body, or his rights in an enforceable contract, *a fortiori* he cannot surrender the persons or the rights of his posterity. This is what the Founding Fathers

---

5. *The Complete Writings of Thomas Paine*, P. Foner, ed. (New York: Citadel Press, 1945), vol. 1, p. 13.

meant by the concept of rights as being "inalienable," or, as George Mason expressed it in his Virginia Declaration of Rights:

> [A]ll men are by nature equally free and independent, and have certain inherent natural rights, of which, when they enter into a state of society, they cannot, by any compact, deprive or divest their posterity.[6]

Thus, we have seen (1) that no existing State has been immaculately conceived—quite the contrary; (2) that therefore the only minimal State that could *possibly* be justified is one that would emerge *after* a free-market anarchist world had been established; (3) that therefore Nozick, on his own grounds, should become an anarchist and then wait for the Nozickian invisible hand to operate afterward, and finally (4) that *even if* any State had been founded immaculately, the fallacies of social-contract theory would mean that no present State, even a minimal one, could be justified.

Let us now proceed to examine the Nozickian stages, particularly the alleged necessity as well as the morality of the ways in which the various stages develop out of the preceding ones. Nozick begins by assuming that each anarchist protective agency acts morally and non-aggressively, that is, "attempts in good faith to act within the limits of Locke's law of nature."[7]

First, Nozick assumes that each protective agency would require that each of its clients renounce the right of private retaliation against aggression, by refusing to protect them against counter-retaliation.[8] Perhaps, perhaps not. This would be up to the various protection agencies, acting on the market, and is certainly not self-evident. It is certainly possible, if not probable, that they would be out-competed by other agencies that do not restrict their clients in that way.

---

6. Reprinted in Robert A. Rutland, *George Mason* (Williamsburg, Va.: Colonial Williamsburg, 1961), p. 111. On the invalidity of the alienability of the human will, see chap. 19, footnote 18 above. The great seventeenth century English Leveller leader Richard Overton wrote:

> To every individual in nature is given an individual property by nature, not to be invaded or usurped by any: for every one as he is himself, so he hath a self propriety, else he could not be himself. . . . Mine and thine cannot be, except this be: No man hath power over my rights and liberties and I over no man's; I may be but an individual, enjoy myself and my self propriety.

Quoted in Sylvester Petro, "Feudalism, Property, and Praxeology," in S. Blumenfeld, ed., *Property in a Humane Economy* (LaSalle, Ill.: Open Court, 1974), p. 162.

7. Nozick, *Anarchy, State, and Utopia*, p. 17.

8. Ibid., p. 15.

Nozick then proceeds to discuss disputes between clients of different protection agencies. He offers three scenarios on how they might proceed. But two of these scenarios (and part of the third) involve physical battles between the agencies. In the first place, these scenarios contradict Nozick's own assumption of good-faith, nonaggressive behavior *by each of* his agencies, since, in any combat, clearly at least one of the agencies would be committing aggression. Furthermore, economically, it would be absurd to expect the protective agencies to battle each other physically; such warfare would alienate clients and be highly expensive to boot. It is absurd to think that, on the market, protective agencies would fail to agree in advance on private appeals courts or arbitrators whom they would turn to, in order to resolve any dispute. Indeed, a vital part of the protective or judicial service which a private agency or court would offer to its clients would *be* that it had agreements to turn disputes over to a certain appeals court or a certain arbitrator or group of arbitrators.

Let us turn then to Nozick's crucial scenario 3, in which he writes:

> the two agencies . . . agree to resolve peacefully those cases about which they reach differing judgments. They agree to set up, and abide by the decisions of, some third judge or court to which they can turn when their respective judgments differ. (Or they might establish rules determining which agency had jurisdiction under which circumstances).[9]

So far so good. But then there comes a giant leap: "Thus emerges a system of appeals courts and agreed upon rules. . . . Though different agencies operate, there is one unified federal judicial system of which they are all components." I submit that the "thus" is totally illegitimate, and that the rest is a *non sequitur*.[10] The fact that every protective agency will have agreements with every other to submit disputes to particular appeals courts or arbitrators does *not* imply "one unified federal judicial system."

On the contrary, there may well be, and probably would be, hundreds, even thousands, of arbitrators or appeals judges who would be selected, and there is no need to consider them part of one "judicial system." There is no need, for example, to envision or to establish one unified Supreme Court to decide upon disputes. Since every dispute has two and only two parties, there need be only one third party, judge or arbitrator; there are in the United States, at the present time, for example, over 23,000

---

9. Ibid., p. 16

10. For a similar criticism of Nozick, see the review by Hillel Steiner in *Mind* 86 (1977): 120–29.

professional arbitrators, and presumably there would be many thousands more if the present government court system were to be abolished. Each one of these arbitrators could serve an appeals or arbitration function.

Nozick claims that out of anarchy there would inevitably emerge, as by an invisible hand, one *dominant* protection agency in each territorial area, in which "almost all the persons" in that area are included. But we have seen that his major support for that conclusion is totally invalid. Nozick's other arguments for this proposition are equally invalid. He writes, for example, that "unlike other goods that are comparatively evaluated, maximal competing protective services cannot exist."[11] Why *cannot*, surely a strong term?

First, because "the nature of the service brings different agencies . . . into violent conflict with each other" rather than just competing for customers. But we have seen that this conflict assumption is incorrect; first, on Nozick's own grounds of each agency acting non-aggressively, and, second, on his own scenario 3, that each will enter into agreements with the others for peaceful settlement of disputes. Nozick's second argument for this contention is that "since the worth of the less-than-maximal product declines disproportionately with the number who purchase the maximal product, customers will not stably settle for the lesser good, and competing companies are caught in a declining spiral." But *why*? Nozick is here making statements about the economics of a protection market which are totally unsupported. *Why* is there such an "economy of scale" in the protection business that Nozick feels will lead inevitably to a near-natural monopoly in each geographical area? This is scarcely self-evident.

On the contrary, all the facts—and here the empirical facts of contemporary and past history are again directly relevant—cut precisely the other way. There are, as was mentioned above, tens of thousands of professional arbitrators in the U.S.; there are also tens of thousands of lawyers and judges, and a large number of private protection agencies that supply nightwatchmen, guards, etc. with no sign whatsoever of a geographical natural monopoly in any of these fields. Why then for protection agencies under anarchism?

And, if we look at approximations to anarchist court and protective systems in history, we again see a great deal of evidence of the falsity of Nozick's contention. For hundreds of years, the fairs of Champagne were the major international trade mart in Europe. A number of courts, by merchants, nobles, the Church, etc. competed for customers. Not only did no one dominant agency ever emerge, but they did not even feel the

---

11. Nozick, *Anarchy, State, and Utopia*, p. 17.

need for appeals courts. For a thousand years, ancient Ireland, until the Cromwellian conquest, enjoyed a system of numerous jurists and schools of jurists, and numerous protection agencies, which competed within geographical areas without any one becoming dominant. After the fall of Rome, various coexisting barbarian tribes peacefully adjudicated their disputes *within* each area, with each tribesman coming under his own law, and with agreed-upon peaceful adjudications between these courts and laws. Furthermore, in these days of modern technology and low-cost transportation and communication, it would be even easier to compete across geographical boundaries; the "Metropolitan," "Equitable," "Prudential" protection agencies, for example, could easily maintain branch offices over a large geographical area.

In fact, there is a far better case for *insurance* being a natural monopoly than protection, since a larger insurance pool would tend to reduce premiums; and yet, it is clear that there is a great deal of competition between insurance companies, and there would be more if it were not restricted by state regulation.

The Nozick contention that a dominant agency would develop in each geographical area, then, is an example of an illegitimate *a priori* attempt to decide what the free market would do, and it is an attempt that flies in the face of concrete historical and institutional knowledge. Certainly, a dominant protective agency *could conceivably* emerge in a particular geographical area, but it is not very likely. And, as Roy Childs points out in his critique of Nozick, even if it did, it would not likely be a "unified federal system." Childs also correctly points out that it is no more legitimate to lump all protective services together and call it a unified monopoly, than it would be to lump all the food growers and producers on the market together and say that they have a collective "system" or "monopoly" of food production.[12]

Furthermore, law and the State are both conceptually and historically separable, and law would develop in an anarchistic market society without any form of State. Specifically, the concrete *form* of anarchist legal institutions—judges, arbitrators, procedural methods for resolving disputes, etc.—would indeed grow by a market invisible-hand process, while the basic Law Code (requiring that no one invade any one else's person and property) would have to be agreed upon by all the judicial agencies, just as all the competing judges once agreed to apply and extend the basic principles of the customary or common law.[13] But the latter, again, would

12. Roy Childs, "Invisible Hand," p. 25.

13. Cf., Bruno Leoni, *Freedom and the Law* (Los Angeles: Nash Publishing, 1972), and F.A. Hayek, *Law, Legislation, and Liberty*, vol. 1 (Chicago: University of Chicago Press, 1973).

imply no unified legal system or dominant protective agency. Any agencies that transgressed the basic libertarian code would be open outlaws and aggressors, and Nozick himself concedes that, lacking legitimacy, such outlaw agencies would probably not do very well in an anarchist society.[14]

Let us now assume that a dominant protective agency has come into being, as unlikely as that may be. How then do we proceed, without violation of anyone's rights, to Nozick's ultra-minimal state? Nozick writes[15] of the plight of the dominant protective agency which sees the independents, with their unreliable procedures, rashly and unreliably retaliating against its own clients. Shouldn't the dominant agency have the right to defend its clients against these rash actions? Nozick claims that the dominant agency *has* a right to prohibit risky procedures against its clients, and that this prohibition *thereby* establishes the "ultra-minimal state," in which one agency coercively prohibits all other agencies from enforcing the rights of individuals.

There are two problems here at the very beginning. In the first place, what has happened to the peaceful resolution of disputes that marked scenario 3? Why can't the dominant agency and the independents agree to arbitrate or adjudicate their disputes, preferably in advance? Ah, but here we encounter Nozick's curious "thus" clause, which incorporated such voluntary agreements into one "unified federal judicial system." In short, if every time that the dominant agency and the independents work out their disputes in advance, Nozick then *calls this* "one agency," then by definition he precludes the peaceful settlement of disputes *without* a move onward to the compulsory monopoly of the ultra-minimal state.

But suppose, for the sake of continuing the argument, that we grant Nozick his question-begging definition of "one agency." Would the dominant agency still be justified in outlawing competitors? Certainly not, even if it wishes to preclude fighting. For what of the many cases in which the independents are enforcing justice for their own clients, and have nothing to do with the clients of the dominant agency? By what conceivable right does the dominant agency step in to outlaw peaceful arbitration and adjudication between the independents' own clients, with no impact on *its* clients? The answer is no right whatsoever, so that the dominant agency, in outlawing competitors, is aggressing against their rights, and against the rights of their actual or potential customers. Furthermore, as Roy Childs emphasizes, this decision to enforce their monopoly is scarcely

14. Nozick, *Anarchy, State, and Utopia*, p. 17.
15. Ibid., pp. 55–56.

the action of an invisible hand; it is a *conscious*, highly visible decision, and must be treated accordingly.[16]

The dominant agency, Nozick claims, has the right to bar "risky" activities engaged in by independents. But what then of the independents? Do not *they* have the right to bar the risky activities of the dominant? And must not a war of all against all again ensue, in violation of scenario 3 and also necessarily engaging in some aggression against rights along the way? Where, then, are the moral activities of the state of nature assumed by Nozick all along? Furthermore, as Childs points out, what about the risk involved in having a compulsory monopoly protection agency? As Childs writes:

> What is to check its power? What happens in the event of its assuming even more powers? Since it has a monopoly, any disputes over its functions are solved and judged exclusively by itself. Since careful prosecution procedures are costly, there is every reason to assume that it will become less careful without competition and, again, only it can judge the legitimacy of its own procedures, as Nozick explicitly tells us.[17]

Competing agencies, whether the competition be real or potential, not only insure high-quality protection at the lowest cost, as compared to a compulsory monopoly, but they also provide the genuine checks and balances of the market against any one agency yielding to the temptations of being an "outlaw," that is, of aggressing against the persons and properties of its clients or non-clients. If one agency among many becomes outlaw, there are others around to do battle against it on behalf of the rights of their clients; but who is there to protect anyone against the State, whether ultra-minimal or minimal? If we may be permitted to return once more to the historical record, the grisly annals of the crimes and murders of the State throughout history give one very little confidence in the non-risky nature of *its* activities. I submit that the risks of State tyranny are far greater than the risks of worrying about one or two unreliable procedures of competing defense agencies.

But this is scarcely all. For once it is permitted to proceed beyond defense against an overt act of actual aggression, once one can use force against someone because of his " risky" activities, the sky is then the limit, and there is virtually no limit to aggression against the rights of others. Once permit someone's "fear" of the "risky" activities of others to lead to

---

16. Childs, "Invisible Hand," p. 32.

17. Ibid., pp. 27–28.

coercive action, then *any* tyranny becomes justified, and Nozick's "minimal" state quickly becomes the "maximal" State. I maintain, in fact, that there is no Nozickian stopping point from his ultra-minimal state to the maximal, totalitarian state. There is no stopping point to so-called preventive restraint or detention. Surely Nozick's rather grotesque suggestion of "compensation" in the form of "resort detention centers" is scarcely sufficient to ward off the specter of totalitarianism.[18]

A few examples: Perhaps the largest criminal class today in the United States is teenage black males. The risk of this class committing crime is far greater than any other age, gender, or color group. Why not, then, lock up all teenage black males until they are old enough for the risk to diminish? And then I suppose we could "compensate" them by giving them healthful food, clothing, playgrounds, and teaching them a useful trade in the "resort" detention camp. If not, why not? Example: the most important argument for Prohibition was the undoubted fact that people commit significantly more crimes, more acts of negligence on the highways, when under the influence of alcohol than when cold sober. So why not prohibit alcohol, and thereby reduce risk and fear, perhaps "compensating" the unfortunate victims of the law by free, tax-financed supplies of healthful grape juice? Or the infamous Dr. Arnold Hutschneker's plan of "identifying" allegedly future criminals in the grade schools, and then locking them away for suitable brainwashing? If not, why not?

In each case, I submit that there is only *one* why not, and this should be no news to libertarians who presumably believe in inalienable individual rights: namely, that no one has the *right* to coerce anyone not himself directly engaged in an *overt* act of aggression against rights. Any loosening of this criterion, to included coercion against remote "risks," is to sanction impermissible aggression against the rights of others. Any loosening of this criterion, furthermore, is a passport to unlimited despotism. Any state founded on *these* principles has been conceived, not immaculately (i.e., without interfering with anyone's rights), but by a savage act of rape.

Thus, even if risk were measurable, even if Nozick could provide us with a cutoff point of when activities are "too" risky, his rite of passage from dominant agency to ultraminimal state would still be aggressive, invasive, and illegitimate. But, furthermore, as Childs has pointed out, there is no way to measure the probability of such "risk," let alone the fear, (both of which are purely subjective).[19] The only risk that can be measured is found in those rare situations—such as a lottery or a roulette

---

18. Nozick, *Anarchy, State, and Utopia*, pp. 142 ff.
19. Childs, "Invisible Hand," pp. 28–29.

wheel—where the individual events are random, strictly homogeneous, and repeated a very large number of times. In almost all cases of actual human action, these conditions do not apply, and so there is no measurable cut-off point of risk.

This brings us to Williamson Evers's extremely useful concept of the "proper assumption of risk." We live in a world of ineluctable and unmeasurable varieties of uncertainty and risk. In a free society, possessing full individual rights, the proper assumption of risk is by each individual over his own person and his justly owned property. No one, then, can have the right to coerce anyone else into reducing *his* risks; such coercive assumption is aggression and invasion to be properly stopped and punished by the legal system. Of course, in a free society, anyone may take steps to reduce risks that do not invade someone else's rights and property; for example, by taking out insurance, hedging operations, performance bonding, etc. But all of this is voluntary, and none involves either taxation or compulsory monopoly. And, as Roy Childs states, any coercive intervention in the market's provision for risk shifts the societal provision for risk away *from* the optimal, and hence *increases* risk to society.[20]

One example of Nozick's sanctioning aggression against property rights is his concern[21] with the private landowner who is surrounded by enemy landholders who won't let him leave. To the libertarian reply that any rational landowner would have first purchased access rights from surrounding owners, Nozick brings up the problem of being surrounded by such a set of numerous enemies that he *still* would not be able to go anywhere. But the point is that this is not simply a problem of landownership. Not only in the free society, but even now, suppose that one man is so hated by the whole world that no one will trade with him or allow him on their property. Well, then, the only reply is that this is his own proper assumption of risk. Any attempt to break that voluntary boycott by physical coercion is illegitimate aggression against the boycotters' rights. This fellow had better find some friends, or at least purchase allies, as quickly as possible.

How then does Nozick proceed from his "ultra-minimal" to his "minimal" State? He maintains that the ultra-minimal state is morally bound to "compensate" the prohibited, would-be purchasers of the services of independents by supplying them with protective services—and *hence* the "night-watchman" or minimal state.[22] In the first place,

20. Ibid., p. 29.
21. Nozick, *Anarchy, State, and Utopia*, p. 55n.

this decision too is a conscious and visible one, and scarcely the process of an invisible hand. But, more importantly, Nozick's principle of compensation is in even worse philosophical shape, if that is possible, than his theory of risk. For first, compensation, in the theory of punishment, is simply a method of trying to recompense the victim of crime; it must in no sense be considered a moral sanction for crime itself.

Nozick asks[23] whether property rights means that people are permitted to perform invasive actions "provided that they compensate the person whose boundary has been crossed?" In contrast to Nozick, the answer must be no, in every case. As Randy Barnett states, in his critique of Nozick, "Contrary to Nozick's principle of compensation, all violations of rights should be prohibited. That's what right means." And, "while voluntarily paying a purchase price makes an exchange permissible, compensation does not make an aggression permissible or justified."[24] Rights must not be transgressed, period, compensation being simply one method of restitution or punishment after the fact; I must not be permitted to cavalierly invade someone's home and break his furniture, simply because I am prepared to "compensate" him afterward.[25]

Secondly, there is no way of knowing, in any case, what the compensation is supposed to be. Nozick's theory depends on people's utility scales being constant, measurable, and knowable to outside observers, none of which is the case.[26] Austrian subjective value theory shows us that people's utility scales are always subject to change, and that they can neither be measured nor known to any outside observer. If I buy a newspaper for 15 cents, then *all* that we can say about my value scale is that, at the moment of purchase, the newspaper is worth more to me than the 15 cents, and that is all. That evaluation can change tomorrow, and no other part of my utility scale is knowable to others at all. (A minor point:

---

22. Furthermore, in Nozick's progression, every stage of the derivation of the state is supposed to be moral, since it supposedly proceeds without violating anyone's moral rights. In that case, the ultra-minimal state is supposed to be moral. But if so, how then can Nozick hold that the ultra-minimal state is *morally obliged* to proceed onward to the minimal state? For if the ultra-minimal state does not do so, then it is apparently immoral, which contradicts Nozick's original supposition. For this point, see R.L. Holmes, "Nozick on Anarchism," *Political Theory* 5 (1977): 247ff.

23. Nozick, *Anarchy, State, and Utopia*, p. 57.

24. Barnett, "Whither Anarchy?" p. 20.

25. Nozick, furthermore, compounds the burdens on the victim by compensating him only for actions that respond "adaptively" to the aggression. *Anarchy, State, and Utopia*, p. 58.

26. Nozick, ibid., p. 58, explicitly assumes the measurability of utility.

Nozick's pretentious use of the "indifference curve" concept is not even necessary for his case, and it adds still further fallacies, for indifference is *never* by definition exhibited in action, in actual exchanges, and is therefore unknowable and objectively meaningless. Moreover, an indifference curve postulates two commodity axes—and *what* are the axes to Nozick's alleged curve?)[27] But if there is no way of knowing what will make a person as well off as before any particular change, then there is no way for an outside observer, such as the minimal state, to discover how much compensation is needed.

The Chicago School tries to resolve this problem by simply assuming that a person's utility loss is measured by the money-price of the loss; so if someone slashes my painting, and outside appraisers determine that I could have sold it for $2000, then that is my proper compensation. But first, no one really knows what the market price would have been, since tomorrow's market may well differ from yesterday's; and second and more important, my psychic attachment to the painting may be worth far more to me than the money price, and there is *no way* for anyone to determine what the psychic attachment might be worth; *asking* is invalid since there is nothing to prevent me from lying grossly in order to drive up the "compensation."[28]

Moreover, Nozick says nothing about the dominant agency compensating *its* clients for the shutting down of *their* opportunities in being able to shift their purchases to competing agencies. Yet their opportunities are shut off by compulsion, and furthermore, they may well perceive themselves as benefiting from the competitive check on the possible tyrannical impulses of the dominant agency. But *how* is the extent of such compensation to be determined? Furthermore, if compensation to the deprived clients of the dominant agency is forgotten by Nozick, what about the dedicated anarchists in the anarchistic state of nature? What about their trauma at seeing the far-from-immaculate emergence of the State? Are *they* to be compensated for their horror at seeing the State emerge? And *how much* are they to be paid? In fact, the existence of only *one* fervent anarchist who *could not* be compensated for the psychic trauma inflicted on him by the emergence of the State is enough by itself to scuttle Nozick's allegedly

---

27. I am indebted for this latter point to Professor Roger Garrison of the economics department, Auburn University.

28. Nozick also employs the concept of "transaction costs" and other costs in arriving at what activities may be prohibited with compensation. But this is invalid on the same grounds, namely because transaction and other costs are all *subjective* to each individual, and not objective, and hence are unknowable by any outside observer.

noninvasive model for the origin of the minimal state. For that absolutist anarchist, no amount of compensation would suffice to assuage his grief.

This brings us to another flaw in the Nozickian scheme: the curious fact that the compensation paid by the dominant agency is paid, not in cash, but in the extension of its sometimes dubious services to the clients of other agencies. And yet, advocates of the compensation principle have demonstrated that *cash*—which leaves the recipients free to buy whatever they wish—is far better from their point of view than any compensation in kind. Yet, Nozick, in postulating the extension of protection as the form of compensation, never considers the cash payment alternative. In fact, for the anarchist, this form of "compensation"—the institution of the State itself— is a grisly and ironic one indeed. As Childs forcefully points out, Nozick

> wishes to prohibit us from turning to any of a number of competing agencies, other than the dominant protection agency. What is he willing to offer us as *compensation* for being so prohibited? He is generous to a fault. He will give us nothing less than *the State*. Let me be the first to publicly reject this admittedly generous offer. But . . . the point is, we *can't* reject it. It is foisted upon us whether we like it or not, whether we are willing to accept the state as compensation or not.[29]

Furthermore, there is no warrant whatever, even on Nozick's own terms, for the minimal state's compensating every one uniformly, as he postulates; surely, there is no likelihood of everyone's value-scales being identical. But then *how* are the differences to be discovered and differential compensation paid?

Even confining ourselves to Nozick's compensated people—the former or current would-be clients of competing agencies—*who* are they? How can they be found? For, on Nozick's own terms, *only* such actual or would-be competing clients need compensation. But how does one distinguish, as proper compensation must, between those who have been deprived of their desired independent agencies and who therefore deserve compensation, and those who wouldn't have patronized the independents anyway, i.e., who therefore don't need compensation? By not making such distinctions, Nozick's minimal state doesn't even engage in proper compensation on Nozick's own terms.

Childs raises another excellent point on Nozick's own prescribed form of compensation—the dire consequences for the minimal state of the

---

29. Childs, "Invisible Hand," p. 27.

fact that the payment of such compensation will necessarily raise the costs, and therefore the prices charged, by the dominant agency. As Childs states:

> If the minimal state must protect everyone, even those who cannot pay, and if it must compensate those others for prohibiting their risky actions, then this must mean that it will charge its original customers more than it would have in the case of the ultra-minimal state. But this would, ipso facto, increase the number of those who, because of their demand curves, would have chosen non-dominant agencies . . . over dominant agency-turned ultra-minimal state-turned minimal state. Must the minimal state then protect them at no charge, or compensate them for prohibiting them from turning to the other agencies? If so, then once again, it must either increase its price to its remaining customers, or decrease its services. In either case, this again produces those who, given the nature and shape of their demand curves, would have chosen the non-dominant agencies over the dominant agency. Must these then be compensated? If so, then the process leads on, to the point where no one but a few wealthy fanatics advocating a minimal state would be willing to pay for greatly reduced services. If this happened, there is reason to believe that very soon the minimal state would be thrown into the invisible dustbin of history, which it would, I suggest, richly deserve.[30]

A tangential but important point on compensation: adopting Locke's unfortunate "proviso," on homesteading property rights in unused land, Nozick declares that no one may appropriate unused land if the remaining population who desire access to land are "worse off."[31] But again, how do we know if they are worse off or not? In fact, Locke's proviso may lead to the outlawry of all private ownership of land, since one can always say that the reduction of available land leaves everyone else, who could have appropriated the land, worse off. In fact, there is no way of measuring or knowing when they are worse off or not. And even if they are, I submit that this, too, is their proper assumption of risk. Everyone should have the right to appropriate as his property previously unowned land or other resources. If latecomers are worse off, well then that is their proper assumption of risk in this free and uncertain world. There is no longer a vast frontier in the United States, and there is no point in crying over the fact. In fact, we can generally achieve as much "access" as we want to these resources by paying a market price for them; but even if the owners

30. Ibid., p. 31.

31. Nozick, *Anarchy, State, and Utopia*, pp. 178ff.

refused to sell or rent, that should be their right in a free society. Even Locke could nod once in a while.[32]

We come now to another crucial point that Nozick's presumption that he can outlaw risky activities upon compensation rests on his contention that no one has the right to engage in "nonproductive" (including risky) activities or exchanges, and that therefore they can legitimately be prohibited.[33] For Nozick concedes that if the risky activities of others were legitimate, then prohibition and compensation would not be valid, and that we would then be "required instead to negotiate or contract with them, whereby they agree not to do the risky act in question. Why wouldn't we have to offer them an incentive, or hire them, or bribe them, to refrain from doing the act?"[34] In short, if not for Nozick's fallacious theory of illegitimate "nonproductive" activities, he would have to concede people's rights to engage in such activities, the prohibition of risk and compensation principles would fall to the ground, and neither Nozick's ultraminimal nor his minimal state could be justified.

And here we come to what we might call Nozick's "drop dead" principle. For his criterion of a "productive" exchange is one where each party is better off than if the other did not exist at all; whereas a "nonproductive" exchange is one where one party would be better off if the other dropped dead.[35] Thus, "if I pay you for not harming me, I gain nothing from you that I wouldn't possess if either you didn't exist at all or existed without having anything to do with me."[36] Nozick's "principle of compensation" maintains that a "nonproductive" activity can be prohibited provided that the person is compensated by the benefit he was forced to forego from the imposition of the prohibition.

Let us then see how Nozick applies his "nonproductive" and compensation criteria to the problem of blackmail.[37] Nozick tries to

---

32. Nozick also reiterates Hayek's position on charging for the use of one's solitary waterhole. Ibid., p. 180. See also pp. 220–21 above.

33. See Barnett, "Whither Anarchy?" p. 19.

34. Nozick, *Anarchy, State, and Utopia*, pp. 83–84.

35. Let us apply Nozick's concept of "nonproductive exchange" to his own process of arriving at the State. If the dominant protective agency did not exist, then clients of the other, non-dominant agencies would be better off, since they prefer dealing with these independent agencies. But then, on Nozick's own showing, on his own "drop dead" principle, these clients have become the victims of a nonproductive exchange with the dominant protective agency and are therefore entitled to prohibit the activities of the dominant agency. For this scintillating point I am indebted to Dr. David Gordon.

36. Nozick, *Anarchy, State, and Utopia*, p. 84.

37. For our own theory of the permissibility of blackmail contracts, see pp. 124–26 above.

rehabilitate the outlawry of blackmail by asserting that "nonproductive" contracts should be illegal, and that a blackmail contract is nonproductive because a blackmailee is worse off because of the blackmailer's very existence.[38] In short, if blackmailer Smith dropped dead, Jones (the blackmailee) would be better off. Or, to put it another way, Jones is paying not for Smith's making him better off, but for *not* making him *worse off*. But surely the latter is *also* a productive contract, because Jones is still better off making the exchange than he *would have been* if the exchange were not made.

But this theory gets Nozick into very muddy waters indeed, some (though by no means all) of which he recognizes. He concedes, for example, that his reason for outlawing blackmail would force him also to outlaw the following contract: Brown comes to Green, his next-door neighbor, with the following proposition: I intend to build such-and-such a pink building on my property (which he knows that Green will detest). I *won't* build this building, however, if you pay me X amount of money. Nozick concedes that this, too, would have to be illegal in his schema, because Green would be paying Brown for not being worse off, and hence the contract would be "nonproductive." In essence, Green would be better off if Brown dropped dead.

It is difficult, however, for a libertarian to square such outlawry with any plausible theory of property rights, much less the one set forth in the present volume. In analogy with the blackmail example above, furthermore, Nozick concedes that it *would* be legal, in his schema, for Green, on finding out about Brown's projected pink building, to come to Brown and offer to pay him not to go ahead. But why would such an exchange be "productive" just because Green made the offer?[39] What difference does it make *who* makes the offer in this situation? Wouldn't Green *still* be better off if Brown dropped dead? And again, following the analogy, *would* Nozick make it illegal for Brown to refuse Green's offer and *then* ask for more money? Why? Or, again, would Nozick make it illegal for Brown to subtly let Green know about the projected pink building and then let nature take its course, say, by advertising in the paper about the building and sending Green the clipping? Couldn't this be taken as an act of courtesy? And why should merely *advertising* something be illegal?

---

38. Nozick, *Anarchy, State, and Utopia*, pp. 84–86.

39. Nozick doesn't answer this crucial question; he simply asserts that this "will be a productive exchange." Ibid., pp. 84, 240n. 16. Ironically, Nozick was apparently forced into this retreat—conceding the "productivity" of the exchange if Green makes the offer—by the arguments of Professor Ronald Hamowy: ironic because Hamowy, as we have seen above, has also delivered a devastating critique of a somewhat similar definition of coercion by Professor Hayek.

Clearly, Nozick's case becomes ever more flimsy as we consider the implications. Furthermore, Nozick has not at all considered the manifold implications of his "drop dead" principle. If he is saying, as he seems to, that A is illegitimately "coercing" B if B is better off should A drop dead, then consider the following case: Brown and Green are competing at auction for the same painting which they desire. They are the last two customers left. Wouldn't Green be better off if Brown dropped dead? Isn't Brown therefore illegally coercing Green in some way, and therefore shouldn't Brown's participation in the auc-tion be outlawed? Or, *per contra,* isn't Green coercing Brown in the same manner and shouldn't *Green's* participation in the auction be outlawed? If not, why not? Or, suppose that Brown and Green are competing for the hand of the same girl; wouldn't each be better off if the other dropped dead, and shouldn't either or both's participation in the courtship therefore be outlawed? The ramifications are virtually endless.

Nozick, furthermore, gets himself into a deeper quagmire when he adds that a blackmail exchange is not "productive" because outlawing the exchange makes one party (the blackmailee) no worse off. But that of course is not true: as Professor Block has pointed out, outlawing a blackmail contract means that the blackmailer has no further incentive *not to* disseminate the unwelcome, hitherto secret information about the blackmailed party. However, after twice asserting that the victim would be "no worse off" from the outlawing of the blackmail exchange, Nozick immediately and inconsistently concedes that "people value a blackmailer's silence, and pay for it." In that case, if the blackmailer is prohibited from charging for his silence, he need not maintain it and hence the blackmail-payer would indeed be **worse off because of the prohibition!**

Nozick adds, without supporting the assertion, that "his being silent is not a productive activity." Why not? Apparently because "his victims would be as well off if the blackmailer did not exist at all." Back again to the "drop dead" principle. But then, reversing his field once more, Nozick adds—inconsistently with his own assertion that the blackmailer's silence is not productive— that "On the view we take here, a seller of such silence could legitimately charge only for what he forgoes by silence . . . including the payments others would make to him to reveal the information." Nozick adds that while a blackmailer may charge the amount of money he would have received for revealing the information, "he may not charge the best price he could get from the purchaser of his silence."[40]

---

40. Nozick, *Anarchy, State, and Utopia,* pp. 85–86.

Thus, Nozick, waffling inconsistently between outlawing blackmail and permitting only a price that the blackmailer could have received from selling the information, has mired himself into an unsupportable concept of a "just price." Why is it only licit to charge the payment foregone? Why *not* charge whatever the blackmailee is willing to pay? In the first place, both transactions are voluntary, and within the purview of both parties' property rights. Secondly, *no one knows,* either conceptually or in practice, what price the blackmailer could have gotten for his secret on the market. No one can predict a market price in advance of the actual exchange. Thirdly, the blackmailer may not only be gaining money from the exchange; he also possibly gains psychic satisfaction—he may dislike the blackmailee, or he may enjoy selling secrets and therefore he may "earn" from the sale to a third party more than just a monetary return. Here, in fact, Nozick gives away the case by conceding that the blackmailer "who *delights* in selling secrets may charge differently."[41] But, in that case, what outside legal enforcement agency will ever be able to discover *to what extent* the blackmailer delights in revealing secrets and therefore what price he may legally charge to the "victim"? More broadly, it is conceptually impossible ever to discover the existence or the extent of his subjective delight or of any other psychic factors that may enter into his value-scale and therefore into his exchange.

And fourthly, suppose that we take Nozick's worst case, a blackmailer who could not find any monetary price for his secret. But, if blackmail were outlawed either totally or in Nozick's "just price" version, the thwarted blackmailer would simply disseminate the secrets for free—would *give away* the information (Block's "gossip or blabbermouth"). In doing so, the blackmailer would simply be exercising his right to use his body, in this case his freedom of speech. There can be no "just price" for restricting this right, for it has no objectively measurable value.[42] Its value is subjective to the blackmailer, and his right may not be justly restricted. And furthermore, the "protected" victim is, in this case, surely worse off as a result of the prohibition against blackmail.[43]

---

41. Ibid., p. 86n.

42. See Barnett, "Whither Anarchy?" pp. 4–5.

43. Nozick, in *Anarchy, State, and Utopia,* p. 86, compounds his fallacies by going on to liken the blackmailer to a "protection racketeer," pointing out that, whereas protection is productive, selling someone "the racketeers' mere abstention from harming you" is not. But the "harm" threatened by the protection racketeer is not the exercise of free speech but aggressive violence, and the threat to commit aggressive violence is itself aggression. Here the difference is not the fallacious "productive" vs. "nonproductive," but between "voluntary" and "coercive" or "invasive"—the very essence of the libertarian philosophy. As Professor Block points out,

We must conclude, then, with modern, post-medieval economic theory, that the *only* "just price" for any transaction is the price voluntarily agreed upon by the two parties. Furthermore and more broadly, we must also join modern economic theory in labelling *all* voluntary exchanges as "productive," and as making both parties better off from making the exchange. Any good or service voluntarily purchased by a user or consumer benefits him and is therefore "productive" from his point of view. Hence, all of Nozick's attempts to justify either the outlawing of blackmail or the setting of some sort of just blackmail price (as well as for any other contracts that sell someone's inaction) fall completely to the ground. But this means, too, that his attempt to justify the prohibition of *any* "non-productive" activities—including risk—fails as well, and hence fails, on *this ground alone*, Nozick's attempt to justify his ultra-minimal (as well as his minimal) state.

In applying this theory to the risky, fear-inducing "nonproductive" activities of independent agencies which allegedly justify the imposition of the coercive monopoly of the ultra-minimal state, Nozick concentrates on his asserted "procedural rights" of each individual, which he states is the "right to have his guilt determined by the least dangerous of the known procedures for ascertaining guilt, that is, by the one having the lowest probability of finding an innocent party guilty."[44] Here Nozick adds to the usual *substantive* natural rights—to the use of one's person and justly acquired property unimpaired by violence—alleged "procedural rights," or rights to certain procedures for determining innocence or guilt.

But one vital distinction between a genuine and a spurious "right" is that the former requires no positive action by anyone except noninterference. Hence, a right to person and property is not dependent on time, space, or the number or wealth of other people in the society; Crusoe can have such a right against Friday as can anyone in an advanced industrial society. On the other hand, an asserted right "to a living wage" is a spurious one, since fulfilling it requires positive action on the part of other people, as well as the existence of enough people with a high enough wealth or income to satisfy such a claim. Hence such a "right" cannot be independent of time, place, or the number or condition of other persons in society.

But surely a "right" to a less risky procedure requires positive action from enough people of specialized skills to fulfill such a claim; hence it is

---

In aggression what is being threatened is aggressive violence, something that the aggressor has no right to do. In blackmail, however, what is being 'threatened' is something that the blackmailer most certainly *does* have a right to do! To exercise his right of free speech, to gossip about our secrets.

Walter Block, "The Blackmailer as Hero," *Libertarian Forum* (December 1972): 3.

44. Nozick, *Anarchy, State, and Utopia*, p. 96.

not a genuine right. Furthermore, such a right cannot be deduced from
the basic right of self-ownership. On the contrary, everyone has the absolute right to defend his person and property against invasion. The criminal
has no right, on the other hand, to defend his ill-gotten gains. But what
procedure will be adopted by any group of people to defend their rights—
whether for example personal self-defense, or the use of courts or arbitration agencies—depends on the knowledge and skill of the individuals
concerned.

Presumably, a free market will tend to lead to most people choosing
to defend themselves with those private institutions and protection agencies whose procedures will attract the most agreement from people in
society. In short, people who will be willing to abide by their decisions
as the most practical way of approximating the determination of *who*, in
particular cases, are innocent and who are guilty. But these are matters
of utilitarian discovery on the market as to the most efficient means of
arriving at self-defense, and do not imply any such fallacious concepts
as "procedural rights."[45]

Finally, in a scintillating *tour de force*, Roy Childs, after demonstrating
that each of Nozick's stages to the State is accomplished by a visible decision rather than by an "invisible hand," stands Nozick on his head by
demonstrating that the invisible hand, *on Nozick's own terms*, would lead
straight back from his minimal State to anarchism. Childs writes:

> Assume the existence of the minimal state. An agency arises
> which copies the procedures of the minimal state, allows the
> state to sit in on its trials, proceedings, and so forth. Under this
> situation, it cannot be alleged that this agency is any more
> "risky" than the state. If it is still too risky, then we are also
> justified in saying that the state is too risky, and in prohibit-
> ing its activities, providing we compensate those who are
> disadvantaged by such prohibition. If we follow this course,
> the result is anarchy.
>
> If not, then the "dominant agency"-turned minimal state
> finds itself competing against an admittedly watched-over
> competing agency. But wait: the competing, spied upon, op-
> pressed second agency finds that it can charge a lower price

45. For an excellent and detailed critique of Nozick's concept of "procedural rights," see
Barnett, "Whither Anarchy?" pp. 16–19. Professor Jeffrey Paul has also shown that any
concept of "procedural rights" implies a "right" of some other procedure to arrive at
such procedures, and this in turn implies another set of "rights" for methods of deciding
on *those* procedures, and so on to an infinite regress. Paul, "Nozick, Anarchism, and
Procedural Rights."

for its services, since the minimal state has to compensate those who would have patronized agencies using risky procedures. It also has to pay the costs of spying on the new agency.

Since it is only morally bound to provide such compensation, it is likely to cease doing so under severe economic pressure. This sets two processes in motion: those formerly compensated because they would have chosen other agencies over the state, rush to subscribe to the maverick agency, thus reasserting their old preferences. Also, another fateful step has been taken: the once proud minimal state, having ceased compensation, reverts to a lowly ultra-minimal state.

But the process cannot be stopped. The maverick agency must and does establish a good record, to win clients away from the ultra-minimal state. It offers a greater variety of services, toys with different prices, and generally becomes a more attractive alternative, all the time letting the state spy on it, checking its processes and procedures. Other noble entrepreneurs follow suit. Soon, the once lowly ultra-minimal state becomes a mere dominant agency, finding that the other agencies have established a noteworthy record, with safe, non-risky procedures, and stops spying on them, preferring less expensive agreements instead. Its executives have, alas!, grown fat and placid without competition; their calculations of who to protect, how, by what allocation of resources to what ends . . . are adversely affected by their having formerly removed themselves out of a truly competitive market price system. The dominant agency grows inefficient, when compared to the new, dynamic, improved agencies.

Soon—lo! and behold—the mere dominant protection agency becomes simply one agency among many in a market legal network. The sinister minimal state is reduced, by a series of morally permissible steps which violate the rights of no one, to merely one agency among many. In short, the invisible hand strikes back.[46]

Some final brief but important points. Nozick, in common with all other limited government, laissez-faire theorists, has no theory of taxation: of how much it shall be, of who shall pay it, of what kind it should be, etc. Indeed, taxation is scarcely mentioned in Nozick's progression of stages toward his minimal state. It would seem that Nozick's minimal

---

46. Childs, "Invisible Hand," pp. 32–33.

state could only impose taxation on the clients it *would* have had before it became a state, and not on the would-be clients of competing agencies. But clearly, the existing State taxes *everyone*, with no regard whatever for who they *would* have patronized, and indeed it is difficult to see how it could try to find and separate these different hypothetical groups.

Nozick also, in common with his limited-government colleagues, treats "protection"—at least when proferred by his minimal state—as one collective lump. But *how much* protection shall be supplied, and at what cost of resources? And what criteria shall decide? For after all, we can *conceive* of almost the entire national product being devoted to supplying each person with a tank and an armed guard; or, we can conceive of only one policeman and one judge in an entire country. Who decides on the degree of protection, and on what criterion? For, in contrast, all the goods and services on the private market are produced on the basis of relative demands and cost to the consumers on the market. But there is no such criterion for protection in the minimal or any other State.

Moreover, as Childs points out, the minimal State that Nozick attempts to justify is a State *owned* by a private, dominant firm; there is still no explanation or justification in Nozick for the modern form of voting, democracy, checks and balances, etc.[47]

Finally, a grave flaw permeates the entire discussion of rights and government in the Nozick volume: that, as a Kantian intuitionist, he *has* no theory of rights. Rights are simply emotionally intuited, with no groundwork in natural law—in the nature of man or of the universe. At bottom, Nozick has no real argument for the existence of rights.

To conclude: (1) no existing State has been immaculately conceived, and therefore Nozick, on his own grounds, should advocate anarchism and then wait for his State to develop; (2) even if any State *had* been so conceived, individual rights are inalienable and therefore no existing State could be justified; (3) every step of Nozick's invisible hand process is invalid: the process is all too conscious and visible, and the risk and compensation principles are both fallacious and passports to unlimited despotism; (4) there is no warrant, even on Nozick's own grounds, for the dominant protective agency to outlaw procedures by independents that do not injure its own clients, and therefore it cannot arrive at an ultra-minimal state; (5) Nozick's theory of "nonproductive" exchanges is invalid, so that the prohibition of risky activities and hence the ultra-minimal state falls on that account alone; (6) contrary to Nozick, there

---

47. Ibid., p. 27.

are no "procedural rights," and therefore no way to get from his theory of risk and nonproductive exchange to the compulsory monopoly of the ultra-minimal state; (7) there is no warrant, even on Nozick's own grounds, for the minimal state to impose taxation; (8) there is no way, in Nozick's theory, to justify the voting or democratic procedures of any State; (9) Nozick's minimal state would, on his own grounds, justify a maximal State as well; and (10) the only "invisible hand" process, on Nozick's own terms, would move society from his minimal State back to anarchism.

Thus, the most important attempt in this century to rebut anarchism and to justify the State fails totally and in each of its parts.

PART V:

TOWARD A THEORY OF STRATEGY FOR LIBERTY

30. Toward a Theory of Strategy for Liberty

The elaboration of a systematic theory of liberty has been rare enough, but exposition of a *theory of strategy* for liberty has been virtually nonexistent. Indeed, not only for liberty, strategy toward reaching any sort of desired social goal has been generally held to be catch-as-catch-can, a matter of hit-or-miss experimentation, of trial and error. Yet, if philosophy can set down any theoretical guidelines for a strategy for liberty, it is certainly its responsibility to search for them. But the reader should be warned that we are setting out on an uncharted sea.

The responsibility of philosophy to deal with strategy—with the problem of how to move from the present (*any* present) mixed state of affairs to the goal of consistent liberty—is particularly important for a libertarianism grounded in natural law. For as the libertarian historian Lord Acton realized, natural law and natural-rights theory provide an iron benchmark with which to judge—and to find wanting—any existing brand of statism. In contrast to legal positivism or to various brands of historicism, natural law provides a moral and political "higher law" with which to judge the edicts of the State. As we have seen above,[1] natural law, properly interpreted, is "radical" rather than conservative, an implicit questing after the reign of ideal principle. As Acton wrote, "[Classical] Liberalism wishes for what ought to be, irrespective of what is." Hence, as Himmelfarb writes of Acton, "the past was allowed no authority except as it happened to conform to morality." Further, Acton proceeded to distinguish between Whiggism and Liberalism, between, in effect, conservative adherence to the status quo and radical libertarianism:

> The Whig governed by compromise. The Liberal begins the reign of ideas.
>
> How to distinguish the Whigs from the Liberal—One is practical, gradual, ready for compromise. The other works out a principle philosophically. One is a policy aiming at a philosophy. The other is a philosophy seeking a policy.[2]

---

1. See pp. 17–20 above.

2. Gertrude Himmelfarb, *Lord Acton* (Chicago: University of Chicago Press, 1962), pp. 204, 205, 209.

Libertarianism, then, is a philosophy seeking a policy. But what else can a libertarian philosophy say about strategy, about "policy"? In the first place, surely—again in Acton's words—it must say that liberty is the "highest political end," the overriding goal of libertarian philosophy. Highest *political* end, of course, does not mean "highest end" for man in general. Indeed, every individual has a variety of personal ends and differing hierarchies of importance for these goals on his personal scale of values. *Political* philosophy is that subset of ethical philosophy which deals specifically with *politics*, that is, the proper role of *violence* in human life (and hence the explication of such concepts as crime and property). Indeed, a libertarian world would be one in which every individual would at last be free to seek and pursue his own ends—to "pursue happiness," in the felicitous Jeffersonian phrase.

It might be thought that the *libertarian*, the person committed to the "natural system of liberty" (in Adam Smith's phrase), almost by definition holds the goal of liberty as his highest political end. But this is often not true; for many libertarians, the desire for self-expression, or for bearing witness to the truth of the excellence of liberty, frequently takes precedence over the goal of the triumph of liberty in the real world. Yet surely, as will be seen further below, the victory of liberty will never come to pass unless the goal of victory in the real world takes precedence over more esthetic and passive considerations.

If liberty should be the highest political end, then what is the grounding for that goal? It should be clear from this work that, first and foremost, liberty is a *moral principle*, grounded in the nature of man. In particular, it is a principle of *justice*, of the abolition of aggressive violence in the affairs of men. Hence, to be grounded and pursued adequately, the libertarian goal must be sought in the spirit of an overriding devotion to justice. But to possess such devotion on what may well be a long and rocky road, the libertarian must be possessed of a passion for justice, an emotion derived from and channelled by his rational insight into what natural justice requires.[3] Justice, not the weak reed of mere utility, must be the motivating force if liberty is to be attained.[4]

---

3. In an illuminating essay, the natural-law philosopher John Wild points out that our subjective feeling of *obligation*, of an oughtness which raises subjective emotional desire to a higher, binding plane, stems from our rational apprehension of what our human nature requires. John Wild, "Natural Law and Modern Ethical Theory," *Ethics* (October 1952): 5–10.

4. On libertarianism being grounded on a passion for justice, see Murray N. Rothbard, "Why Be Libertarian?" in idem, *Egalitarianism as a Revolt Against Nature, and Other Essays* (Washington, D.C.: Libertarian Review Press, 1974), pp. 147–48.

If liberty is to be the highest political end, then this implies that liberty is to be pursued by the *most efficacious means*, i.e. those means which will most *speedily* and thoroughly arrive at the goal. This means that the libertarian must be an " abolitionist," i.e., he must wish to achieve the goal of liberty as rapidly as possible. If he balks at abolitionism, then he is no longer holding liberty as the highest political end. The libertarian, then, should be an abolitionist who would, if he could, abolish instantaneously all invasions of liberty. Following the classical liberal Leonard Read, who advocated immediate and total abolition of price-and-wage controls after World War II, we might refer to this as the "button-pushing" criterion. Thus, Read declared that "If there were a button on this rostrum, the pressing of which would release all wage-and-price controls instantaneously, I would put my finger on it and push!" The libertarian, then, should be a person who would push a button, if it existed, for the instantaneous abolition of all invasions of liberty—not something, by the way, that any utilitarian would ever be likely to do.[5]

Anti-libertarians, and anti-radicals generally, characteristically make the point that such abolitionism is "unrealistic"; by making such a charge they hopelessly confuse the desired goal with a strategic estimate of the probable path toward that goal. It is essential to make a clear-cut distinction between the ultimate goal itself, and the strategic estimate of how to reach that goal; in short, the goal must be formulated *before* questions of strategy or "realism" enter the scene. The fact that such a magic button does not and is not likely to exist has no relevance to the desirability of abolitionism itself. We might agree, for example, on the goal of liberty and the desirability of abolitionism in liberty's behalf. But this does not mean that we believe that abolition will *in fact* be attainable in the near or far future.

The libertarian goals—including immediate abolition of invasions of liberty—are "realistic" in the sense that they *could* be achieved if enough people agreed on them, and that, *if* achieved, the resulting libertarian system would be viable. The goal of immediate liberty is not unrealistic or "Utopian" because—in contrast to such goals as the "elimination of poverty"—its achievement is entirely dependent on man's will. If, for example, *everyone* suddenly and immediately agreed on the overriding desirability of liberty, then total liberty *would be* immediately achieved.[6] The strategic

---

5. Leonard E. Read, *I'd Push the Button* (New York: Joseph D. McGuire, 1946), p. 3.

6. Elsewhere I have written:

Other traditional radical goals—such as the "abolition of poverty"—are, in contrast to this one [liberty], truly utopian; for man, simply by exerting his will, cannot abolish poverty. Poverty can only be abolished through the operation of certain economic

estimate of *how* the path toward liberty is likely to be achieved is, of course, an entirely separate question.[7]

Thus, the libertarian abolitionist of slavery, William Lloyd Garrison, was not being "unrealistic" when, in the 1830s, he raised the standard of the goal of immediate emancipation of the slaves. His goal was the proper moral and libertarian one, and was unrelated to the "realism," or probability, of its achievement. Indeed, Garrison's strategic realism was expressed by the fact that he did not *expect* the end of slavery to arrive immediately or at a single blow. As Garrison carefully distinguished: "Urge immediate abolition as earnestly as we may, it will, alas! be gradual abolition in the end. We have never said that slavery would be overthrown by a single blow; that it ought to be, we shall always contend."[8] Otherwise, as Garrison trenchantly warned, "Gradualism in theory is perpetuity in practice."

Gradualism in theory, in fact, totally undercuts the overriding goal of liberty itself; its import, therefore, is not simply strategic but an opposition to the end itself and hence impermissible as any part of a strategy toward liberty. The reason is that once immediate abolitionism is abandoned, then the goal is conceded to take second or third place to other, anti-libertarian considerations, for these considerations are now placed higher than liberty. Thus, suppose that the abolitionist of slavery had said: "I advocate an end to slavery—but only after five years' time." But this would imply that abolition in four or three years' time, or *a fortiori* immediately, would be *wrong*, and that therefore it is *better* for slavery to be

---

factors . . . which can only operate by transforming nature over a long period of time . . . But *injustices* are deeds that are inflicted by one set of men on another, they are precisely the actions of men, and, hence, they and their elimination *are* subject to man's instantaneous will. . . . The fact that, of course, such decisions do not take place instantaneously is not the point; the point is that the very failure is an injustice that has been decided upon and imposed by the perpetrators of injustice. . . . In the field of justice, man's will is all; men *can* move mountains, if only men so decide. A passion for instantaneous justice—in short, a radical passion—is therefore *not* utopian, as would be a desire for the instant elimination of poverty or the instant transformation of everyone into a concert pianist. For instant justice could be achieved if enough people so willed.

Rothbard, *Egalitarianism as a Revolt Against Nature*, pp. 148–49.

7. At the conclusion of a brilliant philosophical critique of the charge of "unrealism" and its confusion of the *good* and the *currently probable*, Clarence Philbrook declares, "Only one type of serious defense of a policy is open to an economist or anyone else; he must maintain that the policy is good. True 'realism' is the same thing men have always meant by wisdom: to decide the immediate in the light of the ultimate." Clarence Philbrook, "Realism in Policy Espousal," *American Economic Review* (December 1953): 859.

8. Quoted in William H. and Jane H. Pease, eds., *The Antislavery Argument* (Indianapolis, Ind.: Bobbs-Merrill, 1965), p. xxxv.

continued a while longer. But this would mean that considerations of justice have been abandoned, and that the goal itself is no longer highest on the abolitionist's (or libertarian's) political value-scale. In fact, it would mean that the libertarian advocated the *prolongation* of crime and injustice.

Hence, a strategy for liberty must not include any means which undercut or contradict the end itself—as gradualism-in-theory clearly does. Are we then saying that "the end justifies the means"? This is a common, but totally fallacious, charge often directed toward any group that advocates fundamental or radical social change. For *what else* but an *end* could possibly justify any means? The very concept of "means" implies that this action is merely an instrument toward arriving at an end. If someone is hungry, and eats a sandwich to alleviate his hunger, the act of eating a sandwich is merely a means to an end; its sole justification arises from its use as an end by the consumer. Why else eat the sandwich, or, further down the line, purchase it or its ingredients? Far from being a sinister doctrine, that the end justifies the means is a simple philosophic truth, implicit in the very relationship of "means" and "ends."

What then, do the critics of the "end justifies the means" truly mean when they say that "bad means" can or will lead to "bad ends"? What they are *really* saying is that the means in question will violate *other* ends which the critics deem to be more important or more valuable than the goal of the group being criticized. Thus, suppose that Communists hold that murder is justified if it leads to a dictatorship by the vanguard party of the proletariat. The critics of such murder (or of such advocacy of murder) are really asserting, *not* that the "ends do not justify the means," but rather that murder violates a *more* valuable end (to say the least), namely, the end of "not committing murder," or nonaggression against persons. And, of course, from the libertarian point of view, the critics would be correct.

Hence, the libertarian goal, the victory of liberty, justifies the speediest possible means towards reaching the goal, but those means *cannot* be such as to contradict, and thereby undercut, the goal itself. We have already seen that gradualism-in-theory is such a contradictory means. Another contradictory means would be to commit aggression (e.g., murder or theft) against persons or just property in order to reach the libertarian goal of nonaggression. But this too would be a self-defeating and impermissible means to pursue. For the employment of such aggression would directly violate the goal of nonaggression itself.

If, then, the libertarian must call for immediate abolition of the State as an organized engine of aggression, and if gradualism in theory is contradictory to the overriding end (and therefore impermissible), *what further* strategic stance should a libertarian take in a world in which States continue all too starkly to exist? Must the libertarian necessarily *confine* himself to advocating immediate abolition? Are transitional demands, steps toward liberty in practice, therefore illegitimate? Surely not, since realistically there would then be no hope of achieving the final goal. It is therefore incumbent upon the libertarian, eager to achieve his goal as rapidly as possible, to push the polity ever further in the *direction* of that goal. Clearly, such a course is difficult, for the danger always exists of losing sight of, or even undercutting, the ultimate goal of liberty. But such a course, given the state of the world in the past, present, and foreseeable future, is vital if the victory of liberty is ever to be achieved. The transitional demands, then, must be framed while (a) *always* holding up the ultimate goal of liberty as the desired end of the transitional process; and (b) never taking steps, or using means, which explicitly or implicitly contradict that goal.

Let us consider, for example, a transition demand set forth by various libertarians: namely, that the government budget be reduced by 10 percent each year for ten years, after which the government will have disappeared. Such a proposal might have heuristic or strategic value, *provided* that the proposers always make crystal clear that these are *minimal* demands, and that indeed there would be nothing wrong—in fact, it would be all to the good—to step up the pace to cutting the budget by 25 percent a year for four years, or, most desirably, by cutting it by 100 percent immediately. The danger arises in implying, directly or indirectly, that any *faster* pace than 10 percent would be wrong or undesirable.

An even greater danger of a similar sort is posed by the idea of many libertarians of setting forth a comprehensive and planned program of trasition to total liberty, e.g., that in Year 1 law A should be repealed, law B modified, tax C be cut by 20 percent, etc.; in Year 2 law D be repealed, tax C cut by a further 10 percent, etc. The comprehensive plan is far more misleading than the simple budget cut, because it strongly implies that, for example, law D should *not* be repealed *until* the second year of this planned program. Hence, the trap of philosophic gradualism, of gradualism-in-theory, would be fallen into on a massive scale. The would-be libertarian planners would be virtually falling into a position, or *seeming* to, of *opposing* a faster pace toward liberty.

There is, indeed, another grave flaw in the idea of a comprehensive planned program toward liberty. For the very care and studied pace, the very all-embracing nature of the program, implies that the State is not really the enemy of mankind, that it is possible and desirable to *use* the State in engineering a planned and measured pace toward liberty. The insight that the State *is* the permanent enemy of mankind, on the other hand, leads to a very different strategic outlook: namely that libertarians push for and accept with alacrity *any* reduction of State power or State activity on any front; any such reduction at any time is a reduction in crime and aggression, and is a reduction of the parasitic malignity with which State power rules over and confiscates social power.

For example, libertarians may well push for drastic reduction, or repeal, of the income tax; but they should never do so while at the same time advocating its replacement by a sales or other form of tax. The reduction or, better, the abolition of a tax is always a noncontradictory reduction of State power and a step toward liberty; but its replacement by a new or increased tax elsewhere does just the opposite, for it signifies a new and additional imposition of the State on some other front. The imposition of a new tax is a means that contradicts the libertarian goal itself.

Similarly, in this age of permanent federal deficits, we are all faced with the problem: should we agree to a tax cut, even though it may well mean an increase in the deficit? Conservatives, from their particular perspective of holding budget-balancing as a higher end, invariably oppose, or vote against, a tax cut which is not strictly accompanied by an equivalent or greater cut in government expenditures. But since taxation is an evil act of aggression, any failure to welcome a tax cut with alacrity undercuts and contradicts the libertarian goal. The time to oppose government expenditures is when the budget is being considered or voted upon, when the libertarian should call for drastic slashes in expenditures as well. Government activity must be reduced whenever and wherever it can; any opposition to a particular tax—or expenditure—cut is impermissible for it contradicts libertarian principles and the libertarian goal.

Does this mean that the libertarian may never set priorities, may not concentrate his energy on political issues which he deems of the greatest importance? Clearly not, for since everyone's time and energy is necessarily limited, no one can devote equal time to every particular aspect of the comprehensive libertarian creed. A speaker or writer on political issues must necessarily set priorities of importance, priorities which at least partially depend on the concrete issues and circumstances of the day. Thus, while a libertarian in today's world would certainly advocate the denationalization of lighthouses, it is highly doubtful that he would place a greater priority on the lighthouse question than on conscription or the repeal of the income tax. The libertarian must use his strategic intelligence and knowledge of the issues of the day to set his priorities of political importance. On the other hand, of course, if one were living on a small, highly fog-bound island, dependent on shipping for transportation, it could very well be that the lighthouse question would have a high priority on a libertarian political agenda. And, furthermore, if for some reason the opportunity arose for denationalizing lighthouses even in present-day America, it should certainly not be spurned by the libertarian.

We conclude this part of the strategy question, then, by affirming that the victory of total liberty is the highest political end; that the proper groundwork for this goal is a moral passion for justice; that the end should be pursued by the speediest and most efficacious possible means; that the end must always be kept in sight and sought as rapidly as possible; and that the means taken must never contradict the goal—whether by advocating gradualism, by employing or advocating any aggression against liberty, by advocating planned programs, or by failing to seize any opportunity to reduce State power or by ever increasing it in any area.

The world, at least in the long run, is governed by ideas; and it seems clear that libertarianism is only likely to triumph if the ideas spread to and are adopted by a significantly large number of people. And so "education" becomes a necessary condition for the victory of liberty—all sorts of education, from the most abstract systematic theories down to attention-catching devices that will attract the interest of potential converts. Education, indeed, is the characteristic strategic theory of classical liberalism.

But it should be stressed that ideas do not float by themselves in a vacuum; they are influential only insofar as they are adopted and put forward by *people*. For the idea of liberty to triumph, then, there must be an active group of dedicated libertarians, people who are knowledgeable in liberty and are willing to spread the message to others. In short, there must be an active and self-conscious libertarian *movement*. This may seem self-evident, but there has been a curious reluctance on the part of many libertarians to think of themselves as part of a conscious and ongoing movement, or to become involved in movement activity. Yet consider: has any discipline, or set of ideas in the past, whether it be Buddhism or modern physics, been able to advance itself and win acceptance without the existence of a dedicated "cadre" of Buddhists or physicists?

The mention of physicists points up another requirement of a successful movement: the existence of professionals, of persons making their full-time career in the movement or discipline in question. In the seventeenth and eighteenth centuries, as modern physics emerged as a new science, there were indeed scientific societies which mainly included interested amateurs, "Friends of Physics" as we might call them, who established an atmosphere of encouragement and support of the new discipline. But surely physics would not have advanced very far if there had been no *professional* physicists, people who made a full-time career of physics, and therefore could devote all their energies to engaging in and advancing the discipline. Physics would surely still be a mere amusement for amateurs if the *profession* of physics had not developed. Yet there are few libertarians, despite the spectacular growth of the ideas and of the movement in recent years, who recognize the enormous need for the development of liberty as a profession, as a central core for the advancement of both the theory and the condition of liberty in the real world.

Every new idea and every new discipline necessarily begins with one or a few people, and diffuses outward toward a larger core of converts and adherents. Even at full tide, given the wide variety of interests and abilities among men, there is bound to be only a minority among the professional core or cadre of libertarians. There is nothing sinister or "undemocratic," then, in postulating a "vanguard" group of libertarians any more than there is in talking of a vanguard of Buddhists or of physicists. Hopefully, this vanguard will help to bring about a majority or a large and influential minority of people adhering to (if not centrally devoted to) libertarian ideology. The existence of a libertarian majority among the American Revolutionaries and in nineteenth-century England demonstrates that the feat is not impossible.

In the meanwhile, on the path to that goal, we might conceive of the adoption of libertarianism as a ladder or pyramid, with various individuals and groups on different rungs of the ladder, ranging upward from total collectivism or statism to pure liberty. If the libertarian cannot "raise people's consciousness" fully to the top rung of pure liberty, then he can achieve the lesser but still important goal of helping them advance a few rungs up the ladder.

For this purpose, the libertarian may well find it fruitful to engage in coalitions with non-libertarians around the advancement of some single, *ad hoc* activity. Thus, the libertarian, depending on his priorities of importance at any given condition of society, may engage in such "united front" activities with some conservatives to repeal the income tax or with civil libertarians to repeal conscription or the outlawry of pornography or of "subversive" speech. By engaging in such united fronts on *ad hoc* issues, the libertarian can accomplish a twofold purpose: (a) greatly multiplying his own leverage or influence in working toward a specific libertarian goal—since many non-libertarians are mobilized to cooperate in such actions; and (b) to "raise the consciousness" of his coalition colleagues, to show them that libertarianism is a single interconnected system, and that *a full* pursuit of their particular goal requires the adoption of the entire libertarian schema. Thus, the libertarian can point out to the conservative that property rights or the free market can only be maximized and truly safeguarded if civil liberties are defended or restored; and he can show the opposite to the civil libertarian. Hopefully, this demonstration will raise some of these *ad hoc* allies significantly up the libertarian ladder.

In the progress of any movement dedicated to radical social change, i.e., to transforming social reality toward an ideal system, there are bound to arise, as the Marxists have discovered, two contrasting types of "deviations" from the proper strategic line: what the Marxists have called "right opportunism" and "left sectarianism." So fundamental are these often superficially attractive deviations that we might call it a theoretical rule that one or both will arise to plague a movement at various times in its development. *Which* tendency will triumph in a movement cannot, however, be determined by our theory; the outcome will depend on the subjective strategic understanding of the people constituting the movement. The outcome, then, is a matter of free will and persuasion.

Right opportunism, in its pursuit of instant gains, is willing to abandon the ultimate social goal, and to immerse itself in minor and short-run gains, sometimes in actual contradiction to the ultimate goal itself. In the libertarian movement, the opportunist is willing to join the State establishment rather than to struggle against it, and is willing to deny the ultimate goal on behalf of short-run gains: e.g. to declaim that "while everyone knows we must have taxation, the state of the economy requires a 2 percent tax cut." The left sectarian, on the other hand, scents "immorality" and "betrayal of principle" in every use of strategic intelligence to pursue transitional demands on the path to liberty, even ones that uphold the ultimate goal and do not contradict it. The sectarian discovers "moral principle" and "libertarian principle" everywhere, even in purely strategic, tactical, or organizational concerns. Indeed, the sectarian is likely to attack as an abandonment of principle *any* attempt to go beyond mere reiteration of the ideal social goal, and to select and analyze more specifically political issues of the most urgent priority. In the Marxist movement, the Socialist Labor Party, which meets every political issue with *only* a reiteration of the view that "socialism and only socialism will solve the problem," is a classical example of ultra-sectarianism at work. Thus, the sectarian libertarian might decry a television speaker or a political candidate who, in the necessity to choose priority issues, stresses repeal of the income tax or abolition of the draft, while "neglecting" the goal of denationalizing lighthouses.

In should be clear that both right opportunism and left sectarianism are equally destructive of the task of achieving the ultimate social goal: for the right opportunist abandons the goal while achieving short-run gains, and thereby renders those gains ineffectual; while the left sectarian, in wrapping himself in the mantle of "purity," defeats his own ultimate goal by denouncing any necessary strategic steps in its behalf.

Sometimes, curiously enough, the same individual will undergo alternations from one deviation to the other, in each case scorning the correct, plumb-line path. Thus, despairing after years of futile reiteration of his purity while making no advances in the real world, the left sectarian may leap into the heady thickets of right opportunism, in the quest for *some* short-run advance, even at the cost of the ultimate goal. Or, the right opportunist, growing disgusted at his own or his colleagues' compromise of their intellectual integrity and their ultimate goals, may leap into left sectarianism and decry *any* setting of strategic priorities toward those goals. In this way, the two opposing deviations feed on and reinforce each other, and are both destructive of the major task of effectively reaching the libertarian goal.

The Marxists have correctly perceived that two sets of conditions are necessary for the victory of any program of radical social change; what they call the "objective" and the "subjective" conditions. The subjective conditions are the existence of a self-conscious movement dedicated to the triumph of the particular social ideal—conditions which we have been discussing above. The objective conditions are the objective fact of a "crisis situation" in the existing system, a crisis stark enough to be generally perceived, *and* to be perceived as the fault of the system itself. For people are so constituted that they are not *interested* in exploring the defects of an existing system so long as it seems to be working tolerably well. And even if a few become interested, they will tend to regard the entire problem as an abstract one irrelevant to their daily lives and therefore not an imperative for action—*until* the perceived crisis breakdown. It is such a breakdown that stimulates a sudden search for new social alternatives—and it is then that the cadres of the alternative movement (the "subjective conditions") must be available to supply that alternative, to relate the crisis to the inherent defects of the system itself, and to point out how the alternative system would solve the existing crisis and prevent similar breakdowns in the future. Hopefully, the alternative cadre would have provided a track record of predicting and warning against the existing crisis.

Indeed, if we examine the revolutions in the modern world, we will find that every single one of them (a) was utilized by an existing cadre of seemingly prophetic ideologists of the alternative system, and (b) was precipitated by a breakdown of the system itself. During the American Revolution, a broad cadre and mass of dedicated libertarians were prepared to resist the encroachments of Great Britain in its attempt to end the system of "salutary neglect" of the colonies and to reimpose the chains of the British Empire; in the French Revolution, *libertarian philosophes* had prepared the ideology with which to meet a sharp increase of absolutist burdens on the country caused by the government's fiscal crisis; in Russia, in 1917, a losing war led to the collapse of the Czarist system from within, which radical ideologists were prepared for; in post–World War I Italy and Germany, postwar economic crises and wartime defeats created the conditions for the triumph of the fascist and national socialist alternatives; in China, in 1949, the combination of a lengthy and crippling war and economic crisis caused by runaway inflation and price controls allowed the victory of the Communist rebels.

Both Marxists and libertarians, in their very different and contrasting ways, believe that the inner contradictions of the existing system (in the former case of "capitalism," in the latter of statism and state intervention) will lead inevitably to its long-run collapse. In contrast to conservatism, which can see nothing but long-run despair attendant upon the steady decline of "Western values" from some past century, Marxism and libertarianism are both therefore highly optimistic creeds, at least in the long-run. The problem, of course, for any living beings, is how long they will have to wait for the long-run to arrive. The Marxists, at least in the Western world, have had to face the indefinite postponement of their hoped-for long-run. Libertarians have had to confront a twentieth century which has shifted from the quasi-libertarian system of the nineteenth century to a far more statist and collectivist one—in many ways returning to the despotic world as it existed before the classical liberal revolutions of the seventeenth and eighteenth centuries.

There are good and sufficient reasons, however, for libertarians to be optimistic in the short-run as well as the long run, indeed for a belief that victory for liberty might be near.

But, in the first place, why should libertarians be optimistic *even in the long run?* After all, the annals of recorded history are a chronicle, in one civilization after another, of centuries of varying forms of despotism, stagnation, and totalitarianism. May it not be possible that the great post–seventeenth century thrust toward liberty was only a mighty flash in the pan, to be replaced by sinking back into a gray and permanent despotism? But such superficially plausible despair overlooks a crucial point: the new and irreversible conditions introduced by the Industrial Revolution of the late eighteenth and nineteenth centuries, a revolution itself a consequence of the classical-liberal political revolutions. For agricultural countries, in a preindustrial era, can indeed peg along indefinitely on a subsistence level; despotic kings, nobles and states can tax the peasantry

above subsistence level, and live elegantly off the surplus, while the peasants continue to toil for centuries at the bare minimum. Such a system is
profoundly immoral and exploitative, but it "works" in the sense of being
able to continue indefinitely (provided that the state does not get *too* greedy
and actually kill the goose that lays the golden eggs).

But fortunately for the cause of liberty, economic science has shown
that a modern industrial economy *cannot* survive indefinitely under such
draconian conditions. A modern industrial economy requires a vast network of free-market exchanges and a division of labor, a network that can
only flourish under freedom. *Given* the commitment of the mass of men
to an industrial economy and the modern standard of living that requires
such industry, then the triumph of a free-market economy and an end to
statism becomes inevitable in the long run.

The late-nineteenth and especially the twentieth centuries have seen
many forms of reversion to the statism of the preindustrial era. These
forms (notably socialism and various brands of "state capitalism"), in contrast to the frankly anti-industrial and reactionary Conservatism of early
nineteenth-century Europe, have tried to preserve and even extend the
industrial economy while scuttling the very political requirements (freedom and the free-market) which are in the long-run necessary for its
survival.[9] State planning, operation, controls, high and crippling taxation,
and paper money inflation must all inevitably lead to the collapse of the
statist economic system.

If then, the world is irreversibly committed to industrialism and its
attendant living standards, and if industrialism requires freedom, then
the libertarian must indeed be a long-run optimist, for the libertarian triumph must eventually occur. But why short-run optimism for the present
day? Because it fortunately happens to be true that the various forms of
statism imposed on the Western world during the first half of the
twentieth century are now in process of imminent breakdown. The long-
run is now at hand. For half a century, statist intervention could wreak
its depredations and not cause clear and *evident* crises and dislocations,
because the quasi–laissez-faire industrialization of the nineteenth century
had created a vast cushion against such depredations. The government
could impose taxes or inflation upon the system and not reap evidently
bad effects. But now statism has advanced so far and been in power so
long that the cushion, or fat, has been exhausted. As economist Ludwig
von Mises pointed out, the "reserve fund" created by laissez faire has

---

9. For a more extended historical analysis of this problem, see Murray N. Rothbard, *Left
and Right: The Prospects for Liberty* (San Francisco: Cato Institute, 1979).

now been "exhausted," *whatever* the government does now leads to an instantaneous negative feedback that is evident to the formerly indifferent and even to many of the most ardent apologists for statism.

In the Communist countries of Eastern Europe, the Communists themselves have increasingly perceived that socialist central planning simply does not work, particularly for an industrial economy. Hence the rapid retreat, in recent years, away from central planning and toward free markets, throughout Eastern Europe, especially in Yugoslavia. In the Western world, too, state capitalism is everywhere in a period of crisis, as it becomes perceived that, in the most profound way, the government has run out of money: that increasing taxes will cripple industry and incentives beyond repair, while increased printing of new money (either directly or through the government-controlled banking system) will lead to a disastrous runaway inflation. And so we hear more and more about the "necessity of lowered expectations from government" even among the State's once most ardent champions. In West Germany, the Social Democratic party has long abandoned the call for socialism. In Great Britain, suffering from a tax-crippled economy and aggravated inflation, the Tory party, for years in the hands of dedicated statists, has now been taken over by its free-market oriented faction, while even the Labor party has begun to draw back from the planned chaos of galloping statism.

In the United States, conditions are particularly hopeful; for here, in the last few years, there has coincidentally occurred (a) a systemic breakdown of statism across the board, in economic, foreign, social, and moral policies; and (b) a great and growing rise of a libertarian movement and the diffusion of libertarian ideas throughout the population, among opinion moulders and average citizens alike. Let us examine in turn both sets of necessary conditions for a libertarian triumph.

Surprisingly enough, the systemic breakdown of statism in the United States can be given a virtually precise date: the years 1973–74. The breakdown has been particularly glaring in the economic sphere. From the fall of 1973 through 1975, America experienced an inflationary depression, in which the worst recession of the postwar world coincided with an aggravated inflation of prices. After forty years of Keynesian policies which were supposed to "fine tune" the economy so as to eliminate the boom–bust cycle of inflation and depression, the United States managed to experience both at the same time—an event that cannot be explained by orthodox economic theory. Orthodox economics has been thrown into disarray, and economists and laymen alike are increasingly ready to turn to the "Austrian," free-market alternative, both in the realms of theoretical paradigms and of political policy. The award of the Nobel prize in economics during 1974 to F.A. Hayek for his long-forgotten Austrian business-cycle theory is but one indication of the new currents coming to the surface after decades of neglect. And even though the economy recovered from the depression, the economic crisis is not ended, since inflation only accelerated still further, while unemployment remained high. Only a free-market program of abandoning monetary inflation and slashing government expenditures will solve the crisis.

The partial financial default of the New York City government during 1975 and the victory of Proposition 13 in California in 1978 have highlighted for the entire country the fact that local and state reserve funds have been exhausted, and that government must at last begin a drastic cutback in its operations and expenditures. For higher taxes will drive businesses and middle-class citizens out of any given area, and therefore the only way to avoid default will be radical cuts in expenditure. (If default arrives, the result will be the same and more drastically, since access to bond markets in the future by state and local governments will prove impossible.)

It is also becoming increasingly clear that the combination of decades of high and crippling taxes on income, savings, and investment, combined with inflationary distortions of business calculation, has led to an increasing scarcity of capital, and to an imminent danger of consuming America's vital stock of capital equipment. Hence, lower taxes are rapidly perceived to be an economic necessity. Lower government expenditures are also evidently necessary to avoid the "crowding out" of private loans and investments from the capital markets by wasteful federal government deficits.

There is a particularly hopeful reason for expecting the public and the opinion-moulders to grasp at the proper libertarian solution to this grave and continuing economic crisis: the fact that everyone knows that the State has controlled and manipulated the economy for the last forty years. When government credit and interventionary policies brought about the Great Depression of the 1930s, the myth that the 1920s had been an era of laissez faire was prevalent, and so it seemed plausible to assert that "capitalism had failed," and that economic prosperity and progress required a giant leap toward statism and state control. But the current crisis comes after many decades of statism, and its nature is such that the public can now correctly perceive Big Government to be at fault.

Furthermore, all the various forms of statism have now been tried, and have failed. At the turn of the twentieth century, businessmen, politicians, and intellectuals throughout the Western world began to turn to a "new" system of mixed economy, of State rule, to replace the relative laissez faire of the previous century. Such new and seemingly exciting panaceas as socialism, the corporate state, the Welfare–Warfare State, etc., have all been tried and have manifestly failed. The call for socialism or state planning is now a call for an old, tired, and failed system. What is there left to try but freedom?

On the social front, a similar crisis has occurred in recent years. The public school system, once a sacrosanct part of the American heritage, is now under severe and accelerated criticism from people across the ideological spectrum. It is now becoming clear (a) that public schools do not properly educate their charges; (b) that they are costly, wasteful, and require high taxes; and (c) that the uniformity of the public school system creates deep and unresolvable social conflicts over vital educational issues—over such matters as integration vs. segregation, progressive vs. traditional methods, religion or secularism, sex education, and the ideological content of learning. *Whatever* decision the public school makes in any of these areas, either a majority or a substantial minority of parents and children are irreparably injured. Furthermore, compulsory attendance laws are being increasingly perceived as dragooning unhappy or uninterested children into a prison not of their or their parents' making.

In the field of moral policies, there is a growing realization that the rampant Prohibitionism of government policy—not simply in the field of alcohol, but also in such matters as pornography, prostitution, sexual practices between "consenting adults," drugs, and abortion—are both an immoral and unjustified invasion of the right of each individual to make his or her *own* moral choices, and also cannot *practically* be enforced. Attempts at enforcement only bring about hardship and a virtual police state. The time is approaching when prohibitionism in these areas of personal morality will be recognized to be fully as unjust and ineffective as in the case of alcohol.

In the wake of Watergate, there is also an increased awareness of the dangers to individual liberty and privacy, to the freedom to dissent from government, in habitual actions and activities of government. Here, too, we may expect public pressure to keep government from fulfilling its age-old desire to invade privacy and repress dissent.

Perhaps the best sign of all, the most favorable indication of the breakdown of the mystique of the State, was the Watergate exposures of 1973–74. For Watergate instigated a radical shift in the attitude of *everyone*—regardless of their explicit ideology—toward government itself. Watergate indeed awakened the public to the invasions of personal liberty by government. More important, by bringing about the impeachment of the President, it permanently *desanctified* an office that had almost been considered sovereign by the American public. But most importantly, government *itself* has been to a large extent desanctified. No one trusts any politician or government official anymore; all government is viewed with abiding hostility and distrust, thus returning to that healthy distrust of government that marked the American public and the American revolutionaries of the eighteenth century. In the wake of Watergate, no one would dare today to intone that "we are the government," and therefore that anything elected officials may do is legitimate and proper. For the success of liberty, the most vital condition is the desanctification, the delegitimation of government in the eyes of the public; and that Watergate has managed to accomplish.

Thus, the objective conditions for the triumph of liberty have now, in the past few years, begun to appear, at least in the United States. Furthermore, the nature of this systemic crisis is such that government is now perceived as the culprit; it cannot be relieved except through a sharp turn toward liberty. What is basically needed now, therefore, is the growth of the "subjective conditions," of libertarian ideas and particularly of a dedicated libertarian movement to advance those ideas in the public forum. Surely it is no coincidence that it is precisely in these years—since 1971 and particularly since 1973, that these subjective conditions have made their greatest strides in this century. For the breakdown of statism has undoubtedly spurred many more people into becoming partial or full libertarians, and hence the objective conditions help to generate the subjective. Furthermore, in the United States at least, the splendid heritage of freedom and of libertarian ideas, going back beyond revolutionary times, has never been fully lost. Present-day libertarians, therefore, have solid historical ground on which to build.

The rapid growth in these last years of libertarian ideas and movements has pervaded many fields of scholarship, especially among younger scholars, and in the areas of journalism, the media, business, and politics. Because of the continuing objective conditions, it seems clear that this eruption of libertarianism in many new and unexpected places is not a mere media-concocted fad, but an inevitably growing response to the perceived conditions of objective reality. Given free will, no one can predict with certainty that the growing libertarian mood in America will solidify in a brief period of time, and press forward without faltering to the success of the entire libertarian program. But certainly, both theory and analysis of current historical conditions lead to the conclusion that the current prospects of liberty, even in the short-run, are highly encouraging.

BIBLIOGRAPHY

Adler, Felix. "The Relation of Ethics to Social Science." *In Congress of Arts and Science*, edited by H. J. Rogers. Boston: Houghton Mifflin, 1906.

Allen, Francis A. "Criminal Justice, Legal Values and the Rehabilitative Ideal." In *Theories of Punishment*, edited by Stanley E. Grupp. Bloomington: Indiana University Press, 1971.

Allen, Lawrence S. "Parent and Child—Tort Liability of Parent to Unemancipated Child." *Case Western Law Review* 19, no. 1 (November 1967): 139–46.

Ames, James Barr. "The History of Assumpsit." *Harvard Law Review* 2, no. 1 (April 1888): 1–19.

Anscombe, G. E. M. "Does Oxford Moral Philosophy Corrupt the Youth?" *The Listener*, 14 February 1957.

_____ . "Modern Moral Philosophy." *Philosophy* 33 (1958): 1–19.

_____ . *Mr. Truman's Degree*. Oxford: privately printed, 1956.

_____ . "The Two Kinds of Error in Action." *Journal of Philosophy* 60 (1963): 393–401.

Anson, William. *Principles of the English Law of Contract*, 2nd ed. 1882.

Armstrong, K. G. "The Retributivist Hits Back." In *Theories of Punishment*, edited by Stanley E. Grupp. Bloomington: Indiana University Press, 1971.

Bailyn, Bernard. *The Ideological Origin of the American Revolution*. Cambridge, Mass.: The Belknap Press of Harvard University Press, 1967.

Barnett, Randy E. "Fuller, Law and Anarchism." *The Libertarian Forum*, February 1976.

_____ . "Whither Anarchy? Has Nozick Justified the State?" *Journal of Libertarian Studies* 1 (Winter 1977): 15–22.

Barth, Fredrik. "The Land Use Pattern of Migratory Tribes of South Persia." *Norsk Geografisk Tidsskrift*, Bind 17 (1959–60).

Barth, Karl. *Church Dogmatics* 3, no. 4. Edinburgh: T. and T. Clark, 1961.

Becker, Carl L. *The Heavenly City of the Eighteenth Century Philosophers.* New Haven, Conn.: Yale University Press, 1957.

Bekemeyer, Dennis L. "A Child's Rights Against His Parent: Evolution of the Parental Immunity Doctrine." *University of Illinois Law Forum* (Winter 1967): 805–16.

Berlin, Isaiah. *Two Concepts of Liberty.* Oxford: Oxford University Press, 1958.
_____ . *Four Essays on Liberty.* Oxford: Oxford University Press, 1969.

Berns, Walter. "The Behavioral Sciences and the Study of Political Things: The Case of Christian Bay's *The Structure of Freedom.*" *American Political Science Review* 55, no. 3 (September 1961): 550–59.

Betz, Colonel F. "Minor's Right to Consent to an Abortion." *Santa Clara Lawyer* 11, no. 2 (Spring 1971): 469–78.

Binchy, David. *Anglo-Saxon and Irish Kingship.* London: Oxford University Press, 1970.

Blackstone, W. T. *Commentaries on the Laws of England,* book 1.

Bloch, Marc. *Feudal Society.* Chicago: University of Chicago Press, 1961.

Block, Walter, "The Blackmailer as Hero." *The Libertarian Forum,* December 1972.
_____ . "Coase and Demsetz on Private Property Rights." *Journal of Libertarian Studies* 1, no. 2 (Spring 1977): 111–16.

Bondy, Sebastian Salazar. "Andes and Sierra Maestra." In *Whither Latin America?* New York: Monthly Review Press, 1963.

Bourne, Randolph. *War and the Intellectuals,* edited by C. Resek. New York: Harper and Row, 1964.

Bradley, F. H. *Ethical Studies*, 2nd ed. Oxford: Oxford University Press, 1927.

Bremner, Robert H. ed. *Children and Youth in America*. Cambridge, Mass.: Harvard University Press, 1970–74.

Bresler, Robert J. *The Ideology of the Executive State: Legacy of Liberal Internationalism*. Menlo Park, Calif.: Institute for Human Studies, n.d.

Buchanan, James, and Warren J. Samuels. "On Some Fundamental Issues in Political Economy: An Exchange of Correspondence." *Journal of Economic Issues* 9, no. 1 (March 1975): 15–38.

Calhoun, John C. *A Disquisition on Government*. New York: Liberal Arts Press, 1953.

Carmichael, Leonard. "Absolutes, Relativism and the Scientific Psychology of Human Nature." In *Relativism and the Study of Man*, edited by H. Schoeck and J. W. Wiggins. Princeton, N.J.: D. Van Nostrand, 1961.

Channing, William Ellery. *Works*. Boston: American Unitarian Association, 1895.

Chesney-Lind, Meda. "Juvenile Delinquency: The Sexualization of Female Crime." *Psychology Today* 8, no. 2 (July 1974): 43–46.

Childs, Roy A. "The Invisible Hand Strikes Back." *Journal of Libertarian Studies* 1, no. 1 (Winter 1977): 23–34.

Chodorov, Frank. "Don't Buy Government Bonds." *Out of Step*. New York: Devin-Adair, 1962.

Copleston, Frederick, C.S.J. *A History of Philosophy*. Westminster, Md.: Newman Press, 1959.

———. *Aquinas*. London: Penguin Books, 1955.

Chroust, A. H. "Hugo Grotius and the Scholastic Natural Law Tradition." *The New Scholasticism* 17 (1943): 101–22.

Cropsey, Joseph. "A Reply to Rothman." *American Political Science Review* 56, no. 2 (June 1962): 353–59.

d'Entreves, A. P. *Natural Law*. London: Hutchinson University Library, 1951.

de Jouvenel, Bertrand. "The Chairman's Problem." *American Political Science Review* 55, no. 2 (June 1961): 368–72.

_____ . *On Power*. New York: Viking Press, 1949.

_____ . "The Treatment of Capitalism by Continental Intellectuals." In *The Intellectuals*, edited by George B. deHuszar, 385–97. Glencoe, Ill.: The Free Press, 1949.

de la Boetie, Etienne. *The Politics of Disobedience: The Discourse of Voluntary Servitude*. New York: Free Life Editions, 1975.

Dalberg-Acton, John Edward Emerich. *Essays on Freedom and Power*. Glencoe, Ill.: The Free Press, 1948.

Daruvala, Pherozeshah N. *The Doctrine of Consideration*. Calcutta: Butterworth, 1914.

Davidson, James Dale. "Note on Anarchy, State, and Utopia." *Journal of Libertarian Studies* 1, no. 4 (Fall 1977): 341–48.

Davitt, Thomas E., S.J. "St. Thomas Aquinas and the Natural Law." In *Origins of the Natural Law Tradition*, edited by Arthur L. Harding, 26–47. Dallas: Southern Methodist University Press, 1954.

Dietze, Gottfried. *In Defense of Property*. Chicago: Regnery, 1963.

Dillard, Irving, ed. *One Man's Stand For Freedom*. New York: Knopf, 1963.

Dillon, Miles. *The Celtic Realms*. London: George Weidenfeld and Nicholson, 1967.

_____ . *Early Irish Society*. Dublin, 1954.

Donahue, Charles. "Early Celtic Laws." (Unpublished paper delivered at the Columbia University Seminar on the History of Legal and Political Thought, Autumn, 1964).

Donisthorpe, Wordsworth. *Law in a Free State*. London: Macmillan, 1895.

Eastman, Clyde, Garrey Carruthers, and James A. Liefer. "Contrasting Attitudes Toward Land in New Mexico." *New Mexico Business* (March 1971). Also reprinted in *Community Grazing: Practice and Potential in New Mexico*, edited by Clyde Eastman and James R. Gray. Albuquerque: University of New Mexico, 1987.

Evers, Williamson M. "Hobbes and Liberalism." *The Libertarian Forum* (May 1975).

_____ . "The Law of Omissions and Neglect of Children." *The Journal of Libertarian Studies* 2, no. 1 (Winter 1978): 1–10.

_____ . "Political Theory and the Legal Rights of Children." (Unpublished manuscript).

_____ . "Social Contract: A Critique." *The Journal of Libertarian Studies* 1, no. 3 (Summer 1977): 3–14.

_____ . "Toward a Reformulation of the Law of Contracts." *Journal of Libertarian Studies* 1 (Winter 1977).

Farnsworth, E. Allan. "The Past of Promise: An Historical Introduction to Contract." *Columbia Law Review* 69, no. 4 (April 1969): 576–607.

Ferson, Merton. *The Rational Basis of Contracts*. Brooklyn: Foundation Press, 1949.

Foner, Phillip, ed. *The Complete Writings of Thomas Paine*. New York: Citadel Press, 1945.

Foot, Philippa R. *Virtues and Vices*. Berkeley: University of California Press, 1978.

Fox, Sanford J. *Cases and Material on Modern Juvenile Justice*. St. Paul, Minn.: West, 1972.

Frey, R. G. *Interests and Rights*. Oxford: Clarendon Press, 1980.

Fuentes, Carlos. "The Argument of Latin America: Words for the North Americans." In *Whither Latin America?* New York: Monthly Review Press, 1963.

Fuller, Lon L. "The Case of the Speluncean Explorers." *Harvard Law Review* (February 1949): 616–45.

_____ . *The Morality of Law.* New Haven: Yale University Press, 1964.

Gahringer, Robert E. "Punishment as Language." *Ethics* 71 (October 1960): 46–48.

Gardner, Richard. *Grito!: Reies Tijerina and the New Mexico Land Grant War of 1967.* New York: Harper and Row, 1971.

Geach, Peter. "Good and Evil." In *Theories of Ethics,* edited by Philippa R. Foot, 74–82. London: Oxford University Press, 1967.

_____ . *The Virtues.* Cambridge: Cambridge University Press, 1977.

_____ . *Providence and Evil.* Cambridge: Cambridge University Press, 1977.

Gierke, Otto. *Natural Law and the Theory of Society, 1500 to 1800.* Boston: Beacon Press, 1957.

Gilbert, James. *Designing the Industrial State.* Chicago: Quandrangle Books, 1972.

Gilfillan, S. Colum. *The Sociology of Invention.* Chicago: Follett Press, 1935.

Gilmore, Grant. *The Death of Contract.* Columbus: Ohio State University Press, 1974.

Gilson, Etienne. *The Christian Philsophy of St. Thomas Aquinas.* New York: Random House, 1956.

Gluckman, Max. *The Ideas in Barotse Jurisprudence.* New Haven, Conn.: Yale University Press, 1965.

Grampp, William D. *The Manchester School of Economics.* Stanford, Calif.: Stanford University Press, 1969.

Grant, George P. "Plato and Popper." *The Canadian Journal of Economics and Political Science* 20, no. 2 (May 1954): 185–94.

Gray, John N. "F. A. Hayek on Liberty and Tradition." *Journal of Libertarian Studies* 4, no. 2 (Fall 1980): 119–38.

Green, Mark J. "The Law of the Young." In *With Justice for Some*, edited by B. Wasserstein and M. Green. Boston: Beacon Press, 1970.

Grisez, Germain. "The First Principle of Practical Reason." *In Aquinas: A Collection of Critical Essays*, edited by Anthony Kenny. New York: Anchor Books, 1969.

Hamowy, Ronald. "Freedom and the Rule of Law in F. A. Hayek." *Il Politico* 36 (1971–72): 349–77.

_____ . "Hayek's Concept of Freedom: A Critique." *New Individualist Review* 1, no. 1 (April 1961): 28–31.

_____ . "Law and the Liberal Society: F. A. Hayek's Constitution of Liberty." *Journal of Libertarian Studies* 2, no. 4 (Winter 1978): 287–98.

Hare, R. M. *The Language of Morals*. Oxford: Clarendon Press, 1952.

Harre, R., and E. H. Madden. *Causal Powers: A Theory of Natural Necessity*. Totowa, N.J.: Rowman and Littlefield, 1975.

Hart, H. L. A. *Punishment and Responsibility*. New York: Oxford University Press, 1968.

Hartwell, R. M. *The Industrial Revolution and Economic Growth*. London: Methuen, 1971.

Hawkins, D. J. B. "Punishment and Moral Responsibility." *The Modern Law Review* (November 1944). Reprinted in *Theories of Punishment*, edited by Stanley E. Grupp. Bloomington: Indiana University Press, 1971.

Hayek, F. A. *Law, Legislation and Liberty*. Vol. 1. *Rules and Order*. Chicago: University of Chicago Press, 1973.

_____ ."Freedom and Coercion: Some Comments on a Critique by Mr. Ronald Hamowy." In *Studies in Philosophy, Politics, and Economics*, edited by F. A. Hayek. Chicago: University of Chicago Press, 1967.

_____ . *The Constitution of Liberty*. Chicago: University of Chicago Press, 1960.

_____ , ed., *Capitalism and the Historians*. Chicago: University of Chicago Press, 1958.

_____ . *The Road to Serfdom*. Chicago: University of Chicago Press, 1944.

Hazlitt, Henry. "The Economics of Freedom." *National Review* 13, no. 12 (September 1962): 231–32.

Henry, Robert L. *Contract in Local Courts of Medieval England*. London: Longmans, Green, 1926.

Herbert, Auberon, and J. H. Levy. *Taxation and Anarchism*. London: The Personal Rights Society, 1912.

Hess, Karl. *The End of the Draft*. New York: Viking Books, 1970.

Hesselberg, A. Kenneth. "Hume, Natural Law and Justice." *Duquesne Review* (Spring 1961).

Himmelfarb, Gertrude. *Lord Acton: A Study in Conscience and Politics*. Chicago: University of Chicago Press, 1962.

Holmes, Oliver Wendell, Jr. *The Common Law*, edited by Mark de Wolfe Howe. Cambridge, Mass.: Belknap Press of Harvard University, 1963.

Holmes, R. L. "Nozick on Anarchism." *Political Theory* 5, no. 2 (1977): 247–56.

Holton, James. "Is Political Philosophy Dead?" *Western Political Quarterly* 13, no. 3 (September 1961): 75–77.

Hoopes, Townsend. "The Persistence of Illusion: The Soviet Economic Drive and American National Interest." *Yale Review* 49, no. 3 (March 1960): 321–37.

Howlett, Frederick W. "Is the YSB All It's Cracked Up to Be?" *Crime and Delinquency* 19, no. 4 (October 1973): 485–92.

Hume, David. *A Treatise of Human Nature*. Quoted in A. Kenneth. "Hume, Natural Law and Justice." *Duquesne Review* (Spring 1961).

_____ . *Essays, Literary, Moral and Political*. London: Ward, Locke, and Taylor, n. d..

Huntington, Samuel P. "Conservatism as an Ideology." *American Political Science Review* 51, no. 2 (June 1957): 454–73.

Hurlbut, Elisha P. *Essays on Human Rights and Their Political Guarantees*. (1845). Cited in Wright, *American Interpretations of Natural Law*.

Irmen, J. Douglas. "Children's Liberation—Reforming Juvenile Justice." *University of Kansas Law Review* (1972–73).

Jacobson, D. L., ed. *The English Libertarian Heritage*. Indianapolis, Ind.: Bobbs-Merrill, 1965.

Jefferson, Thomas. "A Bill for Proportioning Crimes and Punishments." *In The Writings of Thomas Jefferson*, edited by A. Lipscomb and A. Bergh. Washington, D.C.: Thomas Jefferson Memorial Association, 1904.

Jenks, Edward. *The History of the Doctrine of Consideration in English Law*. London: C. J. Clay and Sons, 1892.

Joseph, H.W.B. *An Introduction to Logic*. 2nd rev. ed. Oxford: Clarendon Press, 1916.

Kant, Immanuel. *Groundwork of the Metaphysics of Morals*, translated by H. J. Paton. New York: Harper and Row, 1964.

_____ . *The Philosophy of Law: An Exposition of the Fundamental Principles of Jurisprudence as the Science of Right*. Edinburgh: T. and T. Clark, 1887.

Katz, Sanford. *When Parents Fail*. Boston: Beacon Press, 1971.

Kelsen, Hans. *General Theory of Law and State*. New York: Russell and Russell, 1961.

Kenealey, William J., S. J. "The Majesty of the Law." *Loyola Law Review* (1949–50): 106–9, 112–13. Reprinted in *The Natural Law Reader*, edited by Brendan F. Brown. New York: Oceana Publications, 1960.

Klapmuts, Nora. "Children's Rights: The Legal Rights of Minors in Conflict with Law or Social Custom." *Crime and Delinquency Literature* (September 1972).

Knowlton, Clark S. "Land-Grant Problems Among the State's Spanish–Americans," *New Mexico Business* (June 1967).

Leoni, Bruno. *Freedom and the Law*. Princeton, N.J.: Van Nostrand Press, 1961, and Los Angeles: Nash Publishing, 1972.

Lehrman, Paul. "Child Convicts," *Transaction* 8, no. 10 (July–August 1971): 35–44.

Levidow, Beatrice. "Overdue Process for Juveniles: For the Retroactive Restoration of Constitutional Rights." *Howard Law Journal* 17, no. 2 (1972): 402.

Lewis, C. S. "The Humanitarian Theory of Punishment." *Twentieth Century* (Autumn 1948–49). In *Theories of Punishment*, edited by Stanley E. Grupp. Bloomington: Indiana University Press, 1971.

Levine, Richard S. "Caveat Parens: A Demystification of the Child Protection System." *University of Pittsburgh Law Review* 35 (Fall 1973): 1–52.

Lieber, Francis. *Manual of Political Ethics*. 1838. Cited in Wright, *American Interpretations of Natural Law*.

List, Lawrence. "A Child and a Wall: A Study of 'Religious Protection' Laws." *Buffalo Law Review* 13 (1963–64). Cited in Evers, "Political Theory and the Legal Rights of Children."

Locke, John. *An Essay Concerning the True Origin, Extent, and End of Civil Government in Two Treatises of Government*, edited by P. Laslett. Cambridge: Cambridge University Press, 1960.

Lougee, Robert W. "German Romanticism and Political Thought." *Review of Politics* 21 (October 1959): 631–45.

Lottin, Odon. *Psychologie et morale aux xiie at xiiie siecles*. 6 vols. (Louvain, 1942–1960).

Lukacs, John. "Intellectual Class or Intellectual Profession?" *In The Intellectuals*, edited by George B. deHuszar. Glencoe, Ill.: The Free Press, 1949.

Lucas, J. R. *The Freedom of the Will*. Oxford: Clarendon Press, 1970.

McAvoy, Thomas T., C.S.C. "Orestes A. Brownson and Archbishop John Hughes in 1860 Bt." *Review of Politics* 24, no. 1 (January 1962): 19–47.

McCloskey, H. J. "A Non-Utilitarian Approach to Punishment." *Inquiry* (1965). Reprinted in *Philosophical Perspectives on Punishment*, edited by Gertrude Ezorsky. Albany: State University of New York Press, 1972.

McCloskey, Kenneth D. "Parental Liability to a Minor Child for Injuries Caused by Excessive Punishment." *Hastings Law Journal* 11 (February 1960): 335.

MacIntyre, A. C. "Hume on 'Is' and 'Ought'." In *The Is-Ought Question*, edited by W. D. Hudson. London: Macmillan, 1969.

McNamara, Ellen M. "The Minor's Right to Abortion and the Requirement of Parental Consent." *Virginia Law Review* 60, no. 2 (February 1974): 305–32.

McPherson, James M. *The Struggle for Equality: Abolitionists and the Negro in the Civil War and Reconstruction*. Princeton, N.J.: Princeton University Press, 1964.

Mack, Eric. "Individualism, Rights, and the Open Society." *In The Libertarian Alternative*, edited by Tibor R. Machan. Chicago: Nelson Hall, 1974, 29–31.

Maine, Henry. *Ancient Law*. New York: E. P. Dutton, 1917.

Martin, James J. *Men Against the State*. DeKalb, Ill.: Adrian Allen Associates, 1953.

Mayne, John D. *Treatise on Hindu Law and Usage*, 11th ed. Edited by N. C. Aiyar. Madras: Higginbothams, 1953.

Mencken, H. L. *A Mencken Chrestomathy*. New York: Alfred A. Knopf, 1949.

_____ . *Happy Days: 1880–1892*. New York: Alfred Knopf, 1947.

Miller, Margaret. "Markets in Russia." In M. Miller, T. Piotrowicz, L. Sirc, and H. Smith, *Communist Economy Under Change*. London: Institute for Economic Affairs, 1963.

Mises, Ludwig von. *Liberalism*. 2nd. ed. Kansas City: Sheed Andrews and McMeel, 1978.

_____ . "Epistemological Relativism in the Sciences of Human Action." In *Relativism and the Study of Man*, edited by H. Schoeck and J. W. Wiggins. Princeton, N.J.: D. Van Nostrand, 1961.

_____ . *Socialism*. New Haven: Yale University Press, 1951.

_____ . *Human Action*. New Haven, Yale University Press, 1949.

Moore, G. E. *Ethics*. Oxford, 1963–1912.

Mora, Jose Ferrater. "Suarez and Modern Philosophy." *Journal of the History of Ideas* 14, no. 4 (October 1953): 528–47.

Morris, Herbert. *On Guilt and Innocence*. Berkeley: University of California Press, 1976.

_____ . "Persons and Punishment." *The Monist* 52, no. 4 (October 1968): 475–501.

Murphy, Patrick T. *Our Kindly Parent–The State*. New York: Viking Press, 1974.

Needham, Joseph. "Review of Karl A. Wittfogel, *Oriental Despotism*." *Science and Society* 23 no. 1 (Winter 1959): 58–65.

Neustadt, Richard. "Presidency at Mid-Century." *Law and Contemporary Problems* 21 no. 4 (Autumn 1956): 609–45.

Nisbet, Robert. *The Social Impact of the Revolution*. Washington, D.C.: American Enterprise Institute for Public Policy Research, 1974.

Nock, Albert Jay. *On Doing the Right Thing, and Other Essays*. New York: Harper and Brothers, 1928.

Noel, F. Regis. "A History of the Bankruptcy Clause of the Constitution of the United States of America." Doctoral dissertation. Washington, D.C.: Catholic University of America, 1920.

Nozick, Robert. *Anarchy, State, and Utopia.* New York: Basic Books, 1974.

_____ . "Moral Complications and Moral Structures." *Natural Law Forum* 13 (1968): 1.

Oppenheimer, Franz. *The State.* New York: Free Life Editions, 1975.

Oubre, Claude F. *Forty Acres and a Mule: The Freedmen's Bureau and Black Land Ownership.* Baton Rouge: Louisiana State University Press, 1978.

Paul, Jeffrey. "Nozick, Anarchism and Procedural Rights." *Journal of Libertarian Studies* 1 no. 4 (Fall 1977): 337–40.

Parent, William A. "Some Recent Work on the Concept of Liberty." *American Philosophical Quarterly* 11, no. 3 (July 1974): 149–67.

Parfit, Derek. "Personal Identity." *Philosophical Review* 80 no. 1 (January 1971): 3–27.

Parrish, Michael. "Iran: The Portrait of a U. S. Ally." *The Minority of One* (December 1962).

Parthemos, George S. "Contemporary Juristic Theory, Civil Rights, and American Politics." *Annals of the American Academy of Political and Social Science* 34 no. 4 (November 1962): 95–107.

Patterson, Edwin W. *Jurisprudence: Men and Ideas of the Law.* Brooklyn: The Foundation Press, 1953.

Peden, Jospeh R. "Property Rights in Celtic Irish Law." *Journal of Libertarian Studies* 1, no. 2 (Spring 1977): 81–86.

_____ . "Stateless Societies: Ancient Ireland." *The Libertarian Forum* (April 1971).

Pease, William H., and Jane H., eds. *The Antislavery Argument.* Indianapolis: Bobbs-Merrill, 1965.

Petro, Sylvester. "Feudalism, Property, and Praxeology." In *Property in a Human Society*, edited by S. Blumenfeld. LaSalle, Ill.: Open Court, 1974.

Philbrook, Clarence. "Realism in Policy Espousal." *American Economic Review* 5, no. 1 (December 1953): 846–59.

Phillips, R. P. *Modern Thomistic Philosophy*. Westminster, Md.: The Newman Bookshop, 1934–35.

Plantinga, Alvin. *The Nature of Necessity*. Oxford: Clarendon Press, 1974.

Platt, Anthony. *The Child Savers*. Chicago: University of Chicago Press, 1961.

Pollock, Frederick. *Principles of Contract*. 12th ed. Edited by P. Winfield. London: Stevens and Sons, 1946.

Pomeroy, John Norton, Jr., and John C. Mann. *A Treatise on the Specific Performances of Contracts*. 3rd ed. Albany, N.Y.: Banks, 1926.

Pound, Roscoe. *Jurisprudence*. St. Paul, Minn.: West, 1959.

Rappard, William E. "On Reading von Mises." In *On Freedom and Free Enterprise*, edited by Mary Sennholz. Princeton, N.J.: D. Van Nostrand, 1956.

Raskin, Marcus. "The Megadeath Intellectuals." *New York Review of Books* (14 November 1963): 6–7.

Rawls, John. *A Theory of Justice*. Cambridge, Mass.: Harvard University Press, 1971.

Read, Leonard. *I'd Push the Button*. New York: Joseph D. Maguire, 1946.

Riemersma, Jelle C. "Economic Enterprise and Political Powers After the Reformation." *Economic Development and Cultural Change* 3(1954–55): 297–308.

Rickenbacker, William F. *The Twelve-Year Sentence*. LaSalle, Ill.: Open Court, 1974.

Robertson, John A. "Involuntary Euthanasia of Defective Newborns: A Legal Analysis." *Stanford Law Review* 27, no. 2 (January 1975): 213–70.

Rodham, Hillary. "Children Under the Law." *Harvard Educational Review* 43, no. 4 (1973): 487–514.

Rose, Willie Lee. *Rehearsal for Reconstruction: The Port Royal Experiment.* Indianapolis, Ind.: Bobbs-Merrill, 1964.

Rothbard, Murray N. *Individualism and the Philosophy of Social Sciences.* San Francisco: Cato Institute, 1979.

_____.*Left and Right: Prospects for Liberty.* San Francisco: Cato Institute, 1979.

_____ . *For a New Liberty.* rev. ed. New York: Macmillan, 1978.

_____ . *Power and Market.* 2nd ed. Kansas City: Sheed Andrews and McMeel, 1977.

_____ . "Punishment and Proportionality." In *Assessing the Criminal: Restitution, Retribution, and the Legal Process,* edited by Randy Barnett and John Hagel III. Cambridge, Mass.: Ballinger Publishing, 1977.

_____ . "Robert Nozick and the Immaculate Conception of the State." *Journal of Libertarian Studies* 1, no. 1 (Winter 1977): 45–58.

_____ . *Toward a Reconstruction of Utility and Welfare Economics.* New York: Center for Libertarian Studies, 1977.

_____ . "Praxeology, Value Judgments, and Public Policy." In *The Foundations of Modern Austrian Economics,* edited by Edwin Dolan. Kansas City: Sheed and Ward, 1976.

_____ .*Conceived in Liberty.* New York: Arlington House, 1975.

_____ . "The Anatomy of the State." In Rothbard, *Egalitarianism as a Revolt Against Nature, and Other Essays.* Washington, D.C.: Libertarian Review Press, 1974.

_____ . "Why Be Libertarian?" In Rothbard, *Egalitarianism as a Revolt Against Nature, and Other Essays.*

_____ . "Value Implications of Economic Theory," *The American Economist,* 17, no. 1 (Spring 1973): 35–39.

_____ . "Bertrand de Jouvenel e i diritti di proprieta." *Biblioteca della Liberta* 2 (1966).

_____ . *Man, Economy, and State*. Princeton, N.J.: D. Van Nostrand, 1962.

_____ . "Huntington on Conservatism." *American Political Science Review* 51 (September 1957): 784–87.

Rousseau, Jean-Jacques. *The Social Contract*, edited by E. Barker. New York: Oxford University Press, 1948.

Rubin, Sol. "Children as Victims of Institutionalization." *Child Welfare* 61, no. 1 (January 1972): 6–18.

Rutland, Robert A. *George Mason*. Williamsburg, Va.: Colonial Williamsburg, 1961.

Sadowsky, James A., S.J. "Private Property and Collective Ownership." *The Libertarian Alternative*, edited by Tibor Machan. Chicago: Nelson-Hall, 1974.

Salmond, John W. *Jurispridence*. 2d ed. London: Stevens and Haynes, 1907.

Sanders, John T. "The Free Market Model Versus Government: A Reply to Nozick." *Journal of Libertarian Studies* 1, no. 1 (Winter 1977): 35, 44.

Schafer, Stephen. *Restitution to Victims of Crime*. Chicago: Quadrangle Books, 1960.

Schmitt, Carl. *Der Leviathan in der Staatslehre Thomas Hobbes*. Hamburg, 1938.

Schultz, J. Lawrence. "The Cycle of Juvenile Court History." *Crime and Delinquency*. (October 1973).

Schumpeter, Joseph A. *Capitalism, Socialism, and Democracy*. New York: Harper and Brothers, 1942.

Sheridan, William H. "Juveniles Who Commit Non-Criminal Acts: Why Treat in a Correctional System?" *Federal Probation* 31, no. 1 (March 1967): 26–30.

Sidman, Lawrence R. "The Massachusetts Stubborn Child Law: Law and Order in the Home." *Family Law Quarterly* 6, no. 1 (Spring 1972): 35–58.

_____ . "The Penal Bond With Conditional Defeasance." *The Law Quarterly Review* (July 1966).

Singer, Peter. "The Right to Be Rich or Poor." *New York Review of Books* 22, no. 3 (6 March 1975): 19–24.

Singer, Marcus. *Generalization in Ethics.* New York: Knopf, 1961.

Sombart, Werner. *A New Social Philosophy.* Princeton, N.J.: Princeton University Press, 1937.

_____ . *Vom Menschen.* Berlin, 1938.

Spencer, Herbert. *Social Statics* (New York: Robert Schalkenbach Foundation, 1970).

_____ . *An Autobiography.* New York: D. Appleton, 1904.

Spooner, Lysander. *No Treason: The Constitution of No Authority,* edited by James J. Martin. Colorado Springs, Colo.: Ralph Myles, 1973.

Strauss, Leo. *Natural Right and History.* Chicago: University of Chicago Press, 1953.

_____ . "Relativism." In *Relativism and the Study of Man,* edited by H. Schoeck and J. W. Wiggins. Princeton, N.J.: D. Van Nostrand, 1961.

Suarez, Franciscus. *De Legibus ac Deo* (1619). Quoted in d'Entreves *Natural Law.*

Sullivan, Michael F. "Child Neglect: The Environmental Aspects." *Ohio State Law Journal* 29 (1968): 85.

Tallack, William. *Reparation to the Injured and the Rights of Victims of Crime to Compensation.* London: 1900.

Thomson, Judith Jarvis. "A Defense of Abortion." *Philosophy and Pubic Affairs* 1, no. 1 (Fall 1971): 47–66.

Thorson, Thomas Landon. "Political Values and Analytic Philosophy." *Journal of Politics* 23, no. 4 (November 1961): 711–24.

Toohey, John J. *Notes on Epistemology*. Washington, D.C.: Georgetown University, 1952.

Tucker, Benjamin R. *Instead of a Book*. New York: B. R. Tucker, 1893.

Veale, F. J. P. *Advance to Barbarism*. Appleton, Wis.: C. C. Nelson, 1953.

Veatch, Henry. *For an Ontology of Morals: A Critique of Contemporary Ethical Theory*. Evanston, Ill.: Northwestern University Press, 1971.

_____ . *Rational Man: A Modern Introduction to Aristotelian Ethics*. Bloomington: University of Indiana Press, 1962.

Watkins, J. W. N. "Philosophy." In *Agenda for a Free Society: Essays on Hayek's The Constitution of Liberty*, edited by Arthur Seldon. London: Institute for Economic Affairs, 1961.

White, Lawrence H. "Bankruptcy and Risk." Unpublished paper.

Wild, John. *Plato's Modern Enemies and the Theory of Natural Law*. Chicago: University of Chicago Press, 1953.

_____ . "Natural Law and Modern Ethical Theory." *Ethics* 63 (October 1952): 1–13.

Williston, Samuel. "Mutual Assent in the Formation of Contracts." In Williston, *Selected Readings on the Law of Contracts*. New York: Macmillan, 1931.

Wittgenstein, Ludwig. *Philosophical Investigations*. New York: Macmillan, 1958.

Wolk, Lawrence J. "Juvenile Court Statutes–Are They Void for Vagueness?" *New York University Review of Law and Social Change* (Winter 1974).

Wolowski, Leon, and Emile Levasseur. "Property." *Lalor's Cyclopedia of Political Science*. Vol. 3. Chicago: M. B. Carey, 1884.

Woolsey, Theodore. *Political Science*. 1877. Cited in Wright, *American Interpretations of Natural Law*.

Wright, Benjamin F. Jr., ed. *American Interpretations of Natural Law.* Cambridge: Harvard University Press, 1931.

Zajdlic, W. "The Limitations of Social Sciences." *Kyklos* 9 (1956): 65–74.

INDEX

Wines, Frederick, 112n
Wiretapping, 122
With Justice For Some (Wasserstein and
   Green), 108n
Wittfogel, Karl, 171
Wittgenstein, Ludwig, 156n
Wolk, Lawrence J., 109n
Wolowski, Leon, 64n
Woodside, Justice, 106–107
Woolsey, Theodore, 23

Works (Channing), 23n
World War II, 259
Wright, Benjamin F., Jr., 23n, 24n
Writings of Thomas Jefferson, The (Lipscomb
   and Bergh), 92n

Yale Review, 172n
Yugoslavia, 270

Zajdlic, W., 25n